AF352134

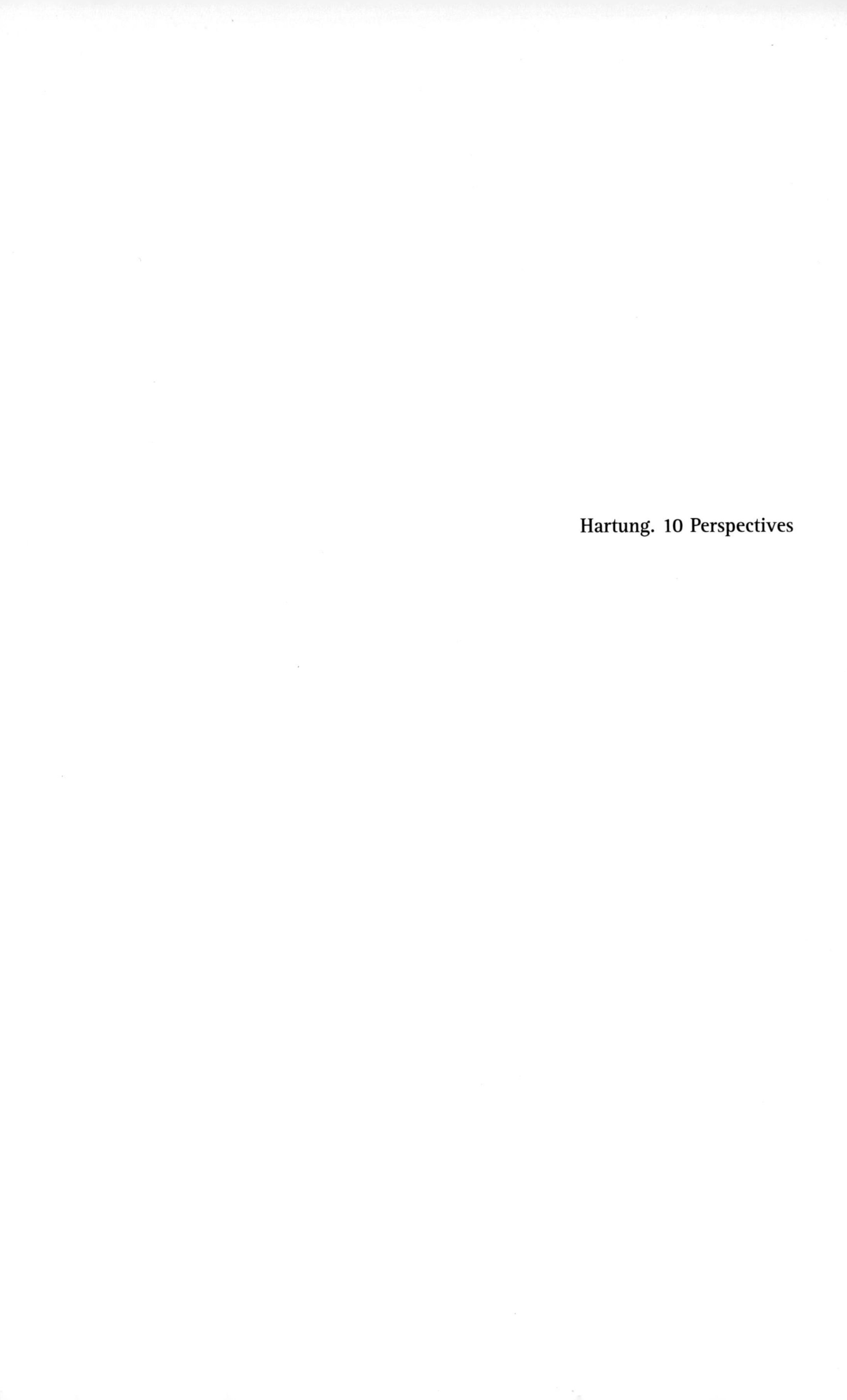

Hartung. 10 Perspectives

Hartung

10 Perspectives

edited by Anne Pontégnie

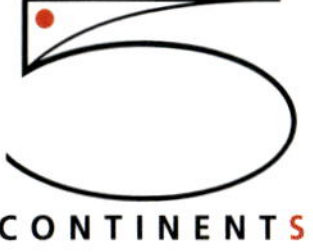

Translation from German
Sara Ogger

Translation from French
Emiliano Battista

Rainer Michael Mason's text has been
translated by John O'Toole

Photographic Credits
Fondation Hans Hartung Anna-Eva Bergman

5 Continents Editions

Editorial Coordinator
Paola Gallerani
Laura Maggioni

Editing
Timothy Stroud

Design and Layout
Lara Gariboldi

Acknowledgments

I would like, first of all, to express my gratitude
to François Hers, artist and director of the Fondation
Hans Hartung Anna-Eva Bergman, for the trust
he has shown me throughout this project.

I would also like to thank the staff at the
foundation, in particular: Jean-Luc Uro, without
whom no research on Hartung would be possible;
Marie Aanderaa for being always so attentive
and available; Bernard Derderian, for the pleasure
he took in sharing with me all he knows about
Hartung's work; and Marcelle Driessen, for her
warm welcome.

At 5 Continents Editions, I would like to thank
Paola Gallerani for her patience and precision,
and Eric Ghysels for his commitment.

Thanks also to Xavier Douroux and Annie Claustres,
for all those long conversations about Hans
Hartung's work.

And, of course, to all the authors.

ISBN 5 Continents Editions: 88-7439-187-0
info@5continentseditions.com

Contents

Introduction

It wasn't so long ago that the foundation that now houses a great part of Hans Hartung's work—the house, the studios and their inhabitants, many of whom were already there when the artist was still alive—emerged from the disarray and confusion into which the death of the artist had plunged it. The thousands of works the artist produced and kept from the 1920s until his death in 1989 weighed all the more since, at the end of the day, only very few of them had ever been shown, seen and analysed, much less understood. The team at the foundation worked intelligently and diligently at archiving, classifying, and understanding that body of work; they have also rearranged the spaces in order to give the ever-growing number of visitors—curators, critics, researchers and artists—the best possible access to this complex and neglected treasure. Thanks to their unflagging efforts, the works have regained life and meaning through new shows and interpretations. Slowly but surely, Hartung's hunch seems to have been confirmed. What would have become of his oeuvre, one wonders, had he not bet on the ability of a foundation to prolong it, to restore what had been forgotten and to correct bad interpretations?

Yes, Hartung is one of the most important European artists of the second half of the twentieth century, and yes, he did enjoy thirty-five years of recognition and prosperity. And yet it is only a minute part of his vast oeuvre, namely his output in the 1950s, that seems to have gained any recognition. No-one would think of comparing his current stature—in critical and commercial terms, or in terms of museum space—with that of some of the artists who crossed paths with him, such as Kandinsky, Pollock or Rothko.

The desire to put together different perspectives on Hartung's work didn't originate in the desire to raise it to the heights occupied by these giants of the history of twentieth-century art. Such an attempt, even if it proved possible, would not benefit Hartung in the least. The fact that he is not one of these giants is precisely what we must look at.

If Hartung's production of the 1950s is what brought his work into the spotlight and secured for it a place in history, it is because, as Christine Mehring has brilliantly intuited, that was the only time his work went hand-in-hand with the spirit of the times. Hartung was a German whose exile in France was indefinitely prolonged by the rise of Nazism, and his abstraction, it turned out, could quite opportunely be claimed by the postwar politics of France and Germany, as is explained from the perspective of each of these countries by Laurence Bertrand-Dorléac and Chantal Eschenfleder. Moreover, the forms and the range of colours Hartung was using during that period mesh with the forms and colours favoured by the design that prevailed during the 1950s. And, as is also the case for design, the seeds of this production date back to the days right before the war. Hartung's formal intuitions, which had come to full bloom by the end of the 1940s and which were to identify him from then on, had their roots in the confrontation with Cubism and, in particular, as Annie Claustres explains, with the work of González, who became, however briefly, his father-in-law.

Hartung never stopped stressing the importance of his production of the 1920s, which already bore the marks of the specificity of his work and of his abstraction. The influence that these early, almost informal, abstract watercolours and ink pieces exerted on his entire work has never been denied, and yet Hartung never succeeded in gaining the recognition he thought he warranted as a pioneer of abstraction. In some ways, the fact that recognition was so slow in coming—he was 45 when it finally materialised—had the effect of obscuring the origins of his work, which in turn explains why it has been so misunderstood. This is confirmed by my own research into the reasons for the failure of his exhibition at the Metropolitan Museum of Art in New York and, more broadly, for the very poor reception he has had in the United States.

Every text gathered here invariably evokes the misconceived notion that portrays Hartung as an artist of the spontaneous gesture when in fact his paintings, all the way up to the 1960s, were the fruit of painstakingly meticulous work. That nobody has highlighted this paradox is a clear enough sign of the absence of a detailed study of Hartung's work right up to the end of the 1980s. This book has offered an opportunity at least to start some of this much-needed research and analysis, and we can only hope that it will stimulate further work in this area. Rainer Mason has been working for the past eight years on a catalogue raisonné of Hartung's printed work; his contribution, an impressively thorough text, presents that work for the very first time. As for Jennifer Mundy, she has undertaken what might be termed a police investigation in order to shed light on the conditions under which Hartung produced his last works. Along with her findings, she also gives us a very beautiful portrait of the artist at the end of his life.

Other authors have opted to approach Hartung's work from a more personal perspective. Franz Kaiser was interested by Hartung's conceptual approach. In John C. Welchman's hand, Hartung's *Autoportrait* exploded into a baroque abecedary. And lastly, Christopher Wool has paid homage to a fellow artist by editing a notebook that, in no more than a few pages, lets us appreciate Hartung's audacity and virtuosity.

These ten texts don't strive to be exhaustive. An artwork doesn't have a single truth. Its capacity to stimulate readings and interpretations prolongs the work's interest beyond the fads and orthodoxies of the moment. Hartung's independence kept his work from securing its place in the history of modern art, though it is this singularity and independence that give it the strength to make some cracks in the altogether too smooth surface of this still recent history. Long, dense, and complex, it is a work whose myriad passageways a book such as the present one would never be able to exhaust. The photography, the notebooks from his youth, the transition period of the 1960s, the 1930s in Paris ... so many topics that we would have loved to explore. We hope the essays gathered here will make others want to continue the work.

John C. Welchman Hans Hartung

Abcedarium: Reading Between the Lines

Franz-W. Kaiser A Case Study on the Caducity of Categories in Art Criticism Annie Claustres

Hans Hartung Clandestine Artist 1937-1942: the Decisive Years

Christine Mehring Hans Hartung Mid-Century Modern Rainer Michael Mason Hartung and Printmaking Christopher Wool

According to Hartung, it was in 1922, when he was only sixteen years old, that the "alphabet" of his designs first emerged in a group of "*informel*" watercolours and paintings which built on the graphic style of Rembrandt, Goya and the German Expressionists while simultaneously eliminating the figurative elements he had inherited from Emil Nolde. In 1922, then, he arrived at a style which he termed, *avant la lettre*, of course, *tachisme*. The following year, in 1923, his genealogical abcedarium was consolidated into the "fundamental elements" of his "future painting" in a second series of works using "black and sanguine crayons" (p. 196, *Autoportrait*[1]). Hartung's "vocabulary" was now a mix of present "signs" and "future rhythms", a blend of "taches", "curves", and lines (p. 60).

The arrival and sequencing of this language of forms is clearly the central alphabet in Hartung's career, but it was far from the only one. His *Autoportrait* is studded with alphabet-like declensions, mostly taking the form of lists or series—such as that cluster of artists from Rembrandt to Nolde whose styles and techniques influenced the emergence of his. Hartung's series are collective concentrations, persons or things strung together with the minimum of qualification, so that certain compulsive differences—and similarities—open up in the spaces between them.

These are Hartung's favourite writers: Knut Hamsun, Thomas Mann, Franz Werfel and, "above all", Kafka whose "phantasmagorical world fascinates me" (p. 219). These are the ancient gods with which he was familiar from his early boyhood: Saturn, Jupiter, Neptune, Venus, Mercury, Artemis and Athena (p. 26). These are professions which he couldn't imagine following: shopkeeper, industrialist, banker; and these he could: astronomer, archaeologist, photographer, film-maker, scholar of religion or philosophy, medical researcher, scientific inventor (p. 218). These are the composers whose music he prefers in the studio: Schütz, Bach (above all), Corelli, Vivaldi, Rameau, Telemann, Haendel [*sic*], Purcell, Guillaume de Machaut, Marc-Antoine Charpentier, Couperin. And these are too "demanding and intrusive": Schoenberg, Webern, Varese, Boulez. These are the national influences gathered up in the School of Paris, which he encountered in the mid-1920s, shortly after discovering the alphabetic epiphany of his own style: Spain, Russia, Germany, Romania, Holland, Italy (and their "colonies and yet more countries"). And these, the artists and movements that he self-consciously "distilled" once more on his return to Dresden: El Greco, Cézanne, Van Gogh, Cubism, abstraction (p. 196). These, finally, are the artists he collected: Goya (a first edition of the *Caprices*), Manet (a Chinese ink drawing), Emil Nolde (a rare lithograph), Gavarni (an original book), Julio González ("one of the best collections of drawings and sculptures"), and Picasso (several works) (pp. 223-24). The last gasp of Hartung's impulsive serial nature comes, fittingly enough, in the concluding pages of the autobiography, in which the artist meditates on the relation of his work to the widest questions of the human and the divine (see V).

In a response to Hartung's largely unqualified lists and sequences, here is an alternative ABC for the artist's work, set out in dialogue with his own, but also conceived

| 1. Hartung working in his studio, 1960

between the lines of his autobiography and the critical and historical record of his work and life. It is a retort to received opinion and a response to the general evasion, both by the artist himself and the majority of his commentators, of larger questions about the meaning of Hartung's oeuvre. My parallel ABC aims not so much to supply a series of specific answers to the riddle of signification posed by Hartung's abstractions, nor to privilege one or other of the several interpretative modes visited on his prodigious output of paintings, drawings and photographs—biographical, psychological, historical, formal etc. Instead, I want to use the scaffolding of the ABC to trace Hartung's subliminal engagement with the abstruse semantics of an oeuvre hitherto caught up in a series of implicit final reckonings that consign it to formal design, expressive agency or calligraphic allusionism. To put it another way, this is a kind of miniature emblem book, arranged around

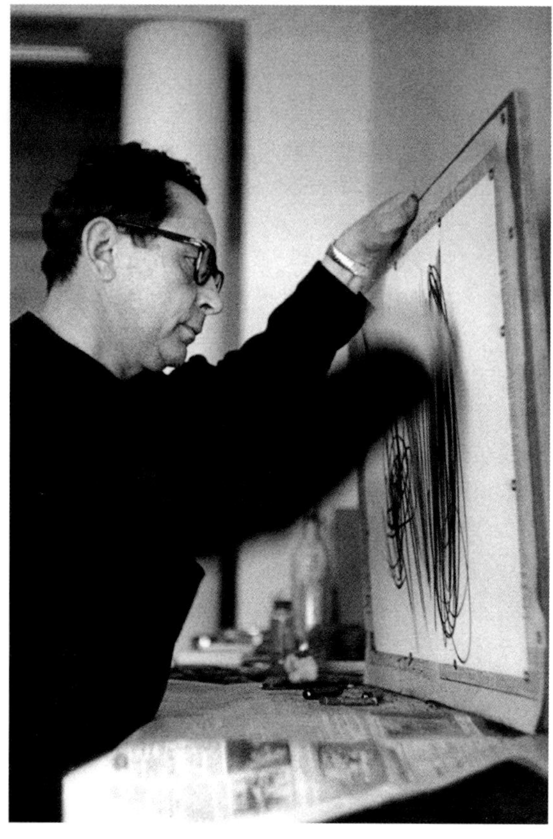

key things and concepts and drawn with a cross-hatching of words, that tries, in its own modest way, to make up for some of the deficit in Hartung's own interpretational and iconographical readings.

A – Abstraction

In the middle of *Autoportrait*, just after the photographic inserts, Hartung delivers his most extensive lesson in art history. Developed as a series of lists, chronologies and affiliations, its aim is to sketch a context for the artist's own style of informal abstraction. The final effect of Hartung's historical reckoning, however, is to suspend his work in an index-like ABC that invests quite heavily in sequence and judgment, but all but ignores definition.

Indeed, the suspension of analysis in these pages is announced at the outset in a lengthy discussion of a pantheon of artists whose mature or later work is considered exceptional (Michelangelo, Titian, Rembrandt, Hals, Goya, Turner, Monet, Bonnard), and of an apparent corollary: the necessary deferment of historical evaluation (in the case of twentieth-century artists, he says, until around 2050). The twofold implication of this preamble is clear. First, neither art critics nor, of course, Hartung himself, writing in the mid-1970s, should be expected to provide a clear, accurate assessment of the artist's work while he is still in the middle of a final phase of painting, the value of which might, by implication, be of a similar relative weight to the later periods of the artists cited.

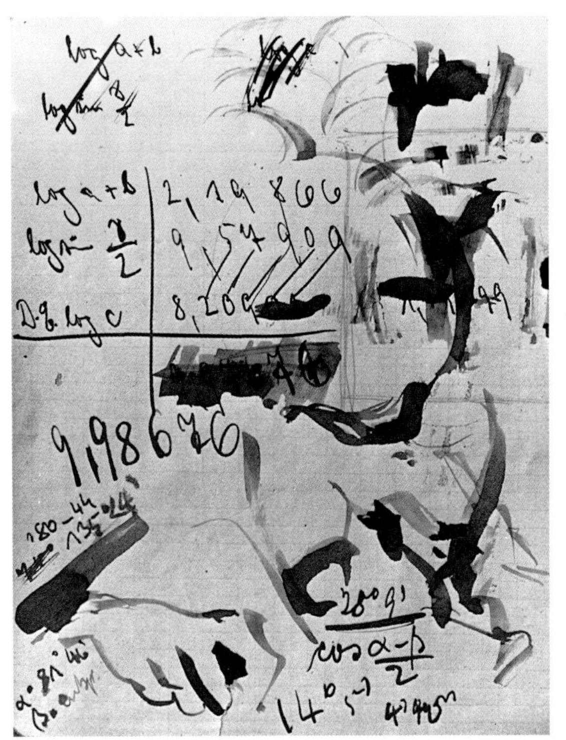

Secondly, any sure judgments about the nature of artistic achievement in the second half of the last century in general are, it is suggested, impossible until halfway through the next one. Hartung clears the way for the presentation of a general map for the location of his work, but excuses the need for any Larousse-like summary of its meanings or effects—apart, that is, from its *grandest* ambitions [see pp. 130–35 of *Autoportrait*].

It is thus that history provides the bulwark for an abstract definition of abstraction validated only by maturity. "One works completely without motif", he noted in 1929, "and the question is to concentrate on the spirit, the rhythm and the tension—to detach oneself from motif, associations and memories and so try to get the purest meaning with the purest optical means".[2]

B – Blessure

On 20 November 1944, while serving in the French Foreign Legion near Dijon, Hartung sustained an injury that lead to the amputation of his gangrenous right leg, first below the knee, then higher up (pp. 166–67). A "clown of horror" in the infirmary, a handicapped husband out of it, the brutal reality of this loss was immediately compounded by another, as he realised from his hospital bed in Toulouse that the folder containing all the drawings and sketches he had made during the war years had also gone missing.

C – Colour

It was in the woods surrounding the Fondation Maeght in Saint-Paul-de-Vence that Hartung learned to work with clay. The resultant joy (see J), which emanated from the unremitting physicality of his struggle with pure material, augmented we might add by his location in the sensory plenitude of the forest (see F), led to an "almost total renunciation of colour" (p. 203). This was a battle that Hartung waged throughout his career. On one side, the sensuous purity of form and line, his black and white reproductions of Matisse and Picasso (p. 68), the pessimistic "smudges of ink" made around 1938 (p. 116), the brown and black masses of the work between 1962 and 1967, his delight with the

2. HH, untitled, 1922, ink on paper, 19.9 cm x 15 cm
3. HH, untitled, 1922, ink on paper, 19.9 cm x 15.5 cm
4. HH, untitled, 1922, ink on paper, 15.3 x 9.7 cm

finesse of lithography and its "noble" monochromatic forms (see L); on the other, the waves of bright aniline in his early watercolours, the would-be aesthetic autonomy of red, blue, yellow and green noted by Will Grohmann (see W), and the bright, fresh colours of the work after 1970. All in all a conflict that could never be resolved, for despite Hartung's projections, who (apart from Kandinsky, see K) could truly know in by what color might be "strident, joyous, or sinister" (p. 252)?

D – Darkness

Even when he emerged from his "dark years" in the 1930s, Hartung writes exorbitantly of his preference for working at night, in darkness and "obscurity" (p. 215). His studio near Antibes, located in one of the most celebrated, light-filled corners of Europe, faced north to avoid direct sunlight and exploit the projection of shadows from the adjacent olive trees.

Night, darkness and obscurity form one axis in a general retreat from exposure, governed by his relentless flight from clarity. Other symptoms include the walls of his living quarters, which he deliberately left unadorned, hanging on them neither his own paintings nor the work he had acquired from friends and acquaintances, including Picasso. Living in geometry and surrounded by blankness, this was Hartung's way of reducing his commitment to discourse in general and revision in particular. This spareness crosses with his preference for monochromes and black-and-white photography. And it perhaps finds its widest horizon in his life-long struggle with the beguiling "clarities" of the French language.

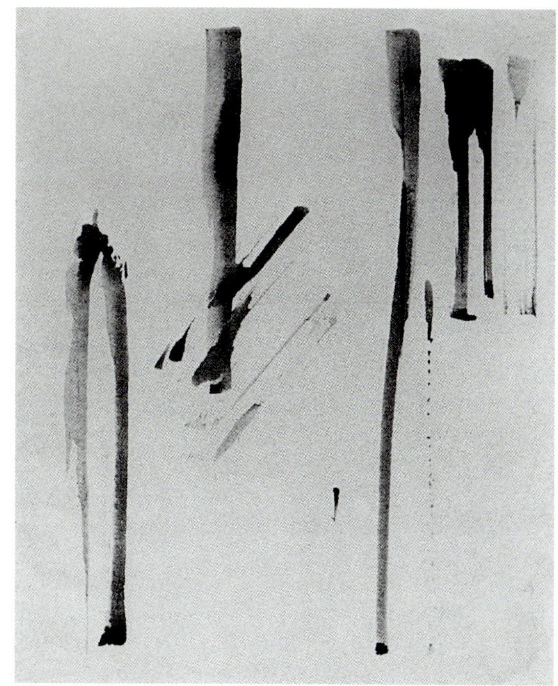

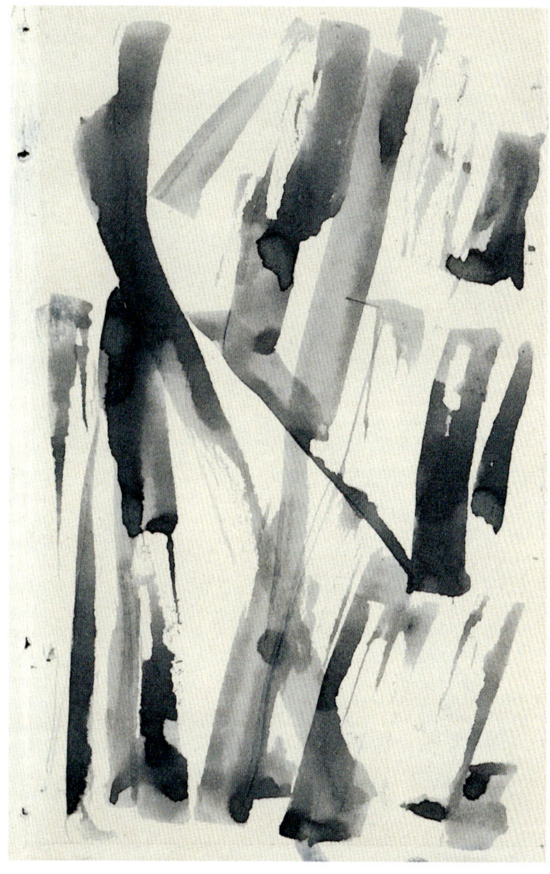

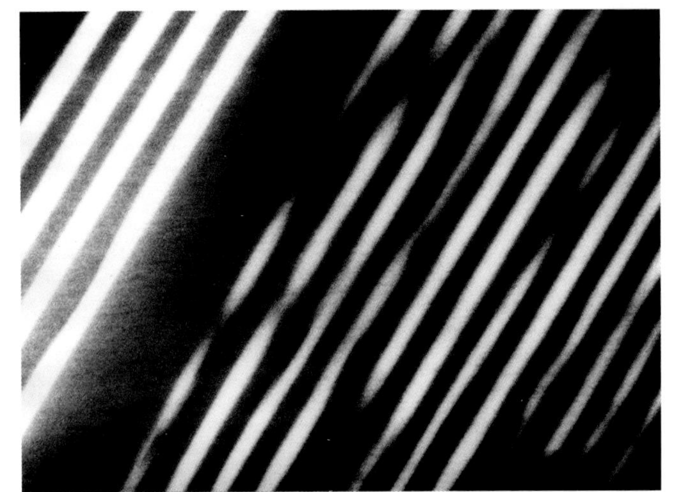

E – Ecriture d'analphabète

This is Hartung's term for a type of mark-making he associates with certain European artists, "Surrealists or informal abstractionists", whose work was executed in trance-like states more or less provoked by drugs (p. 214). He uses it in the course of a "serious" digression sandwiched into his anecdotal account of a trip to Japan in 1966 to participate in the UNESCO-sponsored conference "East–West". The digression comes directly after (or under) the parable of the Chinese painter and his line (see U). Typically, perhaps, the "little adventure[s]" of the journey take precedence over what is probably the most consolidated account Hartung ever offered of the different forms that abstraction could take—and the different kinds of origin and interpretation that accompanied them.

F – Forest

The quasi-pantheistic theory that everything that moves and every predicated movement (see M) must be referred to an ulterior motivating force or intelligence carries with it clear implications for the relationship between sentient nature and that mobile trace of the hand we call a mark or a touch. In the section of *Autoportrait* in which he engages with the ultimate meaning of his most animated pictorial lines, Hartung commences a journey (never quite completed) toward a theory that delivers art as the automatic inscription of the forces governing nature. In this sense he was ever a clandestine Surrealist (see S).

Hartung, however, seems happiest only with the preliminary steps in this series, starting with the tree and moving to the forest. First, the trees of Van Gogh which stand as pure "evidence" of the "vital forces of nature". These loaded representations carry with them such a strong impression of innate force that they become anthropomorphic, or, as Hartung writes, they "take almost human form". It is important here that Hartung's ascription of humanised values to Van Gogh's "expressive" trees arises not because these (or any) trees *look* like human beings, but because the tree is *subject to* and struggles with the same ravaging natural forces—winds, tempests etc.—as a person. To point up the particularity of Van Gogh's trees, Hartung contrasts them with the plural effacement of anything akin to a life-force in the way an Impressionist might paint a "forest"—another

5. HH, untitled, 1976, photo
6. HH, untitled, 1985, photo

example of the conjectural logic that underwrites a good number of Hartung's more complicated parables on the purport of art (see T). Hartung declares that the putative Impressionist would "express nothing of the forest" because his mark-making is organised by memory or "reminiscence"—so that a "blue band" laid down by the Impressionist as the memorial trace of a "brown band" would quite literally miss its mark. The

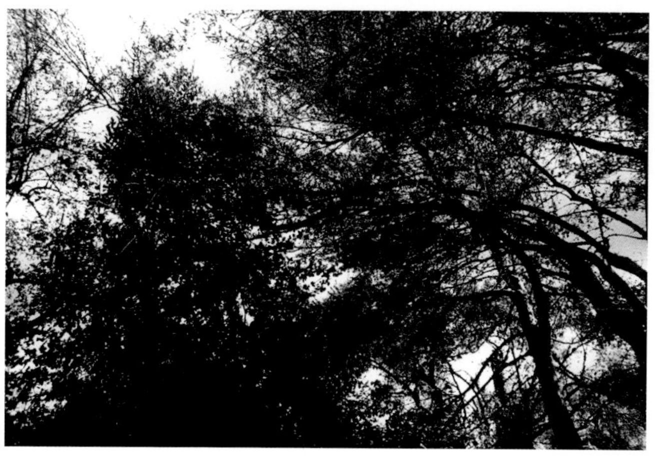

sheerly "optical" rendition of the Impressionist forest drains it of life—and in a double sense, for "the forest doesn't live, and no one lives in the forest".

In one of the most poetic passages of *Autoportrait*, Hartung rehearses the vivacious qualities of the forest that would be foreclosed in the Impressionist image: "neither its warmth, nor its colour, neither its rustling, nor the trees run up against by eye or gesture, neither the beasts that live there, nor the innumerable insects that bustle around under the dead leaves, neither the sarcastic dance of the flies, nor again the songs of the birds" (p. 75).

This is in many ways a strange excursion into the specificity of the sensations that arise from the natural world and that painting is obligated to engage. And it becomes stranger still as Hartung abruptly quits his false forest and takes up with an even more phenomenologically insistent location for necessity of palpable experience: the sea. For the Impressionist, the sea might just be a framework of colours, "green or blue", but not a physical entity in which they could swim—or about which they could entertain such sensations as weightlessness, slipperiness or the scintillation of the sun, let alone the "brutality of a wave" (p. 76).

One understands the theory behind all this, and what Hartung wants for art—even if he rather piles it on. What remains opaque here and elsewhere in his reflections is a sense of how Hartung's own work navigates any of the rhetorically elaborate specifics caught up in the world of powerful sensations that he so avidly describes.

G – Golden Section

Hartung's steadfast respect for the Golden Section exercised a profound influence on the compositional formats of his paintings and drawings as well as on the architecture of the two houses he built, in Minorca and Antibes. It provided him with a diagram for elegant proportion that, he felt, encoded something of the ancient values of beauty, perfection, tranquillity and the divine traditionally associated with its use. Above all, perhaps, the Golden Section offered a measure of "reason" and "mathematical exactness" to the ceaseless social and perceptual relativity of beauty (p. 72). Consciously or otherwise, he argued, it was the invisible figure behind the shapes and designs of the world's great artists and architects.

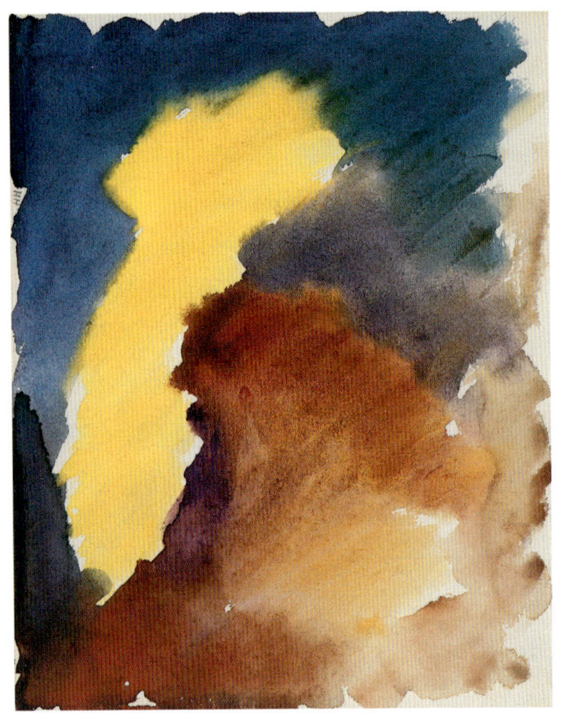

The Golden Section was one of the several ordering systems that Hartung openly acknowledged, and like the stylistic ABC, to the emergence of which he attributed precise times and locations, it too is supplied with a formative date. This is 1928, when Hartung enrolled in the summer semester of the Beaux-Arts in Dresden, where he studied under the supervision of a certain Max Dörner, who had conducted research on the material and technical history of painting.

What resulted was another of the many moves Hartung negotiated in his career that supplied his work not so much with any specific semantic content but with a formatting regime that was rich in historical continuity but at the same time complex, ineffable and "secret". In his Dresden attic that summer, Hartung hung empty canvases here and there, all versions of the Golden Section, and too perfect to be painted. He was searching for the "ideal rectangle" (p. 73) within which he could locate a picture.

The practical application of the Golden Section to the defining edge of his paintings, was the first step in Hartung's quest for a set of "rules", or a defining "law", which would help him convert the chaos of rhythm, movement and colour into visual order, a process he likened to alchemical transmutation. In a formulation that sounds almost neo-Classical, Hartung writes of translating and organising the apparently arbitrary forces of nature into forms that are orderly and harmonious. Of works produced in the late 1920s that look at first glance random and irregular, he pronounces that a sense of regulation can in fact be discerned in their compositional totality or "ensemble" (p. 74). As with the activities of ants or the trajectories of molecules, what seems haphazard when viewed close-up becomes the pattern or trace of a defining natural order when apprehended as a *gestalt* (see M).

Figured against this ground, Hartung's resolution of order, abetted by the Golden Section, becomes both leading method and final subject of the artists' paintings. Like Van Gogh's humanisation of the natural world, Hartung's images, too, are made in "complicity" with nature by offering a visual realisation of its "vital forces".

7. HH, untitled, 1922, watercolour on paper, 22 x 17.7 cm
8. HH, untitled, 1922, watercolour on paper, 26.4 x 16.7 cm
9. HH, untitled, 1922, watercolour on paper, 18 x 27.6 cm

Reminiscing about his "dark years" of poverty and obscurity in the 1930s, especially after he became a refugee in France in 1936, Hartung writes about two encounters with well-known artists (see K). Of the first he significantly says nothing. But his exchange with Hélion gave rise to one of those sanctioned desiderata which shifted from conversation to anecdote to formula, eventually becoming a foundation stone in the artist's legendary self-definition.

Hartung's account of his conversation with Hélion begins with anodyne pleasantries. Hélion, still in his abstract phase, looks at Hartung's paintings, likes them, and counsels a kind of feverish continuation: "You have to go on, you must paint, paint without stopping" (p. 111). This kind of "atta boy" encouragement, neglects, of course, the straightened circumstances of the émigré artist, who in those years could scarcely afford to buy canvas, let alone at the scale of his pictorial ambitions. Hélion's response is part pragmatic, part visionary. He offers up a procedural *economy* based on the preservation of materials—whether canvas or marks—and activated immediacy—what is literally to hand, and what the hand instinctively makes: "if you have the possibility of buying a canvas and painting a sketch that you've made, be faithful to your sketch. Don't change anything. Keep even the accidents, the unpredictable marks

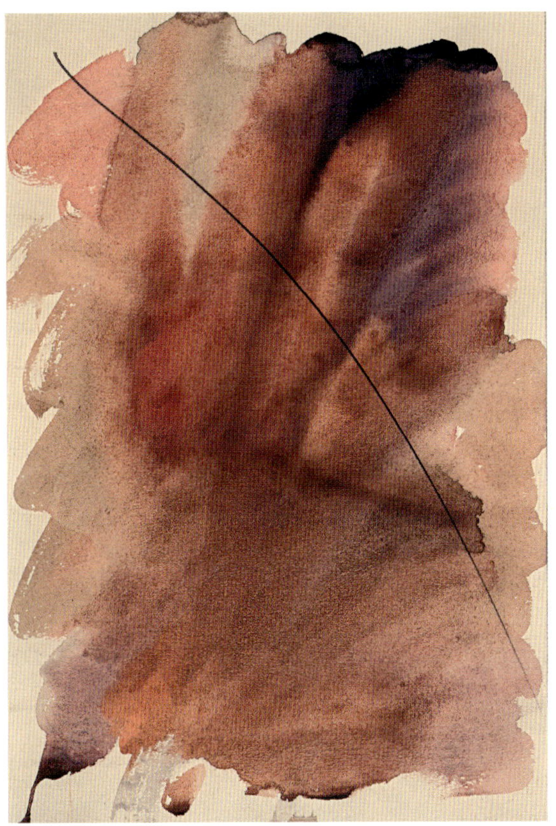

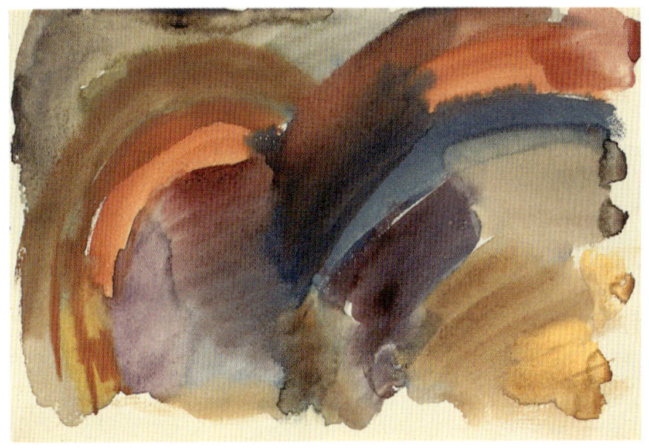

generated by the technique of watercolour, ink or wax [crayon]. Try to remain fresh, natural. It's very difficult, but the painting will benefit" (p. 112).

On Hartung's account, so long as his accidents were "happy" ones, he followed this advice until the 1960s when he began to improvise directly on the canvas. What we encounter here is an important moment in the absorption and domestication of chance or random acts by the contingencies of composition, something, one could argue, that had been hard-wired into the avant-garde ever since Hans Arp let his colourful cuts of paper flutter to the ground and be arranged "according to the laws of chance".

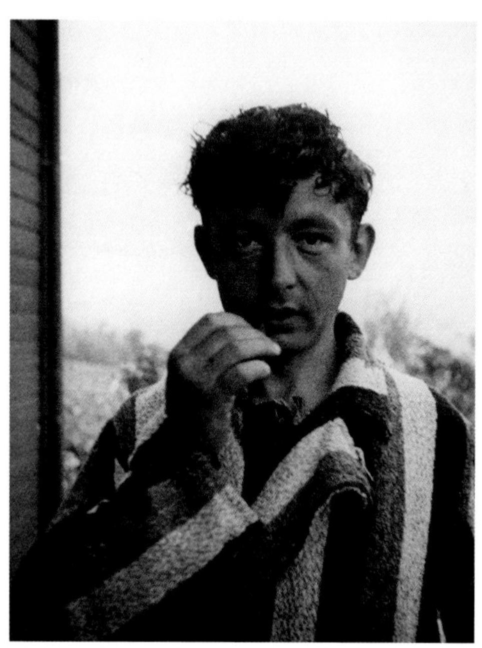

I – Intellectual

For Hartung there were two main forms of abstraction: an intellectual abstraction, the product of artists from Russia, Holland, Italy and France; and a lyrical abstraction, perhaps surreptitiously German (in one paragraph of *Autoportrait* he offers an uncharacteristically brief list of three representatives, Fautrier, Wols and himself, two of whom were German by birth. These were soon joined, however, by Schneider, Soulages, Mathieu and many others, European and American). If the defining feature of intellectual abstraction was its wilful and theoretically self-conscious rupture from the styles of the past, the lyrical variant emerged "simply, naturally and self-evidently" (p. 37), just as it apparently did in the years after 1921 when Hartung commenced his first "adult" sketches and his portraits quietly discarded the figure to become assemblages of forms, marks and rhythms.

One of the main consequences of this split presented itself as an absence, as Hartung was quick to point out: "theories and manifestoes have almost never existed among us, those painters referred to as 'lyrical'" (p. 37). This is the main reason why we are driven to dashing Hartung's ABC onto the rocks of its context and divining new sentences from the closures and elisions that cement it together.

J – Joy

Joy was a somewhat occasional and evasive experience for Hartung. It was there at the very beginning, when his adolescent portraits happily disburdened themselves of the handicaps of physical identity and the "subject" became a simple pretext for the play of "touches": "What joy ensued from letting them play freely amongst each other, accruing their own expressivity, their own relations, their dynamism, without being subject to reality" (p. 37). And, in general, the "pleasure of life" was compounded for him with "the pleasure of painting" (p. 241).

Yet, it can also arise when least expected, as when Hartung recalls the sheer material pleasures of working with soft clay: "You can beat and scrape clay, make deep or light incisions on it. It's a real joy to mass and knead it, to invent irregular forms with it, to mistreat the earth so as to give the surface rhythm!" (p. 203). The excitement here seems caught up in the palpability of beating, thumping and inscribing matter with irregular

10. Anna-Eva Bergman, Portrait of Hans Hartung at Leucate, 1929
11. HH, *T1982-H43*, 1982, acrylic on canvas, 185 x 300 cm

forms and in the transgression of administering punishment to fragments of the earth itself. But pleasure becomes joy as the goal of Hartung's manipulation echoes the foundation of his general abstraction in the "rhythmic" arbitration of surfaces.

A history of art itself might be arranged according to the joyfulness engendered by the work or person of particular artists. Against Rothko's unremitting "pessimism", Hartung celebrates Sonia Delauney who "gave so much joy to humanity" (p. 195). But Hartung's *vie en rose* was ever short-lived. His work cannot be associated, of course, with the sensuousness of Matisse; and his version of joy is even more modest than Kandinsky's *Small Pleasures*.

K – Kandinsky, Wassily

In addition to the meeting with Hélion (see H), Hartung tells us that around 1936 or 1937 he called in at Kandinsky's studio in Paris. And Kandinsky was kind enough, he notes, to repay the visit and look at Hartung's work a little while later. But what follows are two quite monumental silences. Not a word on what Hartung made of the mood-seeking geometric exercises that characterised Kandinsky's often formulaic Paris style. Here were lines and shapes and colours plotted together in a diagrammatic regimen, paintings organised as an unremitting alphabet of visual signs, the interpretation of which was governed by a dictionary of meanings such as the one Kandinsky wrote himself around 1926 while he was at the Bauhaus, *Point and Line to Plane*.

A few years earlier, Hartung attended a lecture by Kandinsky in Leipzig but reported being "neither seduced nor convinced" by his "discourse on the use and symbolism of the circle, the oval, the square and the rectangle" (p. 64). But still, not a word in Paris about

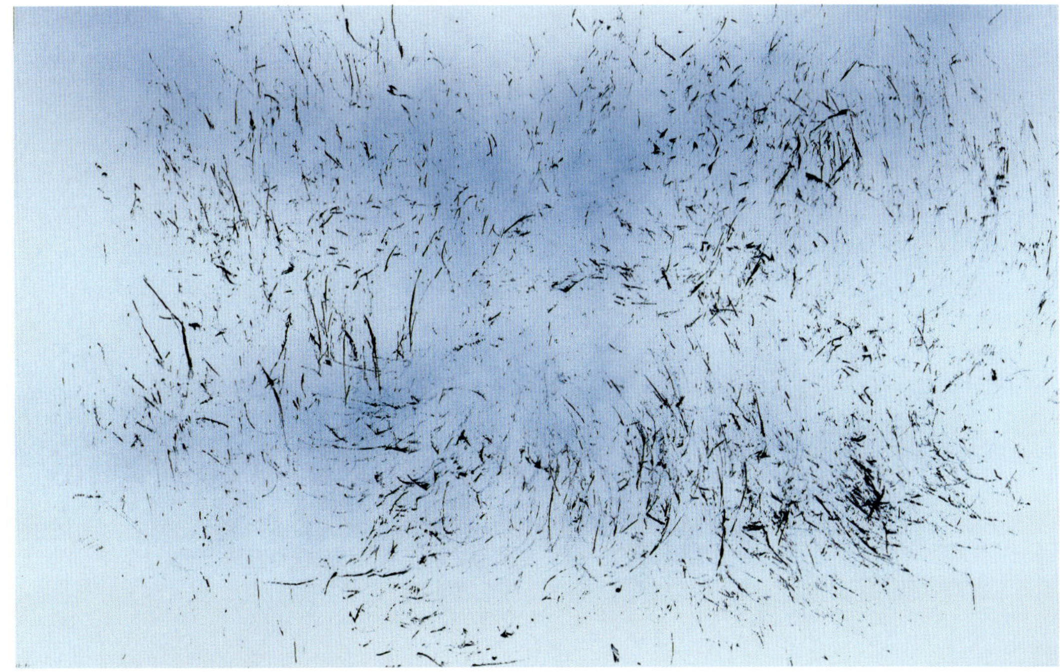

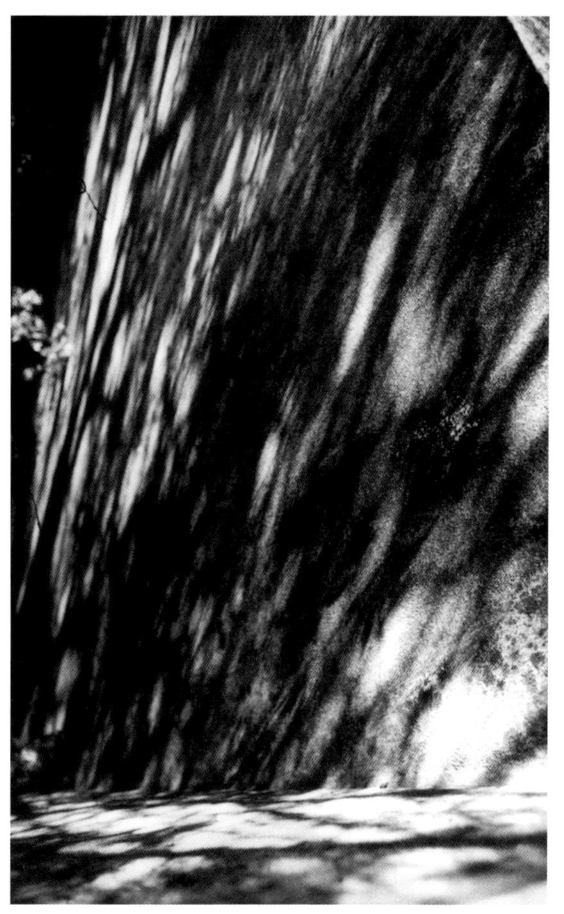

what Kandinsky said to Hartung. Not a single word about anything that transpired in two studio visits that must have been of signal importance to Hartung, at least. But perhaps this was inevitable in a clash between alphabets, one rather fragile and not to be pronounced in words, the other indomitable and almost wholly anchored by every manner of title, equivalence and dependency.

L – Lithography
The somewhat surprising source of a profound liberation from dependence on the *trait* that feeds into the later paintings (p. 202).

M – Movement
On the one hand, that which moves denoted for Hartung the life-force, the very substrate of his theory of representation. Equally, irresolute movement presaged chaos, disorder and lawlessness. Hartung offers a rather impassioned account of a moment in his practice that gave rise to works that "at first sight" appeared chaotic, haphazard and lawless. The better to explain how the "ensemble" effects of such paintings were, in fact, "unified" and "harmonious", he resorts to several elaborate, parable-like comparisons taken from the natural world. We are invited to imagine, first, an anthill on which a certain obstacle has been placed. What transpires in this situation by way of "movement"—and "at what speed"—is simply incredible, he suggests: "the ants run to the left, to the right, perform abrupt about-faces, turn back on themselves, return, go off again, change direction from a straight line without any hesitation". Such movements, he concludes, seem to us absurd, disorganised and the result of some mad panic. It's the same with molecules: "Their directions, their movements seem demented, helter-skelter, random".

Once again, however, the truth of the matter is different, for molecular particles (and ants) do exactly "what is prescribed for them, that which the law, their law, imposes on them" (pp. 74–75). Hartung turns here into the theological cul-de-sac of predetermination, placing his faith in the mechanical inevitability of a natural world in which every action

12. HH, untitled, 1985, photo
13. HH, *Self-portrait*, 1964, photo

is "ordained", and its consequences are always transmitted through one category of eventuating experience: "a calm, assured force" (p. 75). Hartung's utter "complicity" with nature gives rise to another parable, this time more closely tied to the history of representation. This is the exemplum of the forest (see F)—a situation, perhaps, in which one can only see the wood for the trees.

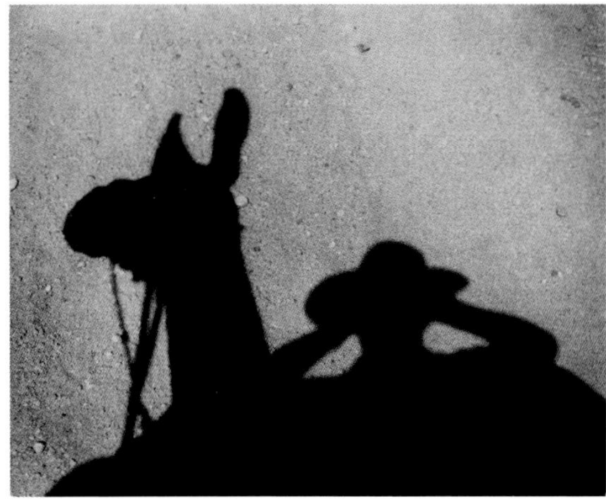

N – Nonsense

Here in the middle of Hartung's Abcedarium, it is appropriate to meditate on the lack of sense and equally the nonsense and the false sense attributed by Hartung and his critics to the artist's lines, forms and colours and the lives lived around them. The artist's Manichean vision was always fixed on the fundamental polarity between chaos and order, and even though he understood his work as promoting a shift from one to the other, the initial randomness of things often confounded and overwhelmed him.

At the centre of his work and thought was a certain half-knowing befuddlement, often brought on by his encounters with the social, and epitomised in the fear, even "panic", induced in him by an exhibition opening—that moment of public declaration for the work of art. He would loose track of etiquette, forget the names of attendees, want to speak… but couldn't: "I stammer, get things wrong, I mumble" (p. 228).

O – O

Let's make this a number (see Y). So, zero. The next step (that can never be taken) after the last line (see U).

P – Photography

One of Hartung's lists reads as follows: "people, clouds, water, mountains, cracking, mould, and all sorts of light and dark effects".[3] In *Autoportrait*, his list is rhetorically abbreviated: "a crack in a wall, clouds, it doesn't really matter" (p. 227). These are, of course, summaries of the subject matter that interested him as a photographer. People and portraiture aside, they reconvene the natural, elemental forms, substances and effects that underwrote the abstract naturalism of his pictorial orientation.

But what was photography to Hartung? Well, it took on both more and less than his work as a draughtsman and painter. More, in that his photographs created images of figures, locations and motifs, all of which were banished from his paintings after the mid-1920s, as well as abstract forms and patterns. Hartung was happy to acknowledge that photography was an *aide-memoire*, or "second memory", that bore witness to the world around him, and resurrected the forms of all the "disappeared faces" that were threaded through his life (p. 226). But it was always less, in that Hartung never claimed that he was a real photographer or that his camera images could be counted as "art" or even photo-journalism. Photography wasn't his metier. He was an amateur, or, better, a painter who photographed.

Yet there was one defining continuity between Hartung's photography and his painting: both practices, in their different but overlapping ways, were agents in the production of the synthetic order solicited by the artist from his early days.

Q – Quant á ma peinture

"As for my painting, I truly think it maintains a relationship, constant but very complex relationships, with that which we have come to term exterior reality".

R – Rembrandt's Robe

What was it that engendered Hartung's almost hallucinatory obsession with a "bit of painting"? Hatching without boundaries; exuberant spirals, occasionally abetted by the contingencies of motifs like the turban; a flurry of round-the-compass reed-pen marks on the cloak in *Portrait of a Man* (1660–65) in the Louvre; ex-orbital bistre and fuzzy washes; dashes of red chalk and Indian ink; immense patterns of shading; singular lines stranded far from their governing volumes. Hartung took all this in, stripping out the subject and fetishising the remainder. The bottom register of *The Holy Family in the Carpenter's Workshop* (Musée Bayonne)[4] was ever his ghostly parergon.

Hartung tells the history of this relation: it began with a lost essay on Rembrandt he wrote as a schoolboy at the Lycée in Dresden, and continued with visits to the Gemäldegallerie in his native city and later, around 1921 or 1922, precisely the date he ascribes to the birth of his symbolic alphabet, to the Musée de Brauchschweig. Here, in front of *La Famille*, he was enraptured by the flurried composition of the robe of the mother with its "abstract form and rhythm". Hartung remembers making his own works in the manner of Rembrandt but these were stored in a family house in Leipzig, and later lost in the allied bombardment. In 1927–28 he began to collect facsimiles of Rembrandt's engravings which became the basis for a more settled retrospective "self-explication" based on the "black-and-white" calligraphy of the master's prints and drawings.

For Hatung Rembrandt's robe is a means of defying time and embodiment.

S – Surrealism

"Its spirit was strange to me: I took no part in it" (p. 83).

T – Titles

Hartung several times insisted that neither his work nor his personal disposition was especially literary: "I am not a literary man" (p. 219). We would not expect, then, that he would indulge with any special enthusiasm in the nomination of his canvases, nor, in particular, that he would relish any form of metaphorical designation. Interestingly, however, Hartung joins a select group of modern artists and critics, reaching back to Charles Baudelaire, James

| 14. HH, *After Frans Hals*, 1920, watercolour on paper, 25 x 34.8 cm

MacNeil Whistler and Paul Gauguin, whose anxieties about the impingement of text into the signifying domain of the image gave rise to a series of parables founded on imaginative projections of speculative titles. Titles were so dangerous (and seductive) to the Symbolist, formalist and exoticist purviews of these three artists that they each directed several agitated paragraphs to the issue, with the purpose of either disavowing titular indulgence alto-

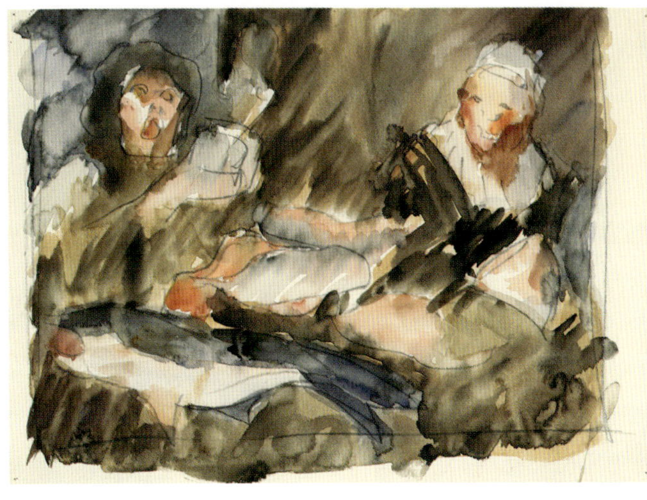

gether (Baudelaire and Whistler), or, in the case of Gauguin, explaining at great length just how a suggestive title should be negotiated. In the course of their mediations all came up with examples of specious titles and titling procedures that should at all costs be resisted[5].

And so did Hartung. Prompted by his war-time experience with the "draconian" Spanish export laws governing works of art, which required the exact dimensions, titles and three photographs for each painting or drawing taken out of the country, Hartung offers a digression on his theory of the title. This begins predictably enough with a version of the anti-titular exhortation raised to vehement abhorrence by Clyfford Still. "From the beginning I have never given titles to my paintings, only numbers". But Hartung clearly felt the necessity of explaining further: his avoidance of titles was based primarily on a commitment not to "influence" or in any way impose on the spectator, whose interpretation of the work should be "completely... free" (p. 102).

It is at this point, before returning to his narrative about the cancellation of a planned exhibition in Oslo, that Hartung writes some of the strangest lines in his autobiography: "If I said [to a spectator], 'this is Zeus, descending from the sky, or this is general depression, or this is neurosis', at that very moment people would look for neurosis" (p. 102).

Strange, it would seem, in two ways. Most immediately because of the apparent bizarreness of the examples he chooses, and secondly, because, as with Baudelaire and company before him, the very specificity (and curiosity) of the subjects cited prompts us to move against the grain of Hartung's argument by questioning how and why it is that they emerge as exemplifications of a viewing and reading process that Hartung doesn't want. It is naturally tempting to look at the three subjects—Zeus, depression and neurosis—in Freudian terms as repressive returns. And there is clear sanction for this, as two of Hartung's forbidden titles explicitly name psychological disorders, to which, if we read between the lines of the autobiography, he was prone, at least from time to time.

The third subject, Zeus, the father of the Greek gods, the epitome of allegorical or historical forms of representation, appears to be an altogether more inexplicable inclusion. Perhaps Hartung was simply citing a random example of a type of representation diametrically opposed to his own? But there is surely more to his choice than this. Zeus is king of the cosmos, chief orderer of the firmament and architect of providence. Hartung has him descending from the sky, moving from the transcendent to the terrestrial, mediating between here and the beyond. The magus of the zigzag (see Z) is caught inscribing himself in the visible, and in this condition it is surely not impossible to imagine him as a figure of Hartung himself, or the artist in general. Nor is it now farfetched to argue that this shift from heaven to earth is posed in opposition to two forms of disorder bound to the anxieties of the inner self. For Hartung, art was always an attempt to find an eloquent short-circuit between the inner self and the cosmological, without making recourse to the precipitating clarities—or obfuscating uncertainties—of language.

U – Underline

Two senses interest me here: first, the emphatic; and secondly, the regime beneath the line, all that transpires under its mark. The general question of linearity in Hartung is clearly crucial, but even more important are those moments in the artist's thinking when consideration of the line itself is elevated. In this regard, the decisive passage in his *Autoportrait* is another parable, one of the most extended—and heartfelt—in Hartung's writings. This is the story of the Chinese artist commissioned by the emperor to paint a work commemorating his victory in a famous battle. The artist withdraws and is not heard of for months. The emperor eventually summons him and the artist shows a sketch marked only with three lines. The emperor is angry, but out of respect for the reputation and good faith of the artist, grants him an extension to complete the work. Once more months and years pass by. The emperor summons the painter again, and is once more presented with the same sketch, except that it now bears only two lines. The emperor is exasperated and thinks that the painter is mocking him. But the artist assures his master that the work is the product of long meditation and patient research. And the emperor allows him to leave once more to finish the painting. When the painter returns with the canvas it has only one line. Now older and more reflective, the emperor is not angry. He understands what the painter wants to express: "In this sole line, this unique mark, he had concentrated and united in the absolute all the energy, courage and value that the emperor has himself deployed to win the battle" (p. 213). And the emperor makes him court painter.

Of course, not a word of commentary from Hartung. For the ultimate wisdom of reduction needs no explication. In a sense, all of Hartung's work falls under this final line. The line itself becomes an emblem of the gestalt of cumulative knowledge, painstaking abstraction, and reflective essentialism that distils pictorial signification into a summary form of the absolute.

V – Vertigo

Hartung's struggle to overcome this "feebleness" allowed him to take his place as a superior "biped" (his term) and to participate in the defining equilibrium that secured his

15. HH, *T1981-H19*, 1981, acrylic on canvas, 114 x 146 cm

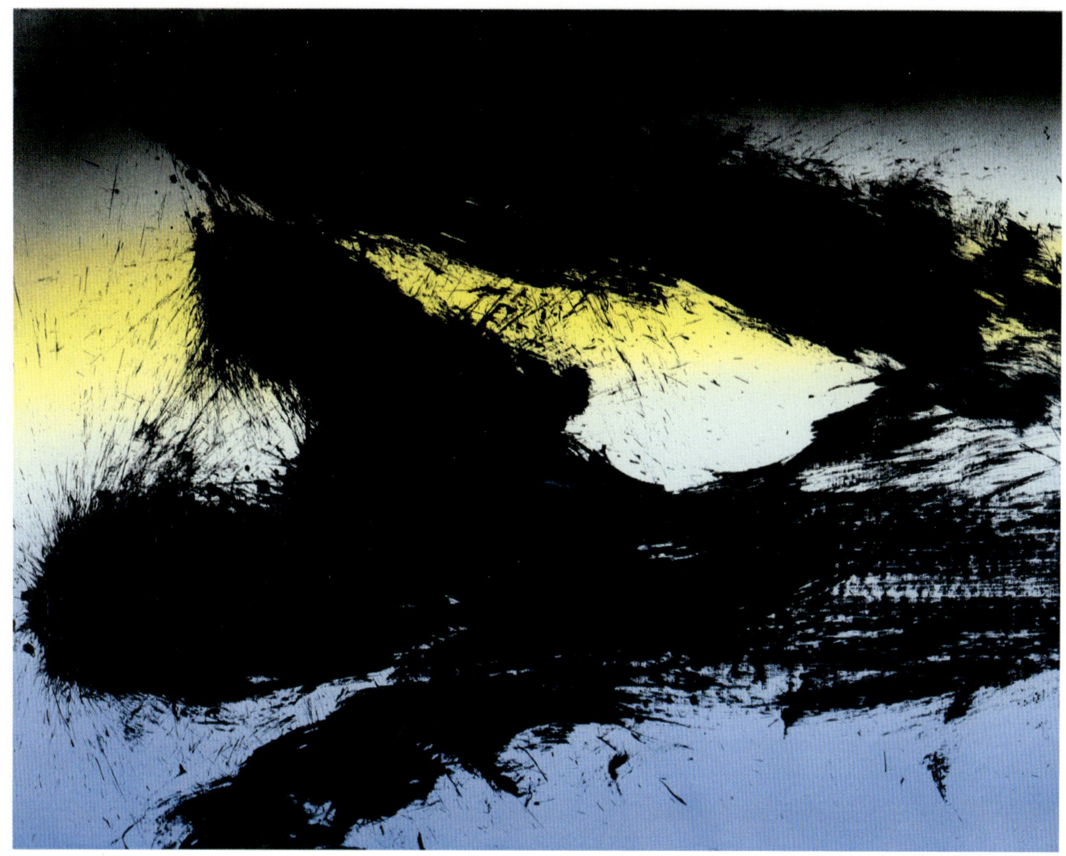

proper relation to gravity and thence to the physical world. His lines—whether "subtle and flexible, curved or straight, rigid or powerful"—and his colour touches—whether strident, joyous (see J), or sinister—were emblems of this continuity, stretching out between the self and universe as "particular incarnations" of the life spirit he encapsulated in his most organically transcendent list: "a budding plant, pulsing blood, everything that is germination, consciousness, *élan vital*, living force, resistance, sadness or joy (see J)" (p. 252).

W – Will Grohmann (and watercolours)

The noted German critic became a friend of Hartung's "for life" following his appearance at the artist's exhibition in Dresden in the winter of 1931. It was on this occasion that Grohmann offered one of the first of those commentaries-cum-advisories that Hartung preserved throughout his career with unflinching fidelity. In *Autoportrait*, Hartung even compares Grohmann's sage recommendations to the advice he received half a decade later from Hélion (see H). Unattended as ever by any gloss or qualification from the artist himself, Grohmann's observations point to a central issue in the signification of Hartung's work: "Your painting seems interesting to me, but you haven't given it any explicit content. Only red, blue, yellow, green, that's all. So you must replace the figuration that you've repressed with the aesthetic, with the perfection of plastic forms. Your canvases must be beautiful"

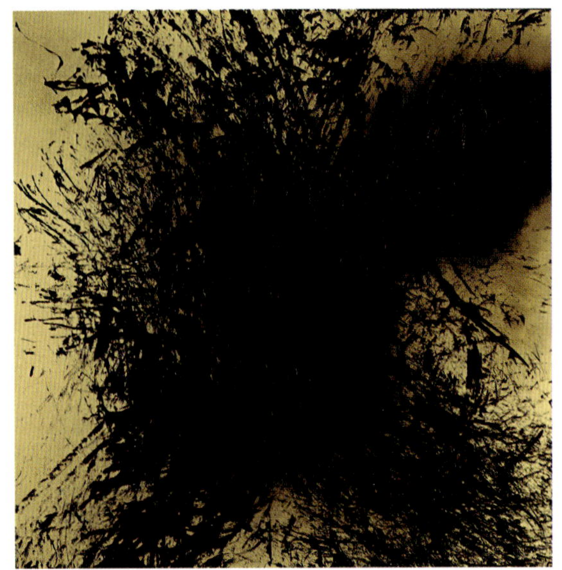

(pp. 88–89). There is something almost frightening in this remark, for beauty and necessity make awkward bedfellows, especially in the work of an abstract painter.

From a historical point of view, Grohmann pointed here to what he clearly perceived as Hartung's manifest destiny. He was surely aware that Hartung's paintings had largely disavowed all forms of subject-matter, whether based on the reduction of a motif, on the expression of the self, or a correlation between form and feeling. Hartung's works were fundamentally different from those of the artists discussed by Grohmann throughout his distinguished career—the lines, colours and shapes of Kandinsky, which purportedly conducted the spirit from mark to mood, or the work of Paul Klee, whose motifs were seldom unaccompanied by doses of wit and whimsy or a network of subterranean references.

The need for beauty was the aesthetic cost, then, of an abstraction wholly untethered from reference except of an extremely general—or cosmological—kind. Curiously, when Grohmann wrote his most extended remarks on the work of Hartung in 1966, the terms recalled by the artist in his autobiography were nowhere to be seen. First, Grohmann dates his first encounter with Hartung's work (his watercolours of 1922) to their exhibition in the late 1920s. Second, while he grapples extensively with the problem of signification in this work, Grohmann never mentions the theory of necessary beauty narrated by Hartung, preferring instead to speculate on the relation of the watercolours to language—thus offering the first few letters of his own ABC. Grohmann accounts for what he determines is Hartung's "interior vision" by correlating it with an "interior language", which, while "free" is not without either "grammar" and "syntax" or even its own "dialectic".[6] As ever, no grammar is even attempted, and Grohmann, like Hartung himself when he points to the concept of "analphabetic writing" (see E), avoids entirely the communicative implications of language. The empty predicates behind the necessity of beauty (attributed by Hartung to Grohmann) meet the absent semantics of language symptomatic in the textual circumlocutions of both artist and critic.

X – Xénophilie/Xénophobie

Though an immigrant himself, who was dispatched around North Africa and Europe in the French Foreign Legion during World War II, it's not especially clear if Hartung entertained

16. HH, *T1980-R37*, 1980, acrylic on canvas, 180 x 180 cm
17. HH, *T1977-R42*, 1977, acrylic on canvas, 100 x 81 cm

any special sympathy for strangers. One side of his relation to travel was a form of solitary adventure, such as that he relates directly after his remarks on the forest (see F), in which he aimed to immerse himself in nature so that he could "comprehend" it—and, most importantly, not "betray" it in his painting. In these circumstances at least, nature itself certainly took precedence over any participation in human groups. And it was as a kind of ultimate reparation with the natural world and its logical expressions that he worked out his own accommodation with the totality of outside forces. At the most abstract and general level of his convictions there were no strangers and no strangeness for Hartung, and thus no xenophobia or xenophilia. All differences were merely brief uneven moments in the play of preconditioned terms. Or, to put it another way, all movement (see M), including migration and journeying, no matter how superficially stressful or complicated, was the product of an ulterior directive, fraught with greater purpose and therefore never without its inner logic.

This said, Hartung was continually wrestling with the strangenesses and alienations that beset him—whether the disarming clarities of the French language, the lack of mobility and sensation that went with the loss of his leg, or the aggravating misdirections of artists and movements (such as the Impressionists) who were unable to engage with the visceral closeness of sensation.

Y – Years

The diary or chronicle is the chronological equivalent of the ABC, offering a framework of digits and days for the sequencing of a life. *Autoportrait* neither embraces nor eschews the logic of the diary. Published in 1976, its drift and spacing are broadly chronological, and it reaches thus from the beginning of Hartung's life (1904) to a decade or so before its end in 1989. Yet what really animates it are the counter-narrative outbreaks of the text—the string of parable-like tales; disquisitions on the nature of art; a series of premonitions, foreshadowings, and regressions; and the para-chronological return of certain characters and events (including Kandinsky [see K]; Will Grohmann [see W]; and Jean Hélion [see H]).

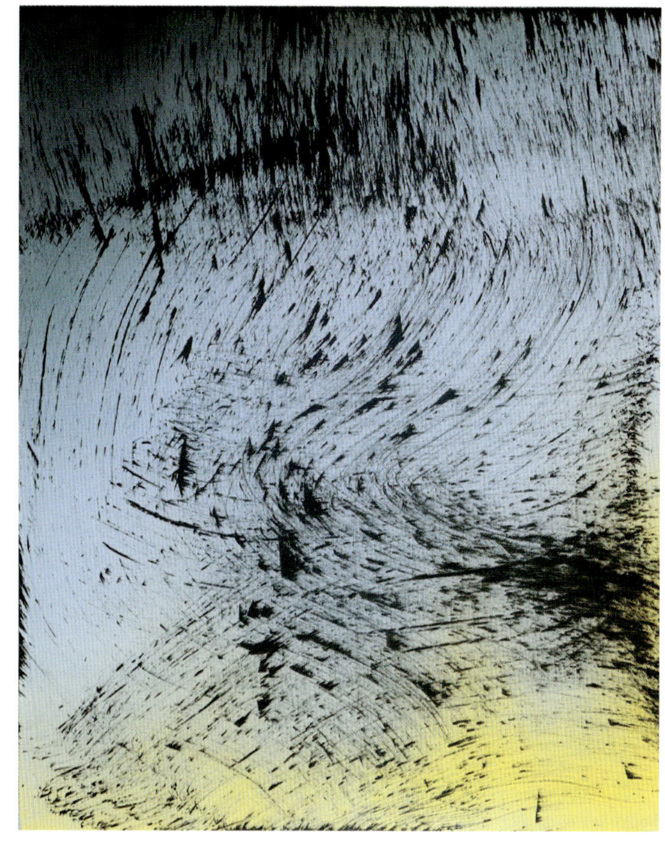

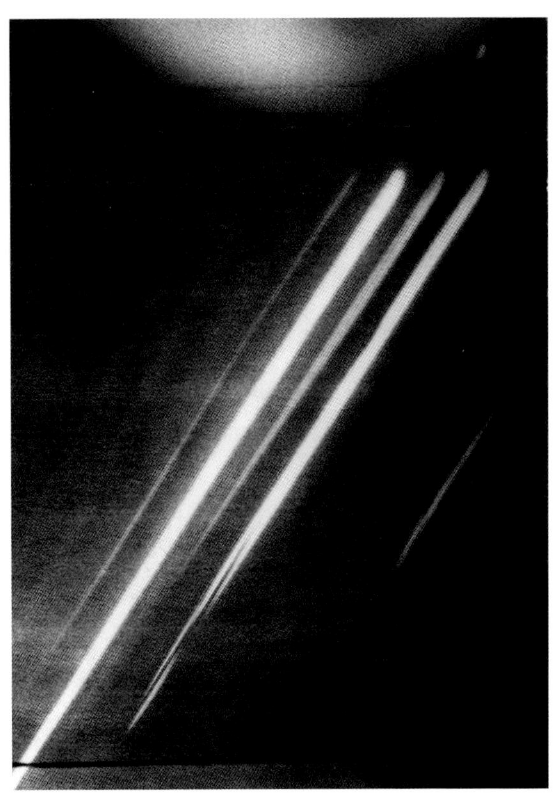

These detours and spaces in the annual progression of the text are the building blocks for this ABC, while its syntax is formed from the hidden connections that link them.

But we should also call attention to the title (see T) of Hartung's book. It is not termed an autobiography, a memoir or a life—it is called, surely with deliberation, a "self-portrait". There is a clear suggestion in this that the destiny of its vast accumulation of written lines corresponds to that of the mass of pictorial lines gathered up in the totality of the artist's oeuvre. And that both must be referred to the same destiny that Hartung alludes to (rather than insists on) throughout his textual self-representation, as ciphers for the expressive play of natural forces.

Z – Zigzag

We must end with the beginning, with the *éclair* or bolt of lightning that is the founding image of Hartung's childhood recollections, the point of origin of his *Autoportrait* and a defining and recurrent motif in the development of his art. The visceral fear of storms passed down from his grandmother and over-sensitive mother was effectively diffused by the young Hartung, who, according to his own account, summoned up the courage not simply to confront the shocking, apocalyptic double strike of sound and light, but to exorcise his minor pathology through representation. Refusing to be incarcerated in the "storm corridor" of the family home, Hartung literally drew the psychological sting out of lightning by tracing its elemental form. His drawings were rapid and repetitive and the zigzag pattern proliferated wildly across his school books, which his father called Hans' *Blitzbücher*.

As both author and subject of these foundational sketches, Hartung, of course, offers an account of their implications for his future practice as an artist, how they influenced what he terms his "manner of painting" (p. 8). His reflections converge on three ideas or experiences generated by this primal scene of representation. The lightning bolts he drew engendered, he suggested, first, "a sense of the speed of the mark [*trait*]"; secondly, "the desire to seize the instantaneous with crayon or pen", and, thirdly, they made him "understand the urgency of spontaneity". Speed, urgency, instantaneousness, and

18. HH, untitled, 1976, photo
19. HH, untitled, 1922, India ink on paper, 20.1 x 15.3 cm

spontaneity—these were the founding tropes established by critics and associated with expressive, gestural abstraction on both sides of the Atlantic, as Hartung's work emerged into the public domain in the late 1940s and 1950s.

As is well-known, however, Hartung's paintings in general, but especially those produced in the years during which this gesturalist discourse was first elaborated, were seldom spontaneous. Instead, the artist used drawings, often made months or years beforehand, as the basis for quite literal, even painstaking, *simulations* of the earlier pen or charcoal compositions. While he would add or change the colouristic register, he would seldom undertake a major recasting of the config-uration of lines and shapes. Instead he used small brushes and precise, controlled

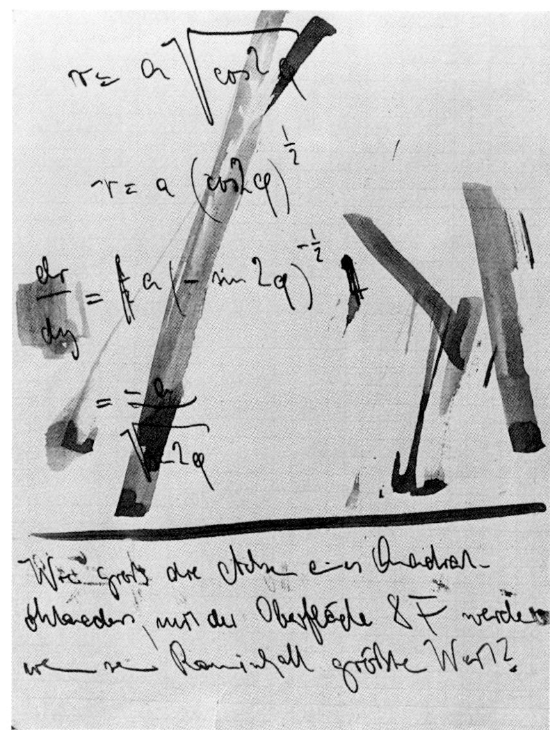

strokes to confect an analogous pattern of swirls, meshes and zigzags.

What does this mean for the allegory of instantaneousness emblematized in the zigzag that we encounter in his *Autoportrait*? Is it an autobiographic dissimulation couched in psychobiographical terms that both answers to, and vicariously seeks to originate, the mythology of gesture? Well, in part, maybe. But while there is evidently an element of fabrication or, at least, of *reading-in*, in the zigzag narrative, it also couples with a grain of truth. In order to understand the creative duplicity of this story we need to confront the nature of the sign around which it is organised and its function as a double agent of signification.

Three things stand out. First, the zigzag is a diagrammatic or shorthand representation of a moment of atmospheric pyrotechnics in which electricity appears as a jagged line of light. In relation to this celestial script, the zigzag both simplifies and embellishes. It sim-plifies in that the lightning of an electric storm, while "forked" or diagonal, seldom declares itself in the simplicity of a "Z". Nor, on the other hand, does it often appear with the horizontal head and tail which extend on opposite sides of the diagonal line that con-nects them in this figure. The "Z" is thus too complex and too linear to act as an index for lightning. The signs "I" or a "Y" just might be more appropriate.

Secondly, the zigzag is a sign for a split, the mark of a rupture or puncture or cut. At the same time, it is always doubled, a sign that turns back on itself and is subject to eter-nal recurrence. It is a line that becomes a vector only to become a line again. A line that carves through space only to assert its linearity. Its hard edges mark it out from the softer serpentine that Hogarth and the early German art historians took as a sign of beauty. From the "S" to the "Z" we might say, is a journey from the perception of elegance and sensuousness to the incarnation of the sublime: from beauty to the bolt.

Finally, the zigzag is an annunciation. It is a formulation of the first aspect in the dramatic coordination of flashing light and thunderous sound. In a sense it is an apparition that appears only to anticipate what comes after it in another, sonic, dimension. While in English we always say "thunder and lightning", the zigzag is really the alpha and not the omega of elemental signage. The moment of illumination that forms it is also the beginning of an interval, that gradient of time between flash and thunder that indicates the intensity and presence of a storm.

Hartung was clearly aware of some of the implications, at least, caught up in the graphic sign that announced his own career. For his narrative emphasises the prophylactic power encoded in the *situation* of his zigzag marks. No matter where or on what they were drawn—on papers, school books, covers, wherever (there is no formatting yet in Hartung's world of representation)—he maintains that his "Z" signs were formed precisely in the interval between flash and sound. If he could draw his bright, electric model in the second or so between its appearance and the arrival of the thunder, he would have conquered the storm and vanquished his inherited fear: "Nothing could happen to me if my line followed the speed of lightning" (p. 8).

It is a profound manoeuvre. One that allows us to see why Hartung was so uninterested in taking on the correlation of human feelings with expressive style, which is how he read Van Gogh; or in landscape as a geometry, which is how he might have understood Cézanne. If your work is founded in the sublime geometry of the "Z", which also brokers its own passage from line to space (and back), then there is no need to reproduce nature in cubic or conical or cylindrical form. Nor, if you have gone straight to the "Z", is there any use for some dubious alphabet of psychological equivalences, say, Kandinsky's Larousse of planes and points and lines, each with its emotional correlate and mood-seeking equivalent. Hartung's first marks effectively outnature the natural world by duplicating its most aggressive form in order to nullify or ward off its terrifying effects. By this sovereign gesture, Hartung is able to take on and simultaneously dispense with nature by absconding with its force and remaindering it as an abstraction.

1. All the pages cited in this essay refer to *Autoportrait*.

2. Hans Hartung, *Bergens Aftenblad*, 12 Oct. 1936, trans. Maria Aanderaa, Fondation Hans Hartung et Anna-Eva Bergman; cited in Jennifer Mundy, "Hans Hartung: A Gestural Draftsman", in *Hans Hartung, works on paper, 1922-1956*, exh. cat., London, Tate Gallery (London: Tate Gallery Publishing, 1996), p. 29.

3. Hans Hartung, *70 Photographies du peintre Hans Hartung*, Le Conseil Régional Provence Alpes Côte d'Azur, 1980, n.p.

4. This work is a preliminary study for a painting of 1645 in St Petersburg; see Seymore Slive, *Drawings of Rembrandt* (New York: Dover, 1965), vol. II, fig. 352. For a discussion of the relation between Rembrandt's drawings and Hartung, see "Rembrandt et l'art contemporain" in *La Gazette Litteraire* (*Gazette de Lausanne*), 25 October 1969, which reproduces details of several works by both artists as well as a letter from Hartung.

5. The history and critical implications of these titles are discussed in John C. Welchman, *Invisible Colors: A Visual History of Titles* (London: Yale University Press, 1997).

6. Extracts from Grohmann's essay of 1966 can be found, in French, at http://www.fondationhartungbergman.fr/pubtemp/engl/grohmann.htm

John C. Welchman Hans Hartung

Abcedarium: Reading Between the Lines

Franz-W. Kaiser A Case Study on the Caducity of Categories in Art Criticism Annie Claustres

Hans Hartung

Clandestine Artist

1937-1942: the Decisive Years

Christine Mehring Hans Hartung

Mid-Century Modern

Rainer Michael Mason Hartung

and Printmaking Christopher Wool

Selected Works

Anne Pontégnie 1975

Hartung at the

Metropolitan Museum

Chronicle of a Failure Chantal Eschenfelder

Hans Hartung in Germany

Laurence Bertrand Dorléac

Germany and France

Two Parts in One Jennifer Mundy

The Very Late Style of Hans Hartung

a Problem?

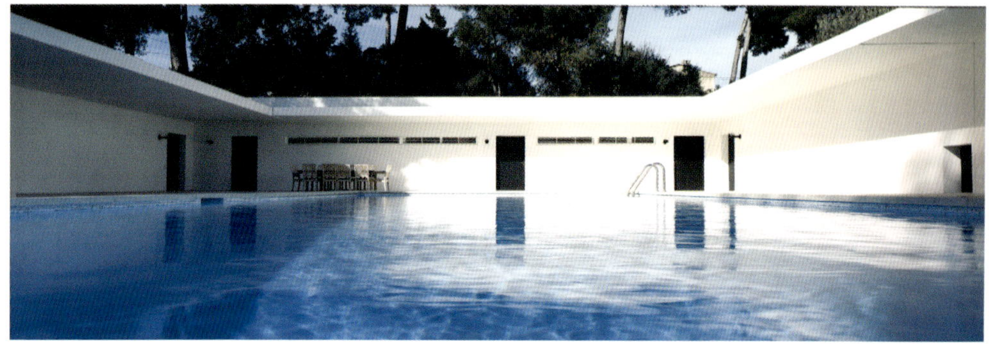

Hans Hartung is regarded as one of the founders of gestural painting in Europe, a variety of expressive or lyrical abstraction, the first truly "international style" to dominate art on both sides of the Atlantic in the mid-twentieth century. The adjectives "lyrical" or "expressive" qualified a direct, almost physical painterly approach to material or form, unlike the pre-war geometrical abstraction characterised by rational construction. However, expressive abstraction's domination did not survive the second half of the century. In the Sixties Pop art rapidly ousted it from the limelight of what by then was a transatlantic art-scene. In the Seventies attention shifted to minimal and conceptual art, in the Eighties back to painting—preferably not abstract—and in the final decade of the twentieth century to politically correct, media-technical or "sensational" art.

Only a relatively small part of the art world is aware of the fact that until his death in 1989 Hartung lived very well from his painting and was extremely productive. This does not tally with his image as a painter who is pigeonholed as a representative of gestural painting, of the lyrical abstraction whose heyday was over by the Fifties. Caricatural though this may sound, it basically reflects the manner in which the art world sees art. Simplification serves here to clarify a mechanism and certainly not to deride it. On the contrary, art's social function depends on such mechanisms, which brings us to the theme of this article. We are dealing here with the gap that yawns between an artist's "image"—the "picture" that the (art) world has of him and the category in which he is consequently filed—and the artistic problem he sets himself, the actual development of his oeuvre. The thesis addressed here is that each follows its own development, the logics of which have much less in common than is usually taken for granted. Public image and its correspondence with the prevailing conceptions of value or art-critical categories at a given point in time are what determine an artist's success. In as far as the image is linked to an era, it has little to do with an oeuvre's timeless value. That value is measured rather by artistic coherence and by a more fundamental appropriateness of the work to the era of its making, and also by its art-historical consequences. Certainly, some artists have been recognised by their epoch as important and nevertheless are still considered as such. But art history is full of examples of the opposite type: the artist unacknowledged while he is alive but whose greatness

1. Patio of the Hartung villa in Antibes, 2000, photo
2. Model of the Hartung villa in Antibes, 1968

is recognised later. The tritest example of this type has to be Van Gogh. The most common case is when the public's taste coincides with an oeuvre's development over a limited period: when a window opens on an artistic oeuvre for a while. Rembrandt is a classical case in point: at the peak of his career he was hailed as the "Dutch Apelles"; twenty years later he died in poverty, but this does not detract a jot from his veneration today. Hartung, too, who regarded Rembrandt as his most important art-historical anchor, is best assigned to this third category. That is why he is not presented here as a gestural painter but as a case study for the thesis that to a considerable extent an artist's oeuvre and its public image develop separately, and that the two must therefore be considered separately. Only then can the nucleus around which the oeuvre develops be separated from its time-bound interpretation.[1] And only then can we identify the influence of prevailing taste on social recognition and possibly on the oeuvre itself. However, separating oeuvre and image is only possible from a sufficient temporal distance and only after prevailing taste has changed.

After Hans Hartung's death on 7 December 1989 in his villa in Antibes, in the south of France, a foundation was set up there for the preservation and administration of his work and that of his wife: the Fondation Hans Hartung et Anna-Eva Bergman. When I first visited the foundation, I was struck by the architecture of the buildings on the property, having been told that the artist himself had designed it. One would not expect from an expressionist artist the design of such a minimalist architecture (figs. 1, 2). Only after having delved a bit deeper into some hardly known aspects of Hartung's working method would I understand how consistent this architecture actually is with his seemingly very different paintings. My interest in these working methods was triggered by my confrontation, again in Antibes, with some unfinished canvases that had come to light, when the foundation had drawn up the studio inventory. The artist appears to have abandoned them while he was still in the stage of drawing the contours. I was intrigued because they contradict the general perception of gestural painting, for the stage of outlining a form that has yet to be painted is only consistent with a more classical notion of painting. As a stage in the genesis of a gestural painting it plainly contradicts the qualification "gestural" (fig. 3). There are also finished versions of some of these unfinished paintings—often in different formats and other colour combinations (fig. 4)—which at first glance really do look as if they were done spontaneously. They are, however, precisely detailed enlargements of ink sketches also belonging to the foundation (fig. 5). What on canvas look like uncontrolled slips made by a few erratic brush-hairs are actually painted with the utmost precision. Could the direct explosion on canvas—the trademark of lyrical abstraction—have been turned into a masquerade by one of its leading protagonists?

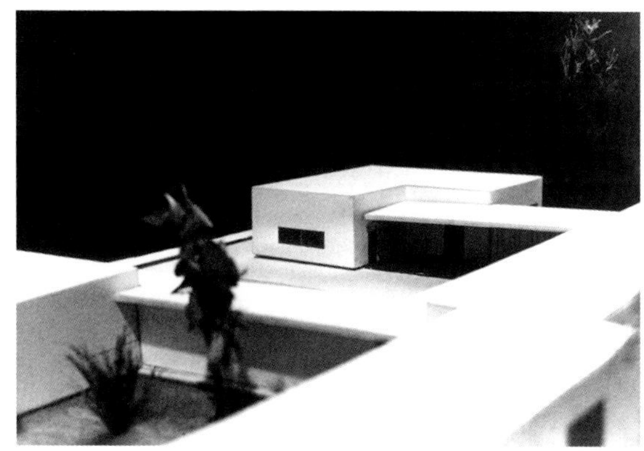

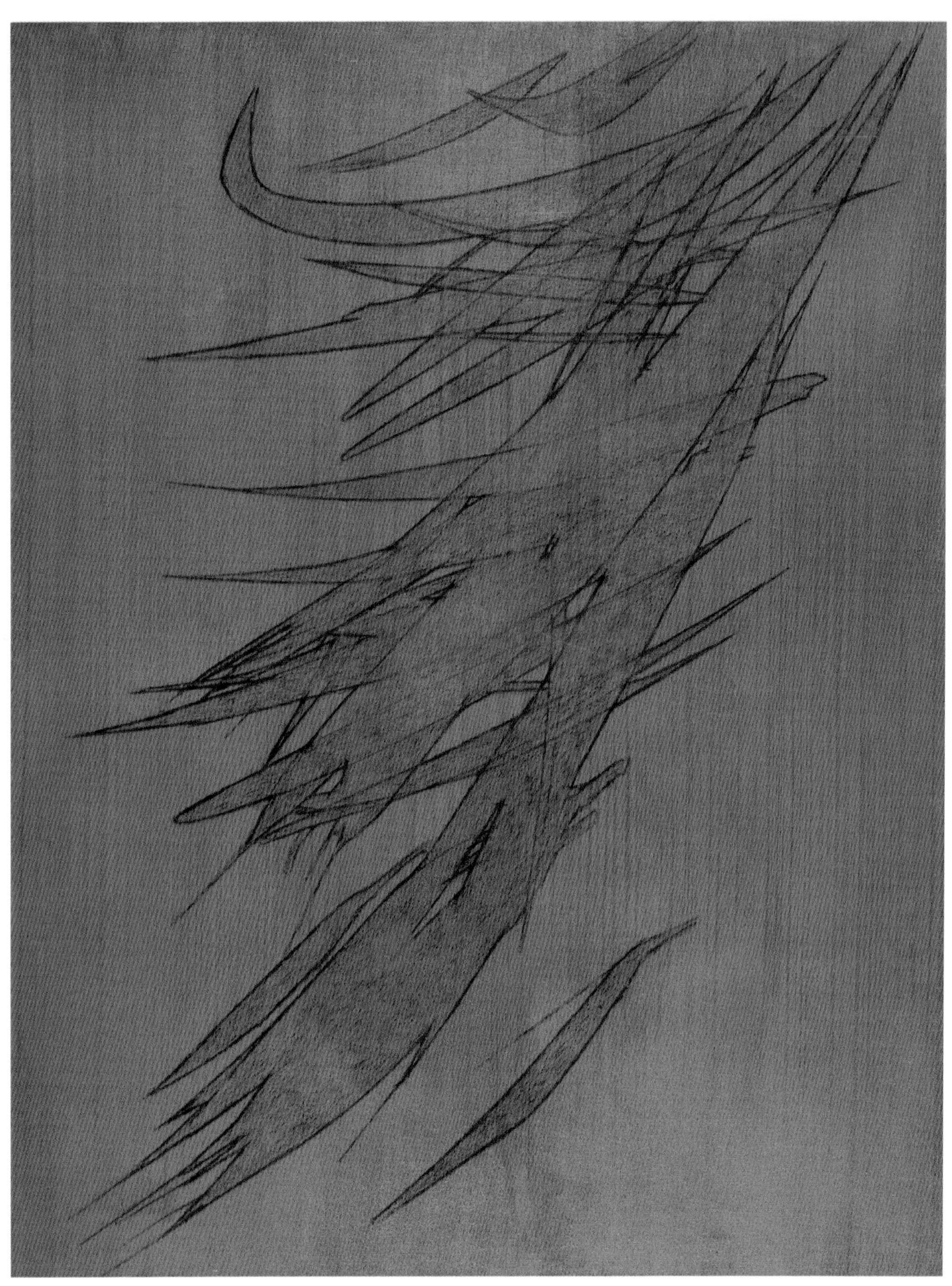

3. HH, unfinished canvas, 1956, charcoal and oil on canvas, 180 x 137 cm

4. HH, *T1958-3*, 1958, oil on canvas, 92 x 73 cm

5. HH, untitled, 1955, ink on paper, 27.2 x 20.2 cm

The collection of the Fondation Hans Hartung et Anna-Eva Bergman holds more evidence that Hans Hartung's image as a vigorous expressionist must be based on a misapprehension. For earlier paintings, too, drawings have been found that served as models: ostensibly uncontrolled scribbling has been transferred to canvas with such precision that there can be no doubt as to their relationship (figs. 10, 11). What is more, paintings with identical compositions occur in various formats (figs. 6, 7, 8, 9). From the exhibition chronology of some of the pairs it can be deduced that at first Hartung sent the smaller versions to exhibitions, later only the larger ones. In some cases there is a time lag of several years between a drawing and the painting derived from it (see for instance figs. 12 and 13). Variations in these related drawings and paintings are confined to format and, occasionally, colours and tiny details; these, too, seem to have been executed with the utmost control.

Hartung made no secret of his method. He would mark, say, the pastels he had used to copy in oils PU, for "*pastel utilisé*" (used pastel) and, when asked, confirmed the existence of a pastel for every oil painting.[2] Interviewed by Roger Bordier on the relation of art and "manner", Hartung stressed his predilection for "action" on canvas, but also that every project needed to ripen before being reduced to the essentials, and that it was imperative to preserve

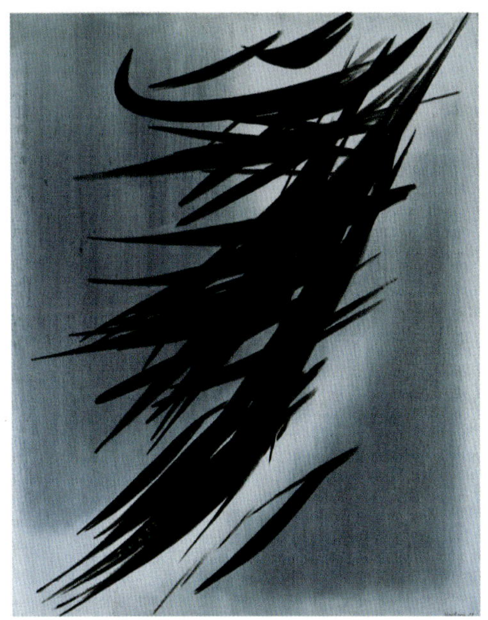

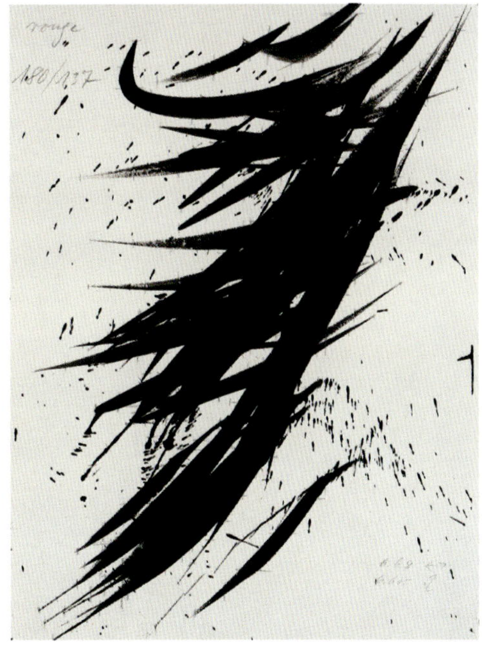

the fresh, spontaneous character throughout the process. The unavoidable exertion must not be visible: "To convey the impression of unprepared improvisation while seeking to achieve convincing perfection. That is the real problem of technique".[3] The passage makes both aspects of Hans Hartung's creative process clear, places them in relationship to one another and has frequently been quoted. Among others by Gindertael, whose monograph on Hartung appeared in 1960–when abstract expressionism was at its height–and who may be considered an excellent witness of the times.[4] He qualified Hartung's method as

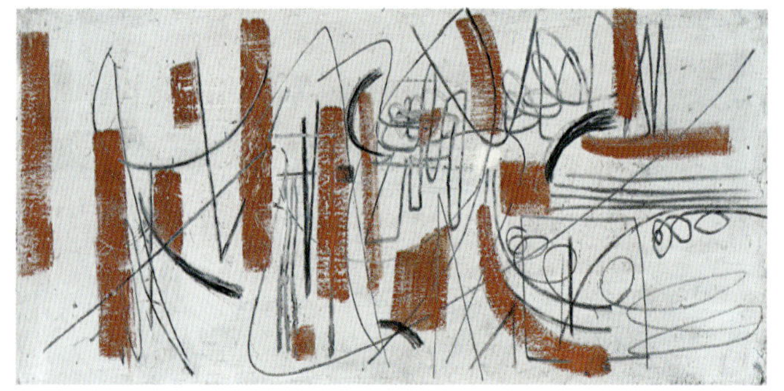

"dialectic", at the same time supplying a recipe for the viewer to follow: "Let us not attempt, then, to know the secrets of a technique that is in fact meant to conceal the effort and the extremely careful and often very long process that enables Hartung to preserve the utmost freshness of his painting."[5] Because painting had to strike a primitive, liberating blow against the canvas and thus also against the rusty traditions of old Europe, whose anachronism had been gruesomely demonstrated by World War II, Hartung's classical method could only be an annoying complication; it was consigned to the artist's secret kitchen and was thus of no significance for the interpretation of his works. Nobody drew what was really the inevitable conclusion, which was that Hartung was *not* a lyrical expressionist in the accepted sense. Hartung himself was less insistent than he would have been before the war, for the acclaim he finally enjoyed in the 1950s was based on that misunderstanding.

Born in 1904 in Leipzig, Hartung was older than most of the lyrical abstractionists of the Fifties, but he was not one of the pioneers of abstract painting either. This in-between position may possibly explain why the seventeen-year-old Dresden schoolboy, with amazing self-assurance, painted a series of watercolours in 1922, some of them completely abstract, although he professed later on to have known nothing about abstract, modern painting at the time. The statement is from his *Autoportrait*, his biography that he dictated in his seventies, which is often used, a bit incautiously, as general reference for details about his life.[6] Whether the statement reflects the truth or is "arranged memory" cannot be checked, and if it were the latter, it would for sure not be the only instance of "arranged memory" within Hartung's *Autoportrait*. Be it as it may, Hartung apparently did not need to master abstraction step by step, as Mondrian and Kandinsky had found necessary. To him, abstraction was self-evident, even before he decided to become a painter, and it developed alongside his figurative experiments as a novice in the Twenties. These initial watercolours were inspired, as he says, by the then new aniline colours; he bought a box as soon as he heard about them.[7] This statement sounds more credible because, throughout his entire artistic career, material and instrument would remain the vital stimuli: the schoolboy's pen and ink inspired his rapid, fluent lines; then came the discovery that he could produce far more varied lines and extremely compact blots with the back of his pen, from which issued his series of abstract ink sketches of 1927, and so on.

6. HH, *T1946–22*, 1946, oil and crayon on paper and canvas, 32.5 x 65 cm
7. HH, *T1946–23*, 1946, oil on canvas, 65 x 130 cm

Nevertheless, he fretted about the legitimacy of his abstract work and sought support in the history of art. In the Twenties he copied famous painters—especially Van Gogh, Cézanne, Picasso and Goya—and was intensely preoccupied with the Golden Section. He sought justification for what was to become the signature of his entire artistic output—the rapid gesture—in Rembrandt, and also in a childhood memory. Studying a drawing of a lion by Rembrandt he realised that a single line was capable of expressing the concentrated strength and force of that king of animals; and the childhood experience with which his autobiography somewhat dramatically opens was a thunderstorm one night in Leipzig. Although scared, he did not hide but went to the window to watch the flashes of lightning. What is more, he drew them.[8] This, incidentally, was the only personal experience that he expressly cited as meaningful for his work, implicitly contradicting existential interpretations according to which his paintings were motivated by his turbulent private life, the separation from his wife, the war, the loss of his leg, etc. Hartung saw his work and its generative processes in a strictly formal manner.[9] He resisted influences from his environment—influences from the context of art too—rather than yielding to them. With regard to expressionist paintings, for example (remember, the expressionist group "Die Brücke" was founded in Dresden), he realised that figuration was not necessary for the orchestration of dynamic rhythms. Likewise he resisted the theoretic systematism practised by the pioneers of abstraction: following a lecture illustrated with slides given by Kandinsky at the Leipzig academy, young Hartung rejected the famous painter's dogmatic definition of the plastic elements of art.[10] In his autobiography he noted later that Kandinsky's lecture had failed to convince him. What interested him most during his studies in Dresden (from 1925) was Kurt Wehlte's class on the technique of painting.[11] The presence in the library of the Fondation Hans Hartung et Anna-Eva Bergman of Wehlte's publications and those of the latter's teacher Max Dörner (whose class at the Munich academy Hartung attended in the summer of 1928), and of like-minded authors (and also the

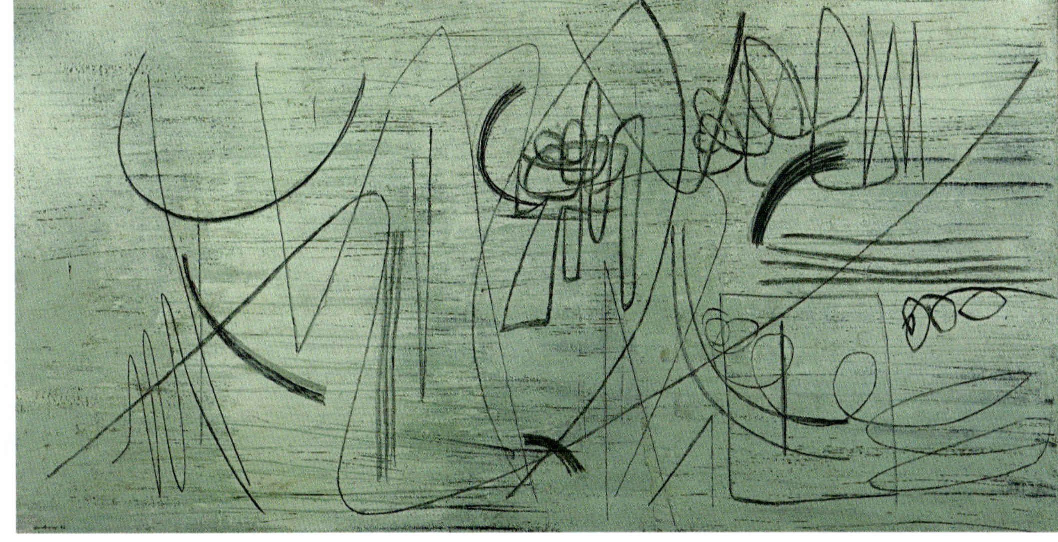

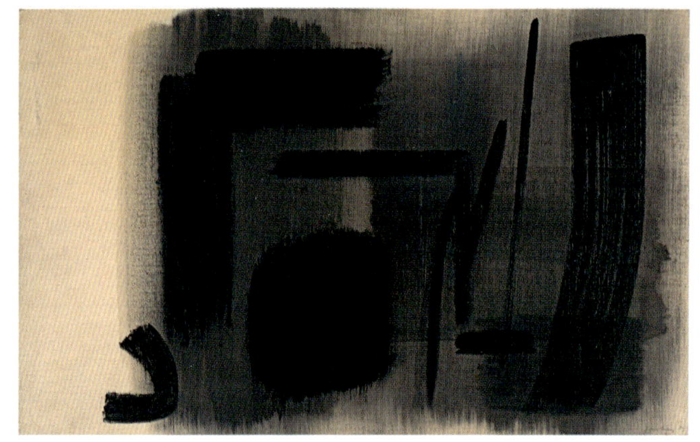

presence of new editions of the same books) bears witness to Hartung's lively and lifelong interest in the techniques of painting.[12] In Dresden he also deveoped an interest in the relation between aesthetics and mathematics—notably with regard to proportion and rhythm. He was surprised at how uncharted this field was, and conducted his own investigations.

One year after Kandinsky's slide lecture in Leipzig, Hartung saw an exhibition of international art in Dresden, which set him firmly on the road of his artistic development. It was there that he saw the new French painting of Picasso, Braque, Gris and Matisse, whose conceptual purity fascinated him, eclipsing everything he had learned up to then.[13] Against the urgent advice of his father and teachers, he did *not* enrol at the Bauhaus, the most advanced artistic training of the time, which was available, so to speak, next door, but went to Paris instead. Thus were these years in Paris (1926–32) an apprenticeship rather than the start of his actual career. A generous allowance from his father enabled him to lead a life relatively free of money troubles, and to undertake some journeys. In Paris he met his wife, Anna-Eva Bergman, who shared his enthusiasm for the Golden Section. Together, they made an intensive study of the principle of harmonic proportions on which classical and European art are based. If Hartung's study of Old Masters and of classical principles of design were initially motivated by his need to counterbalance uncertainties about his artistic identity, he began to feel straitjacketed, as time passed, by his almost superstitious worship of the Golden Section and his ardent admiration of Cubism and other modernistic styles. And so one fine day in 1932 he decided to abandon all these exercises and took a fresh look at the abstract watercolours and drawings he had made in 1922–24.[14] Psychologists would probably pounce eagerly on the fact that he did this shortly after the death of his father, whose commonsense and powers of judgement he had always admired.[15]

The father's death put also an end to the son's carefree material existence. After Hitler came to power he had no access to the resources still in Germany, and his financial situation soon became disastrous. This precarious existence lasted until the end of the war. His work of this period reflects surprisingly little of his tragic experiences or of his bitter poverty. The real influence of these years on his further artistic development is much more prosaic: Hartung had no money to buy canvases and could not afford to spoil a painting.[16] Even if it was Jean Hélion who advised him to copy his drawings onto canvas, there is no

8. HH, *T1951–23*, 1951, oil on canvas, 38 x 61 cm
9. HH, *T1954–21*, 1954, oil on canvas, 97 x 162 cm

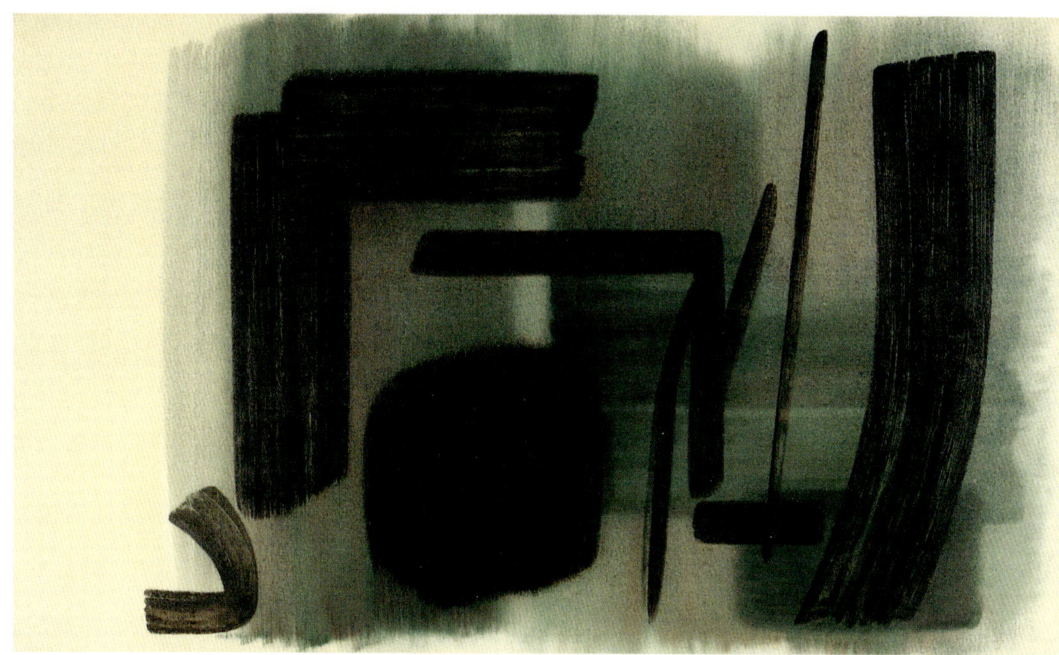

denying that this method was born of necessity. On the other hand it allowed Hartung to remain in keeping with his natural preference for the work on paper. Being conducive to greater flexibility and speed than painting in oils, it was the most obvious medium for Hartung's experiments with the gestural, his primary working method in two steps. Through copying selected drawings in oil on canvas, Hartung could cater to the "real problem of technique" as quoted above from his interview with Roger Bordier of 1954: "To convey the impression of unprepared improvisation while seeking to achieve convincing perfection".[17] This implied a critical distance, a condition for "convincing perfection", while ensuring that even the slightest fortuities and errors were reproduced in minute detail so as to preserve the freshness of the original.

One can imagine Hans Hartung in the Thirties buying a canvas on which to paint a picture: a decision perhaps prompted by a drawing that had turned out particularly well—or by an unexpected financial bonus. In the former case he enlarges the successful drawing—perhaps adding colours; in the latter case he must select from his arsenal of stored drawings one that he judges worthy of being transferred to canvas. We shall never know what his selection criteria were. It may of course be assumed that the Golden Section and Hartung's favourite artistic models influenced his choice. Whatever the case, as long as the arsenal of drawings is limited, they can be laid side-by-side so as to choose the best one. If they are more numerous, the problem is how to proceed if all the drawings are to be equally involved in the selection; and the speed at which a gestural drawing can be made on paper permits large numbers to be produced in a relatively short time. Before long, Hartung no doubt had to address the problem of how to cope with them. And coping with large amounts calls for a system.

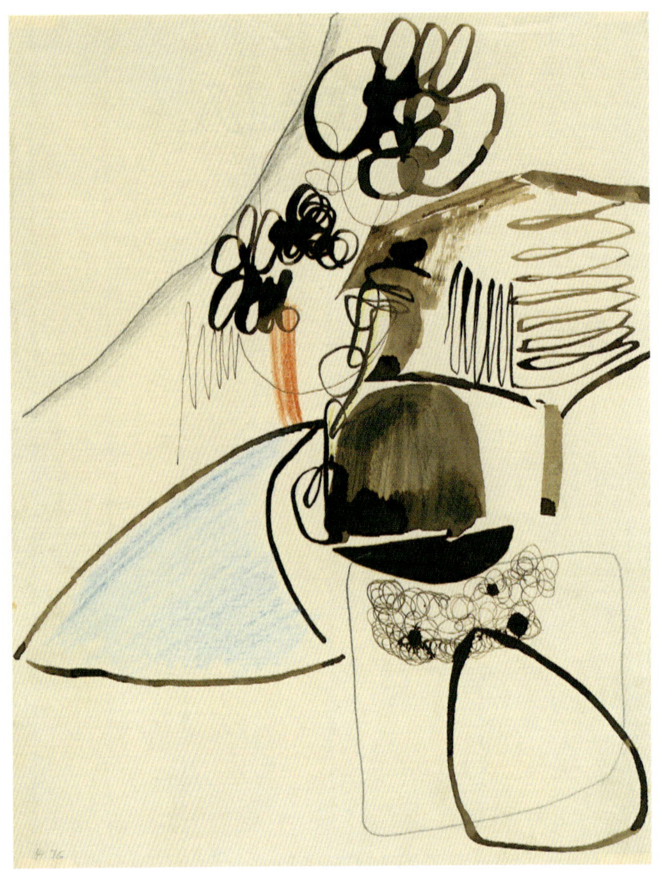

The first sign of systematisation can be seen in the titles he gave his paintings and drawings. It seems that the procedure was prompted by the first extensive monograph on his work by Ottomar Domnick and Madeleine Rousseau, published in 1949.[18] In this and all subsequent publications, the titles of Hartung's works adhere to a rigorous principle: they consist of a letter indicating the technique, followed by the year and a code. His earlier works were re-titled retroactively. The monograph assigns a letter to each technique: A for *aquarelle* (watercolour), C for charcoal, D for drawing, G for gouache. Later, though, the principle was only applied to paintings on canvas—the final product at which his method was aimed.

After the war it seemed quite natural to resume the method that had been born of poverty and uncertainty. In 1945 he reworked the untitled drawing of 1938 into an oil painting (figs. 12, 13) as if nothing unusual had happened in the meantime. The world had changed, however, and the "art world" too: interest in lyrical abstraction grew apace, bringing Hartung the recognition he had been denied for so long and implicitly confirming that his method was the right one. The thick, black lines covering some of his paintings like prison bars, or swirling spirals, were seen as the raw, spontaneous expression of extreme physical or emotional states, as an existential expression of modern humanity. If such interpretations failed to perceive the actual concern of the paintings, this new discourse of critical appreciation nevertheless changed Hartung's life and put paid to his money worries.[19] From 1947 to 1953 he favoured pastels for their flexibility—another technique that gave rise to new forms. The "PU" on the pastels used as models for paintings suggests that he was employing his "dialectic" method more deliberately now. Although critics and collectors were interested first and foremost in his canvases, the works on paper were by no means less important to Hartung; after all, they were the first and hence most authentic formulations of his art.

10. HH, *CP*, 1936, crayon, pastel and ink on paper, 28.5 x 22 cm
11. HH, *T1937–1*, 1937, oil on canvas, 130 x 97 cm

Already before the war he had endeavoured to publicise this aspect of his work—for instance in his first important exhibition in Paris (1939), which brought him no critical esteem whatsoever. Later, following a successful exhibition at the Galerie Lydia Conti in 1947, he decided to show works on paper in the same gallery the year after. His next exhibition in Paris, in 1956, was in the nature of a manifesto: in the Galerie de France he presented recent canvases; a week later, in the Galerie Craven, he opened an exhibition of works on paper done between 1921 and 1938. He selected the works himself; many of them had never been exhibited before. The walls were covered with drawings (fig. 14) so as to provide a complete record of every stage of his development. Now that he was internationally

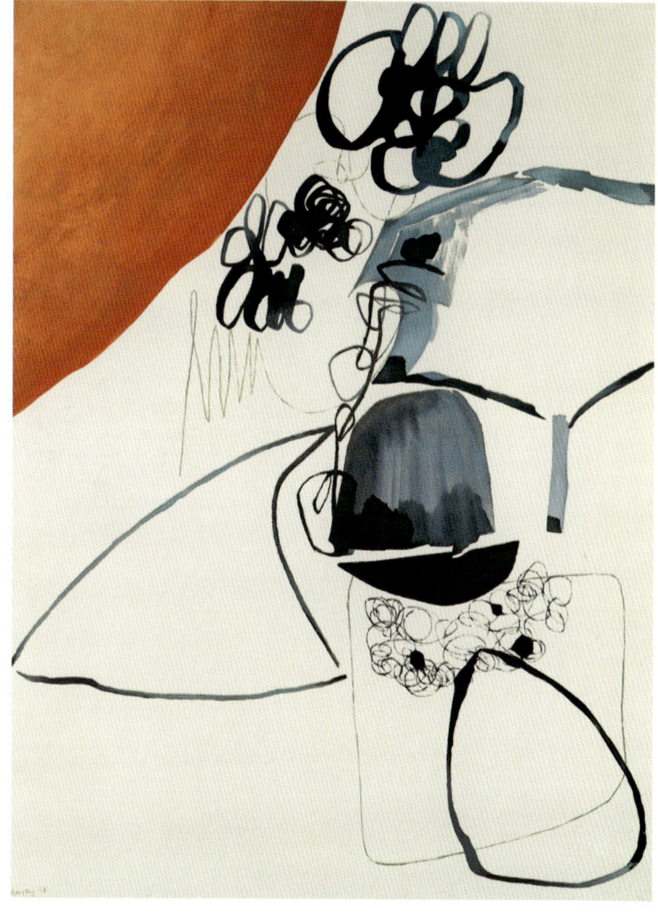

recognised as a key figure in the new École de Paris, his evident intention was to acquaint the public with an aspect of his development that distinguished him from that school's other, younger artists—what René de Solier called his "terrible priority".[20]

This manifesto should be seen in the context of a shift in his method. Around the mid-Fifties Hartung embarked on a new series of ink drawings—a technique dating back to the very beginning of his artistic activity. Now, however, he reduced his vocabulary of forms by employing only one type of tool, a Chinese brush, and by reducing the gesture to a rapid, abrupt movement. Bearing in mind the fascination in implements and materials that is a *leitmotif* of his entire oeuvre, this twofold reduction of artistic means appears like the setup for an analytical experiment: reduce the multifarious artistic means to a few constants, in this case the ink, the Chinese brush, the format of the paper and the straight abrupt and repetitive movement of the hand, in order to examine the remaining variables: the hazards in movements and brush traces. The analytical reduction and serial character of these ink drawings, nearly 3000 of which Hartung produced in less than three years, bear an astonishing conceptual resemblance to Niele Toroni's *Marks of brush no. 50 repeated at regular distances of 30 cm* (fig. 15)—a decade later. There is absolutely no

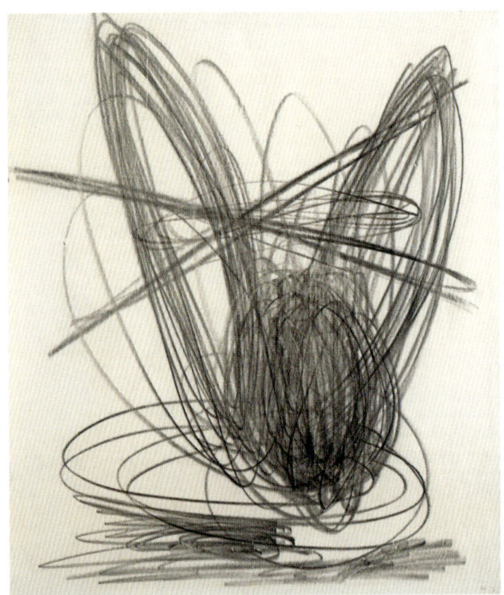

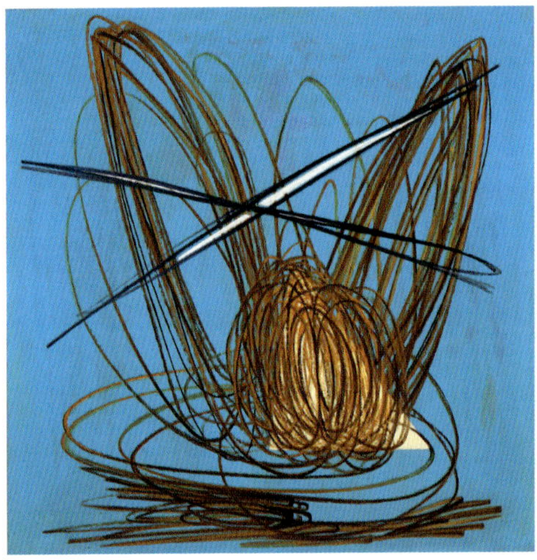

suggestion of Toroni's having been influenced by Hartung. I merely wish to draw attention to an unintentional analogy in the attitude towards art in general and painting in particular: an analogy between the artistic project launched by Hartung with his ink drawings in the latter half of the Fifties and the international project of some 10 years later, which involved an analysis of the output of an art which had become conceptual and was first presented to a shocked public in an exhibition that was to grow into a myth: 'When Attitudes Become Form' (1968).

Like all Hartung's earlier works on paper since the Thirties, the ink drawings formed an arsenal from which those suitable for copying onto canvas could be selected. New were the sheer size of the project, its serial character and the reduction of artistic means, which led to a reduced and easily recognizable vocabulary of forms, the "*formes palmées*", as Hartung called them. The shift appears as having been triggered by the eventual rationalisation of an erratically found method in order to employ it even more systematically. Another sign of rationalisation and systematisation is Hartung's recruitment, from the mid-Fifties on, of assistants for most of the handiwork: stretching canvases, applying background colour and perhaps even the mechanical job of transferring the original onto canvas.[21] With a bit of exaggeration one might say that Hartung's studio became a painting factory, in anticipation of Warhol's. Evidence that Hartung delegated an increasing amount of the technical execution is found in a studio logbook (fig. 16), in which he made thumbnail sketches of selected drawings. Bearing in mind Hartung's phenomenal visual memory, which is confirmed by everybody who knew him, the purpose of these logbooks was less likely to prepare his own work than to communicate with his assistants and to organise their tasks. Beside the thumbnail sketches he

12. HH, untitled, 1938, crayon on paper, 49 x 43 cm
13. HH, *T1945–1*, 1945, oil on wood, 100 x 100 cm
14. Hans Hartung's works at the Galerie Craven, 1956

noted what had been done with them (in what colours, sizes etc.), whether or not the result was satisfactory and what still needed doing. Witness, for instance, the thumbnail sketch, which is obviously related to the painting *T1958-3* and to its unfinished version, referred to above (fig. 17). To its left he noted that a blue outline existed already, to its right that a red one had to be made, suggesting that he had first made

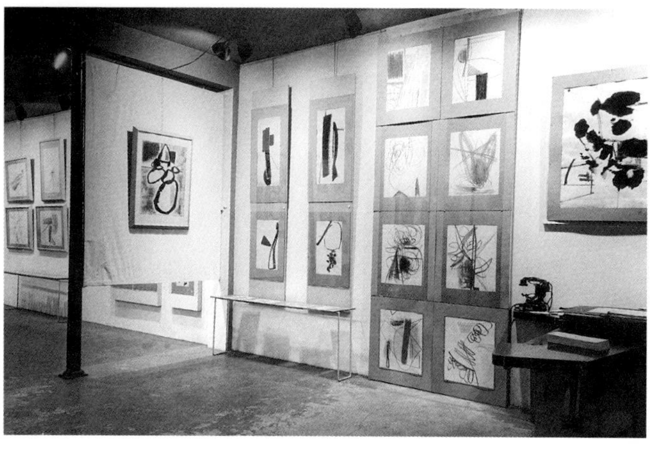

different colour/format combinations in order to select the one to be painted. In this case he decided for the initial version, the smaller blue one, and left the additional red option unfinished. If it is true that the outline drawings on the unfinished canvases in the Fondation Hans Hartung et Anna-Eva Bergman were done by assistants, this could be regarded as the quasi-anticipation of a method normally associated with the minimal artist and initiator of conceptual art, Sol LeWitt. In the early years of his artistic career LeWitt caused a considerable stir by separating the conception of a work of art from its execution.[22] This implies that all decisions were to be made beforehand and that execution was seen as a purely technical matter and could therefore be delegated. The conception or idea became a "machine that makes art".[23] Hartung is unlikely to have left the entire execution to his assistants, although it was rumoured in the late 1980s that he did not paint his pictures himself. He countered this rumour by having his assistants make a video in which he is clearly seen "painting" a picture with a sulphate sprayer. Twenty years after Sol LeWitt's *Sentences on Conceptual Art* were first published, a reaction like this from the art public is curious to say the least, and might have been—still—connected with Hartung's classification in the category of a "gestural painter". Even if by then such a procedure was largely accepted, it was still not for an expressionist artist associated with the Fifties.

A third sign of the deliberate rationalisation of his method, which was heralded in the mid-Fifties, is the "*Catalogue des oeuvres*" on which a start was made at that time. Hans Hartung's first assistant was an artist of German descent who joined him around 1954–55, only to depart towards the end of the Fifties in mysterious circumstances—Hartung always avoided talking about the matter. Because the man died long before Hartung, little is known about the exact division of labour, nor about Hartung's techniques and methods at that time. What we do know is that this man embarked on the systematic inventory of Hartung's works and designed the cataloguing system that made it possible for Hartung to access his ever-growing production. After this first assistant's departure, Hartung hired a professional librarian who continued to catalogue his work until his death, by which time it filled 110 thick files (fig. 18). The analogy with conceptual art works compiled of the same sort of files like *One Million Years* by On Kawara is not merely visual (fig. 19). Basically, each work is

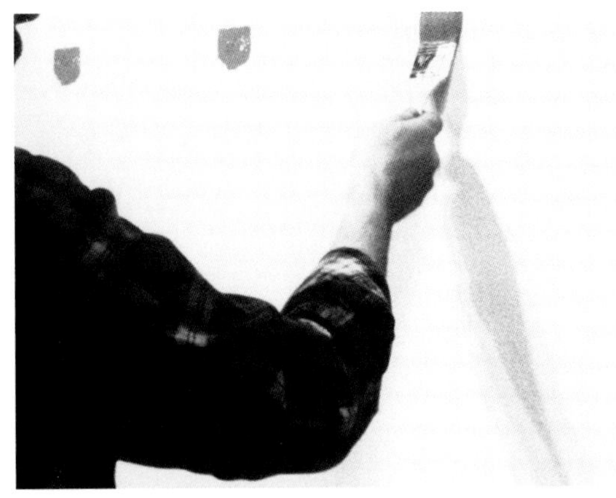

inventoried with a photographic reproduction or, if no photograph was available, a small sketch (at the top right), the name of the collection to which the work belongs (top left), an abbreviated technical and formal description under the photograph,[24] a note as to the whereabouts of a reproducible transparency and details of where the work was reproduced and had been exhibited. This consistently systematic treatment of the entire oeuvre served the Fondation as the basis for the development of a digital database, which is still being complemented with additional information. Thanks to Hartung's spadework the foundation may pride itself on having made astonishing strides in the titanic task of cataloguing his oeuvre in a relatively short time: the digital "catalogue in progress" is, so to speak, a sequel to the systematic inventory begun by the artist.

Put in this a-historical context of strange analogies, Hartung's "conceptualisation" of his method in the mid-Fifties appears to be quite ahead of his time and may even be in breach of his earlier work. It was, however, not a bolt from the blue as we have seen, rather a case of him carrying the rationalisation of all technical processes to extremes—presumably as a means of disguising the effort more effectively and of preserving spontaneous freshness to an even greater extent and perhaps of being able to increase his production. What appears as the real change in his method did not occur until five years later. Maybe conceptualisation, i.e., rationalisation and systematisation, had paved the way for that change, unmasking the method as dangerous routine and, again, as straitjacket. Yet, once more, materials, techniques and environment triggered the change. In 1959 Hartung's move to a new, bigger studio in the Montsouris park district of Paris enabled him to produce large formats; the Sixties saw the advent of new chemical paints like vinyl and acrylic.[25] Those paints are easier to work, dry faster and enabled Hartung to work directly on canvas and intervene more promptly—something he had only been able to do in the drawings up to then. And so the irony of his oeuvre's development is that Hartung only really started to paint gesturally and directly on canvas at a time when the international scene had already abandoned Gestural painting for Pop art and a little later for Conceptual art. This change in Hartung's method was also the parting of the ways for paintings and pastels, for Hartung no longer used the latter as models for the former. He thus benefited from the added advantage that the specific material properties of support and media could be exploited to the full. Working directly on canvas made cataloguing even more neces-

15. Niele Toroni at work
16. Studio Journal, 1957, page with a sketch of *T1958–3*
17. Studio Journal, 1957, detail of the page with sketch of *T1958–3*

sary, for how else could Hartung make sure of being able to access all those big canvases if he needed them for future paintings? Unlike drawings, large paintings cannot be laid side-by-side for comparison. That is why he henceforth also used codes to indicate quality and the possibility of later re-use. For instance, "HH" means that he wanted to keep a work for his personal collection, and "SP" means "*spécial*", indicating a work to be re-addressed some time in the future. Another coding system uses circles and plus-signs: 'o' means 'good', 'oo' means 'better', 'ooo means 'perfect', 'o+' is between good and bad and '+' means bad or "dead-end" and hence available for sale. Sometimes these symbols also occur in the logbook and the catalogue. In the Paris studio they were inscribed on the frame, so that the categories could be recognised at a glance in the storeroom. Later, in Antibes, they were also inscribed on the backs of paintings. Establishing these categories went much further than the normal administrative requirements of a successful artist, for not only the best works were inventoried. Basically, the system enabled Hartung to re-use even errors and unwelcome fortuities in other paintings. Everything was kept and remained accessible. Traditionally, mistakes are over-painted. Hartung analysed

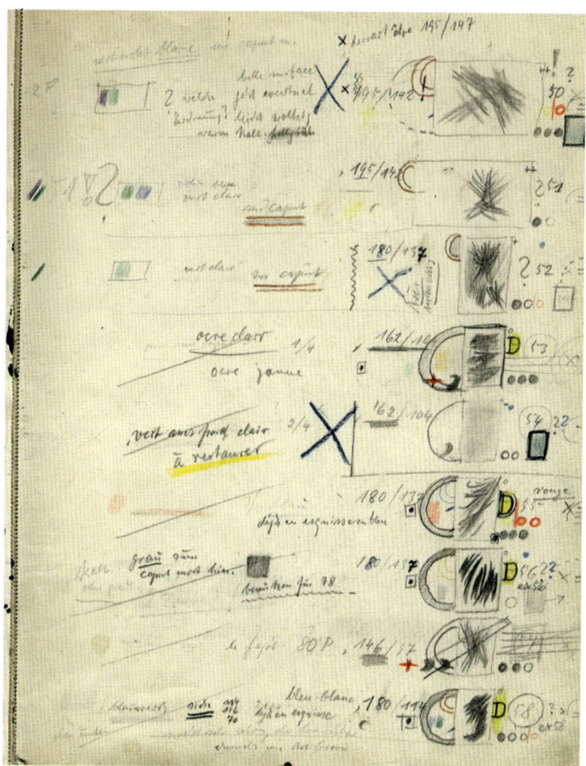

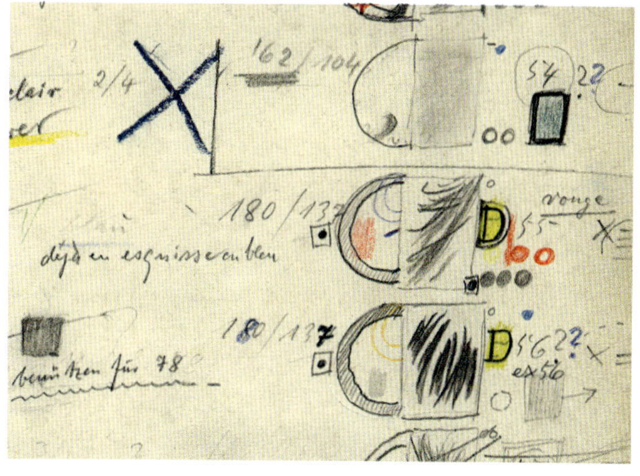

the traditional process of composition by placing various gestures—whether up to standard or not—on separate carriers and keeping them separately with a view to utilising them at a later date. Perhaps one-day the foundation's database will enable us to trace the history of certain "mistakes" in Hans Hartung's oeuvre.

Analysis and systematic access thus became a component of the artistic process.

Colours and especially the tools of painting, in which Hartung had been keenly interested right from the beginning, became vital sources of his inspiration from the Sixties on. In the new studio he had a spray gun installed, for the new colours were diffusible.

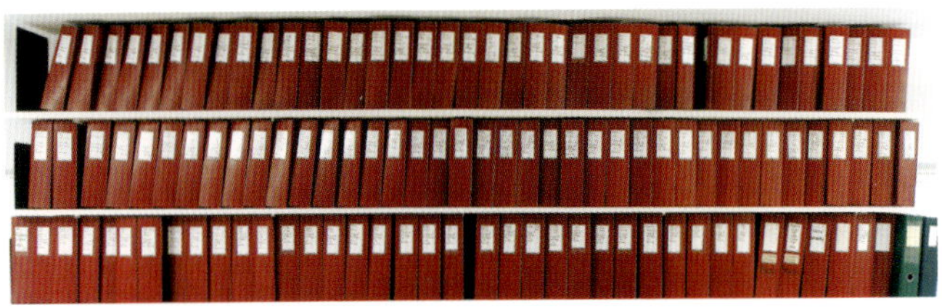

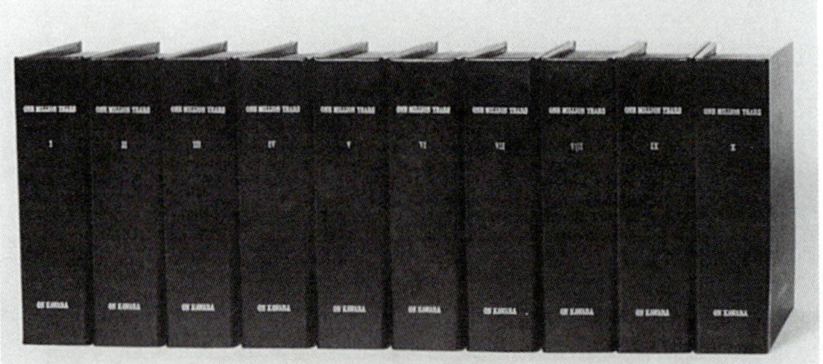

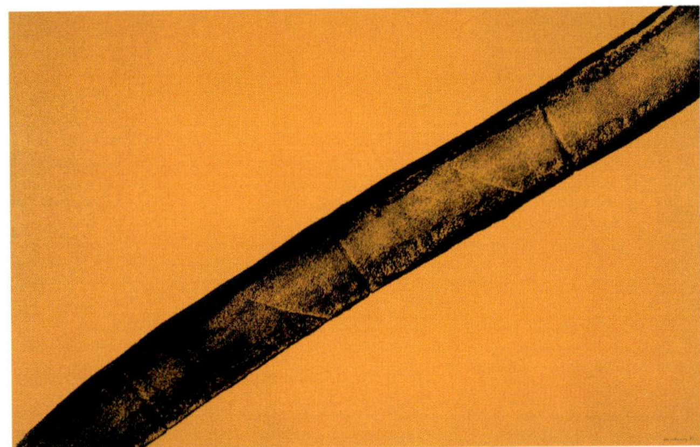

The "cloud paintings" were inspired by this technical innovation. Scratching in wet paint with a variety of implements resulted in the "*grattages*" (fig. 21). At the beginning of the Seventies, when Hartung was fully occupied with the design and construction of his villa and studio in Antibes and had neither the time nor the space to paint, he concentrated on lithography. He subsequently used lithograph rollers directly on his canvas (fig. 20). At the beginning of the Eighties he was using a besom on his canvases (fig. 22) and towards the end of his life he sprayed them with sulphate sprayers (fig. 23). Hartung used many more implements. Adding them to the palette of painting tools became a new task for his assistants. New tools were tested on small samples. As time passed, the arsenal of tools became so large that they, too, had to be inventoried. They were photographed in groups, with a number on each one (fig. 24). When Hartung needed a particular tool he would point to it on the photograph and his assistants knew where to find it.

What constitutes the sustained coherence in Hans Hartung's oeuvre, its thread? According to the logic of his development as outlined here, there are two answers: the primary gesture that was always the starting-point of his artistic work, and the critical distance that Hartung always retained between starting-point and final product. His first abstract sketches at Dresden high school and the start of his work proper at the beginning of the Thirties were separated by his student days in Paris and his study of Old Masters and the

18. Catalogue of works, 2003
19. On Kawara, *One Million Years*, 1970–71, ten volumes
20. HH, *T1975-R23*, 1975, acrylic on canvas, 100 x 162 cm
21. HH, *T1962-U8*, 1962, vinyl on canvas, 180 x 142 cm

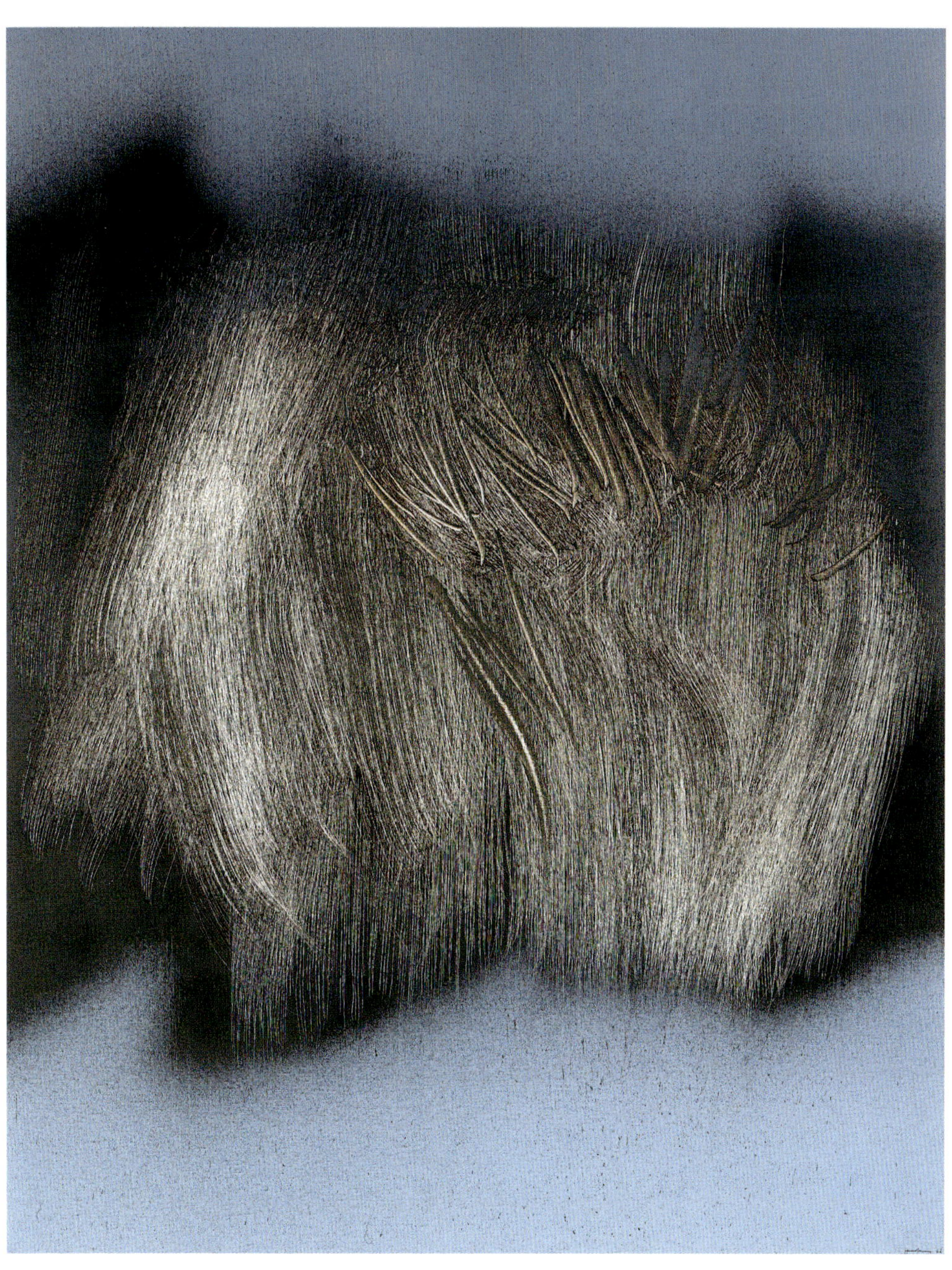

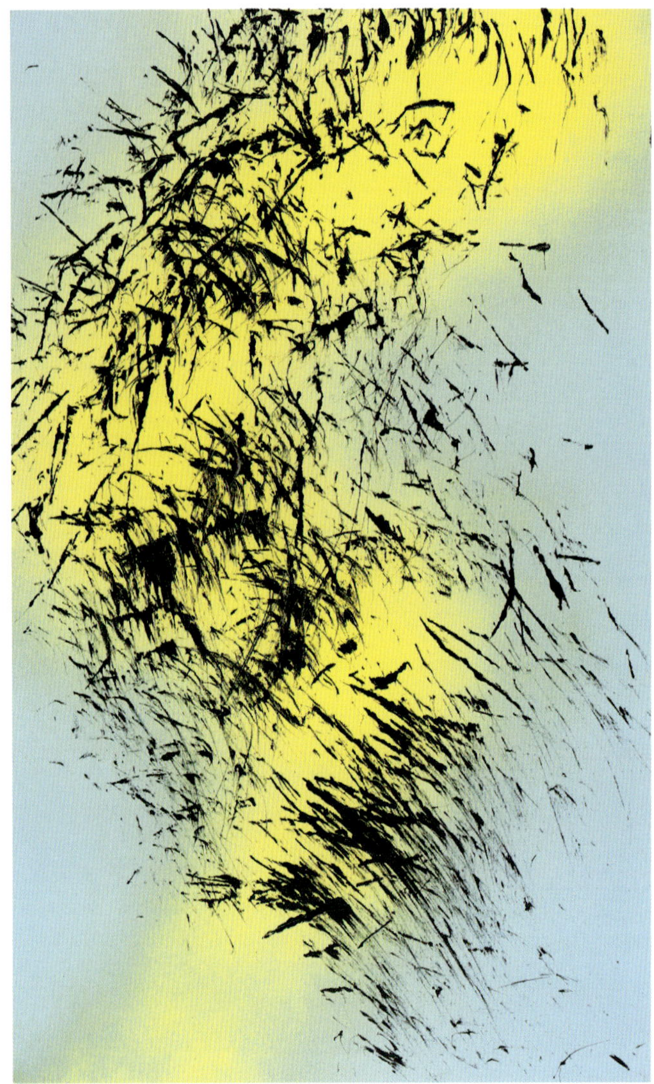

Golden Section. The next distance was between his impulsive works on paper and their painstakingly accurate transference to canvas—not just a technical distance but a temporal one too. Then the complicated system of rationalising the working process came between his impulsion and the final product, and finally it was the physical distance from tool to canvas, the daily rhythm and the division of labour that lay between the assistants' preparations, the artist's intervention, the cataloguing, after which came the critical evaluation—or as the former assistants call it, the "administration" or "management" (*gestion*) of the work.

Conceptual art made a principle of the serial method and the cataloguing or systematisation of large and mostly quite arbitrary stocks, as well as of the division of labour between conception and execution, rendering the seemingly disorganised, indeed chaotic artistic thought process accessible to analysis and systematisation.[26]

If for Sol LeWitt "the idea becomes a machine that makes art", then Hartung assigns virtually the same role to the direct, simple gesture, the trace of a movement performed by the hand. His entire oeuvre is built around the elementary gesture, from the Dresden schoolboy's watercolours to the almost orgiastic, monumental sprayed canvases of his final year, 1989. Distance permits the evaluation of the result of a direct action in accordance with certain criteria that are hard to define but which nevertheless constitute the difference between art and, say, a primal scream.[27] Today, and seen through the filter of Conceptual art (which, too, has become art history in the meantime), Hartung may be assessed as a conceptualist. Of course he was not a precursor of Conceptual art, which he

22. HH, *T1982–E26*, 1982, acrylic on canvas, 180 x 111 cm
23. HH, *T1989–A12*, 1989, acrylic on canvas, 146 x 114 cm

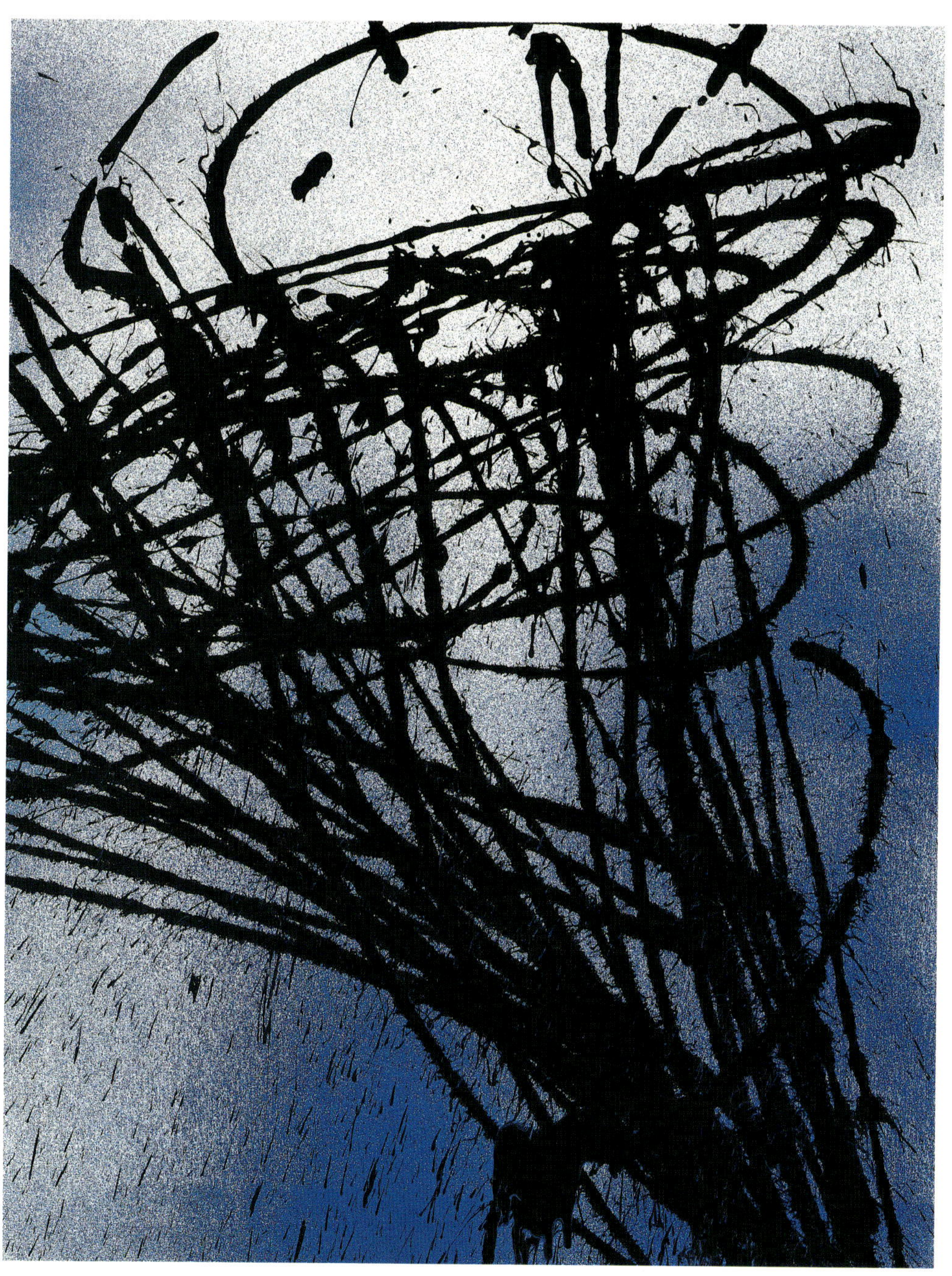

John C. Welchman Hans Hartung Abcedarium: Reading Between the Lines

Franz-W. Kaiser A Case Study on the Caducity of Categories in Art Criticism

Annie Claustres

Hans Hartung Clandestine Artist

1937-1942: the Decisive Years

Christine Mehring Hans Hartung Mid-Century Modern

Rainer Michael Mason Hartung and Printmaking Christopher Wool

Selected Works

At the International Exhibition of Arts and Techniques in Modern Life, held in Paris from 24 May to 26 November 1937, the German and Soviet pavilions directly facing each other bore signs of a menacing future: swastika, hammer and sickle. On the programme from June to November were numerous shows that joined the spectacular effects of light, electricity, cinema and music, and which ran alongside the shows that were part of the Exhibition. The whole point of this major event was to maintain Paris as the artistic capital of the world. And, for the occasion, two new important museums were opened in the city: the state-owned Musée des Artistes vivants and the Musée d'Art Moderne de la Ville de Paris, or Palais de Tokyo.[1] Roughly synchronous with the Exhibition in Paris, in Munich it was possible to visit the exhibition entitled 'Degenerate Art' from July to November. This was organized by the Nazis, who banned, as we know, the works of the avant-garde from the beginning of the century.[2] Abstract art, Expressionism, Dada, New Objectivity, etc., were all subjected to verbal abuse, censure, and destruction on a large scale. Against this background, the International Exhibition in Paris, committed as it was to defending modernity and its international dimension, started to look like a veritable manifestation against totalitarian regimes. The position the Exhibition came to assume was only strengthened by the show entitled 'Masters of Independent Art 1895–1937' at the Petit Palais, which offered a selection of works by a hundred or so French and international artists. But it was the exhibition at the Jeu de Paume, entitled 'Origins and Developments of International Independent Art: From Cézanne to Non-Figurative Art', that boasted the greatest international participation and pertinence. The show at the Jeu de Paume put a strong emphasis on the contributions of international artists to the artistic scene in Paris: "Organizers André Dezarrois and Christian Zervos, the director of Cahiers d'Art, try to show, by recalling the major movements of the twentieth century, the major trends of the avant-garde, Surrealism and Abstraction in particular, whereas the exhibit at the Petit Palais barely mentions these."[3]

It was in this tense and ambivalent historical context that the artists Hans Hartung and Julio González met, as both were part of the exhibition at the Jeu de Paume. For Hartung, this was the beginning of official recognition.

"At the International Exhibition of 1937, held at the Jeu de Paume and entitled 'From Cézanne to Non-Figurative Art', I had the honour, thanks to Christian Zervos, of hanging one of my paintings between a Fernand Léger and a Miró... It was a large painting with thick black lines... There were also at the exhibition sculptures by Julio González, an artist I was already quite interested in after seeing some of his sculptures at the Pierre Loeb Gallery. I met him on the day of the opening of the International Exhibition, and we immediately became fast friends. I admired his work, and he was interested in my paintings."[4]

Hartung's reconstruction of the facts is far from exact: he identifies the International Exhibition with the exhibition at the Jeu de Paume—a perfect example of mnemonic displacement and condensation—and he omits the first part of the title, thus betraying the

1. HH, *T1936-14*, 1936, oil on canvas, 171 x 114 cm, Centre Pompidou, Paris

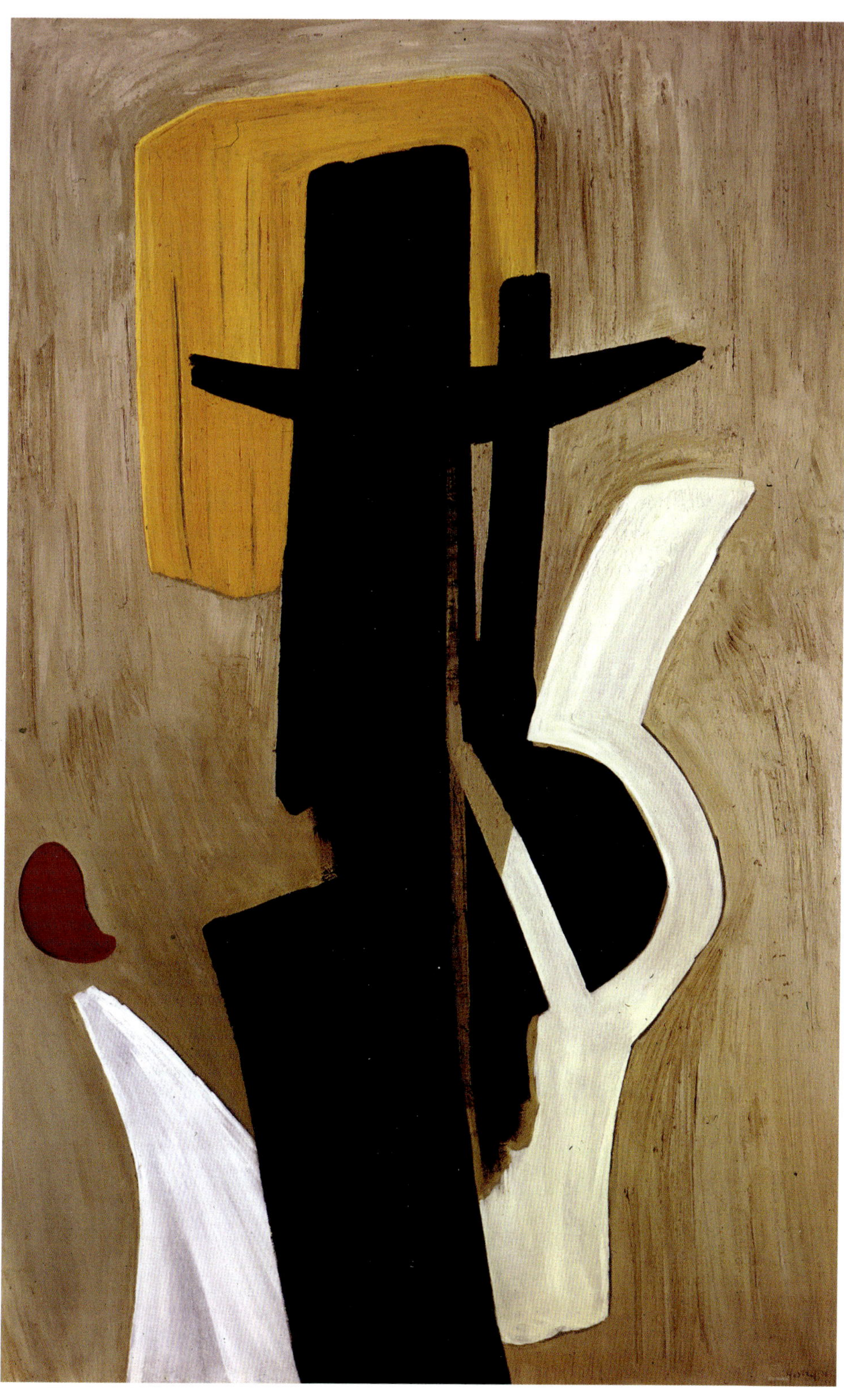

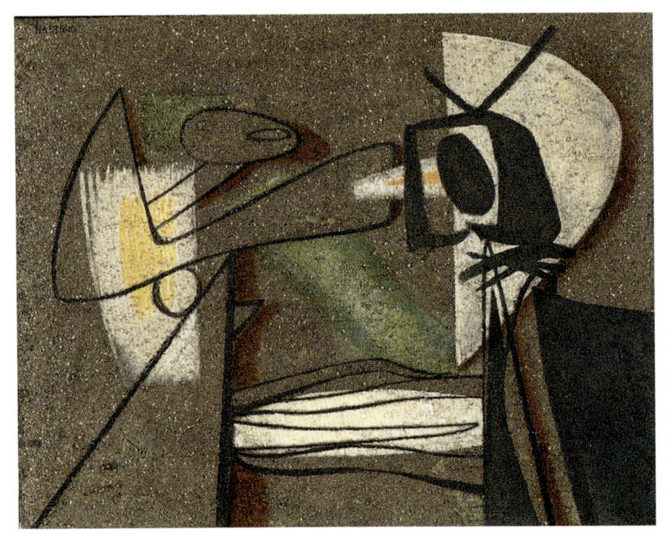

importance the event had for him. It should also be mentioned that when and where the two artists first met has not always been precisely reconstructed in historical accounts. Indeed, one is particularly open to error on this score since the record of their first meeting is based on the words of the artist himself.[5] The exhibition at the Jeu de Paume ran from 30 July to 31 October,[6] and yet the first mention of González's name in Hartung's agenda dates from 12 May 1937.[7] Could the artist have confused the opening of the exhibition at the Jeu de Paume with the opening of the International Exhibition proper? That's out of the question since the International Exhibition opened on 24 May, a bit later than the agenda entry. Are we to take Hartung's words as gospel at this point? The visitors to the Spanish pavilion, dedicated to the theme of war, were greeted by González's *La Montserrat* (1936–37), while his *Woman at the Mirror* (1936–37), the highly abstract nature of which is no doubt what must have caught the eye of the organizers, was on display at the Jeu de Paume, in Gallery XIV. We learn in the catalogue published for the occasion—*Origins and Developments of International Independent Art: From Cézanne to Non-Figurative Art*—of the presence of the painting entitled *Composition* (1937) in Gallery XV, where there were also canvases by Miró and Léger, but also by Magnelli, Hélion and Domela, who were all represented by one work.[8] In fact, it turns out that the work thus referred to in the catalogue was actually *T 1936–14* (171 x 114), which was completed in 1936, not 1937, as the legend on the catalogue indicates.

González only started creating his own pieces, metal sculptures and spatial drawings at the beginning of the 1930s, when he was already over fifty. Gargallo, and later Picasso, both of whom relied on González' help for their metal sculptures due to his training as a metalworker and his know-how in the making of decorative objects, were the ones who encouraged him to start sculpting even though González himself had no particular ambitions at that level. He had settled in Paris in 1900 after selling the workshops adjoining his family's business; he had gone to Paris wishing to become a painter but he made his living from his work as a goldsmith. The collaboration with Picasso in the years 1928 to 1931[9] was quickly transformed into an artistic dialogue that prompted González to make his first sculptures

2. HH, *T1938–20*, 1938, oil on tarred paper and sand, mounted on canvas, 78 x 100 cm

3. HH, *T1938–16*, 1938, collage wood panel, 102 x 91 cm

4. HH, untitled, 1938, iron, 96 x 37 x 43 cm

in 1929, in which he combined work with planes with the expressive power of the line. Although certain motifs are clearly formal borrowings from Picasso's paintings, González brought a personal approach to his use of them and abandoned assemblage in favour of a plastic language traceable to the use of signs and to the practice of welding iron. Although essentially a loner, González was on friendly terms with some of the people on the artistic scene, particularly foreigners who, like himself, were immigrants to France and defenders of the artistic avant-garde, for example, Joaquim Torrès-Garcia, Christian Zervos and Alberto Magnelli. Through these acquaintances, González had regular shows during his most productive years, 1932–39. His pieces could be seen most notably at the Salon des Surindépendants, in galleries like the Galerie de France and the Galerie Percier, as well as in other places affiliated with the programmes organised by the Cahiers d'Art. Mention should also be made of his solo exhibition at the Galerie Pierre from 12 to 26 May 1937. Hartung was there at the opening, which explains why the Catalan sculptor's name shows up in the agenda that day. There is no time specified in the agenda entry of 12 May, but the second instance of González's name in Hartung's agenda, on 8 September 1937, specified the hour as three o'clock. In other words this was an appointment.

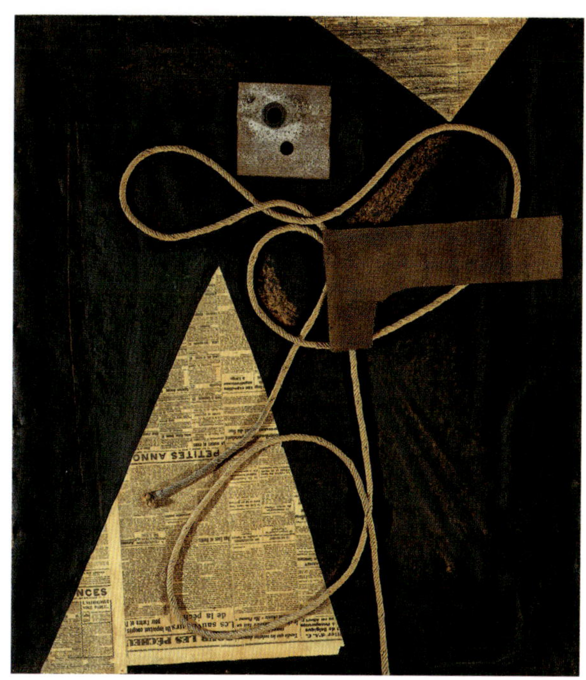

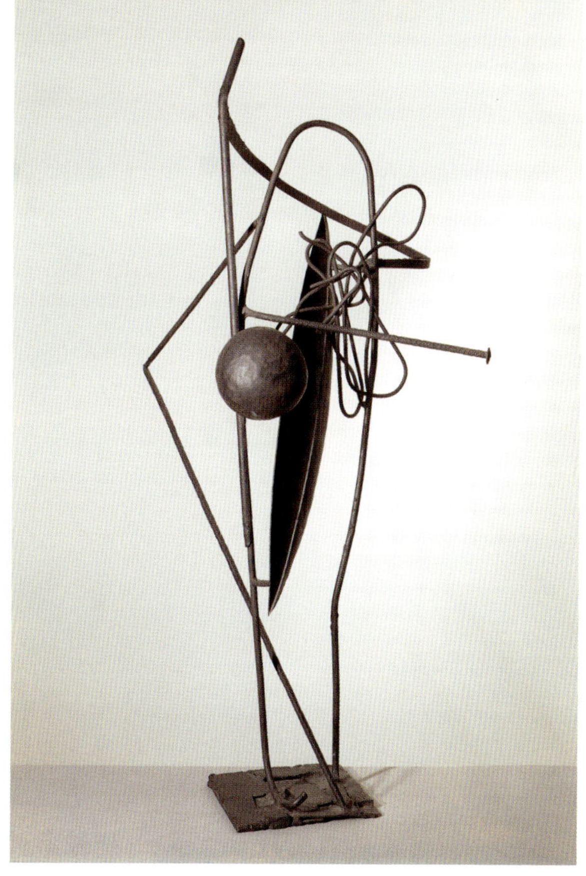

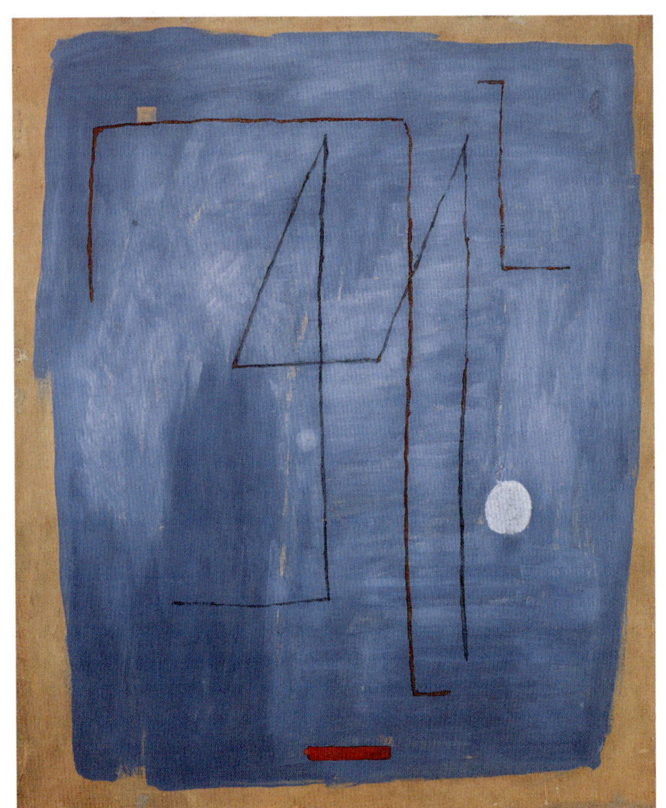

We may then conclude that, though both were present at the opening at the Galerie Pierre, they didn't speak to one another and that their first actual meeting occurred at the opening of the exhibition at the Jeu de Paume. This would explain how they may have subsequently scheduled a meeting for later on in 1937. The following year, González invited the young painter to work in his workshop in Arcueil, which was an exceptional offer considering how reserved he was with his practice. Indeed, he constantly denied access to his workshop to critics and collectors, claiming always that there was "nothing there to show them".[10]

Sometime in the autumn of 1935, Hartung, then a German citizen, arrived in Paris to settle indefinitely in France after being forced into exile by the Nazi regime. Upon Hitler's official appointment as Reichsführer on 2 August 1934, on the death of Hidenburg, the distinction between Germans living in Germany and Germans living abroad insinuated itself in new repressive measures. Hartung, who had been living in Minorca since 1932, was obliged to return to Germany, to Berlin to be exact, to deal with some questions about his material situation, and he remained in the city until 30 September, almost six months. The Nazi government permitted Germans living abroad to receive only a limited sum of money. In addition, the death of Hartung's father in 1932 made life more difficult by paralysing his financial transactions. An avant-garde artist committed to Abstract art from his youth, Hartung knew he was in danger. From the minute he arrived in Berlin he felt that was being followed and his suspicions turned out to be true.

"When I arrived, I met up with many of my old friends from the Academy of Fine Arts. Among them were some Jews and communists, like Fritz Schulze and Eva Knabe who had already been imprisoned once. Nor would it be long before they were arrested again."[11]

5. HH, *T1931-1*, 1931, oil on canvas, 46 x 38 cm, private collection
6. HH, untitled, 1931, black lead on paper, 35.1 x 24 cm

He told of their arrest to one of his cousins who urged him to contact a distant cousin, a "certain Wilcke, the head of Goering's personal guard".[12]

Wilcke scheduled a meeting for him the following morning at Gestapo offices to see how the situation might be solved, but when he arrived Hartung was locked up in a small cell and held under strict surveillance the whole day. A night-time interrogation followed. Hartung was finally let go around two or three in the morning, having by then prevailed upon his torturers to call his cousin, who vouched for him.[13] Will Grohmann and Christian Zervos managed to get him a visa to Paris, where he arrived with his wife, Anna-Eva Bergman, in autumn 1935.

"We became drifters once more, Germans living abroad. And we were penniless. Everything I inherited from my father was blocked in Germany, and there was nothing I could do about that."[14]

They found a place on the Rue Daguerre in November 1935 where they lived for two years. They had Henri Goetz and Christine Boumeester as neighbours, and through them Hartung soon met Jean Hélion, who became a close friend and a staunch supporter in matters of artistic creation. An exiled German artist and an anti-Nazi, Hartung gradually found himself in dialogue with the circles of Concrete Art and Abstraction-Création, though he was careful to keep his distance from their aesthetic foundations and their claims to a universal art. Hartung defended individuality and syncretism by combining spontaneity and construction in his work.[15] Although he liked to work in solitude, Hartung emerged from isolation and thereby secured for his work a first, though quite modest, reception in France, England and the United States: a few group shows (regular participation in the Salon des Surindépendants beginning in 1935, and the Galerie Pierre in 1936), an article in the journal *Axis* by Herta Wescher in spring 1936,[16] and the sale of a painting (*T 1936–1*) to Albert Eugène Gallatin in 1938 for the Museum of Living Art. The efficient network directed by Abstraction-Création was behind the inclusion of Hartung's painting in the exhibition at the Jeu de Paume. Hartung was only 33 when he first met González, who was then 61, but in the years 1932–33 he had already developed a plastic idiom in which the autonomy of black lines and colour determined a non-geometric abstraction that, while owing nothing to Surrealism, retained the plane constructions

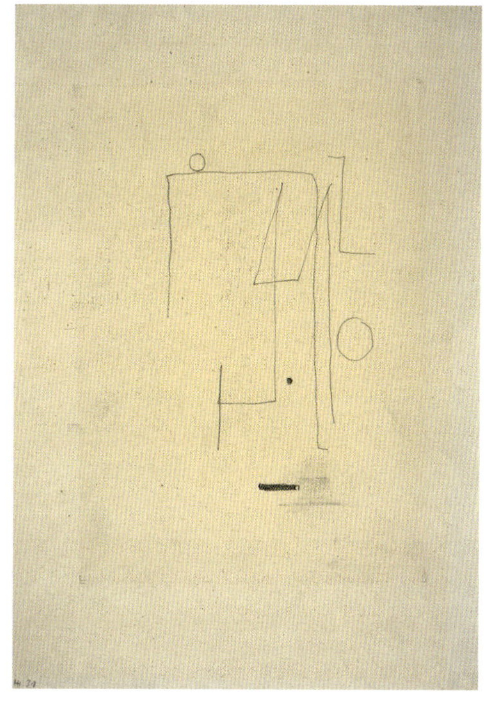

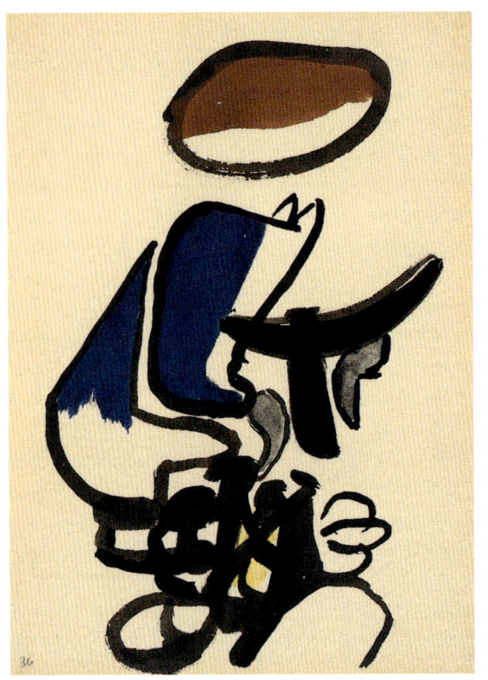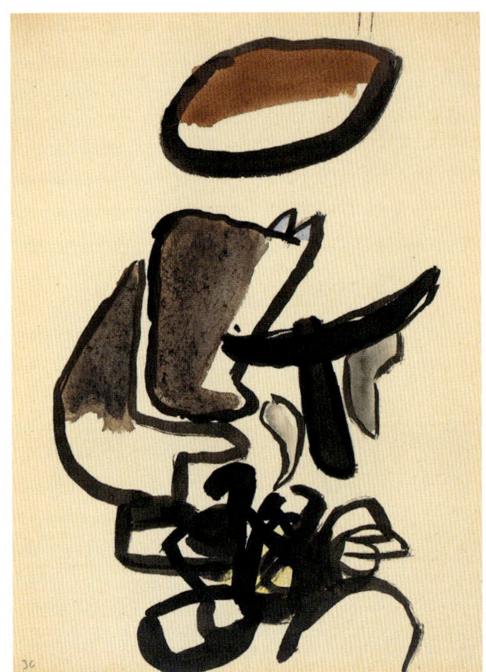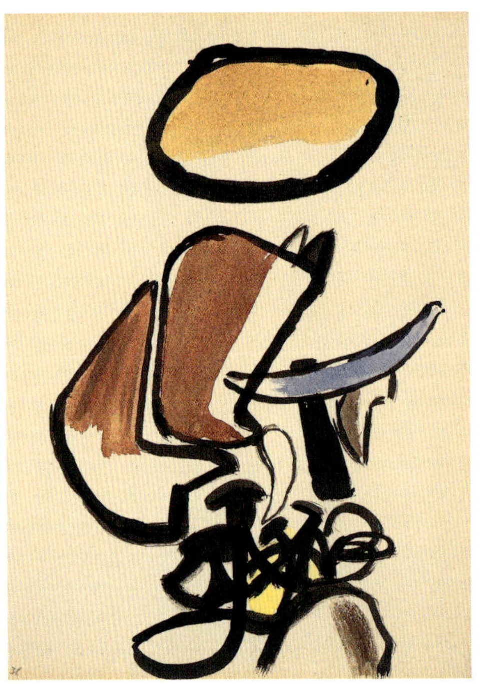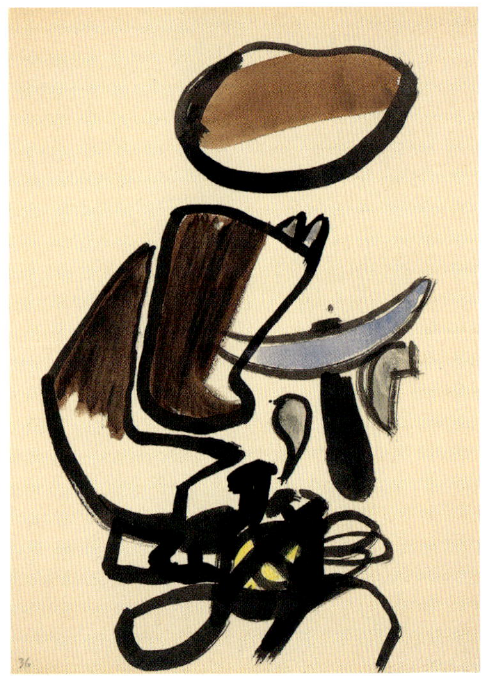

7. HH, untitled, 1936, watercolour and ink on paper, 31 x 23 cm

8. HH, untitled, 1936, watercolour and ink on paper, 31 x 23 cm

9. HH, untitled, 1936, watercolour and ink on paper, 31 x 23 cm

10. HH, untitled, 1936, watercolour and ink on paper, 31 x 23 cm

11. HH, *T1936–20*, 1936, oil on canvas, 116 x 81 cm, private collection

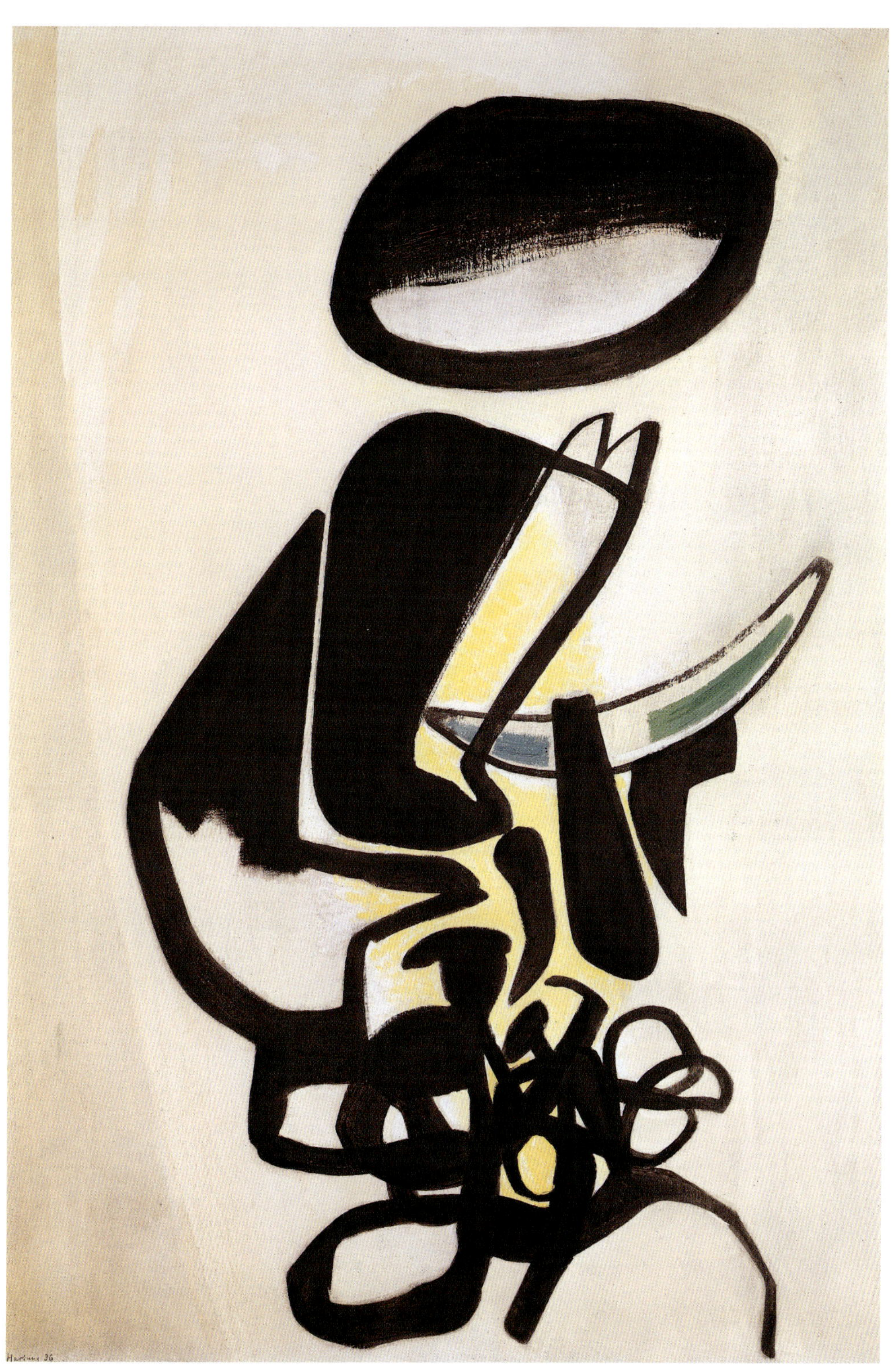

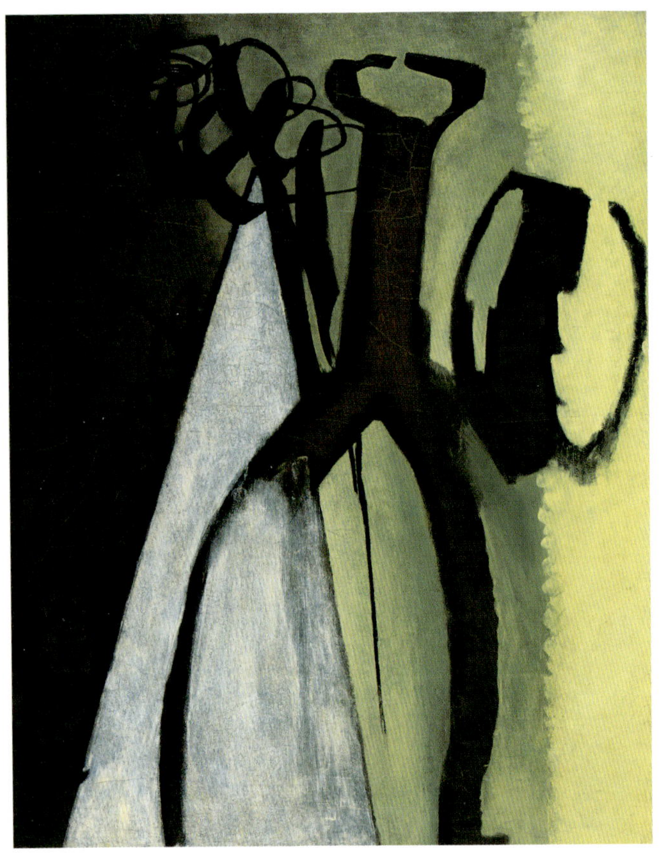

of Cubism. Artistically speaking, Hartung was outside the contemporary scene, much as González was, but for different reasons. González too frequented the circles of Abstraction-Création but he rejected its dogmatic insistence on abstraction. This was not true of Hartung, who had been defending abstract art from the first watercolours and India ink pieces he had done in Germany (1922–27). Hartung's plastic idiom differed from that of the champions of Concrete Art by the fluidity of its lines, the spontaneity of its circumvolutions (*T 1937–1*) and by its refusal to believe in a collective and socio-political mode of creation. He was against Communism, and had been since witnessing the Spartacist uprising as a young man. Albeit in different ways, both Hartung and González were in a similar situation towards their defenders. Daniel Abadie has noted that it is very likely that Hartung had seen pieces by González here and there well before he attended the latter's solo show at the Galerie Pierre. Both men, Abadie argues, belonged to the same coterie, and their eventual meeting simply crystallised their encounter.[17] The two artists also shared the strategy of mutism and were brought closer by their identity as exiles and their opposition to the political regimes then in power in their respective countries. Hartung agreed to participate in the anti-Nazi exhibition 'German Art in the Twentieth Century' at the New Burlington Galleries in London (from 8 July to 27 August 1937), which fashioned itself as a response to the show 'Degenerate Art'.[18] That notwithstanding, Hartung never joined any of the quickly forming groups to fight Nazism. Conversely, González was an inveterate Catalan and he was an active participant in militant activities against the Spanish Civil War and Franco; he attended demonstrations organised by the immigrant Spanish community in aid of the Republicans. Still, neither artist saw militancy as an aesthetic exoneration. For them, the defence of freedom was a catchword that correlated with the space of creation: they were both humanists.

12. HH, *T1938–36*, 1938, oil on canvas, 81 x 65 cm
13. HH, untitled, 1942, black lead and ink on paper, 23.9 x 31 cm

At the beginning of 1938, González invited Hartung to the newly completed studio adjoining his family home in Arcueil, built in 1937.[19] Metal welding and the spontaneity of sculptural practice soon harboured no secrets for him. They started spending their days together in Arcueil, and this became more frequent as Hartung's separation from Anna-Eva Bergman began to take its toll on the artist. She had returned to Norway, exhausted by the hardships that resulted from their financial difficulties and the tension inherent in their situation as exiles. They divorced. The German Embassy in Paris confiscated Hartung's passport but he managed to get a temporary resident's permit that could be renewed every six months. The threat of war tightened the noose around him. Hartung writes:

"Other refugees could justify their presence in France by alleging the persecutions they had suffered in Germany. I, on the other hand, had no such reason to offer the authorities: I wasn't Jewish, communist, or even politically active in some party or another."[20]

The act of creating became a refuge, an act of survival, a form of resistance. González and Hartung believed that the defence of a free act underwrites the artistic act, and this attitude was only strengthened by the historical context. From the start of 1938 to the early days of September 1939, when World War II was declared, the painter's creativity progressed in parallel with that of González (don't forget that in his youth González had dreamed of being a painter). Hartung completed two collages in 1938. A certain matterism appears in *T 1938–20* (fig. 2), where the grainy background (produced using sand) gives weight to the painting and a more consequential density to the black lines. For *T 1938–16* (fig. 3), Hartung inverted the method: the different materials he arranged on the wood panel covered with a layer of vibrant black paint—newspapers cut into triangular forms, wood, metal squares pierced with two holes, string—become so many abstract signs. These works allowed him a tangible experience of the life of abstract forms in the space of the real. González' work made such a strong impact on Hartung that he was moved to make an iron sculpture in 1938 (fig. 4), one that turned out perfectly accomplished.

This was to remain an exception for the painter as he never repeated the experience. His sculptural experimentation in spatial drawing found its match in a painting completed that same year, *T 1938–2*, which is, essentially, an enlarged version of a drawing from 1934. Hartung had been working since 1931 on this relationship, enlarging some of his drawings in order to transpose them into paintings, for example, *T 1931–1* (46 x 38 cm; fig. 5) and

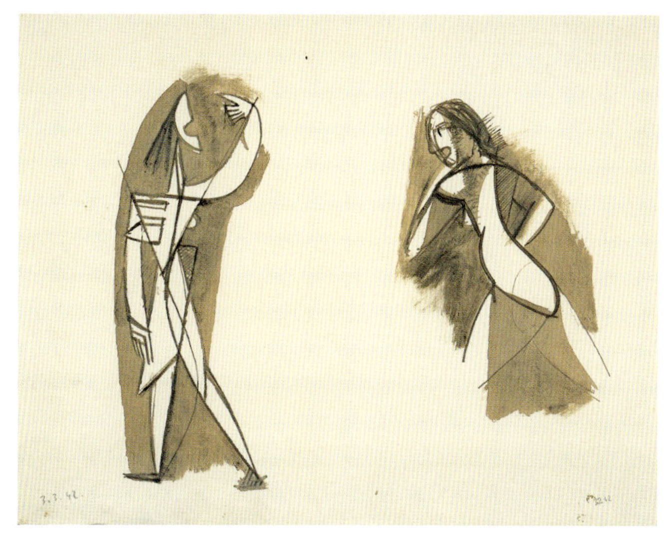

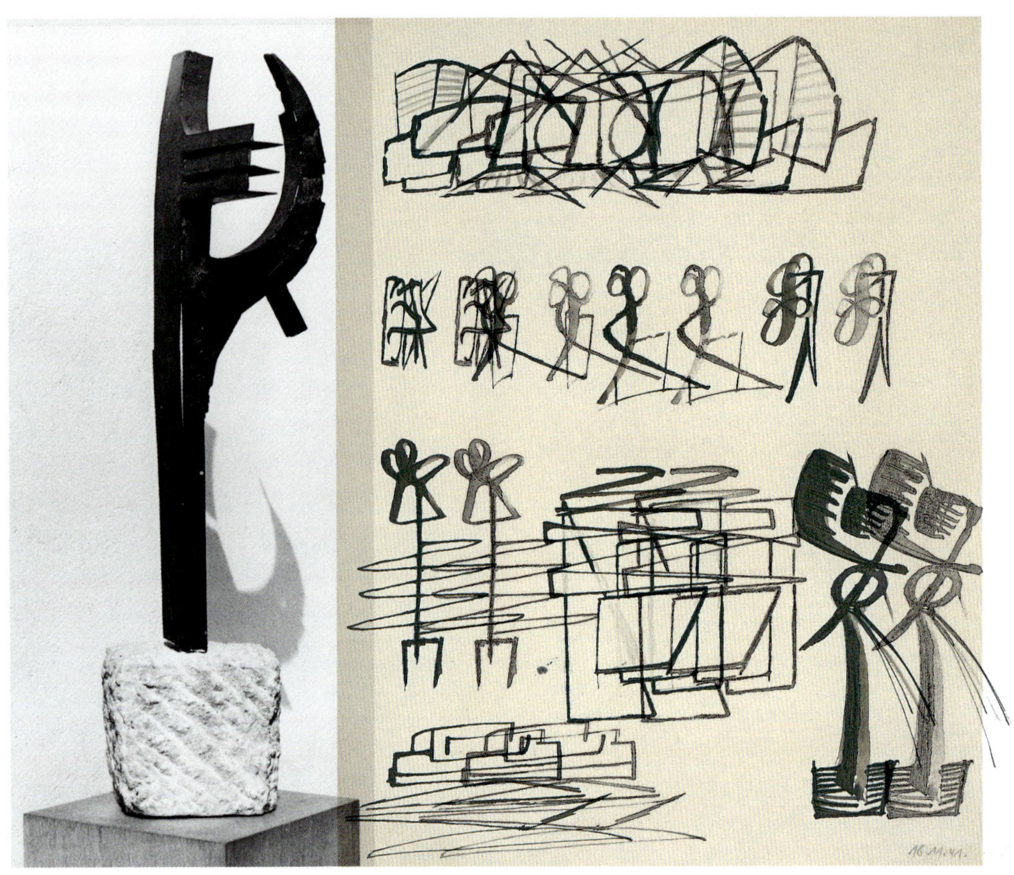

untitled 1931 (35.1 x 24.2 cm; fig. 6); *T 1932–11* (80 x 61 cm) and *untitled* 1932 (15.7 x 12.1 cm); *T 1936–20* (116 x 80 cm; fig. 11), and four untitled drawings (1936, 31 x 33 cm; figs. 7, 8, 9, 10). The point here is to question the myth of spontaneity that Hartung never bought into. Hélion had urged him to develop this practice, which has its origins in the grid method, since he thought it particularly adapted to so-called constructed art. However, we should notice that the slight modification to the original drawing in *T 1938–2* transforms the base of the line into a veritable pedestal. The flattened welded iron of González's art and the tension he produced by crushing metal find an echo in the painting *T 1938–36* (fig. 12), for which there is an outline in India ink (1938). In this painting, Hartung rediscovered the density of the line, which are thick and tense; he had already explored this characteristic in his black crayon work in 1923–24 but it reappears here as if summoned by a system of resonances. There are also echoes of this abstract series that Hartung composed in his younger days in a sculpture called *Petite Vénus* by González (1936–37), which

14. Julio Gonzalez, *Stern Shape*, 1937, iron, 79.2 x 22.3 x 29.1 cm
15. HH, untitled, 1941, black lead and ink on paper, 27.2 x 21 cm
16. Julio Gonzalez, *Cactus Man*, 1939, iron, 65.1 x 27 x 13.8 cm
17. HH, untitled, 1940, gouache, ink and pastel on paper, 37.2 x 27.5 cm

seems to be the perfect translation of Hartung's series into three-dimensional space. A real resonance developed in the work of the two artists but the more González' titles bespeak their link to the real, the more Hartung's remained radically closed within themselves, something that sparked many lively discussions between the two artists.[21] González continued to portray and sustain the human figure in his work. Furthermore, both artists were in the habit of drawing before they committed the design to canvas or sculpture, a habit that allowed them to master the use of gesture. And, given that it had become very difficult to buy canvas in those days, the two artists were naturally more attracted to drawing than anything else. Nor is it trivial to note the presence of the human figure, albeit with a certain degree of abstraction, in the drawings Hartung started composing in 1937. This is something that had not been seen in his own work since his early endeavours, when the paintings of artists he admired had helped him find his own artistic idiom. In 1921–22 Goya's study for *El tres de mayo* (1814), an image of the human drama in the face of oppression, had provided Hartung with the chance to compose three works where he reduced an upright human figure to an X, the arms and legs forming a cross (figs. 25, 26, 27). This abstract sign, however, had not yet found a consequential treatment in Hartung's work. We find him retracing the same path in many of his small drawings (which measured 36.2 x 29.4 cm on average) in the period 1937–38. The themes of the woman with the amphora and the country woman were the objects of many studies drawn by González in 1937, where we see time and again the human form in the same position, but in a subdued

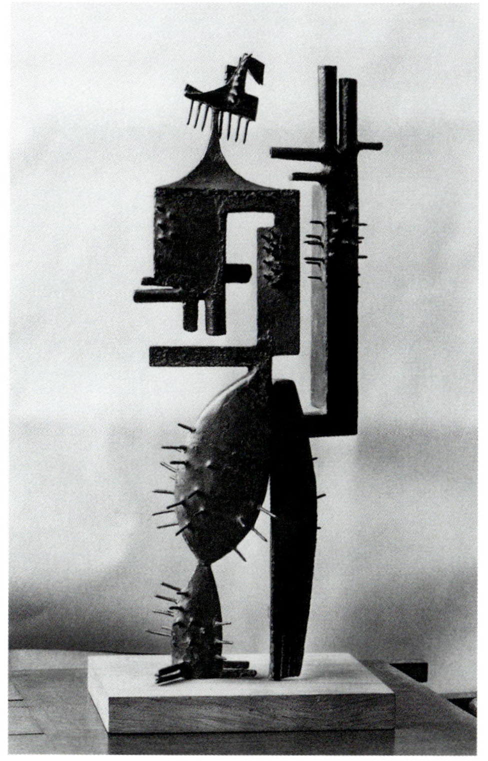

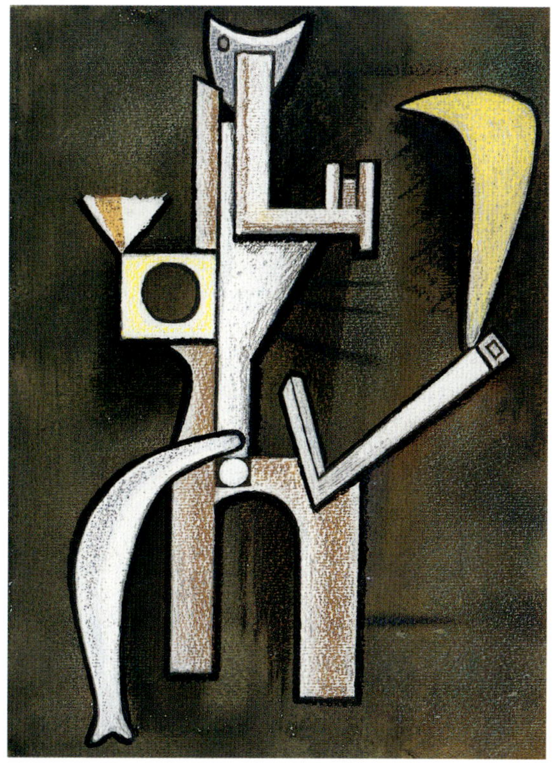

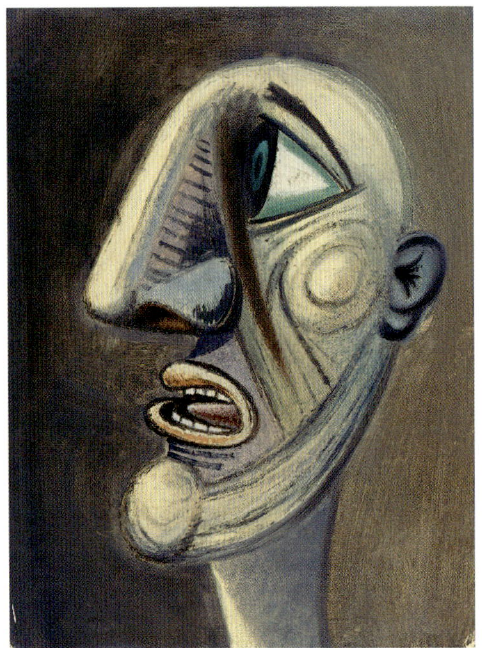

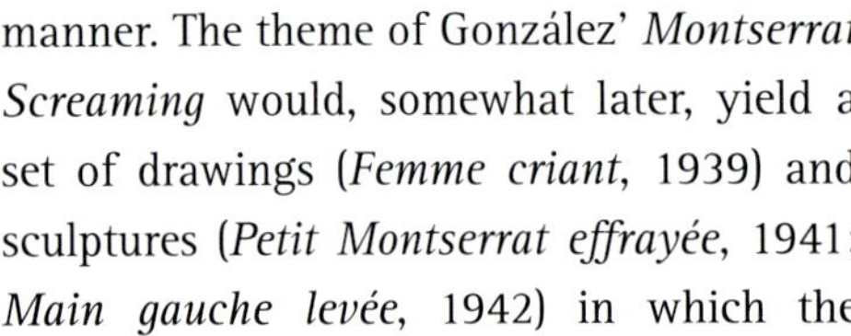

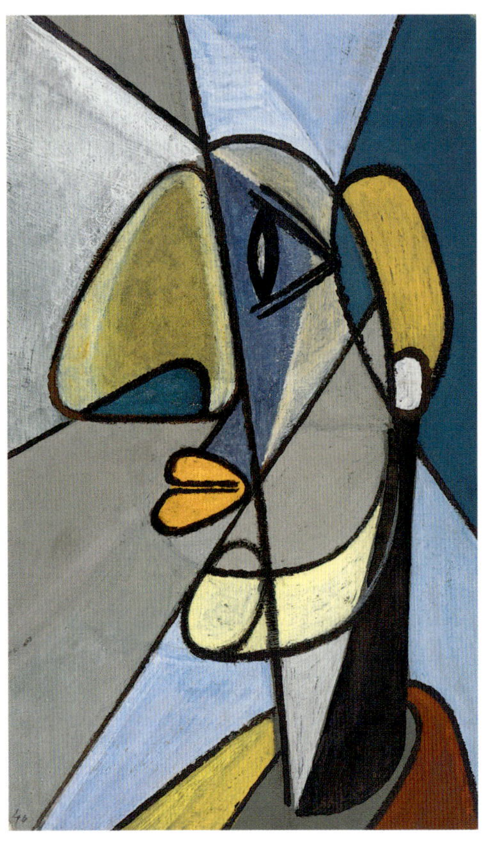

manner. The theme of González' *Montserrat Screaming* would, somewhat later, yield a set of drawings (*Femme criant*, 1939) and sculptures (*Petit Montserrat effrayée*, 1941; *Main gauche levée*, 1942) in which the scream is accompanied by a raised arm that is simultaneously a movement of both protest and fear. Numerous drawings by Hartung from 1939 seem to copy drawings composed by González before making *L'Homme cactus* (1939; fig. 16). Beyond their differences relating to the abstract vs. the figurative, both artists were guided by the same search for an art with a human and expressive content.[22] The intimacy the two men shared in their artistic practice was strengthened by a growing intimacy in their emotional lives. This was sealed by Hartung's second marriage, on 22 July 1939, to Roberta González, herself an artist.

The outbreak of World War II led Hartung to enlist as a volunteer soldier in the French army after a fifteen-day stay in the Stadium of Colombes.[23] On 4 October, Roberta González wrote to Mendès-France in the hopes of securing an attestation signed by him certifying that Hartung sided with France against the Nazis and attesting his status as a professional painter.[24] The artist's situation seemed very delicate indeed. In spite of the difficulties posed by his German citizenship, Hartung managed to enlist on 26 December in the Foreign Legion under the name Jean Gauthier. He arrived in Algeria on

18. HH, untitled, 1940, oil on paper, 32 x 24.5 cm
19. HH, untitled, 1940, gouache on paper, 41 x 24.5 cm
20. HH, untitled, 1940, black lead, gouache, ink and pastel on paper, 30 x 22 cm
21. HH, untitled, 1940, graphite, gouache, pastel and ink on paper, 31.4 x 23.6 cm

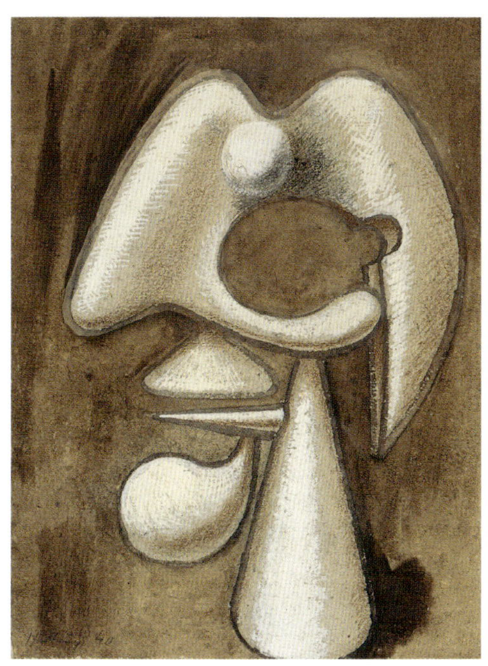 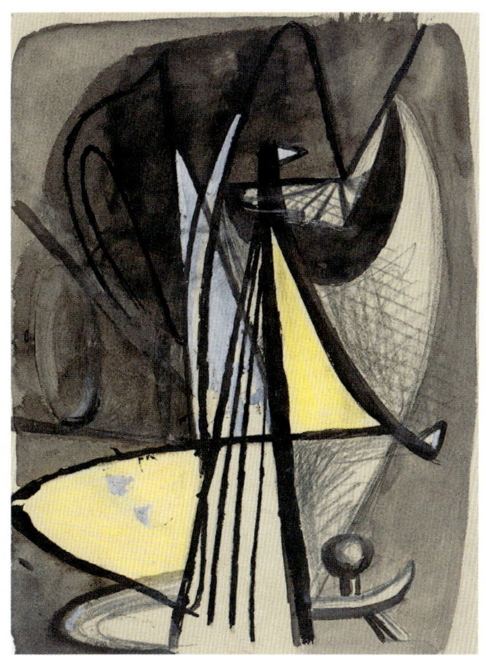

8 January 1940 where he was put in charge of decorating the dining hall of the Legion in Sidi-bel-Abès. Demobilized at the beginning of October, he joined up with the González family in the rural zone of Lasbouygues in the south of France after France had been divided into two zones—one occupied, the other free—by the Armistice. Under the Vichy government, Hartung was obliged to live clandestinely, protected by the González family and the name Jean Gauthier.

Feeling very weak, fragile, and guilty at forcing the González family to live in the south of France to protect him, Hartung was not particularly drawn to artistic work. There is a noticeable slowdown in his output during this period, but, encouraged by his father-in-law and wife, he slowly made his way back to work. In 1940 he completed eight paintings and ten in 1941, but it was in the area of drawing that his production was at its most interesting. In 1939 González had completed the *Masque Montserrat criant* using the repoussé method; the following year he started exploring how he might represent a scream until he alighted upon *Tête Montserrat criant* in 1942. This was a full-relief sculpture made in plaster. Hartung was likewise exploring how to represent the human face but in a different vein and on paper. In a method that had by then become quite standard, Hartung made the figurative works of other artists his starting point and extracted signs from them that he subsequently made his own. The thirty gouaches from 1940 have their reference in the heads produced by Picasso at the end of the Thirties and the heads González had likewise conceived in the same period. Hartung assimilated these figurative works by putting the emphasis on the nodal points of expressivity—the triangle of the nose, the grids sealing the link between planes, the crescent shape of the screaming mouth, the force of the slightly curved line marking the point where the plane of the nose intersects that of the jaw.

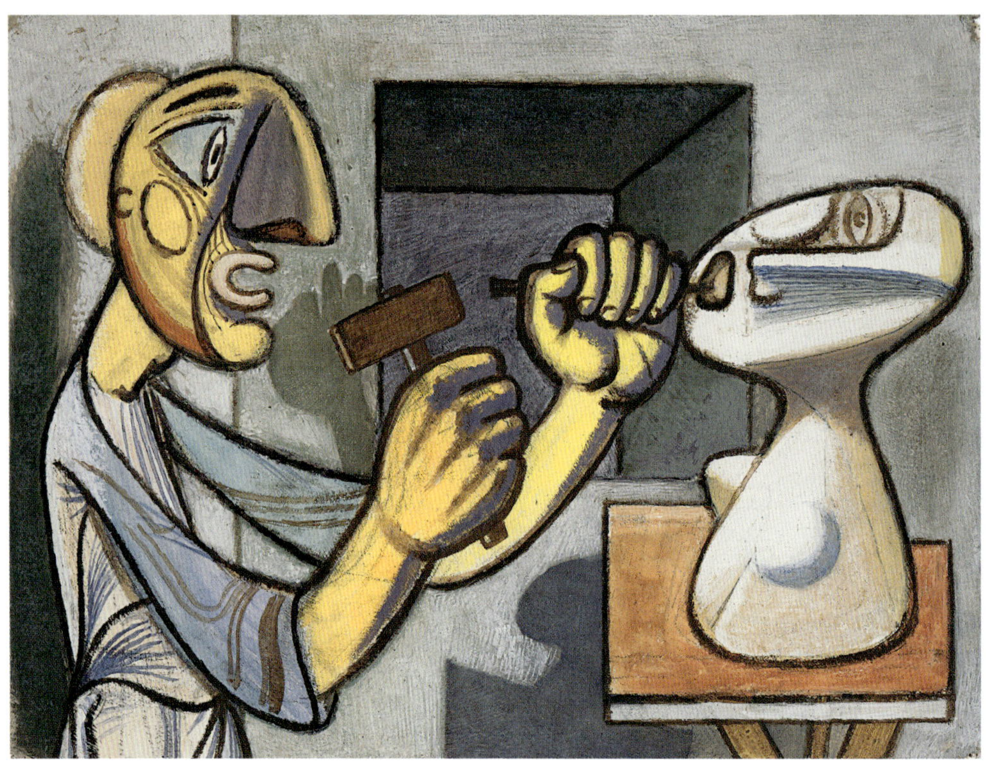

Triangle, crescent, grids... they become so many recurrent signs in these gouaches that their repetition is tantamount to a form of creative experimentation. Hartung transposed them into their proper space, the uniform background that he placed them on investing the signs with an autonomous existence. A set of some fifty small drawings (21 x 27.2 cm on average) 1941–42 essentially formed the second stage of this exploration. During this phase, Hartung freed the signs from all reference to visible reality by randomly arranging them in space. He repeated this experiment over and over again, and succeeded in creating a repertoire of signs with a high degree of abstraction, but they are not to be found in the rare paintings he produced in the same period. Although this body of work, composed under very difficult psychological and material circumstances, amounts more to an investigation than a real plastic achievement, it turned out to determine his future production. These signs—crescents, grids, curved lines—all reappear in Hartung's post-war paintings, where they've become an autonomous vocabulary fully affirmed by the artist.

In 1941 González returned to Paris and left Hartung to pursue his work alone. The sculptor died in March 1942, which Hartung experienced as the loss of a second father.

22. HH, untitled, 1941, watercolor, gouache and ink on paper, 28.2 x 38 cm
23. HH, untitled, 1942, graphite and ink on paper, 21 x 27 cm
24. HH, untitled, 1942, ink on paper, 21 x 27 cm
25. HH, *After Goya y Lucientes' The Third of May*, 1922, oil on cardboard, 23 x 33.5 cm

The invasion of the free zone on 11 November 1942 forced Hartung to flee to Spain to rejoin the Foreign Legion, as he would have been considered a deserter by the German authorities. A large sum of money had to be raised to enable him to escape so his mother-in-law, Marie-Thérèse González, turned to Picasso for help. The end of the story is given in the correspondence between Hartung and Marie-Thérèse well after the Liberation. On 11 February 1944, Hartung wrote:

"Dear Marie-Thérèse, I also want to talk to you about something else. It was some time ago—so many things have happened in the meantime—that Roberta led me to understand that I was totally wrong. Everything was done in such secrecy and through such winding paths—Roberta and I both thought that Picasso had given the 40 thousand francs I needed to flee. Now she tells me that was not at all true, that he only gave 4,000 and that it was you who put up the rest. Dear Marie-Thérèse, I was so confused then and am still confused now. I don't know what to tell you, how to express to you my gratitude for this enormous sacrifice. I'm afraid this must have been quite a privation for you and—who knows—maybe—with all the time that's passed, that you're annoyed. I am so moved I don't even know how to thank you."[25]

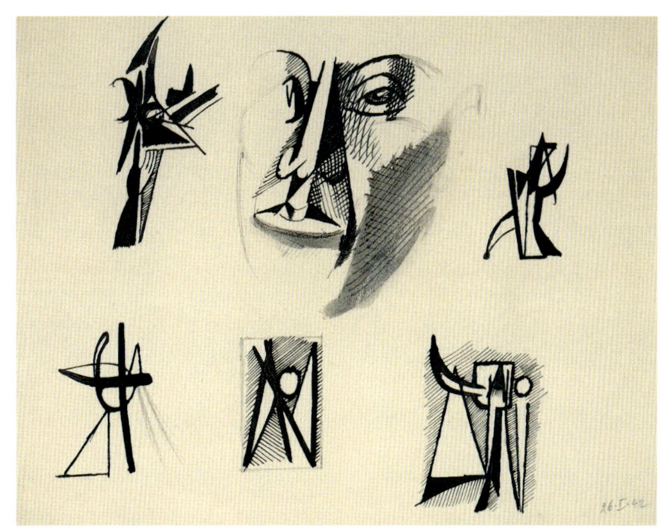

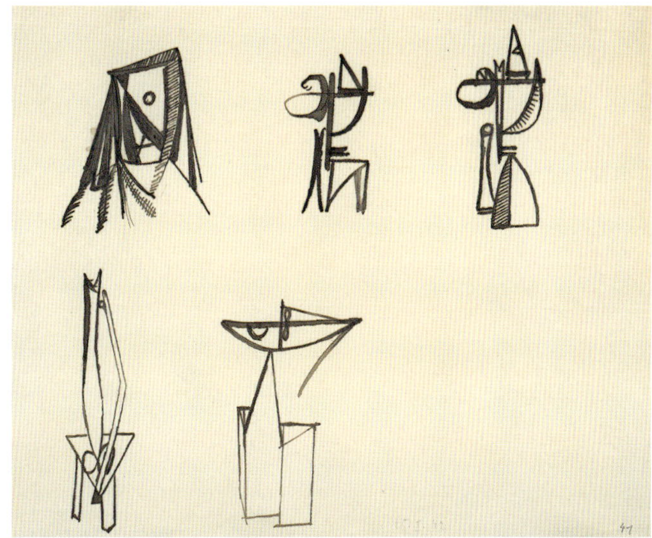

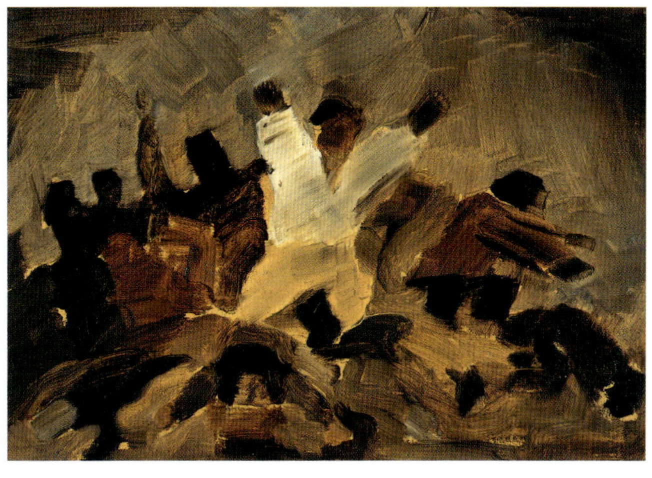

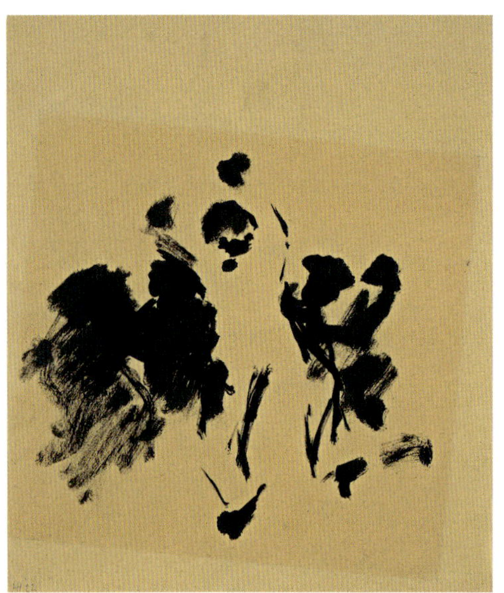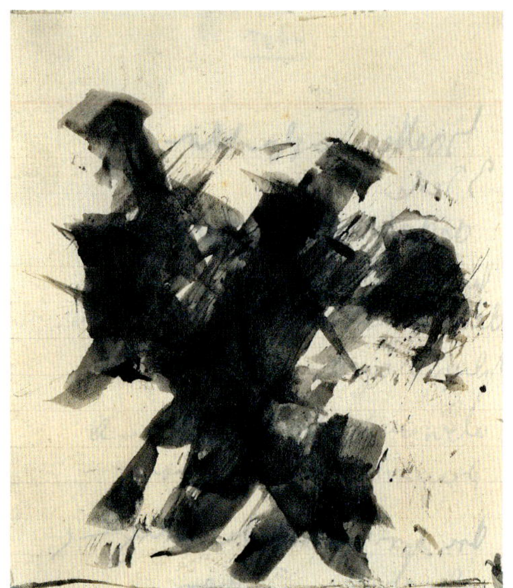

Hartung arrived in Spain in 1943 but was immediately taken prisoner and sent to the Miranda del Ebro POW camp from where he managed to reach North Africa. Seriously wounded on the front on 27 November 1944, his right leg had to be amputated during the first days of December. He was hospitalised and only returned to live in Arcueil in 1945 but was eager to start working as soon as possible. The strategy he devised to organise this reencounter with painting was to use drawings he had done before the war as the basis for oil paintings. Little by little, he developed the pictorial vocabulary that was soon to make him the leader of Lyrical Abstraction. The black lines of his famous paintings from 1946–1954 correspond to the vocabulary of signs he created in 1940–41. Moreover, the method of relating a drawing to its painting equivalent using a grid, which he started developing at the beginning of the Thirties, quickly evolved into a system. But that remained a secret of the studio.

The years 1937–42 turned out to be decisive, but only a posteriori. The plastic vocabulary Hartung created truly embodied an act of resistance that enjoyed victory after the war.[26] A new conception of the act of painting soon imposed an aesthetic value based on subjectivity and on the defence of freedom of action commensurate with the new state of the world. The call to freedom was better understood after 1946, and indeed a number of critics had the sense, as they stood before Hartung's recent paintings, that their origins lay in the experience that creation and survival were indissociable. Hartung petitioned to the French government to be naturalised at the end of the war and his petition was granted in November 1946, so ending his clandestine life. An artist of German origin and French citizenship, Hartung finally triumphed.

26. HH, *After Goya y Lucientes'*, 1922, ink on paper, 23.2 x 24.8 cm
27. HH, untitled, 1923, ink on paper, 11.1 x 9 cm

1. For more details about its coming into being, please see: Bertrand Lemoine, "Le Palais de Tokyo", in *Années 30 en Europe. Le temps menaçant 1929-1939* (Paris: Musée d'art moderne de la ville de Paris, 1997), pp. 501-3.

2. For a more in-depth look at these two exhibitions, see: Serge Fauchereau, "Les expositions de Paris et Munich en 1937", and "Paris, capitale artistique", in *Années 30 en Europe*, pp. 409-14; 489-92. See also Patrick Weiser, "L'Exposition internationale, l'état et les beaux-arts", in *Paris-Paris. 1937-1957* (Paris: Centre Georges Pompidou, 1981; reprinted 1992) pp. 91-95.

3. Sophie Krebs, "1937, l'art 'indépendant' à Paris", in *Années 30 en Europe, op. cit.* note 1, p. 495.

4. Hans Hartung, *Autoportrait. Récit recueilli par Monique Lefebvre* (Paris: Bernard Grasset, 1976), pp. 115-16.

5. See, for example, the anonymous "Biographie", in *Julio González: catalogue raisonné des sculptures* (Milan: Electa, 1987); "*Musée du Jeu de Paume: Exposition 'De Cézanne à nos jours', organizée par Yvonne Zervos. Participation de González. Rencontre Hans Hartung*", p. 314. Daniel Abadie noticed the omission and corrected it but without mentioning that he had done so. See the interview with Daniel Abadie, "Le grand atelier", in *Une rencontre: Hans Hartung et Julio González 1935-1952* (Paris: Galerie de France; Lugano: Galleria Pieter Coray, 1992), p. 11. "Hans Hartung's *Autoportrait* provides the precise answer: in 1937, at the Musée du Jeu de Paume, during the opening of the exhibition Origins and Developments of International Independent Art".

6. Catalogue entitled *Origines et développement de l'art international indépendant* (Paris: Musée du Jeu de Paume, 1937).

7. The agendas are now in the archives of the Hartung Foundation in Antibes.

8. *Origines et développement de l'art international indépendant*, note 6, n.p.

9. On this, see the very detailed study by Margit Rowell, "Julio González: La genèse de la sculpture en fer", in *Julio González: catalogue raisonné des sculptures*, note 5, pp. 11-14. The author traces how, in work after work, a pas-de-deux develops in the practices of the two artists, and then how each one returns to his solitary trajectory with more resolve.

10. Hartung, *Autoportrait*, Rowell, "Julio Gonzalez", p. 10.

11. Hartung, *Autoportrait*, p. 105.

12. Hartung, *Autoportrait*, p. 105.

13. For further details, see Hartung, *Autoportrait*, pp. 103-7.

14. Hartung, *Autoportrait*, p. 107.

15. For a more detailed account of the relationship between Hartung and the protagonists of Concrete Art, I take the liberty of referring the reader to my monograph *Hans Hartung. Les aléas d'une reception* (Dijon: Presses du réel, 2005), pp. 69-74.

16. Herta Wescher, "New Works in Paris", *Axis* 6 (Spring 1936), p. 27.

17. Interview with Daniel Abadie, "Le grand atelier", in *Une rencontre entre Hans Hartung et Julio González. 1935-1942* (Paris: Galerie de France, 1992), note 5, p. 11.

18. On the topic of artists in exile during the 1930s, see: Lionel Richard, "Ténèbres sur l'Europe", in *Années 30*, pp. 45-51.

19. Cf. Hartung, *Autoportrait*, pp. 122-25.

20. Hartung, *Autoportrait*, p. 120.

21. Hartung, *Autoportrait*, pp. 124-25.

22. Cf. Josephine Withers, "Julio González", in *Julio González. Les matériaux et son expression* (Paris: Galerie de France, 1970) n.p.

23. Hartung, *Autoportrait*, p. 135. "The way things were going, war seemed ineluctable to me. I put my name down on the list of volunteers for the French army. In September 1939, I was first taken, like so many other foreigners from central Europe, to the Stadium of Colombes. I was there for fifteen days, the time it took the military authorities to check the identities and motives of all the people there."

24. A transcript of this letter can be found in the catalogue *Une rencontre: Hans Hartung et Julio González*, pp. 99-100. "Dear Mendès-France: My husband, Hans Hartung, has committed himself to serving France. He currently finds himself in the camp where there are rounded-up all those Germans who, like himself, enlisted during the summer. He has written to me indicating that he needs to provide two certificates. He needs, first of all, an attestation from an art dealer indicating that he is indeed a painter who's had exhibitions; since Hartung has exhibited his work at the Surindépendants, I thought to ask you for a written attestation (on unheaded paper), if you would not mind, or if you can do it. The second, and more important, certificate he needs to provide is a certificate signed by a French citizen known either to the Police or the Military vouching for my husband's loyal and sympathetic feelings to France."

25. Handwritten letter from Hartung to Marie-Thérèse González dated 11 February 1944, and signed Jean. The original is now in the archives of the Musée National d'Art Moderne, Paris.

26. For a more detailed analysis of the production and reception of Hans Hartung's work after the war, I take the liberty of referring the reader to my essay, *Hans Hartung. Les aléas d'une réception*, the first chapter in particular, pp. 24-125.

Hans Hartung

John C. Welchman — Abcedarium: Reading Between the Lines

Franz-W. Kaiser — A Case Study on the Caducity of Categories in Art Criticism

Annie Claustres — Hans Hartung Clandestine Artist 1937-1942: the Decisive Years

Christine Mehring — Hans Hartung Mid-Century Modern

Rainer Michael Mason — Hartung and Printmaking

Christopher Wool

Selected Works

Anne Pontégnie 1975

Hartung at the

Metropolitan Museum

a Problem?

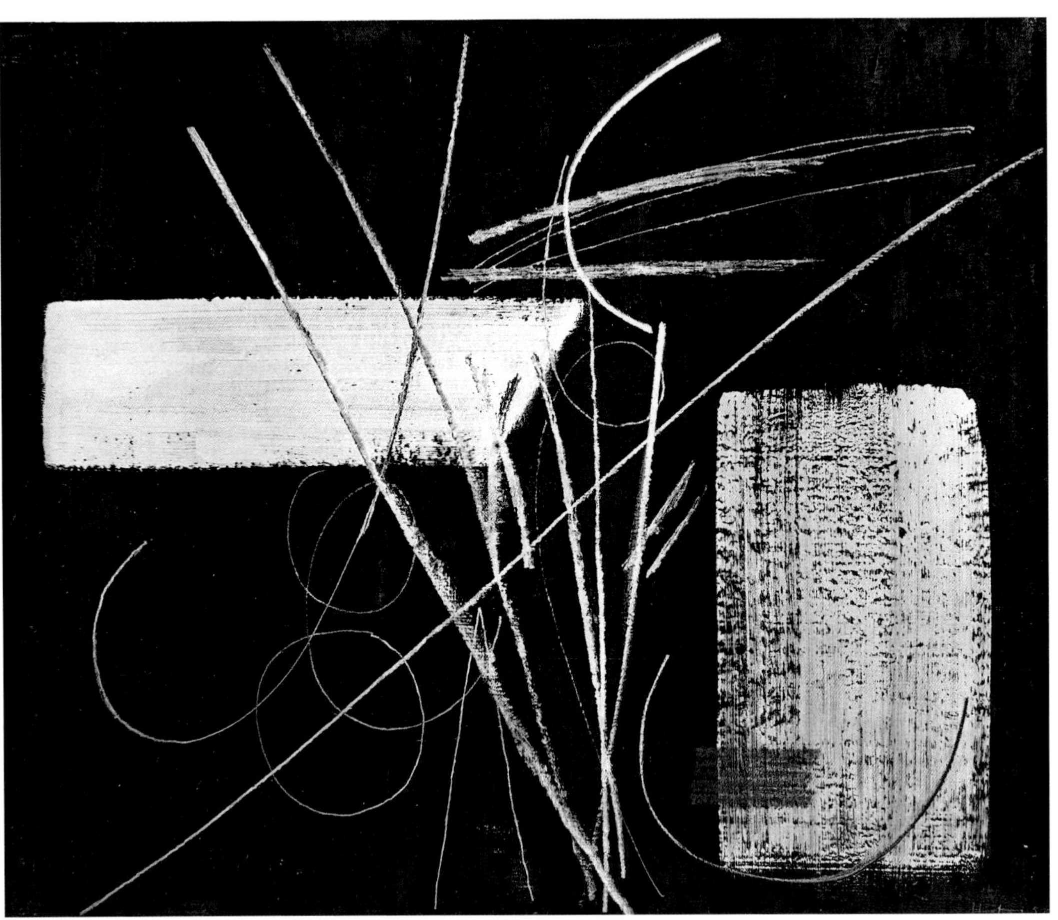

Matching paintings with couches and curtains was far from Hans Hartung's mind, especially coming out of World War II as he did, impoverished and handicapped. And yet match they do. Take the living room of Ottomar Domnick, the artist's most ardent supporter, featuring a moderately-sized 1950 oil painting (*T1950–42*, fig. 1) amidst a thoroughly modern environment (fig. 2).[1] Hartung seems at home here. To start with, the juxtapositions of different textures: in the painting, the smooth black background with a rough, as if perforated, white dry-brushstroke-turned-plane; in the interior, the shag rug with shiny tiles and mat brick walls. Next, lines set against amorphous planes: the armchair, with an undulating seating surface supported by four spiny, splayed legs, echoing the painting's tentative semicircles, the smooth corners of the white plane, and the bundle of lines spreading across the canvas from the centre of its bottom edge. With the strong overall contrast of light and dark, the correspondence is poignant.

In the years after the war, Domnick, based in Stuttgart, made a name for himself by collecting and supporting young abstract artists in Europe. As a practising psychiatrist he took

1. HH, *T1950–42*, 1950, oil on canvas, 53 x 65 cm, Fondation Domnick, Nürtingen
2. Domnick's living room, 1967
3. Wassily Kandinsky, *First Abstract Watercolour*, ca. 1913, Centre Pompidou, Paris

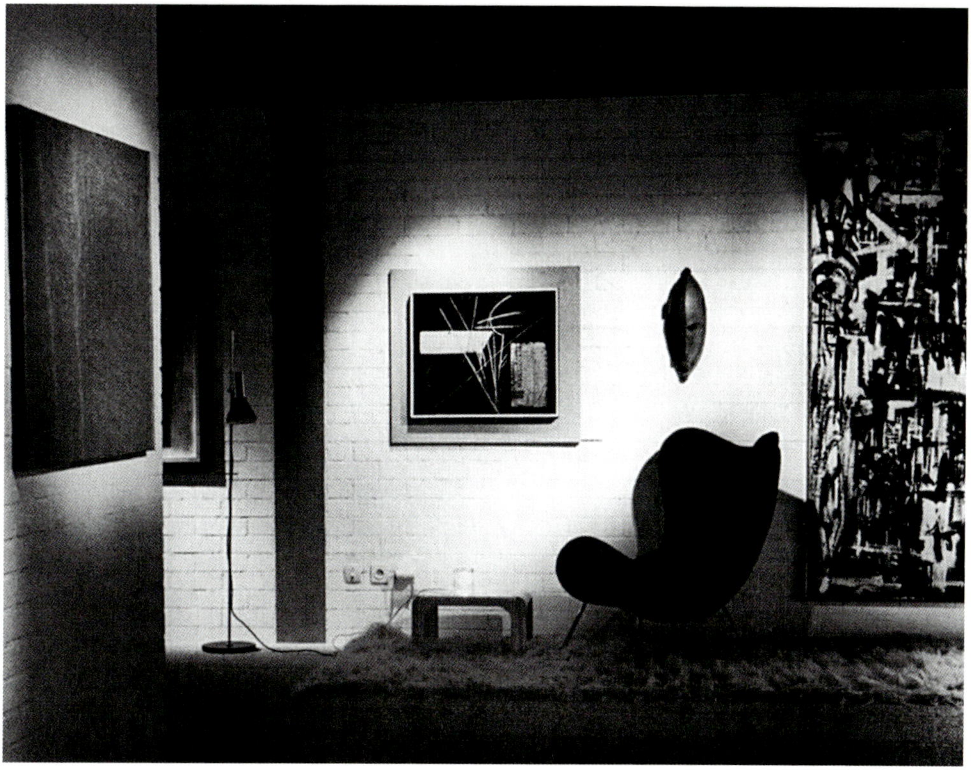

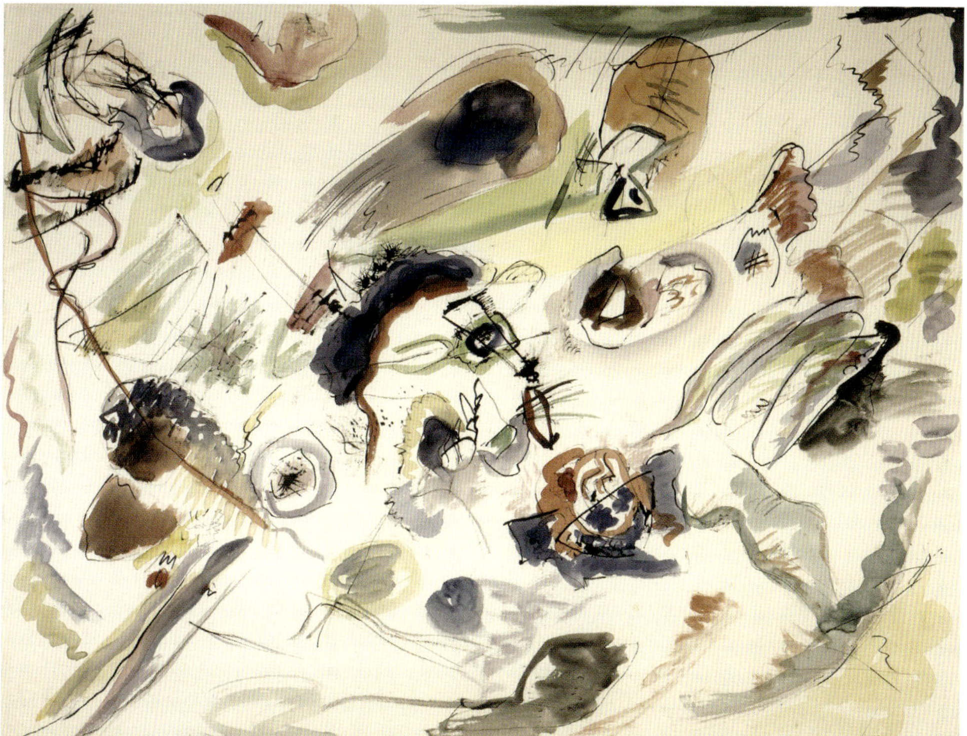

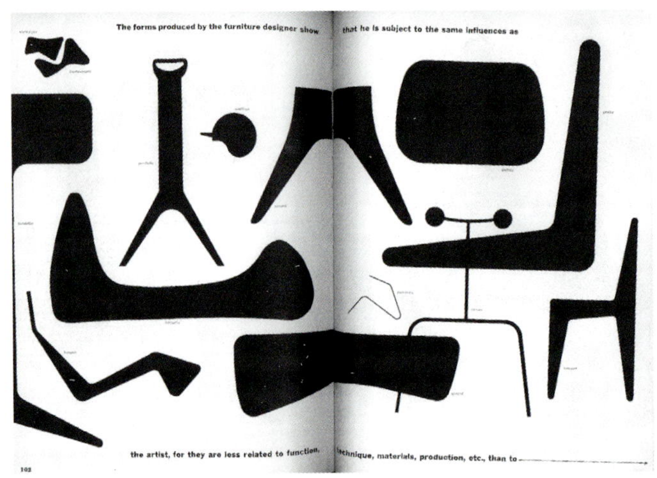

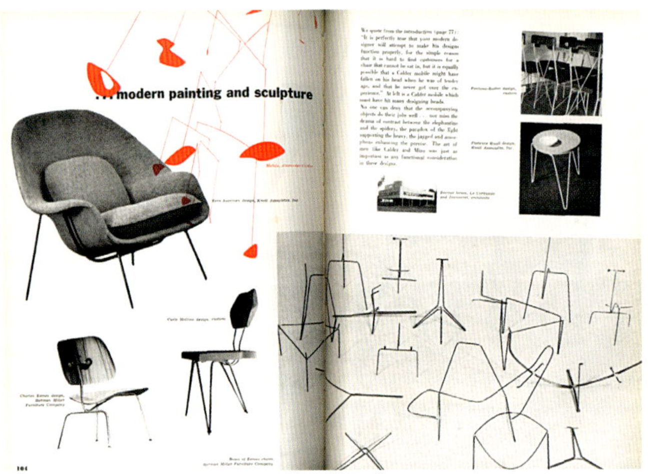

a particular liking to expressionist, abstract painting. Following his first meeting with Hartung while organising the travelling exhibition *Die französische Abstrakte Malerei* in 1948, Domnick was fascinated to such a degree that he published, in the following year, a luscious monograph on the artist. "Hartung is a phenomenon", he raved.[2] In his mind, the painter conveyed emotions by means of lines and texture:

"Hartung's graphic linear play receives its special charm because in its dynamism one can read not only the psychic expression but also the speed of writing... To this is added a tactile element: the pressure of the brushstroke, at one time made by the sensitive hand and another time by the full force of his arm, indicates a structural charm... These two factors, the speed and the pressure of the brush, let us almost feel the motion and convey to us the dynamic experience. Motion and psychic experience are joined."[3]

No doubt Domnick's book was a crucial step towards Hartung's subsequent fame in the European art world. What do we make of this quintessential collector of mid-century existentialist painting in Europe unintentionally tarnishing the work of his favourite protégé with a decorative touch by matching his living room with it?

The need to dissociate abstract art from "the decorative", however vaguely defined, is as old as abstract art itself. Modern artists have worried about producing "mere" decoration ever since they first ventured into abstraction during the second decade of the twentieth century. Around the time of his self-proclaimed *First Abstract Watercolour* (fig. 3), Wassily Kandinsky, for example, noted that "a terrifying abyss of all kinds of questions, a wealth of responsibilities stretched before me. And most important of all: What is to replace the missing object? The danger of ornament revealed itself clearly to

4. George Nelson, *Interiors + Industrial Design* (July 1949), pp. 102–103
5. George Nelson, *Interiors + Industrial Design* (July 1949), pp. 104–105
6. HH, *T1950–21*, 1950, oil on canvas, 50 x 65 cm, Fondation Sonja Henia Niels, Onstad, Oslo

me; the dead semblance of stylized forms I found merely repugnant."[4] Because abstract forms had primarily fulfilled decorative functions in previous centuries, the danger of non-art loomed large for Kandinsky's pioneering generation.

Half a century later critics and artists alike continued to express the same worries, attesting to the forcefulness of the threat and to the still uncertain position of abstract painting in the immediate postwar years. Reviewing Hartung's first solo exhibition after the war at Galerie Lydia Conti in Paris in March 1947, the critic Léon Degand wrote that "the artist opens up an empire of sensations that implicates our whole being, body and soul. He never lapses gratuitously into the decorative, and he impugns the accessory." The artist himself echoed that aversion: "At shows, I can't stand all these high-hats who parade shamelessly before our work, the aggressive motley of their dresses jarring with the colours of the paintings... And I like even less those buyers who choose a painting because the colour matches their couch or curtains. I am not a designer, nor am I an interior decorator, I'm a painter."[5]

Decoration seems particularly threatening to the kind of abstract art which critics believed Hartung—following in the footsteps of the early, improvising Kandinsky—pursued. Prominent, sweeping brushstrokes paired with clusters of swiftly drawn lines made for a painting full of feeling. With prewar abstract, expressionist paintings to his credit—an "*antériorité redoubtable*" in critic René de Solier's words—Hartung in the late Forties and Fifties gained a reputation as the founding father of Art Informel.[6] Alternately called Tachisme, Abstraction Lyrique, and Un Art Autre, "informel" alludes to the crude, shapeless, and casual application of paint with brushes, palette knives, sticks or fingers. These gestural marks were understood to bear witness to an individual artist's emotional states and struggles.[7] Decoration was everything but that: gratuitous, to use Dégand's term, superficial, simplistic, light, insignificant, arbitrary. Degand's rhetorical move of dissociating Hartung's existentialist painting from the decorative thus returns over and over again in the literature that followed, finding its most dramatic articulation in the words of Michel Ragon, one of several defining authorities on Informel. "He never falls to the decorative of the ideogram. His stroke can sometimes 'hurt' like a wound."[8]

Yet it was not simply coincidence that Hartung's painting matched Domnick's furniture. The artist's most celebrated paintings of the Forties and Fifties, especially the "linear play" and "structural charm" singled out by the collector, relate to what decoration actually meant during that period. Defined strictly historically—not in some generic,

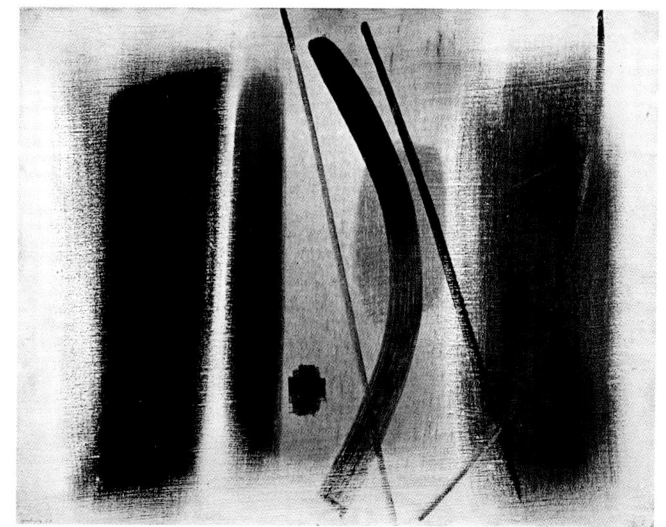

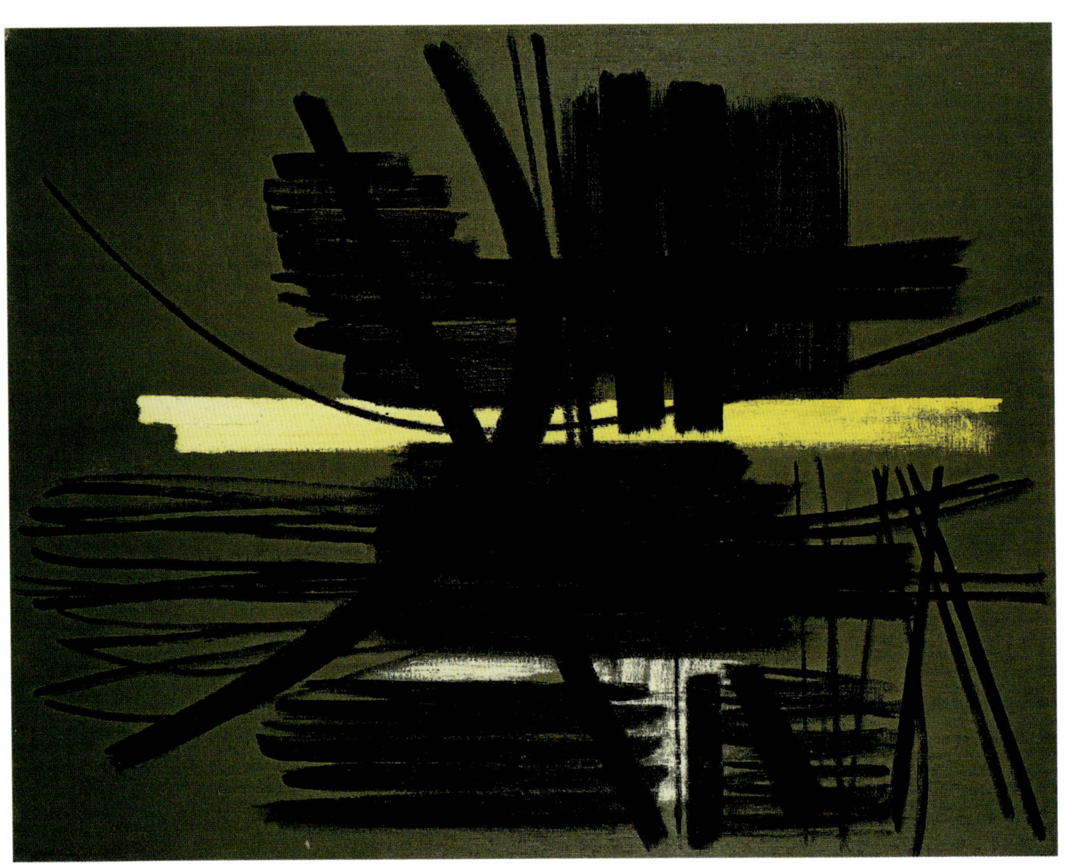

nebulous sense of a scarecrow—decoration in the Forties and Fifties refers to the interior design along with furniture, textile, and product design today known as "mid-century modern". That is precisely the context Domnick chose for displaying his arguably most elegant Hartung painting. In fact, all interiors reproduced in the documentation of this collection of Fifties painting are consistent with the mid-century modern style, ranging from built-in shelving and multifunctional benches to furniture classics like Harry Bertoia's *Diamond Lounge Chair* of 1951–52 made by Knoll (seen in a different home in fig. 8) and Charles Eames' *LCM Chair* of 1946 made by Herman Miller (seen in the lower left corner in fig. 5). Domnick's arrangements are all the more striking because they postdate the Fifties; the building was completed only in 1967. One gets the impression of a curatorial choice.

The mid-century modern style in essence expanded the vocabulary and visibility of modern design. Pushing beyond the constraints of Twenties functionalism, design professionals explored "many kinds of shapes, materials, and techniques", as the designer George Nelson wrote in his quasi-manifesto on the movement's furniture[9] (figs. 4, 5). Smoothly curved forms define our stereotypical image of the Fifties to this day: kidney-

7. HH, *T1952-30*, 1952, oil on canvas, 50 x 65 cm, private collection
8. *Maison et Jardin* 89 (Dec. 1962), p. 192

shaped table tops and undulating profiles of chairs, swelling and bulging shapes reminiscent of boomerangs, palettes, or bulbs, and large indoor plants with heart-shaped leaves. In addition to this "biomorphic look", captured well in Nelson's black silhouettes based on mid-century modern chair elements (fig. 4), the designer lists the "machine look" and the "handicraft look", epitomising the characteristic convergence of modern and traditional elements in mid-century design. Correspondingly, favoured materials were metal and wood. According to Nelson, these were used in order to stress their tactile appeal, like yielding to pressure, and to exploit new structural possibilities, like bending wood laminate and metal tubing (fig. 5).

Returning to Hartung, many of his pastels and oils made between 1945 and 1954 prominently balance planes and lines: the planes come coloured or black, as ovals or other amorphous oblongs with rounded corners; the lines, usually black, come in a range of thicknesses, sometimes tapered, and in a range of configurations, bent or straight by themselves, bundled or hatched in clusters (figs. 1, 6, 10). That same aesthetic, albeit resulting largely from functional considerations, defines many chairs and tables of the period, classics and no-names, with table tops and seats in biomorphic shapes supported on elegantly thin, often splayed, black legs (fig. 5).

In some of Hartung's paintings, what Domnick called "linear play" dominates (fig. 7). These linear configurations parallel other mid-century designs relying more heavily on black wires or tubing—the popular *String* shelving systems designed by the Swedish couple Nisse and Karin Strinning, Jean Prouvé's 1950 *Potence/Swing Jib Lamp*, and Bertoia's *Diamond Lounge Chair*.

When the magazine *Maison & Jardin* ran a spread on Hartung's art as displayed in private collections, a photograph of Monsieur Bernard Gheerbrant's home shows that very Bertoia classic beneath a Hartung painting from the mid-Fifties (fig. 8), a moment when black bundles of lines emerged as central to Hartung's production.[10] In yet other paintings, planes and lines are not so much set in contrast or balance but distributed in more even fashion (fig. 9, 10). Those bring to mind not furniture but textile designs from the Forties and Fifties, when printing (as opposed to weaving) of textile patterns became widespread and made possible run-on configurations of gesturally applied stripes, strokes, and patches (fig. 12).

The most obvious and convincing period feel is evidenced by Hartung's palette. "*J'aime le noir*", he raved and mid-century design shared the love.[11] Graphic

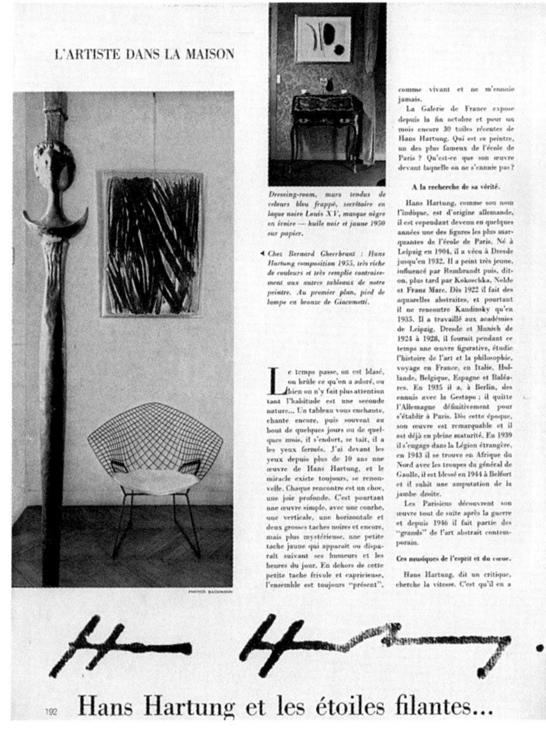

L'ARTISTE DANS LA MAISON

Dressing-room, murs tendus de velours bleu frappé, secrétaire en laque noire Louis XV, masque nègre en ivoire — huile noir et jaune 1950 sur papier.

◀ *Chez Bernard Gheerbrant : Hans Hartung composition 1955, très riche de couleurs et très remplie contrairement aux autres tableaux de notre peintre. Au premier plan, pied de lampe en bronze de Giacometti.*

Le temps passe, on est blasé, on brûle ce qu'on a adoré, ou bien on n'y fait plus attention tant l'habitude est une seconde nature... Un tableau vous enchante, chante encore, puis souvent au bout de quelques jours ou de quelques mois, il s'endort, se tait, il a les yeux fermés. J'ai devant les yeux depuis plus de 10 ans une œuvre de Hans Hartung, et le miracle existe toujours, se renouvelle. Chaque rencontre est un choc, une joie profonde. C'est pourtant une œuvre simple, avec une courbe, une verticale, une horizontale et deux grosses taches noires et encore, mais plus mystérieuse, une petite tache jaune qui apparaît ou disparaît suivant ses humeurs et les heures du jour. En dehors de cette petite tache frivole et capricieuse, l'ensemble est toujours "présent".

comme vivant et ne m'ennuie jamais.

La Galerie de France expose depuis la fin octobre et pour un mois encore 30 toiles récentes de Hans Hartung. Qui est ce peintre, un des plus fameux de l'école de Paris ? Qu'est-ce que son œuvre devant laquelle on ne s'ennuie pas ?

A la recherche de sa vérité.

Hans Hartung, comme son nom l'indique, est d'origine allemande, il est cependant devenu en quelques années une des figures les plus marquantes de l'école de Paris. Né à Leipzig en 1904, il a vécu à Dresde jusqu'en 1932. Il a peint très jeune, influencé par Rembrandt puis, dit-on, plus tard par Kokoschka, Nolde et Franz Marc. Dès 1922 il fait des aquarelles abstraites, et pourtant il ne rencontre Kandinsky qu'en 1935. Il a travaillé aux académies de Leipzig, Dresde et Munich de 1924 à 1928, il fournit pendant ce temps une œuvre figurative, étudie l'histoire de l'art et la philosophie, voyage en France, en Italie, Hollande, Belgique, Espagne et Baléares. En 1935 il a, à Berlin, des ennuis avec la Gestapo : il quitte l'Allemagne définitivement pour s'établir à Paris. Dès cette époque, son œuvre est remarquable et il est déjà en pleine maturité. En 1939 il s'engage dans la Légion étrangère, en 1943 il se trouve en Afrique du Nord avec les troupes du général de Gaulle, il est blessé en 1944 à Belfort et il subit une amputation de la jambe droite.

Les Parisiens découvrent son œuvre tout de suite après la guerre et depuis 1946 il fait partie des "grands" de l'art abstrait contemporain.

Ces musiques de l'esprit et du cœur.

Hans Hartung, dit un critique, cherche la vitesse. C'est qu'il en a

192   Hans Hartung et les étoiles filantes...

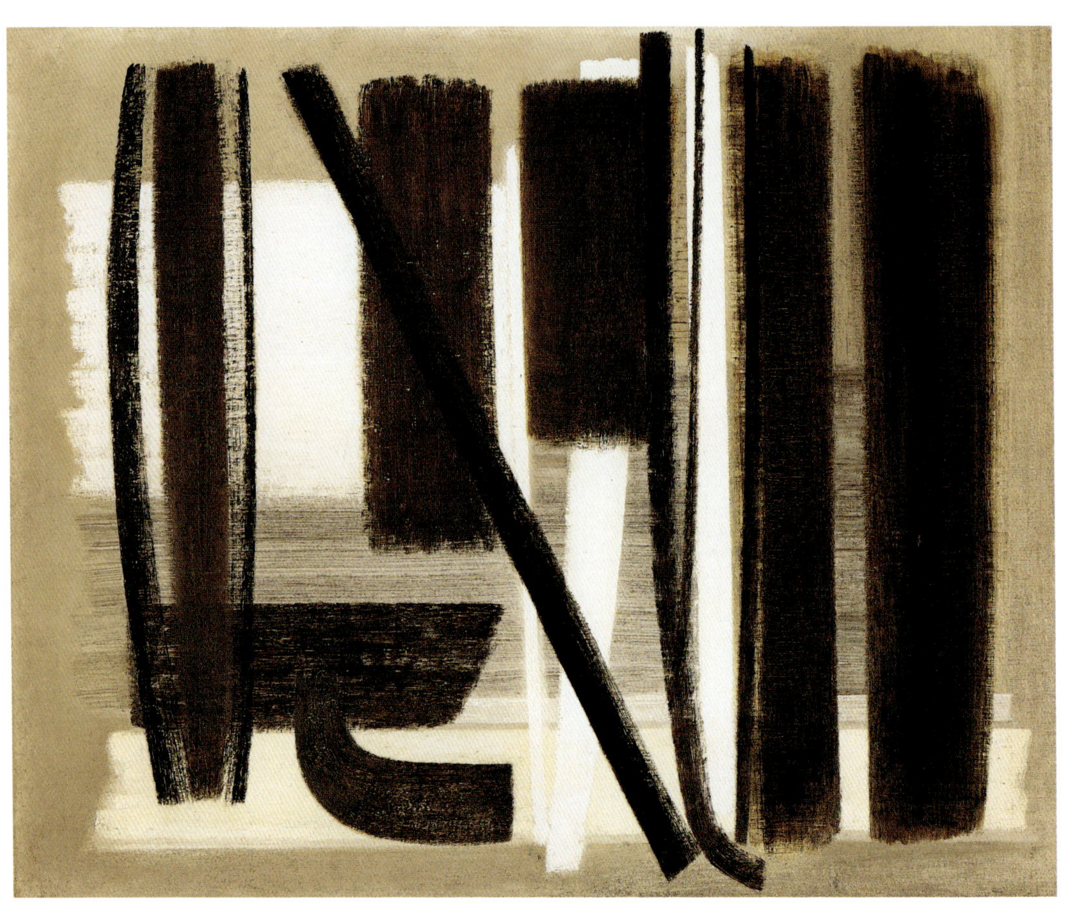

and especially textile designers had a penchant for blacks, set against plain grounds, shapes, or patches in tones closely related to Hartung's: off- or cream-whites and maroons; cool, saturated colours like mustard yellow, turquoise, lemon yellow, and lime green; and yellow, blue, mint, and lavender pastels, never the clean, baby-nursery kind but slightly muddled with warm greys and browns (figs. 6, 7, 9, 11, 12).

Texture plays a dominant role in Hartung's paintings, giving them the "structural charm" that Domnick praised. The prominent planar brushstroke executed with a semi-dry brush loaded with little paint is one means to that end; hatching is another (fig. 10). The artist eloquently built texture even in his works on paper: by superimposing vertical and horizontal sweeps of charcoal stick applied parallel to the paper surface and by evenly applying pastel crayon in a colour almost identical to the ground, thereby accentuating the paper's grain and giving it an illusion of porosity (fig. 11). That in itself conjures up the woven texture of fabrics. Like Hartung, contemporary interior designers appealed to the tactile sense more specifically with textured upholsteries, curtains, rugs,

9. HH, *T1949–33*, 1949, oil on canvas, 81 x 100 cm
10. HH, *T1949–9*, 1949, oil on canvas, 89 x 162 cm, Kunstsammlung Nordrhein-Westfalen, Düsseldorf

and carpets, often used in contrasts that echoed the combinations of wood and metal in furniture designs (fig. 14).

Of course Hartung's abstractions do not literally represent mid-century modern design. But they do share a style—preferences for certain formal strategies, shapes, colours, and their combinations. That said, it seems a foregone conclusion that one influenced the other. Designers had put in place the groundbreaking elements of mid-century modern as early as 1940, while Hartung established his mid-century vocabulary only a few years later. However, those first signature canvases date too close to the war for the painter to have had any exposure to the designs in question—a handful were made within months of the war's end, considerably more followed in 1946. A 1961 story on Hartung's house at the Rue Gauguet in the popular German interior design magazine *Schöner Wohnen* features a host of watered-down versions of mid-century modern designs—*LCM Chair* imitations in the hallway and living room, joined by a variation on the tractor seat stools by the Italian Castiglioni brothers to the left of the fireplace. But it is safe to assume these only entered Hartung's life much later (fig. 15).[12]

What accounts at least to some degree for the parallel but independent development of these mid-century styles in design and painting is that both drew on the same abstract-surrealist sources, especially the art of Alexander Calder and Joan Miró and their use of coloured or black biomorphic shapes paired with black lines. Hartung greatly respected the two, and the Spaniard's impact on his work is well established.[13] Likewise George Nelson in his manifesto illustrated a Calder mobile (fig. 5) and quipped that "it is perfectly true that your modern designer will attempt to make his designs function properly... but it is equally possible that a Calder mobile might have fallen on his head when he was of tender age..." He concluded that "the art of men like Calder and Miró was just as important as any functional consideration in these designs."[14]

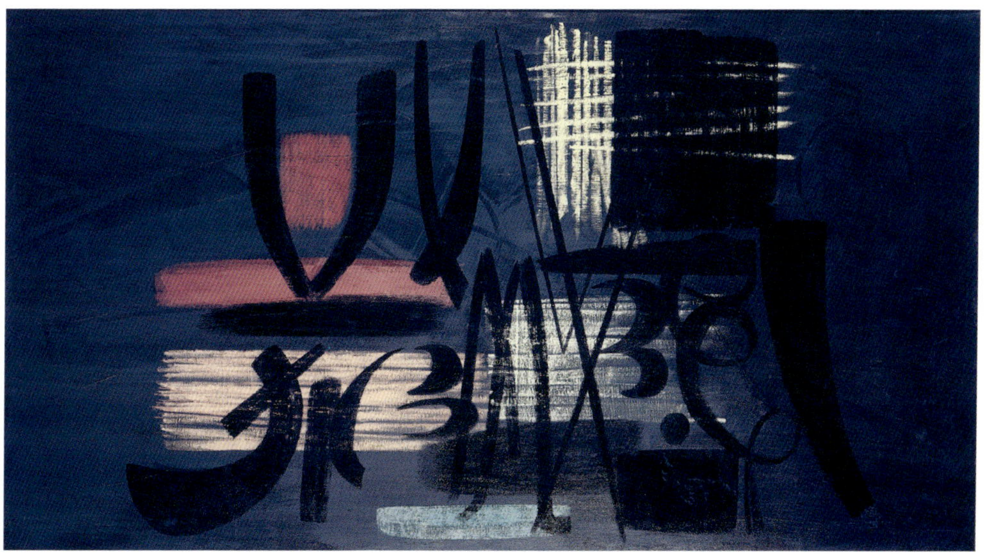

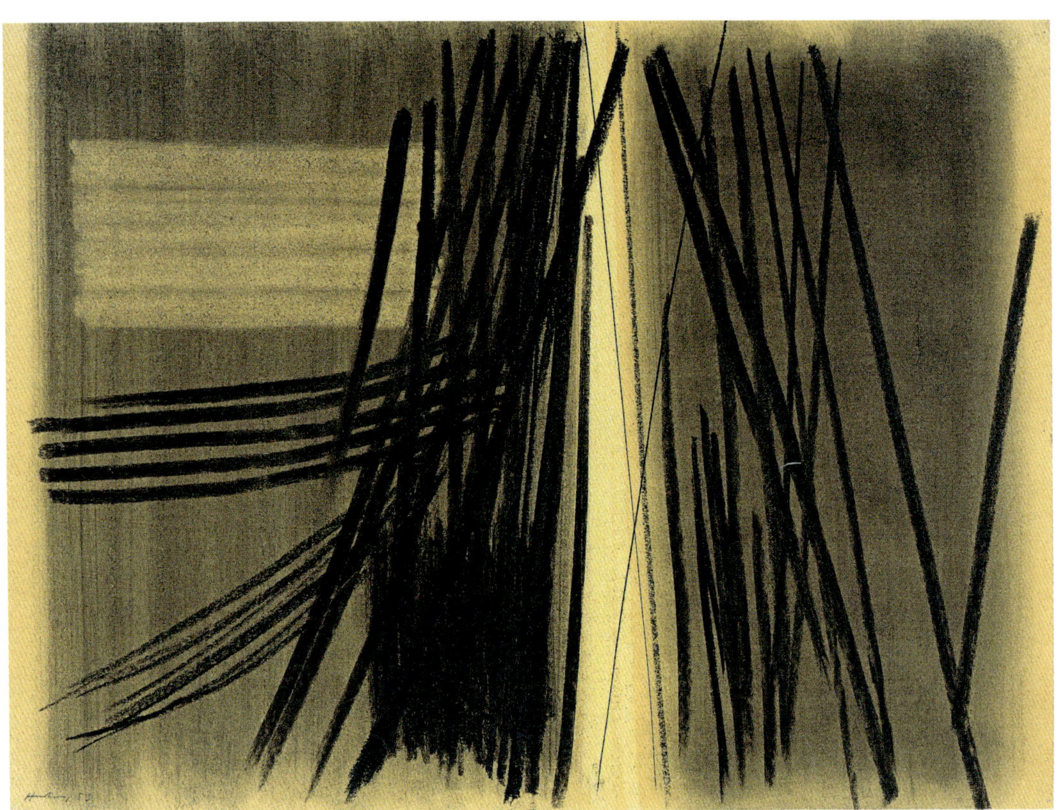

Questions of influence and priority become even less relevant when one considers that "mid-century modern" was a period style typified too by the abstract painting of Hartung's contemporaries, of other French Informel artists (Georges Mathieu and Pierre Soulages), of the German ZEN49 group (Willi Baumeister, Theodor Werner and Fritz Winter) with which Hartung exhibited on several occasions, and even of a handful of Italian painters (Emilio Vedova, for example, whose black and white gestures blend into Domnick's living-room next to Hartung's, (fig. 2)). More or less, these painters favoured the same generous blacks, the same heavy contrasts and textures, the same black lines and organic planes. Only Hartung's period palette outshines them all.

At issue, then, are the historical and conceptual implications of mid-century modern as a shared style. The visual affinities of design and painting from the late Forties through the Fifties, I would argue, caused them to partake in each other's status and meanings. Contrary to the worst fears of Hartung and his critics, the decorative does not condemn his abstract paintings to repugnant gratuitousness. From the perspective of abstraction, always wrestling with how it comes to mean, decoration and design, grounded firmly in the world as they are, can function as bridges to historical and social circumstances. In other words,

11. HH, *P1690–236*, 1960, crayon and pastel on paper, 49 x 64 cm, private collection
12. Textile Designs, 1950s

"the decorative" can imbue abstract forms with importance and meaning rather than necessarily condemn them to insignificance. (Meaning also travels the other way around, but that is not our concern here). In this case, decoration and design inadvertently tied the painting of Hartung and his contemporaries to postwar European history.

The mid-century style not only increased the vocabulary but also the presence of modern design beyond the limited circles of an artistic elite. In 1940, designers Charles Eames and Eero Saarinen had submitted prototypes for moulded chairs to the "Organic Design in Home Furnishings" exhibition and competition held at the Museum of Modern Art in New York. In the following twenty years, the "new look" or "good design" as it was called at the time conquered commercial and residential interiors, first in the United States, then abroad. American firms like Knoll and Herman Miller quickly expanded across the Atlantic and were joined there by European companies like the Danish Fritz Hansen, producer of Arne Jacobsen's chairs. The continent provided fertile ground in the aftermath of World War II. Catalysed by the Marshall Plan, European economies surged and consumers shopped. Public institutions quickly received new interiors and buildings; companies rebuilt or restructured for peacetime needs. And while modern design conquered households more slowly than the needs for reconstruction and our image of the Fifties might suggest, rudimentary and makeshift furnishings were gradually replaced with contemporary ones. By 1959 public opinion polls showed 39% of the German population, for example, preferring a kidney-shaped table over other varieties for their own home.[15] The "new look" swept through France in slightly diluted versions—more bulky and mixed with traditional elements like rattan—not only in Hartung's home but also more generally (fig. 16). Nevertheless, even in France "the modern style of decoration is a complete success, in spite of its youth", wrote Georges Eudes, the author of a 1958 book on modern French interiors, "it is truly the style of the man to-day".[16]

Mid-century modern gave a face to the forward-looking spirit of postwar reconstruction. "The modern style made a clean sweep", Eudes wrote further, "hardly anything from the past has been retained, partly from choice and partly under the influence of a new way of living."[17] Furnished with the same language as design, abstract painting shared that historical resonance of a move into a new, modern era. Young painters who came of age in the Fifties experienced it in just those terms. The painter Markus Lüpertz recalls that as a teenager he regarded Hartung's images as a "translation of Bauhaus thought", exactly what mid-century design aspired to. In that sense, they "stood like a kind of formula for 'modern'. That was iconography for me, that was synonymous for me".[18]

Because their message was mutual, mid-century painting and design easily and increasingly intertwined. They got along. In Germany, where the alliance of the arts and design during the Weimar

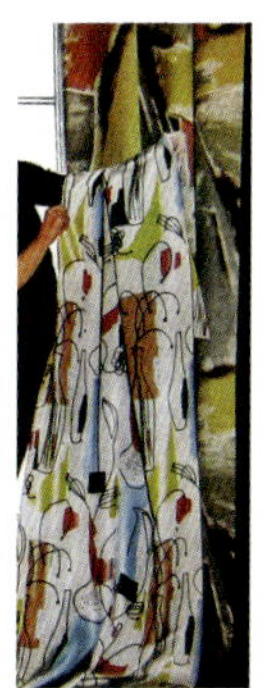
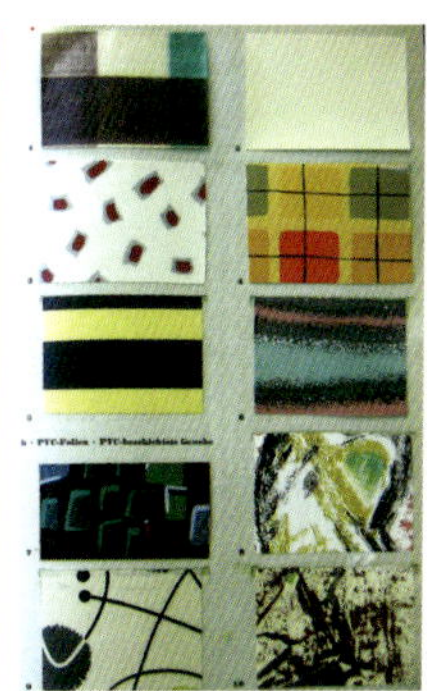
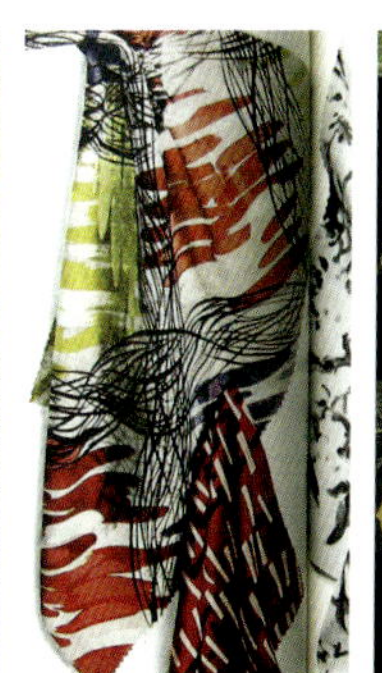
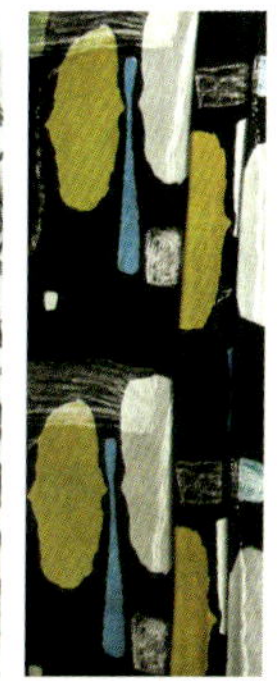

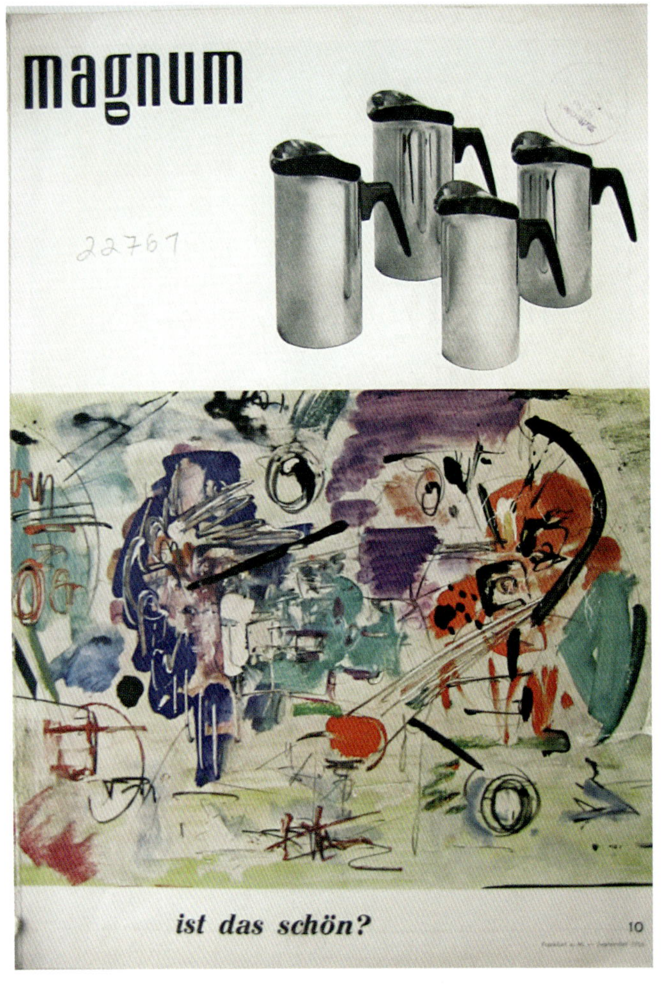

13. Cover for *Magnum* (September 1956)

period was naturally and proudly returned to after the Nazis' shameful banishment of most Twenties art as degenerate, painters ventured into commercial design already in the early Fifties. The young K.O. Götz, who would soon become a well known *Informel* painter and professor of painting, earned a living with advertisements for the chocolate maker Sprengel featuring his signature squeegeed loops and swirls (fig. 17); Willi Baumeister designed fabrics for Pausa AG using the coloured organic shapes from his paintings (fig. 19); Fritz Winter and K.R.H. Sonderborg designed plastic table cloths for the Göppinger Kaliko- und Kunstleder-Werke.[19] The popular interest magazine *Magnum*, in a special 1956 issue posing the question "What is beautiful?", explored the mid-century style with decisive disregard for boundaries between high and low. The cover set the tone with a set of thermal pitchers (designed by the Danish architect Erik Herlöw) that offered surely sceptical readers a visual way into a gestural watercolour (by Vedova); the smooth aluminium bodies were echoed in soft shaded areas of green and purple paints, their linear pattern of reflections in the watercolour's back and forth lines, their black Bakelite handles in an assertive semicircular black brush stroke (fig. 13).

The French followed, Hartung included. In 1959, Informel look-alikes decorated the shopping windows of the Galeries Lafayette flagship store in Paris, as an article reported in the summer of that year: "There can be no doubt that the most important artistic event of the past few months—in terms of dimensions, breadth, and public reach—was the window decorations of the Galleries Lafayette. This is the first time the man in the street

13. Cover for *Magnum* (September 1956)
14. Interior (*Die Kunst und das Schöne Heim*, November 1956)
15. *Schöner Wohnen* 7 (July 1961), pp. 24–25
16. A French interior, 1950 (Georges Eudes, *Intérieurs Modernes*)

found himself face to face with every-thing that is most informal in abstract art: enormous abstract compositions provide the background for all the shop windows lining the Boulevard Haussmann. The multicoloured taches and 'signs' are such that they can easily be mistaken for the work of abstract painters like Hartung, Soulages, and Mathieu."[20]

Popular design and life-style mag-azines ran features on "Hartung at home". *Maison & Jardin*, as already mentioned, reported on collectors' homes displaying Hartung paintings, the German *Schöner Wohnen* on the home into which the artist and his wife had recently moved; others fol-lowed (figs. 8, 15).[21] Surely Hartung's painting on the easel in *Schöner Wohnen* did not just happen to "match" the palette of the new studio; it was a twelve-year-old canvas pulled for the photo op. But enthralled perhaps with a new found fame, Hartung disregarded any wor-ries and went along with the shoot. The painter also ventured more actively into the decorative arts and design. In 1953 he produced two ceramic plates with his signature clusters of black lines for Mme Lacouriére (the owner of a print shop where he had worked extensively dur-ing that year, fig. 18), shortly there-after, a cover for the art magazine *Cimaise*, and in 1959, projections of linear configurations to function as stage sets for Jean Tardieu's *Rythme à 3 temps*. Hartung initially stuck somewhat safely to the types of design media established as classics

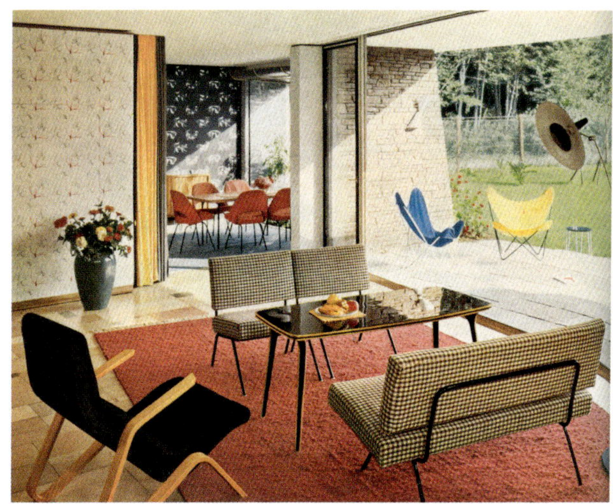

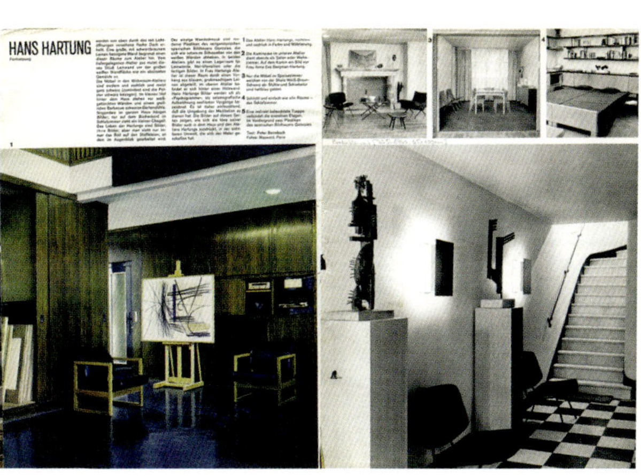

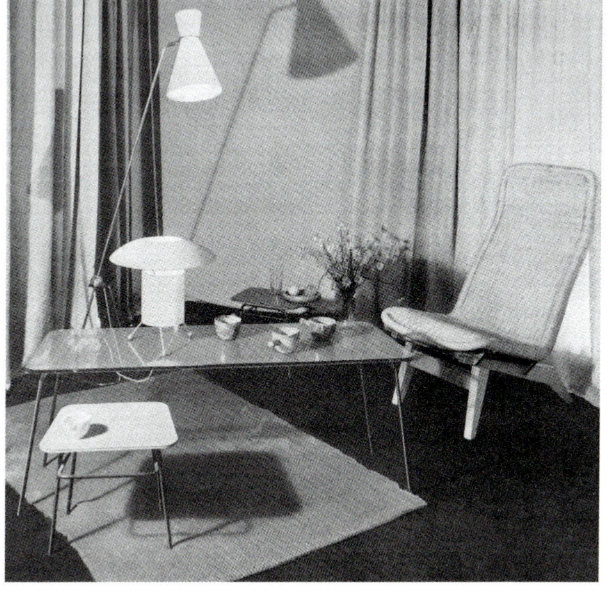

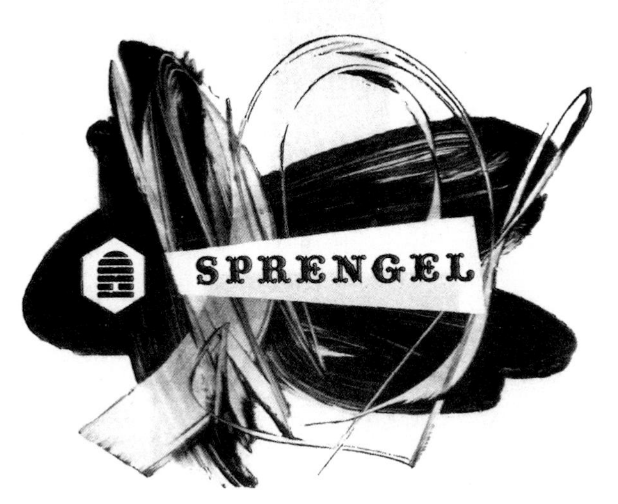

among modern artists: ceramics, cover illustration, and theatre. By the following decade, he had become less restrained, accepting commissions ranging from record covers for classical music to corporate brochures and joining Mathieu, Soulages and other French artists in creating designs for Air France (figs. 20, 21).[22] Hartung went popular. By 1967, an *original* Hartung could be bought *inside* the Galerie Lafayette for 30,000 Francs.[23]

These inroads into the design and consumer worlds, depending on their dates, presented a means towards or a measure of abstraction's success. Mid-century design, it seems in retrospect, happened to ease a wide share of the European population into contemporary abstract art, familiarising them with its forms and colours. The first 'Documenta' exhibitions in 1955 and 1959, the most important showcases for modern and

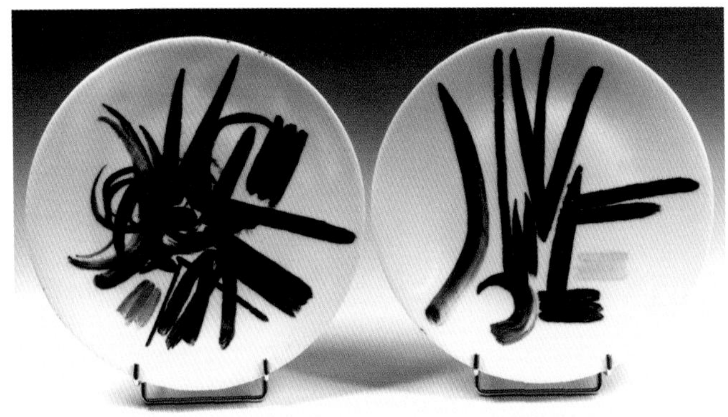

especially abstract art in postwar Europe, drew no fewer than 130,000 visitors.[24] It is the same period in which Hartung became famous. In 1947, the year of his first solo exhibition at Lydia Conti, he had been little known. By 1960, Roger Van Gindertael exclaimed, "Hartung is famous". He continued, in the first monograph on the artist since Domnick's, "his mastery is exemplary, and his renown is universal. Certainly the last ten years have been those where public recognition has been made of Hartung's personality".[25] Much had happened in the interim: the 1957 retrospective with seven venues curated by Werner Schmalenbach; the first solo exhibition in New York during the same year at Kleeman Galleries; acquisitions by renowned public collections such as the Nationalgalerie in Berlin, the Tate Gallery in London, and the Musée d'Art Moderne in Paris; and then, in 1960, the award of the Grand Prix for Painting at the Venice Biennale (the general Grand Prix went to Jean Fautrier).[26] In the Sixties, as we have seen, the now

17. K.O. Götz, advertisement for *Sprengel*, 1954
18. HH, dishes lacourière, 1953
19. Willi Baumeister, *fabric* for Pausa AG, Mössingen, 1954–55, Kunstgewerbemuseum, Berlin

famous (and expensive) Hartung received more and more design commissions. At that point, mid-century modern design became passé and postwar reconstruction grew into full-blown consumer culture. Hartung's abstraction, now with a shrill and psychedelic palette, kept pace with the times. But that is another story.

The "decorative affairs" of mid-century abstraction, with their nods to mass culture and historical conditions, curbed not its artistic legitimacy but its subjectivist, expressionist nature. Hartung, for one, was wary of simplistic, unreflected self-expression all along. On several occasions he stressed his art's relationship to reality as a corrective.

"The inner workings of happiness and sadness, everything we feel, all the rage we experience, against the world or what have you... none of it is, in itself and directly, a subject matter... And it is a great mistake to think that it is. These inner workings can be a basis, an incentive... But a scream, for example, isn't art. A scream is still nothing."

Instead, he elaborated, "I think that it is due to the total experience that we have reality..."[27] What is more, Hartung in a sense "designed" his expressive gestures. Most of his larger works on canvas from the Forties and Fifties were copied meticulously from carefully selected, small, often older pastels—every little line, every sweeping stroke. What had developed out of economic necessity (he could not afford to waste any canvases during the Forties) became a conceptual and aesthetic choice (the Fifties brought Hartung fame and money).[28] With that technique in place, Hartung was only one step away from actual design work. Sure enough, thereafter the transfer to a larger scale no longer served as the basis for oils (that practice ceased in 1960) but led him to the

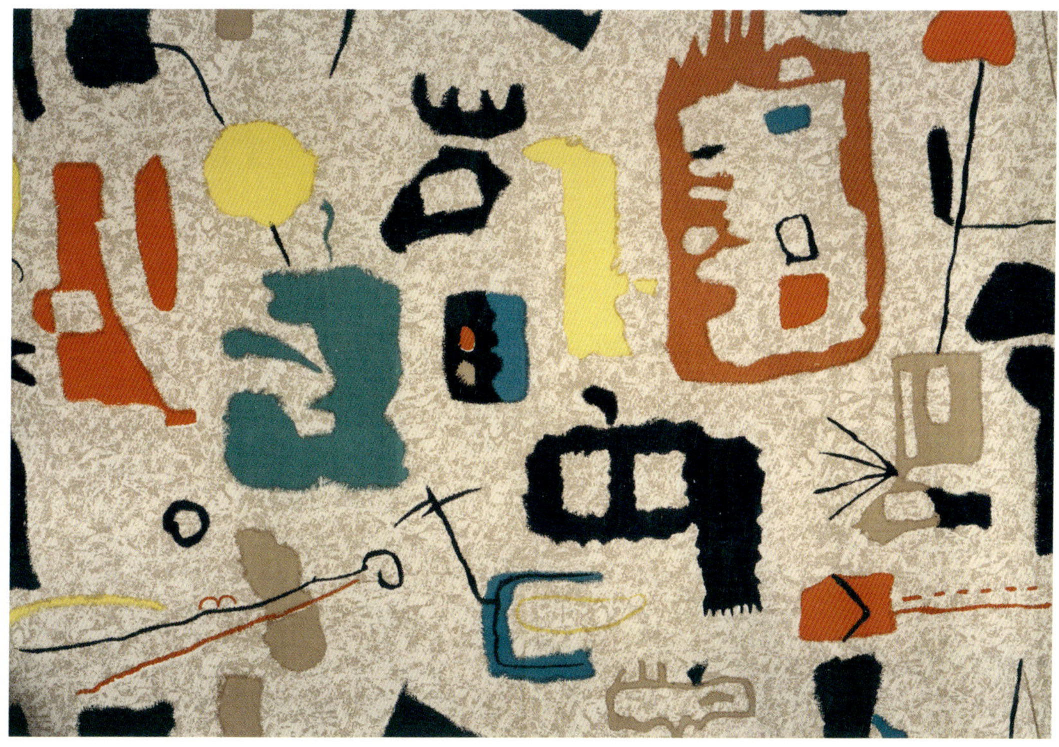

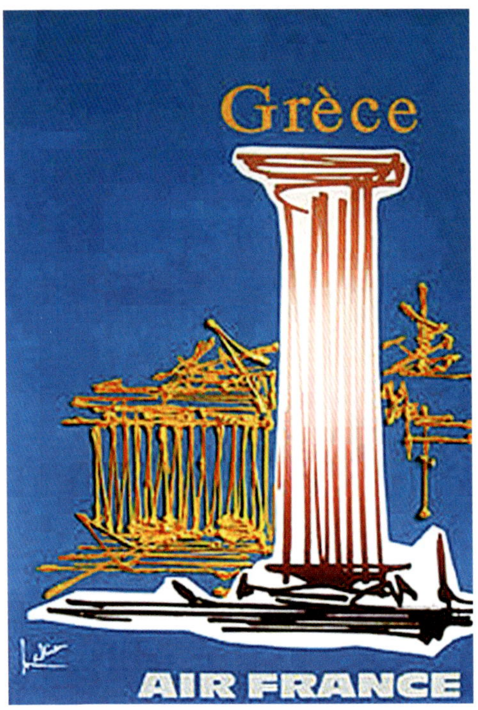

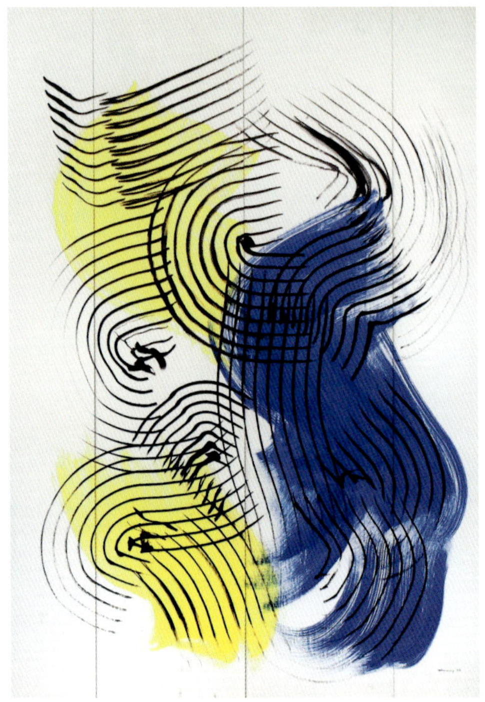

production of decorative tapestries. As the critic François Le Targat relayed, "he was only too happy to use large tapestries for his projects; after all, he had always dreamed of seeing some of his works, of his studies, in a large format that would make their truth all the more persuasive"[29] (fig. 22).

The success of abstraction at mid-century, not only in Europe but also in the United States, has been understood in historical terms before, if not via the role of design. The self-expressive tenet underlying a gamut of individually differing styles grew out of a newfound freedom from fascism and fed into a Western propagation of liberal individualism during the Cold War.[30] To claim a relationship to design and postwar reconstruction is not to refute but to complement and complicate that contention with respect to art made in Europe. By contrast, American Abstract Expressionism bears little if no resemblance to mid-century modern design.[31] The continental experience was marked by a dramatic shift from war to peace, from need to plenty, and from constraint to freedom. In Europe, therefore, the supposed expressive, free subject was wrapped up immediately and inadvertently with the consumption that defined the period of postwar reconstruction following the fall of fascism.[32] That might account for the different feel of abstract painting on each side of the Atlantic. Insightful and eloquent as ever, critic Clement Greenberg put his finger on it: "There is a crucial difference between the French

20. Georges Mathieu, Poster for Air France, 1962
21. HH, proposed decorative motif for Air France, 1970
22. HH, tapestry, 1962

and the American versions of so-called abstract expressionism despite their seeming convergence of aims. In Paris, they finish and unify the abstract picture in a way that makes it more agreeable to standard taste... For all the adventurousness of their 'images', the latest generation in Paris still go in for 'paint quality' in the accepted sense. They 'enrich' the surface with films of oil or varnish, or with buttery paint. Also, they tend to tailor the design so that it hits the eye with a certain patness... The result is softer, more suave and more conventionally imposing than would seem to accord with the 'idea' or inherent tendency of the new kind of abstract painting. If 'abstract expressionism' embodies a vision all its own, that vision is tamed in Paris—not, as the French themselves may think, disciplined."[33]

Looking at Hartung's paintings today, Greenberg's description is still right on; in the age of a transatlantic art world, his competitive tenor less so.[34] As an American armed with a critical apparatus of self-reflexive art, the historical place of "patness" amid so many liberated Europeans busily making modern homes escaped him. To this day, Hartung remains a European phenomenon.

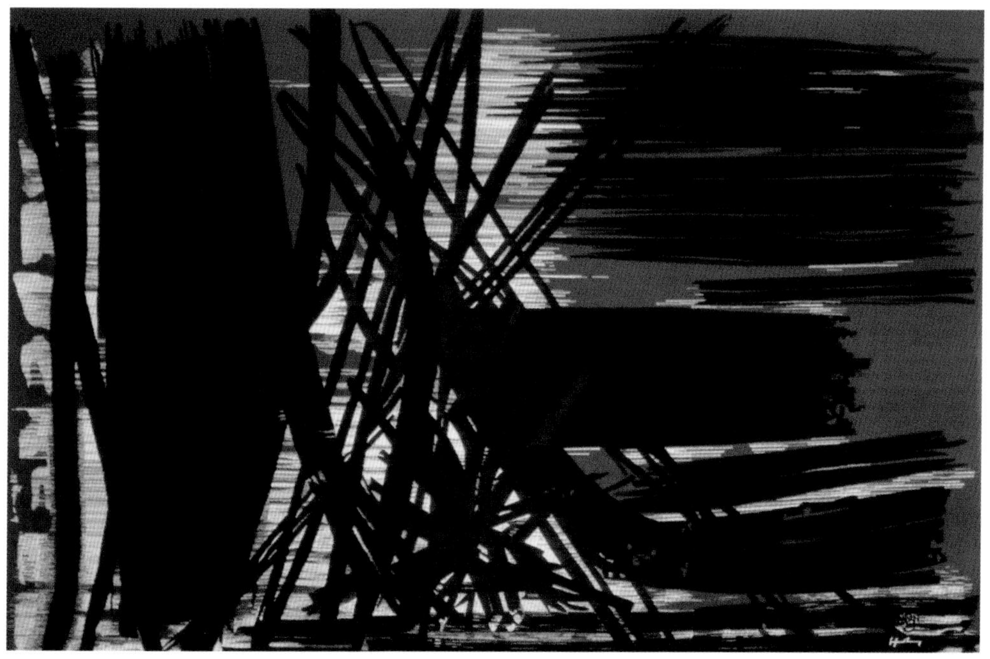

I would like to thank the staff at the Fondation Hans Hartung et Anna-Eva Bergman for their hospitality during my "surprise" visit and for their help in researching this essay, in particular, Marie Aanderaa, Bernard Derderian, and Jean-Luc Uro.

1. The image was first reproduced in Ottomar and Greta Domnick, *Die Sammlung Domnick—ihre Enstehung, ihre Aufgabe, ihre Zukunft* (Stuttgart and Zürich: Belser, 1982), p. 65.

2. Ottomar Domnick, "Aussage und Gestaltung", in *Hans Hartung*, Vol. 1 of an international series on new art, essays by Madeleine Rousseau, James Johnson Sweeney, and Ottomar Domnick, transl. by Virginia H. Fontaine, Matteo Mostacci, Greta Domnick (Stuttgart: Domnick-Verlag, 1949), p. 47. On Domnick, see idem, *Hauptweg und Nebenwege: Psychiatrie, Kunst, Film in meinem Leben* (Hamburg: Hoffmann und Campe, 1977), and O. and G. Domnick, *Die Sammlung Domnick*.

3. Ottomar Domnick, "Aussage und Gestaltung", *op. cit.*, p. 53 (translation slightly modified).

4. Wassily Kandinsky, "Reminiscences/Three Pictures" (1913), in *Wassily Kandinsky: Complete Writings on Art*, ed. Kenneth C. Lindsay and Peter Vergo (New York: DaCapo, 1994 [1982]), p. 370. See also Kandinsky's "Cologne Lecture" (1914), in ibid., p. 399.

5. Léon Degand, "Hans Hartung", *Les Lettres Françaises*, Paris, 21 Mar. 1947; Hans Hartung, *Autoportrait. Récit recueilli par Monique Lefebvre*, (Paris: Bernard Grasset, 1976), p. 239.

6. René de Solier, "Hans Hartung", *Quadrum* 2 (Bruxelles: Nov. 1956), p. 32.

7. An American audience might appreciate the origins of these terms widely used in postwar European art histories. The French critic Michel Tapié first used the term "Informel" in 1951 in reference to Camille Bryen; his book *Un Art Autre* (A Different Art) coined that label a year later. "Tachisme" emphasized the blot- and stain-like marks of mid-century European abstract painting and was popularised by the painter Georges Mathieu's book *Au delà du Tachisme*, published in 1963. "Abstraction Lyrique", too, was long believed to be coined by Mathieu in 1947, but Annie Claustres has recently shown in her brilliant work on Hartung that it in fact originates in that same year with Jean-José Marchand, literary critic and editor of the magazine *Combat*. Annie Claustres, "La Fabrique de Hans Hartung: Un faux expressionisme pictural", *Les Cahiers du Musée d'Art Moderne* 80 (Summer 2002), p. 65. Artists associated with this movement, besides Hartung and Mathieu, were Wols, Pierre Soulages, Camille Bryen, among others.

8. Michel Ragon, "Hans Hartung", *Cimaise* 7 (Paris: Oct.–Dec. 1960), p. 26. [French original: Hartung "*ne tombe jamais dans le décoratif des idéogrammes. C'est un trait qui, parfois, 'fait mal' comme une blessure.*"]

9. George Nelson, "Modern furniture... an attempt to explore its nature, its sources, and its probable future", *Interiors + Industrial Design* (New York: July 1949), p. 78.

10. Jacques Damase, "L'artiste dans la maison: Hans Hartung et les étoiles filantes...", *Maison & Jardin* 89 (Paris: Dec. 1962), pp. 192–93.

11. Hans Hartung, *Autoportrait*, p. 238.

12. Peter Bermbach, "Hans Hartung", *Schöner Wohnen* 7 (Hamburg: July 1961), pp. 22–26.

13. See Hans Hartung, *Autoportrait*, pp. 110, 115–17, and 194; "An Interview with Hans Hartung", *The Paris Reporter*, 13 Aug. 1980. For early references in the literature, see James Johnson Sweeney, "Preface", in *Hans Hartung* (Stuttgart: Domnick-Verlag, 1949), p. 4; and Werner Schmalenbach, "Zur Ausstellung", in *Hans Hartung*, exh. cat. (Hanover: Kestner-Gesellschaft, 1957), p. 7.

14. Nelson, "Modern furniture...", p. 105.

15. *Jahrbuch der öffentlichen Meinung 1958-1964*, ed. Elisabeth Noelle and Erich Peter Neumann (Allensbach and Bonn: Verlag für Demoskopie, 1965), p. 172. The percentages of the population embracing modern design increased over the course of the Fifties, while percentages of the population favouring traditional varieties decreased significantly. Cf. *Jahrbuch der öffentlichen Meinung 1947-1955*, ed. E. Noelle and E.P. Neumann (Allensbach and Bonn: Verlag für Demoskopie, 1956).

16. Georges Eudes, *Modern French Interiors*, transl. M.I. Martin (New York: Thomas Y. Crowell, 1958), p. 2. See also the interiors reproduced throughout for visual examples.

17 *Ibid.*, p. 1.

18. "Markus Lüpertz über Hans Hartung, Gespräch mit Siegfried Gohr, April 2004", in *Hans Hartung: So beschwor ich den Blitz*, exh. cat., ed. Stephan Diederich (Cologne: Museum Ludwig and Verlag der Buchhhandlung Walther König, 2004), p. 145. Fifties painting played a similarly formative "iconographic" role for Sigmar Polke. See for example his paintings *Die 50er Jahre*, 1963–69, *Moderne Kunst* of 1968, and his *Bogen* and *Streifenbilder* of the Sixties.

19. For an advertisement for the plastics of the Göppinger Kaliko- und Kunstleder-Werke, see *Magnum* 17 (Cologne: Apr. 1958), p. 64.

20. J.P. Crespelle, "The window designers of the Galeries Lafayette make abstract art available to the man in the street... thus signalling the triumph, and defeat, of Mathieu, the 'Dali of the informal'", *France Soir* (Paris: 28 June 1959), and *Le Quotidien* (Buenos Aires: 1 July 1959).

21. Jacques Damase, "L'artiste dans la maison..."; Peter Bermbach, "Hans Hartung". Hartung appeared in other popular magazines before then and after. A work was included in a quiz run by *Elle*: "Les Peintres modernes savent-ils dessiner?", *Elle* 353 (Paris: 1 Sep. 1952), pp. 38–39. See also "Georges Robin, un décorateur soucieux d'actualité", *La Maison Française* 205 (Paris: Mar. 1961); J. Capy, "L'appartement d'un collectionneur de peinture", *La Maison Française*, (Paris: Mar, 1967); "Tapis zèbre à faire sur canevas", *Maison de Marie-Claire* (Paris, July 1969).

22. The record covers and corporate brochure were commissioned during the Sixties by Philips. The designs for Air France date from 1967 and 1970. Compare "Bleu, Vieil Or Et Brun... C'est la nouvelle décoration qui habillera désormais les 'Boeing' d'Air France", *Le Soir* (Marseille: 17 June 1968); and "Un 'habit à la française' pour les 'Boeing' d'Air France", *Le Progrès* (Lyon: 4 Dec. 1967). Thereafter, Hartung designed a poster for the 1972 Olympic Games in Munich and gave permission to reproduce a painting from the Fifties on a 1981 French stamp. Hartung objected very strongly when his work or his painting's style were used for design purposes without permission—for example, in advertisements, or on a 1988 series of Puma sneakers. Records for all of these are in the archive of the Fondation Hans Hartung et Anna-Eva Bergman.

    Early on, Hartung did not seem opposed to earning a living by venturing into the decorative arts. In 1951 he told a German newspaper that the situation of artists in France "is not better, perhaps worse, than that of colleagues in Germany. In Germany, there are *Kunstvereine* and patrons willing to make sacrifices, not so in France. And there are few possibilities to work as a stage designer, poster artist, or decorator". Ludwig von Döry, "Der Maler denkt in Farben und Formen: Ein Gespräch mit dem Pariser 'Abstrakten' Hans Hartung", *Frankfurter Rundschau* (Frankfurt: 4-5 Aug. 1951). It is only later in 1976, from a vantage point of fame and wealth, that he dismissed decorative practice, as for example in his autobiography. Telling of the pressures exerted by the families of both his wives to earn a living, he wrote: "But I didn't want to give in. I couldn't

give in. Yes, it's true, I could have accepted the compromise, the dishonest compromises. I could have tried to make more fashionable paintings that would have sold easily, I could have designed patterns for scarves... But then, I could also have gone back to Germany and become a supporter of Hitler and the Nazis", Hans Hartung, *Autoportrait*, pp. 125–26.

23. In 1967, the store placed abstract art by several contemporary painters for sale amidst its camping department. See Frédéric Mégret, "Des Galeries Lafayette aux Beaux-Arts", *Figaro Litteraire* (Paris: 14 July 1966); Peter Bermbach, "Paris: Beim Kaufhausbummel steht man plötzlich vor Moderner Kunst", *Schöner Wohnen* (Hamburg: Dec. 1966); Günter Metken, "New York zwingt Paris zu einer Entfettungskur", *Die Welt* (Hamburg: 3 Mar. 1967).

    The sale of contemporary art in European department stores dates back as early as 1964 and has to be seen in the wider context of the European art market which during the Sixties made a variety of efforts to expand the circles of potential buyers. For various reports about department store art exhibitions and sales, see for example K. Hakiewitz, "Farbexplosion über der Couch und Chiffren an der Bar. Ein Münchner Experiment: Moderne Kunst im Kaufhaus", *Kölner Stadt-Anzeiger* (Cologne: 19 Feb. 1964); "Kunsthandel", *Der Spiegel* 20 (Hamburg: 24 Oct. 1966): 157; and Elsbeth Haller, "Kunst im Kaufhaus", *Kunstwerk* 25 (Baden-Baden: Jan. 1972), p. 73.

24. Dieter Westecker, *documenta–Dokumente 1955-1968* (Kassel: Georg Wenderoth, 1972), pp. 6, 58.

25. Roger Van Gindertael, *Hans Hartung* (Paris: Pierre Tisné, 1960), p. 47. Four years earlier the critic had still restricted that "public recognition" to the artist's personality—excepting that change, the paragraph in the book was lifted from the opening of Gindertael's 1956 essay on Hartung for the journal *Cimaise*. For that earlier publication of the passage, see Van Gindertael, "Hans Hartung", *Cimaise* 4 (Paris: Sep.–Oct. 1956), p. 9 [English translation provided in *Cimaise*].

26. Compare the increasing listings of private and public collections owning Hartung's work in 1949, 1957, and 1960 in O. and G. Domnick, *Die Sammlung Domnick*; *Hans Hartung*, exh. cat. (New York: Kleeman Galleries, 1957); *Hans Hartung*, exh. cat. (Paris: Galerie de France, 1960).

27. Hartung in Georges Charbonnier, "Entretien avec Hans Hartung", *Les Lettres Nouvelles* 7 (Paris: 10 June 1959), p. 39.

28. Compare Hartung, *Autoportrait*, pp. 111–13 and 233. For discussions of this technique, see Jörn Merkert, "Geste, Zeichen und Gestalt–Zum Werk von Hans Hartung", in *idem, Hans Hartung: Malerei, Zeichnung, Photographie*, exh. cat., ed. Ulrich Krempel (Berlin: Akademie der Künste, 1981), pp. 26–27; Xavier Douroux, "–Au Fond", in *Hartung, Peintre Moderne*, exh. cat., ed. Jean-Michel Foray, Fréjus: Centre d'Art Contemporain, (Milan: Skira, 1996), pp. 67–79; Annie Claustres, "La Fabrique de Hans Hartung: Un faux expressionisme pictural", *Les Cahiers du Musée d'Art Moderne* 80 (Summer 2002), pp. 57–79; and Franz-W. Kaiser, "Conceptuel avant la lettre", in Franz-W. Kaiser, Anne Pontégnie, Vicente Todoli, *Hans Hartung x 3* (Antibes: Fondation Hans Hartung et Anna-Eva Bergman, 2003), pp. 7–91.

29. François Le Targat, "Hans Hartung ou le classicisme révolutionnaire", in *Hans Hartung, Anna-Eva Bergman: Tapisseries et Gravures sur Bois*, exh. cat. (Paris: Musée de la Poste, 1980), n.p. Hartung made his first tapestry at the Manufacture de Beauvais in 1962. Anna-Eva Bergman relayed her memories about their tapestry work in Andrea Schomburg, *Manuscript for a Biography of Anna-Eva Bergman* (1985), Archives of the Fondation Hans Hartung et Anna-Eva Bergman. My thanks to Marie-Noël Rio for drawing the passage to my attention.

30. Eva Cockcroft, "Abstract Expressionism, Weapon of the Cold War", *Artforum* 12 (San Francisco: June 1974), pp. 39–41; Serge Guilbaut, *How New York Stole the Idea of Modern Art*, transl. Arthur Goldhammer (Chicago: University of Chicago Press, 1983); Yule Heibel, *Reconstructing the Subject: Modernist Painting in Western Germany, 1945-1950* (Princeton: Princeton University Press, 1995); Sigrid Ruby, *"Have we an American art?" Präsentation und Rezeption amerikanischer Malerei im Westdeutschland und Westeuropa der Nachkriegszeit* (Weimar: VDG, 1999).

31. T.J. Clark has argued for a relationship of Abstract Expressionism to petty bourgeois taste, to the language of its users, evidenced in particular by the paintings of Jackson Pollock, Willem de Kooning, Mark Rothko, and Hans Hofmann. Clark argues that these vulgar traces are the last cheap refuge of any forms of individuality. The exhibition *Vital Forms, American Art and Design in the Atomic Age, 1940-1960*, examined art and design of the period in conjunction through the lens of vitalism and the organic. The stress was on the early, Surrealist-inspired work of the Abstract Expressionists, and concrete relations to design of the period were not elaborated on. *See Vital Forms, American Art and Design in the Atomic Age, 1940-1960*, ed. Brooke Kamin Rapaport and Kevin L. Stayton, exh. cat. (New York: Brooklyn Museum of Art, 2001).
T.J. Clark, "In Defense of Abstract Expressionism", *October* 69 (Summer 1994), pp. 23–48; reprinted in *idem, Farewell to an Idea: Episodes from a History of Modernism* (New Haven and London: Yale University Press, 1999), pp. 371–403.

32. Three other accounts of the relationship between design and art during this period should be mentioned. Christian Borngräber, in his survey of German postwar design, first included examples by Fifties abstract painters. C. Borngräber, "Bruchstücke: Westdeutsches Nachkriegsdesign, 1945–1955", in *Grauzonen Farbwelten: Kunst und Zeitbilder, 1945-1955*, ed. Bernhard Schulz, exh. cat. Berlin, Neue Gesellschaft für Bildende Kunst (Berlin: NGBK/Medusa, 1983), p. 144.
Ruth Wessel draws a series of formal comparisons between Fifties German abstract paintings and Fifties designs, for example, she juxtaposes a Hartung painting with a pretzel basket. What these similarities might mean is not discussed. Ruth Wessel, "Nierentischstil", in *'Flächenland': Die absrakte Malerei im frühen Nachkriegsdeutschland und in der jungen Bundesrepublik*, ed. Hans Körner (Tübingen und Basel: Francke, 1996), pp. 72–98.
Thomas Zaunschirm, in the introduction to his book on the style of the Fifties, works out the central element of contrast in the art and design of that period and relates it to the *Zeitgeist*, "an ambivalent consciousness which fluctuates between the miseries of depression, Cold War, irreconcilable contrasts, existential resignation and... the hope for a new world." T. Zaunschirm, *Die fünfziger Jahre* (Munich: Heyne, 1981), p. 22.

33. Clement Greenberg, "Symposium: Is the French Avant-Garde Overrated?" (1953), reprinted in *Clement Greenberg: The Collected Essays and Criticism, Volume 3*, ed. John O'Brian (Chicago: University of Chicago Press, 1993), pp. 155–56.
Romy Golan, in an excellent recent essay, has taken Greenberg's comments for the symposium as a starting point for arguing that French avant-garde artists' mural paintings and tapestries of the Fifties revealed the way in which French gestural abstraction was about to be pushed aside by Abstract Expressionism, degraded as "nothing more than *belle peinture*". R. Golan, "L'Eternel Décoratif: French Art of the 1950s", *Yale French Studies* 98 (2000), pp. 98–112, esp. 110.

34. For an excellent essay detailing the misunderstandings between the French and the Americans, see Eric de Chassey, "Paris–New York: Rivalry

and Denial", in *Paris: Capital of the Arts, 1900-1968*, exh. cat., ed. Sarah Wilson (London: Royal Academy of Arts, 2002), pp. 344–51.

Consistent with the complaints of many other French artists and critics, Hartung on various occasions dismissed American Abstract Expressionist painters. "Mark Rothko or Hans Hofmann aren't Americans. They emigrated to America... Great art developed once European artists came to America... In America everything is larger... everyone made a big fuzz. That made it seem like the results of the American artists were more profound than those of the Europeans. I believe Jackson Pollock is overrated". Hartung in an interview with Werner Krüger, "Kunst muss immer die Fassung bewahren", *Kölner Stadt-Anzeiger* (Cologne: 21 Sep. 1979). Incidentally, Hartung scribbled "*décoratif*" next to some of these painters' names—James Brooks, Adolph Gottlieb, and Bradley Walker Tomlin—listed in the exhibition catalogue *Regards sur la Peinture Américaine*, exh. cat. (Paris: Galerie de France, 1952). Hartung's annotated copy is in the archive of the Fondation Hans Hartung et Anna-Eva Bergman. My thanks to Franz-W. Kaiser for drawing these notes to my attention. Hartung, in an interview with Henry Geldzahler, relayed that he liked the paintings of Franz Kline. "They impressed me because from one painting to another I could see his working process". It is unclear whether Hartung knew that Kline, like him, transferred small gestural sketches onto large canvases. Unlike Hartung, the American painter did so with the help of a projector. But altogether, Hartung claimed antecedence in that same interview: "I saw exhibitions of American painting in the years 1951–53... And I said to myself, 'We have infected them' and they have acquired a taste for some of our ideas". H. Geldzahler, "Biographical Notes", in *idem, Hans Hartung Paintings 1971-1975*, exh. cat. (New York: The Metropolitan Museum of Art, 1975), n.p. Cf. Hartung, *Autoportrait*, pp. 180–81. Along the same lines, Hartung has often been praised as anticipating American Abstract Expressionism. For example, Sara Moore wrote that "He is... a pioneer of Lyrical Abstraction. Long before America discovered Action Painting, Hartung was a gestural painter, a dynamic action painter." Sara Moore, "Hartung: un Rimbaud qui serait revenu d'Ethiopie", *La Galerie des Arts*, 1 (Paris: Nov. 1962), p. 6.

John C. Welchman Hans Hartung
Abcedarium: Reading Between the Lines
Franz-W. Kaiser A Case Study
on the Caducity of Categories
in Art Criticism Annie Claustres
Hans Hartung
Clandestine Artist
1937-1942: the Decisive Years
Christine Mehring Hans Hartung
Mid-Century Modern
Rainer Michael Mason Hartung
and Printmaking Christopher Wool

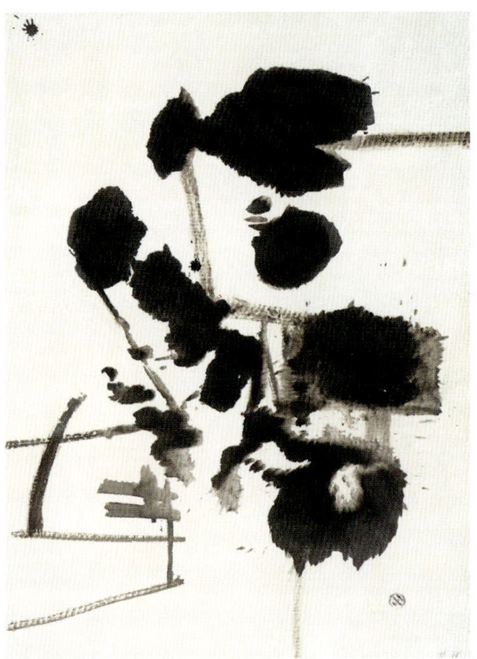

I.

Should we think of Hans Hartung as a *graveur,* an engraver? It is well known that the artist began drawing—"bolts of lightning" and "spots"—at a very early age. He often spoke about his fundamental experience: he would diligently try to trace the zigzags of light before he heard the clap of thunder. "That was my way of warding off lightning", recalled the artist in 1981. "If my pencil was as quick as the lightning, nothing bad would happen to me".[1] In 1921, around the age of sixteen, at school and elsewhere, and even before the colourful "informal" watercolours of 1922, collected in a 1966 album with a preface by Will Grohmann (figs. 7-9, pp. 16, 17),[2] Hartung was turning out what he called his spots, "I was doing ink spots, drawing by using spots, and finally drawing spots for themselves."[3] Hartung was to continue with these abbreviated works, these nascent pieces, until just before the war: "I spent my days at the Café du Dôme. Along with the *café crème* the waiter would bring paper and ink, and I would draw and draw, make spots".[4] These sketches provided the material for his large works, not only during the pre-war period ("In 1938 I redid them on a large scale in oil paint"),[5] but also up to the early 1960s: "I quite simply could not manage to tackle a canvas directly. Until two years ago [1961], without exception the large paintings were preceded by studies, usually drawings. I would then transfer the project to the canvas" (figs. 2, 3).[6]

It is this bolt of lightning, this initial shock that is the start of Hartung's oeuvre, not the deferred (and inevitably slow) transposition which is the province of engraving. Instead, the work of revising and rewriting takes place in his painting. So, despite, or rather because of, this singular circumstance (which would suggest that here the print is, unusually, the medium of the rough draft, the first go), we can ask again the weighty question: is Hans Hartung an engraver, a *graveur?*

II.

What is "printmaking"? While I will not describe here the innumerable techniques that make it up, these exist, of course, and so many that they force (and enable) artists to

1. HH, untitled, 1938, ink on paper, 79 x 60 cm
2. HH, *T1938-30,* 1938, oil on wood, 100 x 100 cm

"rethink" the image from top to bottom before (re)producing it. What the German painter and printmaker Georg Baselitz (1938) would call in 1991 "a complementary analysis" first occurs because printing inverts the image created on the print support, from left to right. A face angled toward the left on the copperplate or stone looks in the opposite direction once printed on the sheet of paper. And that is only one of the delays caused by encoding (a very intellectual operation when all is said and done), of the "pause" that precedes printing and the (potentially) great proliferation and distribution of the work.

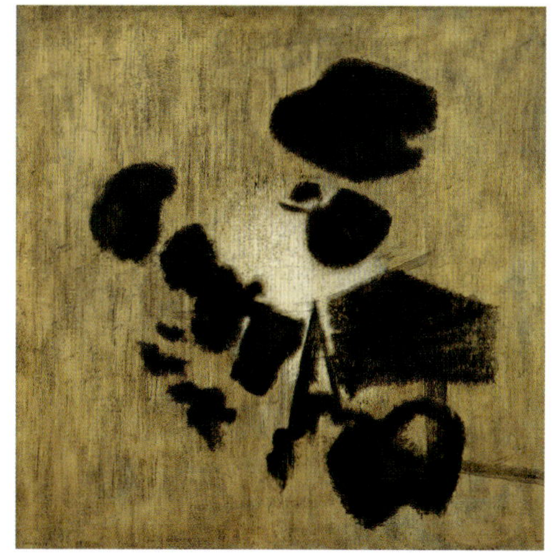

This is not the place, even if these parameters are important, to offer insights into the practices and recipes of the studios, the inking of the matrices (wood, copper or stone), the presses and the printing processes, not to mention the types of paper with their inexhaustible qualities. Without going into the sleight of hand that takes place in the workshop, I can nonetheless point out, at the risk of oversimplification, that "printmaking" revolves around three main points, and Hartung was familiar with all three: *reserve engraving*, or relief printing (woodcut, linocut); *intaglio*, or recessed printing (engraving, etching, dry point, mezzotint, aquatint, photogravure); and *planography* or flat printing (lithography, zincography, offset, stencil, silkscreen, and... even photography).

We shall only keep in mind here that "engraving" involves various physical resistances and responses according to whether the engraved or sensitized support is wood, metal, or stone, and subjected to direct cutting or the chemical action of acid. Whether it reproduces in the end a given image or draws one out *ex nihilo*, as it were, from the depths of the material laid bare by a cutting tool or the surface of the support that has been exposed to an acid, "engraving" (*gravure*) is an art of distancing, of setting apart, between the data "encoded" in the matrix and their restitution on paper. The genius of the printmaker lies in his way of filling the gap between the preliminary image that he imagines on his inner screen and the result that will be fixed in reverse before his eyes. "Engraving" implies a delay between the act and the effect. Its being lies in the united and the separated.

Hartung, who sketched bolts of lightning and dribbled spots, well understood the subservience and the stakes involved in the art of *differance* (a word derived from the verb *defer*) that "engraving" (*gravure*) embodies (inasmuch as that neologism can clarify the argument here). He explained himself this way in 1973: "Basically I prefer engraving tools to the brush. The process is radical, definitive, and I really like the resistance of the material.

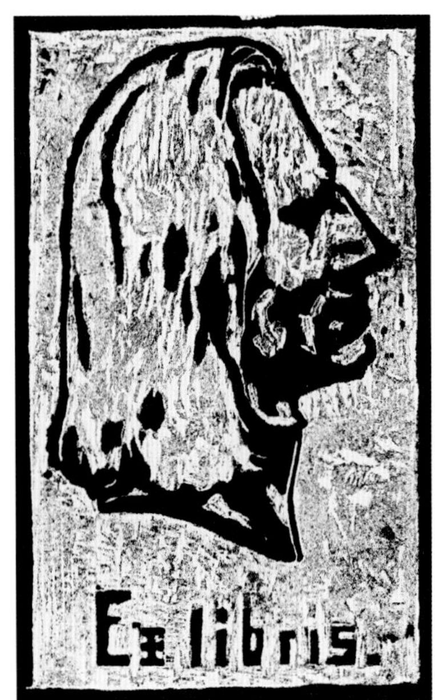

What bothers me in engraving—but I hope to surmount this—is the slowness, the fact that you're interrupted. In lithography I can work quickly, I remain in touch with myself, I associate a quick line and a grainy material, and I feel altogether at home".[7]

What we have here ("I prefer engraving tools to the brush") is a staggering confession from the lips of a man of the "drawn gesture". The painted gesture, in its immediacy, only came later, when the artist was entering his sixties. And it came with a (quantitative) domination of planography, an art of immediate recording.

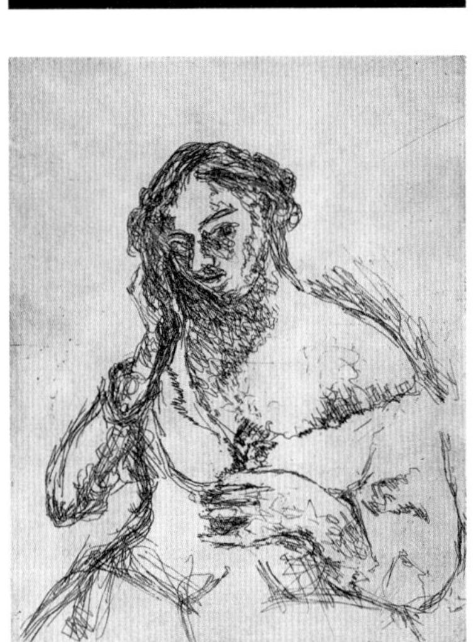

III.

Hans Hartung *graveur*? A printmaker, at least! His printed work, dating from the years 1921 to 1978, was concentrated in the three decades that followed World War II and in some six hundred pieces. To be specific, black-and-white and colour lithography takes up about two-thirds of the output. Intaglio engraving, by which we mean recessed engraving on metal, represents a fourth of the total, the rest is comprised of relief engraving (wood- and linocut).

Although they do not represent some kind of *nec plus ultra*, these figures can be compared with the graphic output (more or less original, i.e., invented or merely reproduced) of other twentieth-century artists, such as Max Beckmann (373 prints), Jean Dubuffet (1,474), Max Ernst (3,041), Jean Fautrier (286), André Masson (285), Henri Matisse (829), Henri Michaux (212), Joan Miró (1,269), Henry Moore (557), Picasso (2,024), Antonio Saura (632), etc.

An initial catalogue raisonné of Hartung's prints listing 191 pieces was published with the artist's blessing in 1965 by Rolf Schmücking.[8] The present author, assisted by Geneviève Laplanche, has undertaken to establish a new catalogue raisonné which will include the truly immense holdings of the Fondation Hans Hartung et Anna-Eva Bergman. The wealth

3. HH, *Portrait of Franz Liszt*, 1921, woodcut, 14.8 x 9.5 cm
4. HH, *Figure of a woman*, after Corot, 1928, etching, 18.6 x 14.9 cm
5. HH, *G5*, 1947, soft-ground etching and dry point, 15.9 x 11.4 cm

of working proofs, editions and documents making up this corpus has set back the publication of a book that will describe over six hundred prints to some future date. Consequently, this incomplete view of Hans Hartung's printed oeuvre only allows us to highlight a series of parameters and questions without going into an analysis of the whole.

IV.

What do we know of Hartung's training as a printmaker? According to Schmücking, his first known print (S. 1; M. 1)[9] dates from 1921, in other words, when the artist was sixteen years old. It is a numismatic portrait of Franz Liszt engraved on wood, which the artist offered to Johannes Landgraf (1905–72) as a book plate (*expressis litteris*, an "ex libris") (fig. 3). Trained as a scientist, Landgraf, a highschool friend in Dresden and an accomplished pianist, discovered music with Hartung, which explains this small woodcut that probably transposes a medal of the good abbot Liszt in a style that is both charming and stiff, while revealing a slight echo of German Expressionism.

The next prints (S. 2 to 10; M. 2 to 24) date in all likelihood from 1927–28, rather than from 1926–28, as Schmücking states. Executed using etching, dry point, or soft-ground etching, either on metal or celluloid (dry point), these pieces are portraits (including his father, Landgraf, and himself), as well as nudes and bathers. All of these works make use of line—a hasty, repeated line, whose light, occasionally vehement, repetition creates forms as much as values of light and shade. Hartung possesses the sense of the blank, of the void. If Slevogt[10] and Corinth can be cited as distant stylistic parameters, there is Impressionism as well, which Hartung discovered at the 1926 International Art Exhibition in Dresden. Perhaps we can detect Cézanne and Corot in these rapid sketches; Hartung, for example, interpreted the latter's *Portrait of a Woman* (S. 6; M. 21), an etching that probably dates from around 1928 (fig. 4).

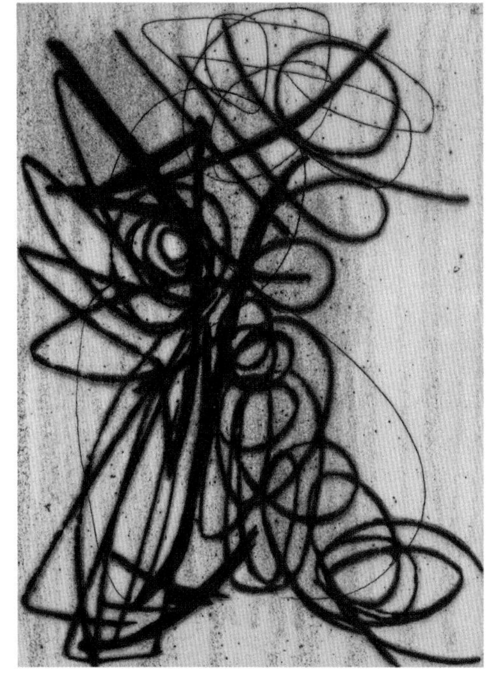

That was the year that Hartung enrolled for a summer semester in Max Dörner's class at the Fine Arts Academy of Munich, where he also took Schinnerer's drawing class. Was it at this time that he executed most of his figurative prints, often faithfully reproducing his drawings (which still exist), the quality of which betrays a certain experience? Or should we postulate that his "etcher's" hand was formed sometime between March 1924

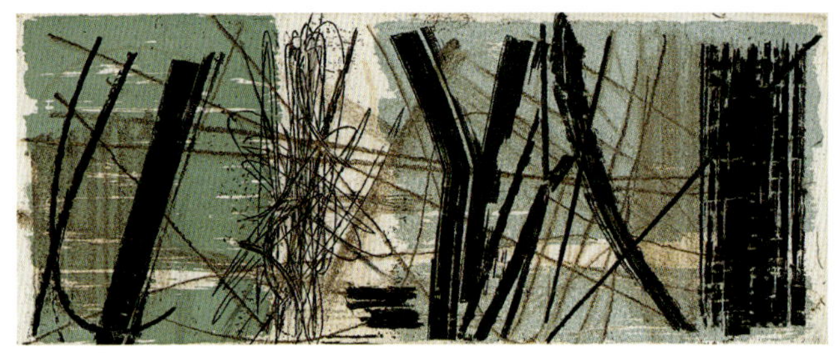

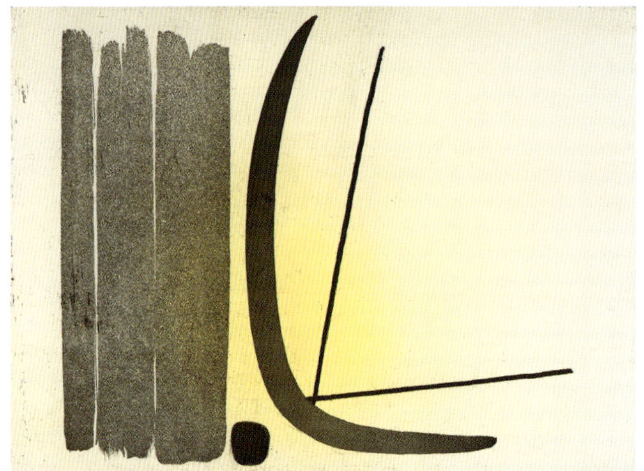

and July 1925 in Leipzig, during his double semester of *Angewandte Graphik in Verbindung mit Werkstatt-übungen*[11] under Professor Buhe—or a bit later, at the end of the summer, when Hartung enrolled at Dresden's Fine Arts Academy?

How not to be surprised then by the discrepancy between the first prints, all of which are figurative, and the watercolour, ink, charcoal and red-chalk drawings of 1922–24, from which all *mimèsis*, if not all psychology, is banished? Very probably, academic demands prescribed a reverence for the descriptive, hence the "lifelike" subjects. Beginning in 1938 Hartung's engraved works were to be abstract compositions designated by simple generic labels (G for *gravure* [etching, dry point], L for lithograph, H for woodcut—*Holz* in German) followed by a date and a series number.

On 27 November 1963, while answering questions put to him by Françoise Adam Woimant from the Bibliothèque nationale, Hartung noted that he began making prints "in 1927, on [his] own because of an interest in the graphic aspect of dry point... [while later] in 1928, deepening [his] technical knowledge as a student of Professor Schinnerer at Munich's Fine Arts Academy".[12] Despite these details, there is no known conclusive document on his training in printmaking (or on the precise chronology and subjects of his studies in Leipzig, Dresden and Munich). When Hartung points out, in conversation with the same person, that he was "naturally drawn to engraving and lithography, techniques that were still at their high point based on black and white and the line", is he thinking of Rembrandt, his benchmark? He spoke of the Dutchman's painting (*The Family Group* in the Herzog Anton Ulrich-Museum in Brunswick) and drawings, but never, that I am aware, of the great artist's etchings.

6. HH, *G2*, 1953, colour intaglio print, 11.5 x 28.4 cm

7. HH, *G8*, 1953, aquatint, 37.5 x 51.1 cm

8. HH, *G7*, 1953, colour intaglio print, 41.3 x 32.7 cm

9. HH, *L2*, 1953, lithography, 30.7 x 50.5 cm

Let us go back then to what Hartung shared with one interviewer on 28 April 1977: "The first woodcut that I did in my life, which is simply my first print, was produced for a friend I had in school who was very much a musician. We often worked together. I would draw and he would play the piano. It was a kind of rhythmic pairing... Because he asked me to, I did a woodcut of Franz Lizst in a traditional manner (fig. 3). Later I learned a little engraving, a little bit of what they call intaglio printing and still later just a little bit of lithography as well at the Academy in Munich; but all of that was not enough and out of date".[13]

For a few years around 1947, and later in 1953, an initial output of engravings took shape, first in black (S. 15 to 26; M. 34 to 45; fig. 5), then in colour when Hartung threw himself into a fruitful exploration of intaglio printing (S. 29 to 55; M. 59 to 85; figs. 6–8). Through Terry Haas (1922), a printmaker who was the head of Hayter's studio in New York, Hartung was given an introduction to Lacourière's own studio: "In 1953 I no longer had a studio, an easel, paint, anything at all, and we [i.e., Anna-Eva Bergman and the artist] were living in a tiny room in a hotel. We couldn't do

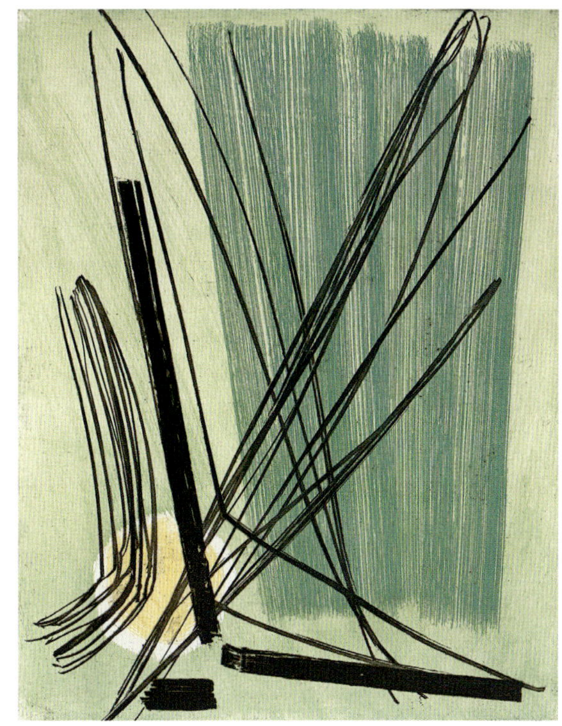

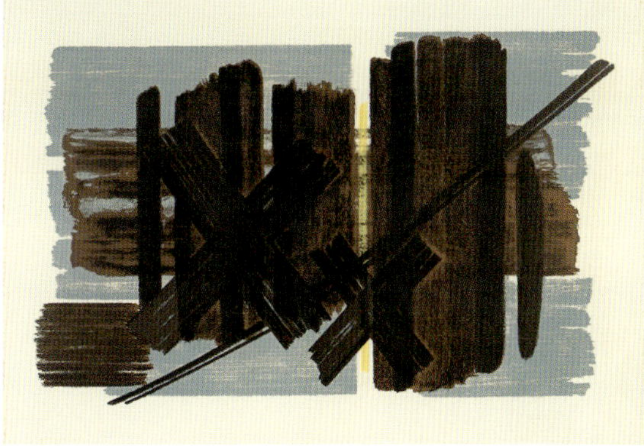

anything there, barely eat and sleep. At that point, the question came up, Why not go and work in a studio where we can do something, engraving, litho...? We went to Lacourière's, where we were very kindly welcomed, it was wonderful. Madame Lacourière was an extraordinary woman, Frélaut really knew his craft and taught us printmaking, Anna-Eva Bergman and me. We spent half a year there, I think, or maybe more. In the end there weren't any copperplates left, or rather any clients left for the prints pulled from the copperplates, so we thought we could perhaps move on to something else. That's how we began the lithographs at Jean Pons's studio" (fig. 9).[14]

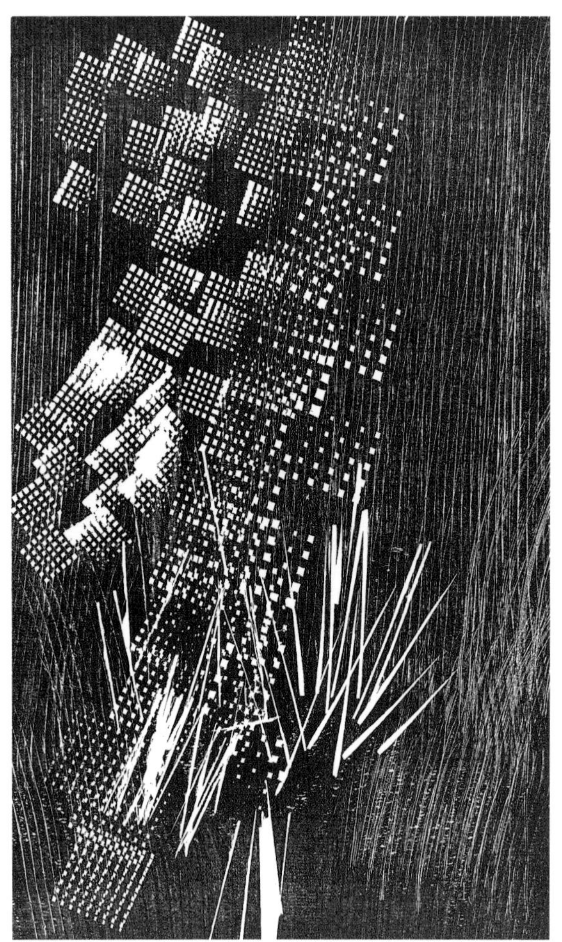

V.

Hartung's printed work developed by phases. That is due, of course, to the need to have a studio at one's disposal (and a favourable work climate, in which music plays a stimulating role), but also to Hartung's way of making art, "What I never do: a single etching or lithograph. Once I've begun, I've got to do a lot right away, to catch fire".[15] These waves of creativity were favoured by lithography, "The great advantage is that it goes very quickly and you don't have to wait for hours while it bubbles away: what you do is there right away."[16] Whereas, as Hartung was to deplore, "what bothers me in printmaking... is the delay, the fact of being interrupted",[17] because one has to wait "for it to begin to boil".[18]

His practice of intaglio printing peaked in 1947, in 1953 (Lacourrière, Paris; figs. 6-8), in 1970 (this was the Barcelona period, with Poligrafa, Cometa and Gustavo Gili), in 1973 (the Crommelynck studio, Paris) and in 1978 (Jacques Frélaut). Woodcuts were produced in number during Hartung's 1973 stay at Erker-Presse in St Gallen, Switzerland (figs. 10, 11). Lithography came to the fore in Paris in 1952–53, and again in 1957 at Jean Pons's studio (fig. 12), while 1958 witnessed a series of lithographs from the Patris studio (fig. 13). In 1961 Hartung continued his lithographic work of 1957 using transfer paper at Erker-Presse, where he would return in 1963 and 1966 (the interval may seem long but studios need time to print). The printing of the 1966 lithographs (fig. 14) was to stretch over several years, from 1969 to 1971. The twenty plates of *La farandole* date from 1970 (pulled in 1971), at Poligrafa in Barcelona (fig. 15). From the Erker studio in St Gallen, we have some sixty additional lithographs in 1973, twenty-four in 1974, and twenty-seven in 1976. In addition to these there are the thirteen later lithographs from the Chave studio in Vence.

10. HH, *H1973-1*, 1973, woodcut, 50 x 30.3 cm
11. HH, *H1973-6*, 1973, woodcut, 40 x 40 cm

VI.

The more sequential process introduced by the serial operations of etching, for example, produces "states"–that is to say, different phases in the evolution of the image. Working with a lithography stone also gives rise to such phases, of course, although fewer in number. Hartung always took great care to keep his proofs. It seems that from an early date he was seduced by their varied charms. We thus possess, from [?: 1928], the series of nine states of his *Femme aux mains croisées, de face* (S.–; M. 13; figs. 16, 17)[19] and the fifteen states of *Jeune femme nue allongée sur un divan* (S.–; M. 14). Of the colour intaglio print *G1* from 1953 (S. 30;

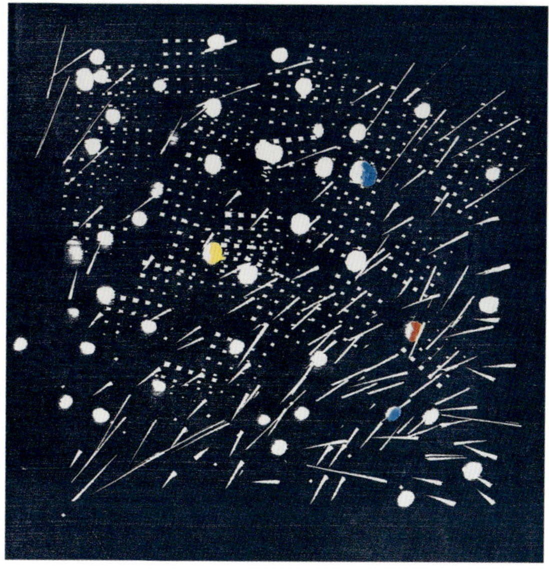

M. 60), we can trace thirteen states produced by the differently combined superimpressions of two plates comprising twelve and three states respectively. The 1953 colour print *G13* (S. 42; M. 71) reaches its ultimate phase in the eighth state, which is actually the result of a back-and-forth play of five plates that yielded one to four states respectively. Later, from the start of the 1970s on, Hartung would not exceed four states, whether working in intaglio or lithography. One could conclude that he now "saw" more rapidly what he was trying to achieve.

Yet in working the different states, the artist was offered another perception of the passage of time, not as fugitive, but embodied step by step. And this experience is significant as well. In the movement of the work, improvisation and objectivation through maturation occasionally go hand in hand. The "payoff" is on view on his internal screen, as a kind of "subconversation". Because there is something that eludes him, this interiorisation offers the attraction of contradiction, particularly to an artist devoted to the speed of sketch and gesture. Thus, Hartung is not being altogether paradoxical when he declares: "Normally I prefer direct, short-lived inspiration, and all the colour lithos and more so the colour engravings are produced in two, three, or four stages. You have to do first the yellow plate, then the black, then the green, wait for that to dry, come back two days later, four or six days later, then it is Sunday, then Monday, eventually you're no longer in the swing of things. If, at that point, I want to improve or rework something, it is no good, you've no longer got the initial spontaneity that I look for in art"[20]–an immediacy that does not appear, however, to exclude the pleasure of resistance, as he confessed in 1973.[21]

VII.

To what motivations does printmaking correspond in Hans Hartung's work, and what is its status? When Françoise Adam Woimant asked him in 1963 in what spirit he practised

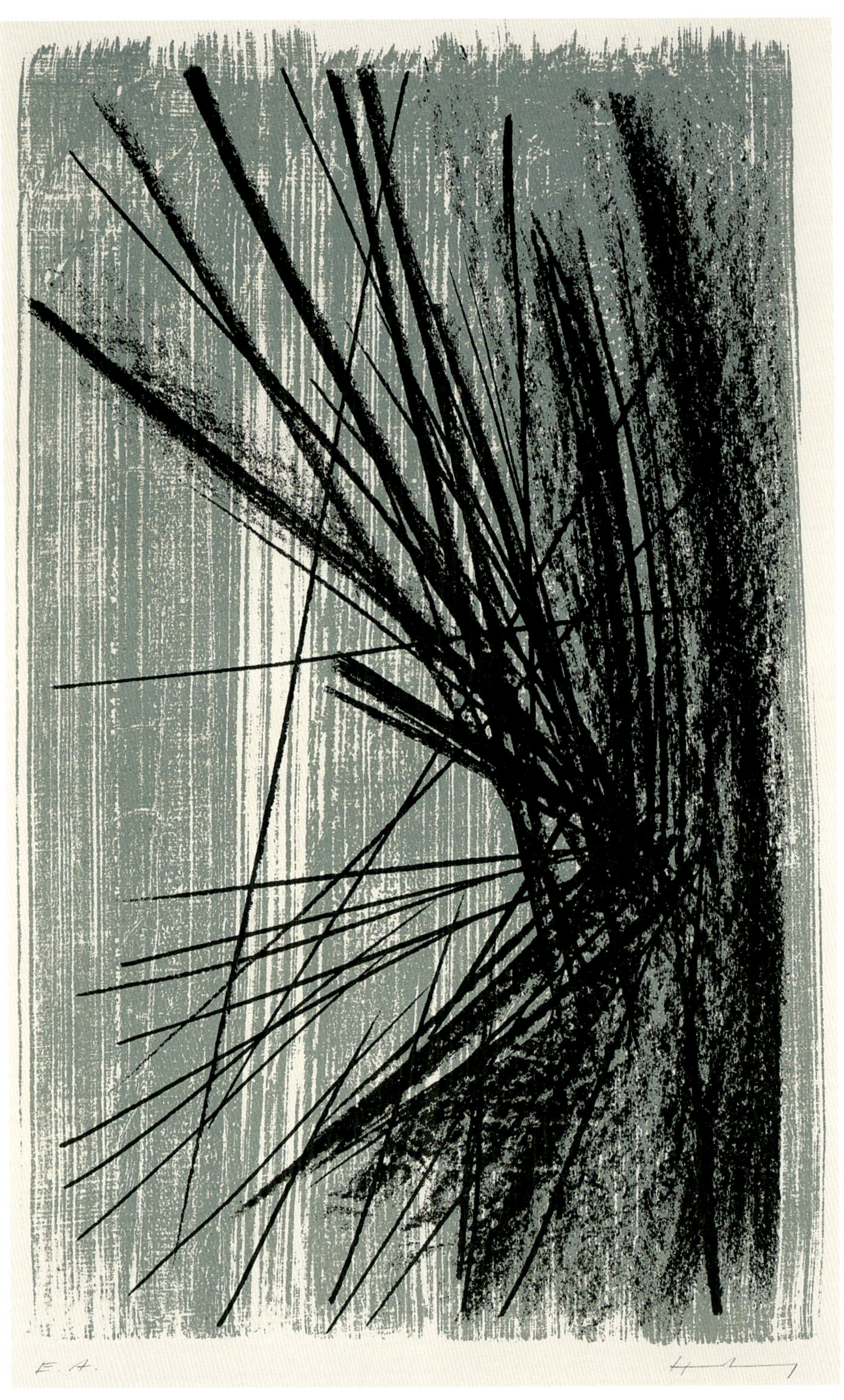

12. HH, *L34*, 1957, autography transfered on stone (transfer lithography), 49.2 x 30.4 cm
13. HH, *L72*, 1958, autography transfered on zinc (transfer zincography), 47.5 x 59.2 cm
14. HH, *L1966-40*, 1966, lithography, 21.4 x 17.2 cm

engraving, with what techniques he worked, and finally how engraving fit into his oeuvre, he gave a banal enough answer, saying that in the plastic arts he favours "everything having to do with graphics".[22] It was on other occasions, however, that he would throw light on his singular and fruitful relationship—a rather instrumental one—with engraving and painting. What is certain is that Hartung was not motivated by the printed restitution of his works. He is not a reproductive engraver, although we can identify a very limited number of prints related to paintings or drawings—related, rather than deliberately preparatory. Hartung rightly stated that interpretative lithography, especially when put in the hands of workshop assistants, ran counter to his work, "They have often offered me the chance but I have practically never done it".[23]

We do find exceptions to this principle of the initial draft. Thus, at least four of the lithographs executed in 1946 at Desjobert's in Paris, namely, *L02* to *L05* (S. 58 to 61; M. 30 to 33), go back to sketches dating from 1938, which were done on paper in India ink and, for the last of the series, pastel. In the case of *L03* (224 x 169 mm; S. 59, M. 31; fig. 21), we originally have a drawing (135 x 100 mm; FHH inv. 4866-0; fig. 18) that gave rise to two oil paintings, one on panel (18 x 12 cm; FHH inv. 2241; fig. 19) and a second on cellotex (*T1938–12*; 102 x 80 cm; FHH inv. 1822-0; fig. 20).[24] Thus, since the actualisation of the drawing occurred first in two paintings, the 1946 lithography can hardly pass for a kind of test; it is a reflection of the drawing, subject to it and devoid of any exploratory breakthrough. All three "echo-modalities" attest, if need be, to Hartung's ability to "re-produce" a *princeps* composition far removed from any and all "spontaneity".[25] This delayed transfer to the lithographic stone, enlarged point by point, may have been helped along by a photograph, though this is not confirmed, and we can trust both the master artist's hand and the tricks of the studio to explain the faithful character of the result.

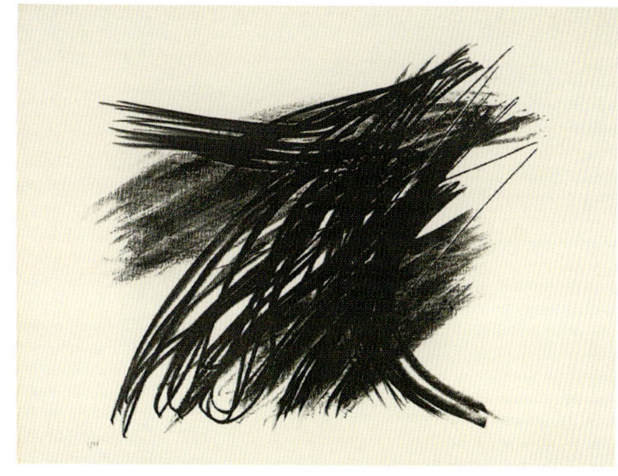

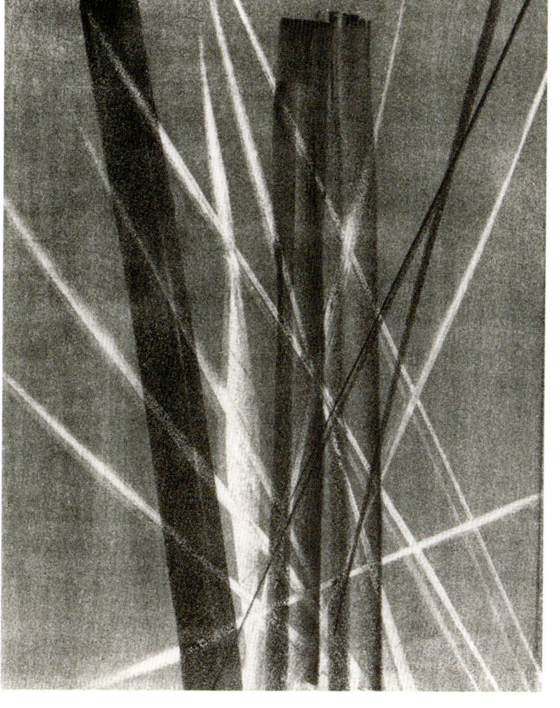

VIII.

I would add here parenthetically that the "spontaneous" Hartung clearly favoured direct contact with the print matrix, at least starting in the 1960s. But at first he did not balk at behaving like a draftsman whose compositions are transferred, perhaps because the quality of the "Parisian" stones did not encourage him to "let go" directly: "At the Pons studio, unfortunately there were no large stones, and very often the edges were more or less damaged". Yet "[they] had remained in quite good shape—you would use them to the utmost, right away, and those stones were an inspiration from the start", he said in 1977.[26]

In his print output, then, we can distinguish a fair number of lithographs, executed at Jean Pons's studio in 1957 and the Patris workshop in 1958 (figs. 12, 13),[27] made by the transfer process, by which we mean drawings created on ad hoc paper and transferred to the lithographic stone or zinc plate. Later, in 1970, in keeping with practices at the Arte/Adrien Maeght printing house in Paris, we are dealing with what I call "photo transfer prints".[28] When Hartung cautiously undertook in 1961 his collaboration with Franz Larese, the driving force, along with Jürg Janett, of Bodensee-Verlag in Amriswil and later Erker-Presse

15. HH, *L1970-1*, 1970, lithography, 49.3 x 74.9 cm
16. HH, *Woman with folded hands, frontal view* (fourth state out of nine), 1928, etched engraving, 10.5 x 7.7 cm
17. HH, *Woman with folded hands, frontal view* (fifth state out of nine), 1928, etched engraving, 10.5 x 7.7 cm

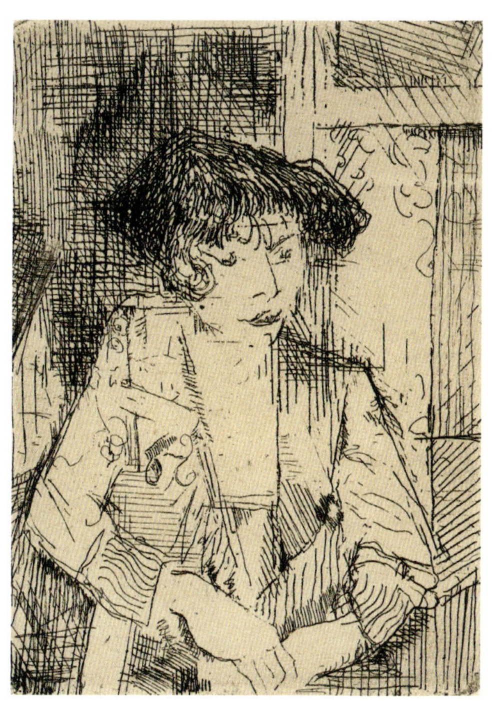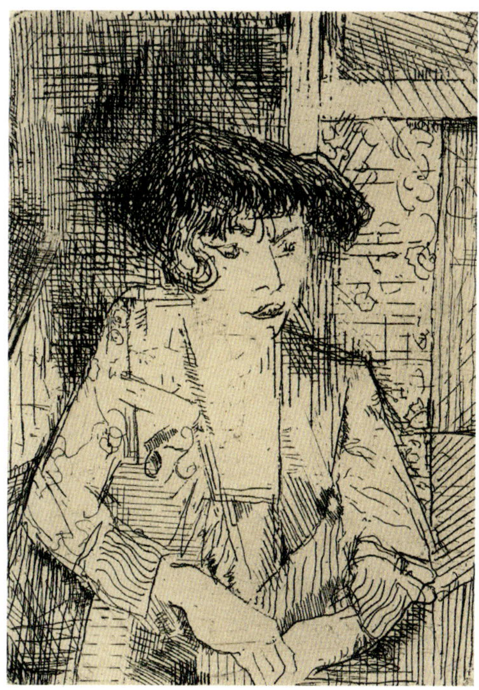

(and Galerie Im Erker) in St Gallen, he began by sending transfer sheets to Switzerland. These sheets may have been originally prepared for Jean Pons and date from 1957 (and not 1958, as Schmücking has it). The initial attempts gave rise to the lithographs *L81* to *L89* (S. 144 to 152; M. 158 to 166). With several transfer sheets that appeared to be unusable, they were returned to Paris and are still conserved in perfect condition at Hans Hartung and Eva Bergmann Foundation (FHH & AEB).[29] They correspond exactly to the prints *L86* to *L88*, for example, (S. 149 to 151; M. 163 to 165)—which of course strongly supports the hypothesis of a *photographic transfer* for their later execution as lithographs.

The use of photography, i.e., the transfer of a painted or drawn image to copperplate by photogravure, corresponds to two rather rare circumstances in Hartung's work. In one situation, to his disappointment, the artist no longer possessed the actual intaglio plates, only paper proofs, so a photo of the proof was transferred to a copperplate. The new matrix allowed the artist to "continue" printing the image without necessarily guaranteeing the same subtleties. Such was the case with *L'Homme au chapeau* [1928] (S. 9; M. 19; fig. 22) and a series of eight plates from 1947 (*G03, G04, G06* to *G09, G011, G012*; S. 14, 18, 20 to 23, 25, 26; M. 36, 37, 39 to 42, 44, 45). These photogravures (fig. 23) are associated with Terry Haas, who steered Hartung to Lacourière's studio; we should date them to around 1952–53 or 1959 at the latest. Another use of photogravure brings us back once again to the Lacourière studio and the complex elaboration of colour engravings, which required between two and four individual plates in the course of four to thirteen state proofs. These are *G1, G2, G13, G19* (S. 30, 31, 42, 48; M. 60, 61, 71, 78), in 1953, and *G27* (S. 56, M. 115) in 1957.]

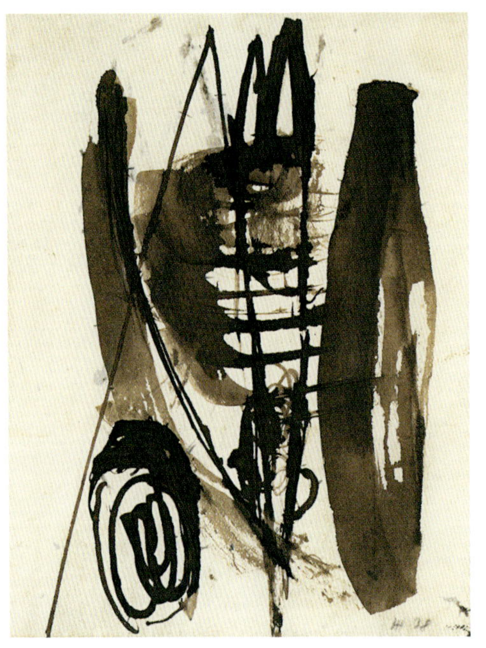

IX.

The year 1973, which Anne Pontégnie has very usefully examined in depth,[30] was quite productive in terms of volume of work, range of techniques used by the artist and the symphonic texture deployed in the process. Hartung worked in etching, aquatint, soft ground, even burin at the printing house of the brothers Aldo and Piero Commelynck in Paris, producing thirteen engravings (*G1973–1* to *G1973–13*; M. 361–373). At Erker-Presse in St Gallen, thanks to two prolonged visits from 2 April to 1 May and subsequently 1 to November, he tackled reserve engraving, making twenty-six woodcuts (*H1973–1* to *H1973–26*; M. 374 to 399) and two linocuts (*Lino 1973–1* and *Lino 1973–2*; M. 401, 402). His parallel campaign in lithography amounted to sixty pieces (*L1973–1* to *L1973–60*; M. 402 to 461), not to mention the several hundred drawings and paintings also dating from 1973.

Of course it is hardly possible to single out either the direct transpositions, which would justify speaking about interpretative pieces, or oblique derivations. But an entire system of allusions and echoes is articulated between the prints, paintings and drawings, which resonate with forms and structures, materials and textures, line and signs, actions and gestures, bubbling ideas and patient mastery, premeditation and improvisation—even the artist's hand and the tools he employed.

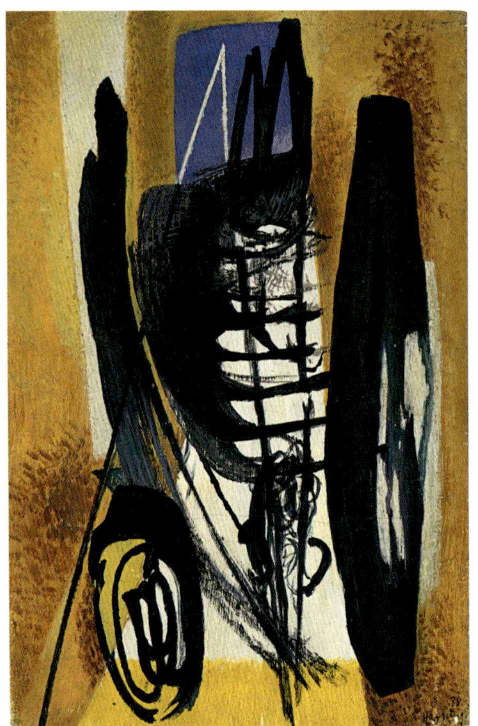

18. HH, untitled, Indian ink on paper, 1938, 13.5 x 10 cm
19. HH, *T1938*, 1938, oil on wood, 18 x 12 cm
20. HH, *T1938–12*, 1938, oil on wood, 18 x 12 cm
21. HH, *L03*, 1946, lithography, 22.4 x 16.9 cm

Hartung's turning to one or another technique does not occur synchronically, but diachronically. In other words, one process at a time! The work of printing or painting is materially distinct, serial. We are not able to detail the sequences of individuation and to attest—regardless of whether the origin of a piece goes back to a print or drawing—the more or less strict realization of *Vorlagen*, of *modelli*. The dates that have been determined either precisely (for works on cardboard or canvas) or globally (for the prints) nevertheless allow us to establish connections, even in his past work, and hence the modalities of the thematic account and repetitive insistence on certain patterns.

A few examples. *P1973–A26* (ink and pastel, 74.7 x 104.4 cm; fig. 24)[31] from 26 March 1973 features the halving of a rectangular surface, the right of which boasts a lively circular whisking movement of tangled line. The left-hand zone almost overwhelms or erases these lines in the dark triple sweep of a broad brush that affirms the composition's verticality over the perception of its width. Hartung's treatment, using two different masses and two different kinds of light, pairs the positive vertical trace on the left with the negative (scratched) linear tangle on the right. This match suggests that we might view the lithograph *L1973–51* (M. 452; fig. 25), which brings together the brayer (or ink roller), the spatula, and the scraper (the piece was printed in dark indigo), as a true

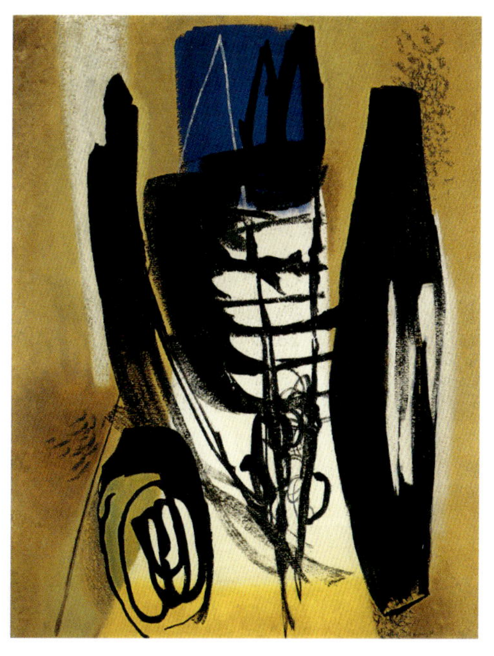

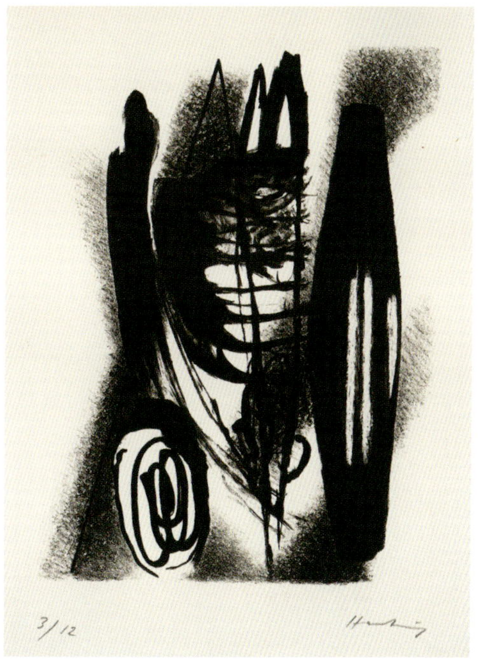

development of *P1973–A26*, since the lithograph dates at the earliest from the beginning of April 1973.

The lithograph *L1973–23* (M. 424; fig. 26) superimposes a screen of parallel curved and crossed furrows on a background of dark-to-light layers applied with an ink roller. Does this piece precede or follow the acrylic canvases *T1973–E33* (fig. 27), *T1973–E35*,

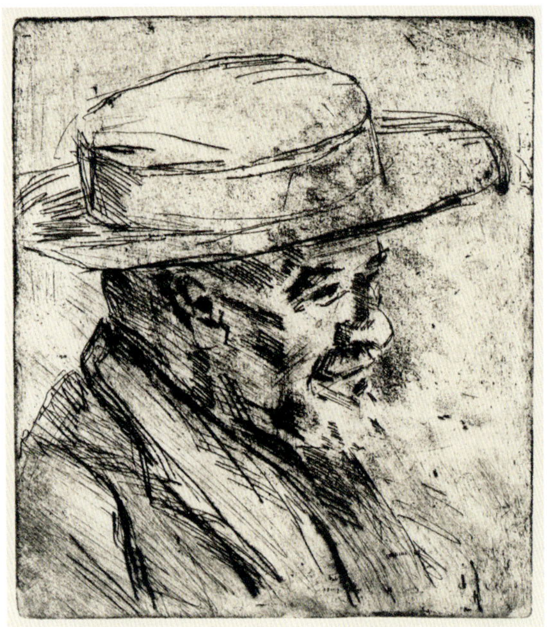

T1973–E36, *T1973–37*, from 6 October 1973, and *T1973–44* to *T1973–49* from 10 October 1973?[32] Here, similar lines are ploughed in for emphasis and stand out against one or two areas of colour. In both cases, the multi-brush tool he used derives from an adaptation of the *vélo* (literally the bicycle), a type of metal-engraving instrument made up of a row of blades or roulettes.

The style and the space, the coloured material of grainy earth and the ink roller (an instrument that moves forward through regular revolutions) clearly evince a genuine kinship between two acrylic paintings dating from 12 October 1973, *T1973–R14* and *T1973–R15* and in particular the lithographs *L1973–25* and *L1973–26* (M. 426, 427). Unlike almost all of the prints from 1973, these two show no margins (probably due to the cut of the paper in the 350 x 350 mm format).[33] They also infer a framing in a continuum, an off-screen space filled with potential developments, something found in many of the paintings, including *T1973–R14* and *T1973–R15*.

Of course *L1973–25* and *L1973–26* were meant to enrich the deluxe edition of a work on the drawings and watercolours from 1922–28 (with a text by Bernard Dorival): this editorial "constraint" explains the square format and the absence of white edges (which are the rule normally, as we know, in printed works of art). This clean cut spontaneously links the lithographs to the paintings that, from more or less early 1973 on, tended to abandon the motif fixed in a given area for one that invaded the entire surface of the canvas, in a kind of all-over process. Prints were to remain "affected" by their margins because the tradition in printing prescribes them. But Hartung considered the lithographic stone (or woodblock or copperplate) as a unified field that he would encompass and treat in its totality, from one edge to the other, like his canvases. The "window" is soon enough finished, over and done with. Space opens up.

22. HH, Man with a hat, 1928, photogravure, 23.9 x 21.7 cm
23. HH, G07, 1947, photogravure, 17.8 x 13 cm

[A series done in pastel and ink (in that order!) on horizontal cardboard (*PM1973–24* to *PM1973–31*), dating from 8 and 9 February 1973, demonstrates that the question of delimiting the work ("breaking open the frame" and, to accomplish this, first putting it to the test) clearly preoccupied Hartung at this time.[34] Networks of lines furiously scribbled in pastel, drawn side by side, practically mirroring one another, interconnected by their excesses, are in the end isolated from each other by broad sweeps of India ink (?) turning them into two rectangular sections posed upright.

By a movement in the opposite direction (a return upstream?), we shall pull up from memory and the storeroom of FHH & AEB a painting on canvas from 1965, *T1965–H34* (54 x 81 cm; fig. 28). The piece features a brushed-on hazel surface spread over a black background, hence its appearance of being framed in black (like the white margins of a print). In this broad expanse of colour Hartung nimbly scratched with dry point, *vélo*, and crayon a drawing that is read in reverse and which displays, in the "grain" of the boldest lines, the look of a lithograph (using scraping and pencil). Clearly the artist "depicted" a print here. The exchanges within Hartung's work are not a one-way conversation. As he explained: "In my youth (between 1928 and 1938) I executed a few etchings, and I did more in 1953. I'm really made for the job of scraping the copper or zinc plate, and that passion has followed me to the point of having still—twenty to thirty years later—a clear influence on my painting—especially in the years 1961 to 1965, when I got into the habit of scraping with different instruments the fresh layer of colours, colours that were often dark."[35] When Daniel Abadie raised the question in 1977 of "the difference between engraving and lithography", Hartung provided a response that—paradoxically?—alters the light shed on his relationship to intaglio, an art of delay: "Engraving has a character that is a bit aggressive, caustic, even cutting sometimes. I mean I really like cutting, scraping, mistreating a material if I can, leaving there the precise, exact trace of those actions. That's the great advantage of engraving. You scrape the varnish, let the acid bite in, and things reach a boiling point..."[36]]

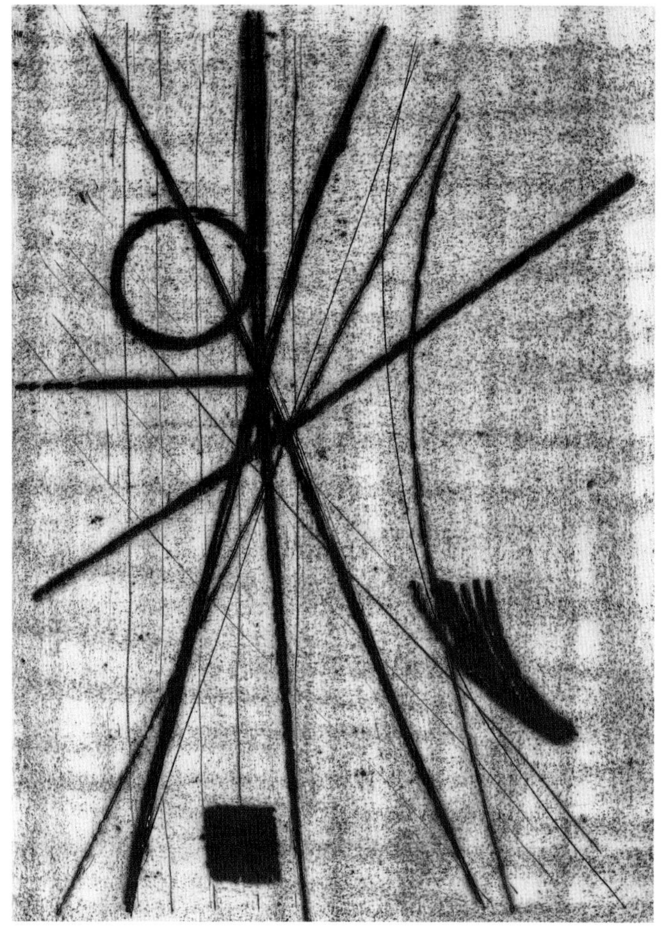

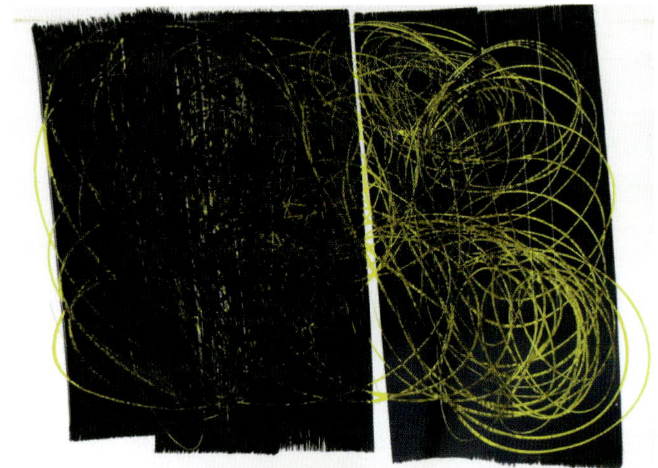

X.

Let us make a digression to touch on the techniques of woodcut and linocut (*H1973–1* to *H1973–26* [M. 374 to 399], and *Lino 1* and *Lino 2* [M. 400, 401]). According to Heidi Bürklin, Hartung apparently took up woodcutting "at the suggestion of [Franz] Larese",[37] one of the two owners of Erker in St Gallen. With Daniel Abadie in 1977, on the other hand, the story takes a different turn: "At Larèse's, I must have observed my wife [Anna-Eva Bergman], who worked with wood a lot. Finally I was jealous. I said to myself, Why don't I do a woodcut too? Only I'm not the kind of guy who takes up wood, for example, generally hardwood—the harder it is the better—and begins making a line. When you go off course you take up another block and you redo your line... If you could do your woodcut rapidly—because I can't work slowly, I can't manage, I haven't got the patience— I would have done it like everyone else. I had to invent. I went to a joiner's workshop, I asked for big blocks of wood, an axe, a large hammer, one of those that has a broad end and a narrower one, all the instruments of the carpenter's trade. Then I let loose on the blocks of wood, which were clamped down—because otherwise they jump around—and that's the way I did the engravings".[38]

If they involved nothing more than the use of the customary knives, chisels, and gouges, Hartung's twenty-six woodcuts[39] would merely translate—unsurprisingly—the sets and bundles of lines, the flashes of light, the removal of material. These pieces, printed in black or bluish black—broken by a few patches of lemon yellow or tangerine, turquoise or Caribbean blue, Swiss red, raspberry or madder which are sometimes applied by lithography or sometimes by stencil—do not hold our attention by their colour but through the rhythmic character of the graphic style, or rather the hammering, the trace. It is as if the artist, in perfecting his formal vocabulary, were acting like a percussionist working in circles or slight shifts to do riffs with his drumsticks, mallets or brushes. *H1973–1* (M. 374) makes use of a simple gouge for the lines, bush hammers for the chequered structures, and a metal brush for lightening the background with scratches (fig. 10). These interventions not only cut the wood, they are registered there by crushing or driving in the surface when, for example, in *H1973–5* (M. 378), Hartung used structured round-headed hammers or round punches. With this the engraved image adds modular structures, with their firework highlights, in a clear affirmation of the black panel. A comparable effect, of coarsely

24. HH, *P1973–A26*, 1973, ink and pastel on cardboard, 74.7 x 104 cm
25. HH, *T1973–E33*, 1973, acrylic on canvas, 73 x 100 cm

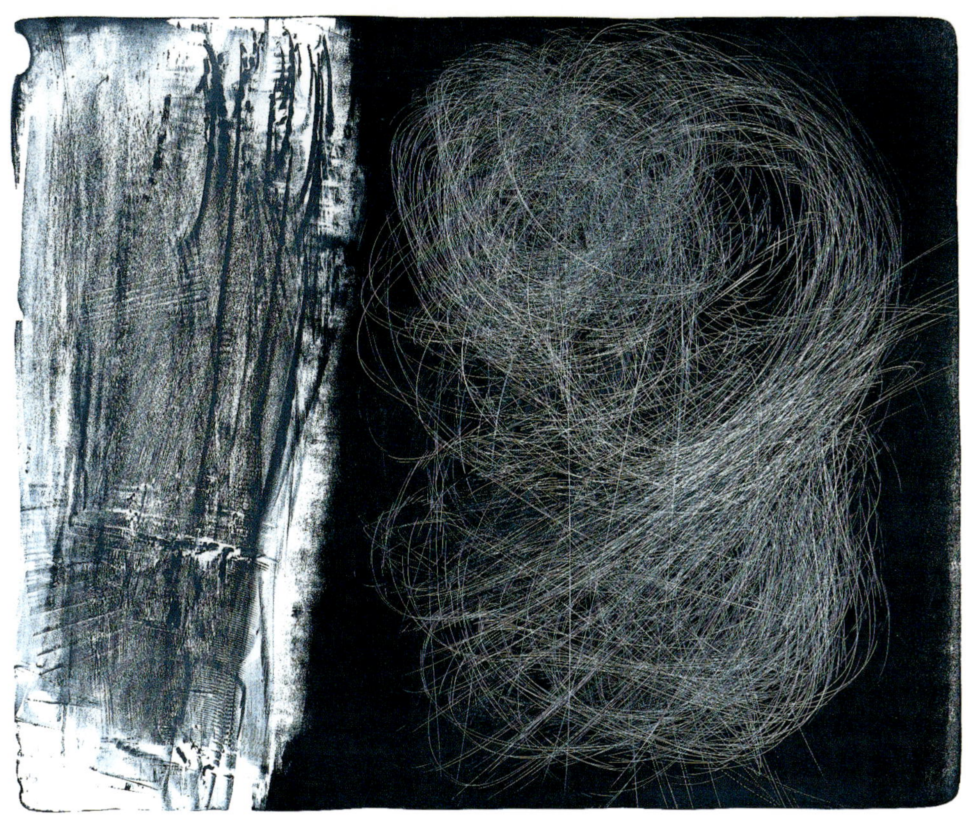

stippled or latticed networks achieved with an instrument for circular repetitive pattern can be seen in certain acrylics on cardboard dating from 13 August 1973 (*P1973–B21, P1973–B23*),[40] though much more uniform and unadorned.

We need not see in Hartung's use of all these tools, be it bush hammers or multiple rollers (structured or smooth), the search for a disparity between the gesture and the printing support, as in the disparity between the gesture and the pictorial surface. Except for finger-painting, in the work of every painter and every printmaker there is always some instrument that comes into play, leaving behind its trace, its "print", whether it is a brush, a dry-point engraver, a litho crayon, etc. Naturally the aim of such an instrument is less to create distance than to prolong (the hand). Hartung, tool in hand, does not tend to mask the use of the instrument or to alter its function (like Brice Marden [1938], who, in the 1980s and '90s, used to attach a brush to the end of a long stick to better achieve calligraphically a "letting go"): rather, Hartung wields it as directly as possible.

XI.

It is frequently said that Hartung's painting in the 1970s often resulted from his involvement in printmaking. Moreover, he himself insisted on this: "Along with those pictorial experiments

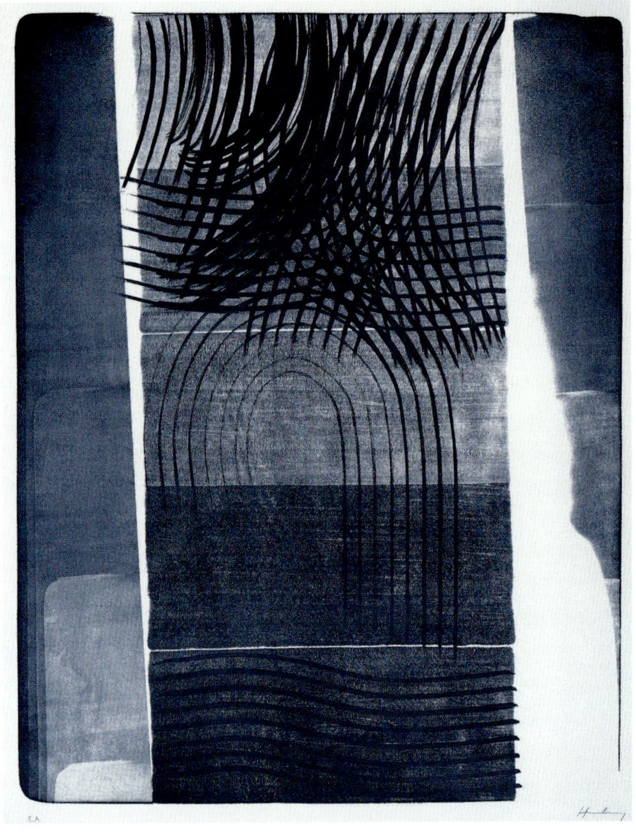

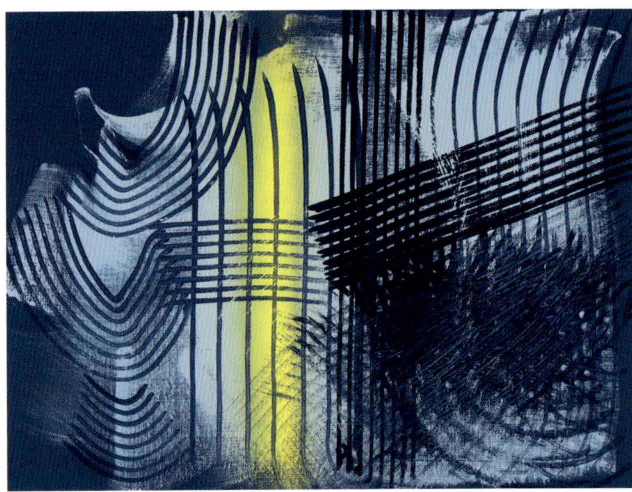

[beginning in 1970], these last few years I've had the good fortune to increase my possibilities of expression using a new material, the lithographic stone. I've worked with it periodically since the war and it has become one of my favourite techniques... Working with lithography has also brought a renewal to my painting. You have to let yourself be guided by the material when it attracts you, and above all search for it with persistence when it becomes a necessity. Over the last few years a new way of painting has developed that is, in a certain sense, the result of my long period of experimentation in lithography. That medium gave me the inspiration for massive constructions and freed me from my dependence on the line, which was my usual way of doing things almost my whole life."[41]

What lithography did in this case was not immediately and exclusively visible in the 1973 output, but soon thereafter. If we consider, for example, the acrylics on canvas *T1974–R25*, *T1974–R12*, *T1975–H24*, *T1975–H25* (fig. 20) and *T1975–E37*,[42] which feature striated *glissandi* that are both firm in their progression and emphatic in the sign they leave on the surface of the painting, we can well

26. HH, *L1973-23*, 1973, lithography, 80.6 x 63.7 cm
27. HH, *L1973-51*, 1973, lithography, 64.6 x 79.9 cm
28. HH, *T1965-H34*, 1965, vinyl on canvas, 54 x 81 cm

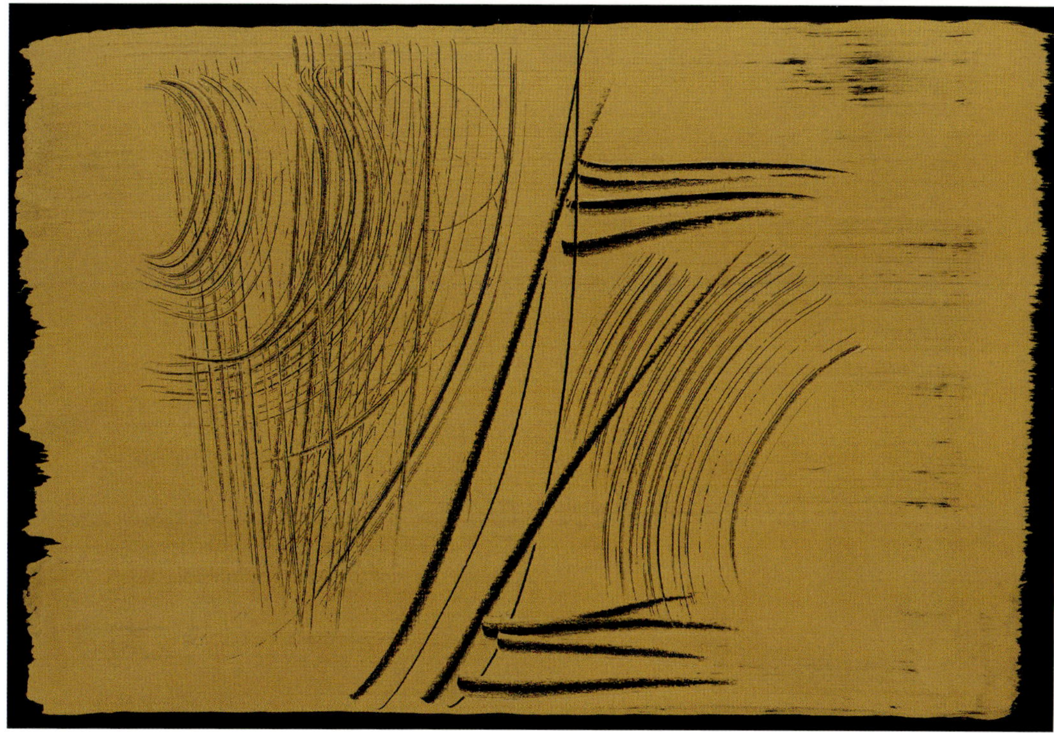

imagine the regularly-spaced notched roller Hartung made use of to produce them. A similar process can be seen at work in *L1973–1*, *L1973–2*, *L1973–4*, *L1973–11* and *L1973–36* (M. 402, 403, 405, 412, 437). But we should probably assume that the artist used, unless we are mistaken, not a roller but a large faceted stick of (litho) crayon, which he rolled with the palm of his hand over the stone.

There is nonetheless an undeniable correspondence—style and image—between the lithographs *L1973–6* (fig. 30), *L1973–7*, *L1973–18*, *L1973–28*, *L1973–33*, *L1973–39*, *L1973–43* and *L1973–45* (M. 407, 408, 419, 429, 434, 440, 444 and 446), which use the ink roller alone, turning it to good advantage as a "brush", and such paintings as *T 1975–R46* (fig. 31), *T1975–E11*, *T1975–E12*, *T1975–K9* and *T1975–K10*.[43] The roller lays down, like so many grand movements of sweeping curves (we can no longer speak of motifs in this case), the transparency or opacity of the film of pictorial "material", both stable and varied, with its patches of massed, thinned or overflowing pigment on uniform backgrounds, which the fine spray of the airbrush occasionally softens in cloudy zones. This way of creating, of articulating space and "form", is completely indebted to lithography.

XII.

When considering the lithographic stone and the canvas, Hartung listed the many advantages (and limits) of the technology of lithography: "You can work with broad or narrow

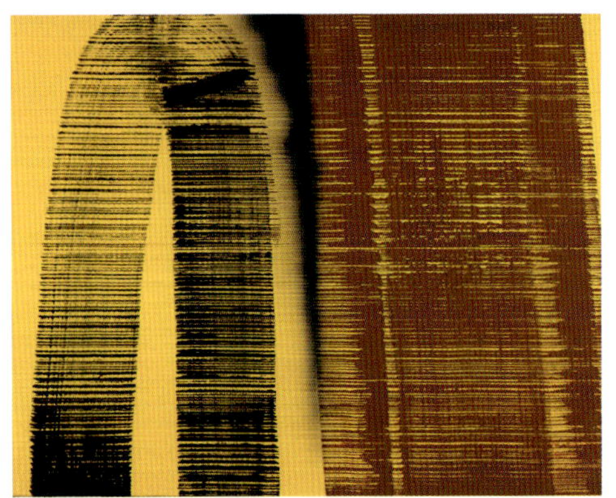

crayons, lightly or very rigorously, on the point of the stone's pores (granular surface), and you can scrape, too, take material away more than once. Very often all of that yields something that's a bit slack; on the other hand, over time I've found that litho offers lots of other possibilities. You can work with rollers and thick ink, which, because of the pores of the stone, give a kind of transparency that's very beautiful. That also allows you to make rather large patches of colour, to play with rather large masses, and to dominate a surface of a certain scale more easily. The big advantage is that it goes very quickly, you don't have to wait for things to come to a boil for hours. What you do is there straight off". And Hartung concluded, "Engravings and lithographs really have very different, decisive characters, and for me these two techniques subsequently influenced my painting".[44]

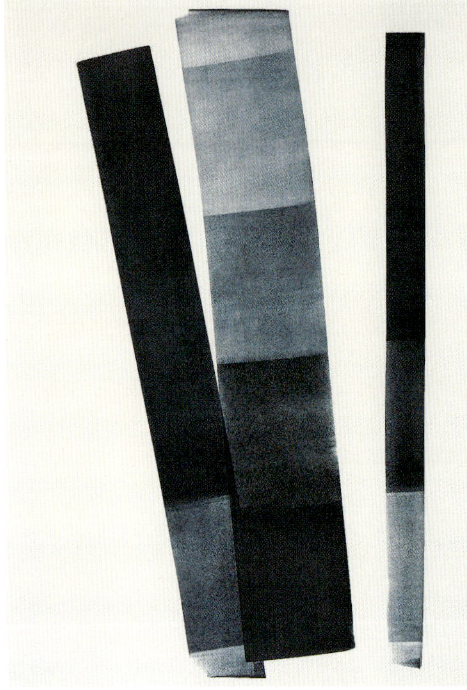

In the same interview, when asked again by Abadie how lithography and engraving affected his work in painting, Hartung replied: "For instance, and this is certain, in the use of the roller in painting, but also scraping into a surface, which yields very clear and sharp transparencies, if you bring it off. The very way of scraping in my own painting, in the layer I have just applied, comes from engraving; finally, and above all, I have used in painting the same treatment of large surfaces as in lithographs, by varying the roller's movements, or the object with which you're applying the colour to the stone, which leaves it visible and perceptible by placing, for example, a dark colour under white and another light colour. So much so that you sense through it what's already taken place beneath. An action and a rhythm have already occurred, (...) the latter remains noticeable and is contradicted, emphasised by the rhythm superimposed on it".[45]

29. HH, *T1975-H25*, 1975, acrylic on canvas, 102 x 130 cm
30. HH, *L1973–6*, 1973, lithography, 86.2 x 46.6 cm
31. HH, *T1975-R46*, 1975, acrylic on hardboard panel, 81 x 130 cm

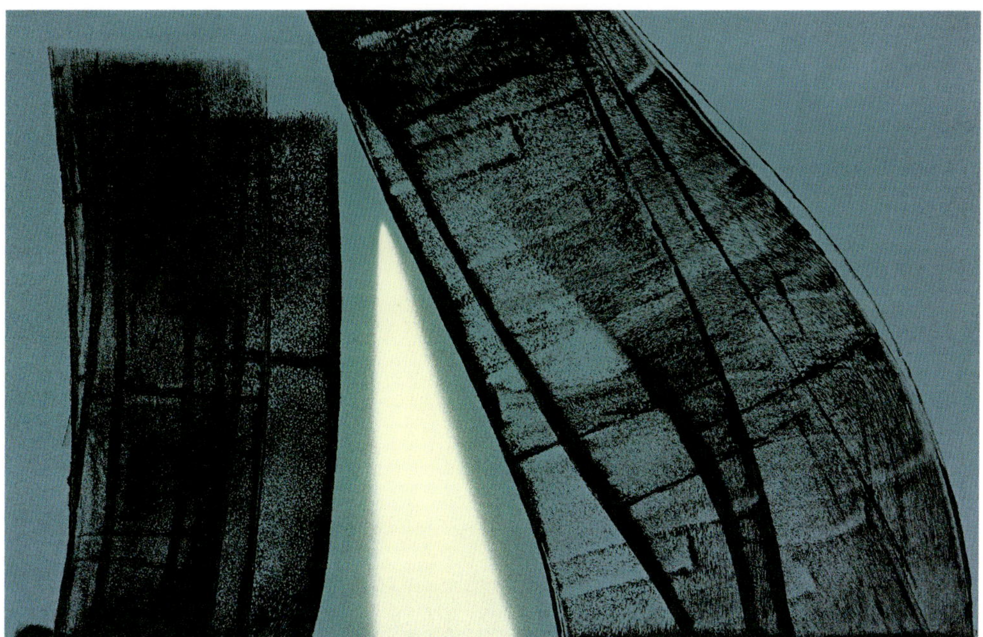

Painting often acts as a palimpsest of the printed work. Hence, the print enjoys a status in Hartung's work that is far more central than simply as an agent of reproduction and dissemination. It participates in the infinite debate at the heart of the artist's output. The question "Hartung as a *graveur*", an engraver (more specific than printmaker) can no longer be answered on a single level. Especially since the highly rational Hartung was made up of contradictions, meanders, and second thoughts.[46]

We can simply recall here what René de Solier (1914–74), the husband of the sculptor Germaine Richier (1902–59), wrote with such clear-sightedness in 1954 in his preface to the Palais des Beaux-Arts show in Brussels, which featured forty-six paintings, twenty pastels, and fifteen prints: "If the 'drawings' are at the very least partially related to the painting, Hans Hartung's prints display great independence: painting has found its means of expression on the fringe, one might say, thanks to the invented 'tools', the ingenuity that characterises the artist, from the moment he takes up a new means of expression. The (bone) rubbing devices, the sponge-like element, and the grainy effects, combs or scrapers were used by a painter who hardly thought about conventions. The discovery of these necessary 'tools', particular to an art, is the work of an investigator (he does not settle for established modes), and the 'interlacing' that seems studied is flung down, direct. The lines are like an imprint, the graphic mark of the gesture. In a word, we have here a unique experiment in the history of printmaking."[47] What more can be said?

XIII.

Since the time of Adam Bartsch (1757–1821), the father of the modern science of cataloguing, the term *peintre-graveur* (painter-engraver) has been readily used to speak about those particular artists who produce prints of their own invention, not reproductions of other works of art. Perhaps we could invert this formula and introduce for Hans Hartung the term *graveur-peintre* ("engraver-painter"), for such is the development (by modal attraction, Hellenists would say) of printmaking in his art as a painter.

In memoriam Maurice Pianzola (1917-2004)

Translated from French by John O'Toole
and edited by Madeleine Goodrich Noble with the author

1. "Monsieur Hans et le docteur Hartung", interview with France Huser, *Le Nouvel observateur* (Paris: 18–24 July 1981), p. 15.
2. Will Grohmann, *Hans Hartung · Aquarelle 1922* (St Gallen: Erker-Verlag, 1966).
3. "De l'homme à l'univers : un médiateur, l'artiste", interview with Valérie Brière-Maroger, *Réforme* (Paris: 12 Aug. 1978), p. 6.
4. Note supra 1.
5. Note supra 3. Cf. infra p. 109 and note 24.
6. "Die herbe Vision | LR-Gespräch mit Hans Hartung", interview with Jürgen Claus, *Literatur Revue*, 12 (Würzburg: 1963); reprinted in Jürgen Claus, *Theorien zeitgenössischer Malerei in Selbstzeugnissen* (Hamburg: Rowohlt, 1963), p. 84. Translated here from the author's French translation of the passage. Cf. infra p. 109 and note 24.
7. Interview with Heidi Bürklin, in *Hans Hartung. Grafik aus der Erker-Presse 1973. Lithografien. Holzschnitte. Linolschnitte* (St Gallen: Erker, 1974), p. 5. Translated here from the author's French translation of the passage.
8. Rolf Schmücking, *Hans Hartung. Werkverzeichnis der Graphik. 1921-1965* (Brunswick: Verlag Galerie Schmücking, 1965); second edition, (including the critical response of 1965 (Basel: Verlag Galerie Schmücking, 1990).
9. S. = Schmücking, note supra 8; M. = Mason
10. "I liked Slevogt's engravings, done in a cursory way with a quick line that is already a bit cut loose from realism, as if it were aiming to be a short-hand of the represented subjects." In *Autoportrait*, as told to Monique Lefebvre (Paris: Bernard Grasset, 1976), pp. 57–58.
11. Applied graphic arts in connection with studio exercises.
12. FHH & AEB archives.
13. "Hans Hartung: sur la gravure et la lithographie | Entretien avec Daniel Abadie · 28 avril 1977", *Hartung*, catalogue of a travelling print exhibition curated by MNAM (Paris: Centre Georges Pompidou, 1977), p. 3.
14. Note supra 13, p. 2.
15. Note supra 7, p. 5.
16. Note supra 13, p. 3.
17. Note supra 7, p. 2.
18. Note supra 13, p. 3.
19. A photograph (FHH) bearing no date shows that there exists an oil on canvas that corresponds to the engraving; this painting could be the work entitled *Femme au boa.*
20. Note supra 13, p. 4.
21. Cf. note 7 supra; cf. also note 36 infra.
22. Cf. note 12 supra.
23. Note supra 13, p. 2.
24. Repr. in Franz-W. Kaiser, Anne Pontégnie, Vicente Todoli, *Hartung x 3* (Angers: Expressions contemporaines, 2003), p. 16. HH offered the former to AEB, who was then in Norway; in a letter to AEB dated 1.3.1939, HH judges it to be better than the larger one.
25. Cf. *Hartung. Peintre moderne*, exh. cat., Fréjus, Le Capitou. Centre d'art contemporain (Milan: Skira editore, 1996).
26. Note supra 13, p. 2.
27. Schmücking indicates them with the letter *U* for *Umdruck* (report).
28. Drawing executed on a semi-transparent acetate sheet (one glossy and one "frosted" side), which very likely allowed a transfer to the zinc through exposure to light.
29. These three autograph sheets display at the bottom of the page on the right in lead pencil the indication *H–t–g 57*: a. in litho crayon (495 x 325 mm), inv. 2585-646; b. in ink, MONFOURAT watermark (495 x 325 mm), inv. 2585-645; c. in ink, MONFOURAT watermark (495 x 325 mm), inv. 2585-343.
30. "Mille neuf cent soixante-treize" in *Hartung x 3* (note 24 supra), pp. 93–159.
31. Repr. in *Hartung x 3*, note 24 supra, p. 114.
32. Repr. in *Hartung x 3*, note 24 supra, pp. 145–51.
33. I would add *L 1973–32* and *L 1973–37* (M. 433, 438).
34. Repr. in *Hartung x 3*, note 24 supra, pp. 110–11.
35. *Autoportrait*, pp. 198–99.
36. Note 13 supra: p. 2; cf. also note 21 supra.
37. Note 7 supra, *ibid.*
38. Note 13 supra, p. 3.
39. For this series of woodcuts the artist photographed a large selection of instruments arranged like a butterfly collection; on the back of one photograph is the inscription *"The instruments that I had / with me in St. Gallen 1973 / April".*
40. Repr. in *Hartung x 3*, note 24 supra, p. 122.
41. Note 35 supra, pp. 201–202.
42. Repr. in *Hartung x 3*, note 24 supra, pp. 194, 195, 199, 202.
43. Repr. in *Hartung x 3*, note 24 supra, pp. 201, 49, 51, 53.
44. Note 13 supra, p. 3.
45. Note 13 supra, p. 4.
46. I shall pass over in silence for now some of the artist's habits such as the neurotic demand for the least proof left lying about at the printer's, the creation of an artificial shortage at print dealers, the supplementary and superfluous printings, the hoarding of innumerable editions, etc.
47. In *Hartung*, exh. cat. (Brussels: Palais des Beaux-Arts, 1954), pp. 1–2.

John C. Welchman Hans Hartung

Abcedarium: Reading Between the Lines

Franz-W. Kaiser A Case Study

on the Caducity of Categories

in Art Criticism Annie Claustres

Hans Hartung

Clandestine Artist

1937-1942: the Decisive Years

Christine Mehring Hans Hartung

Mid-Century Modern

Rainer Michael Mason Hartung

and Printmaking Christopher Wool

Selected Works

Anne Pontégnie 1975

Hartung at the Metropolitan Museum

Chronicle of a Failure Chantal Eschenfelder

Hans Hartung in Germany

Laurence Bertrand Dorléac

Germany and France

Two Parts in One Jennifer Mundy

The Very Late Style of Hans Hartung

a Problem?

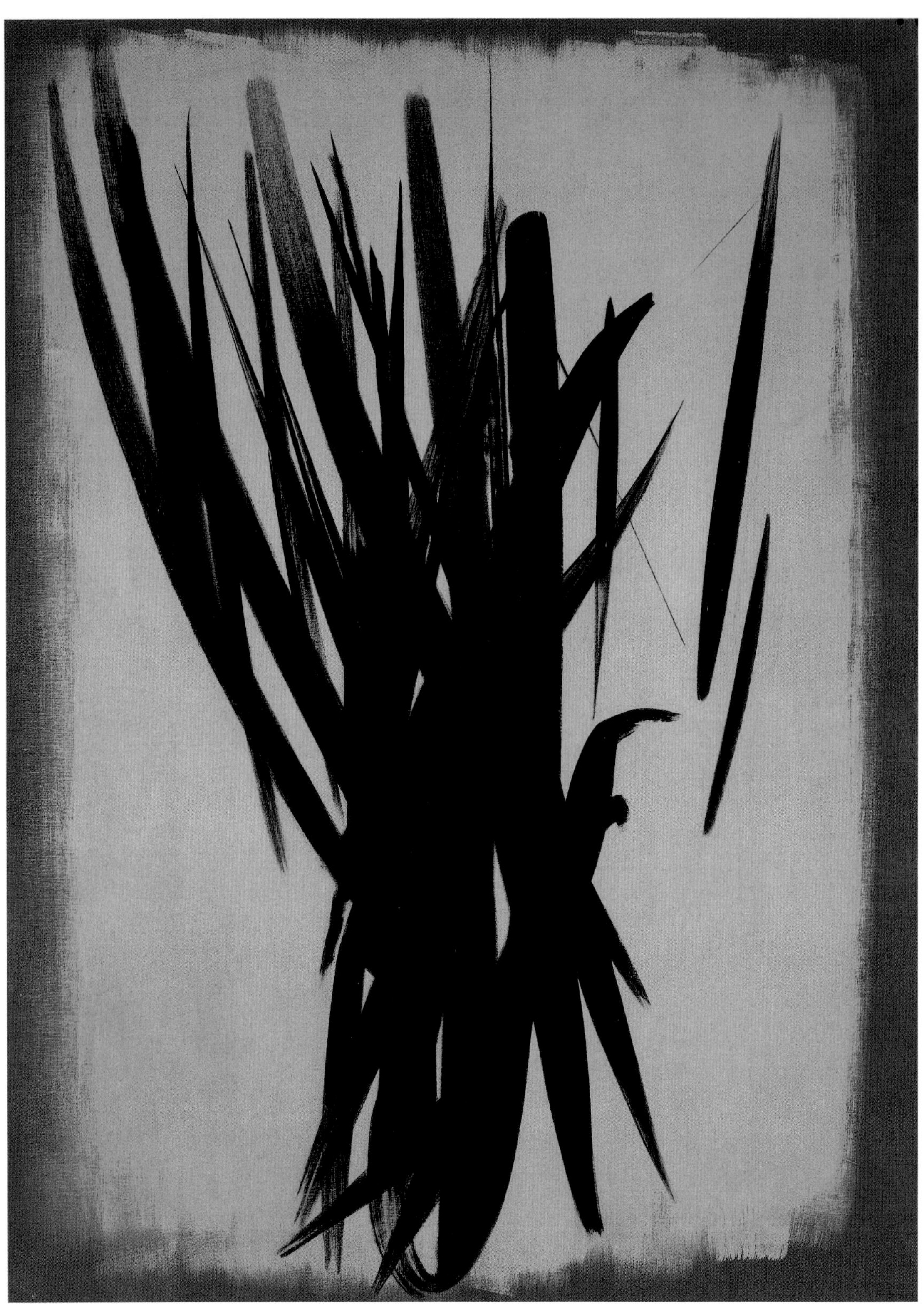

 Christopher Wool

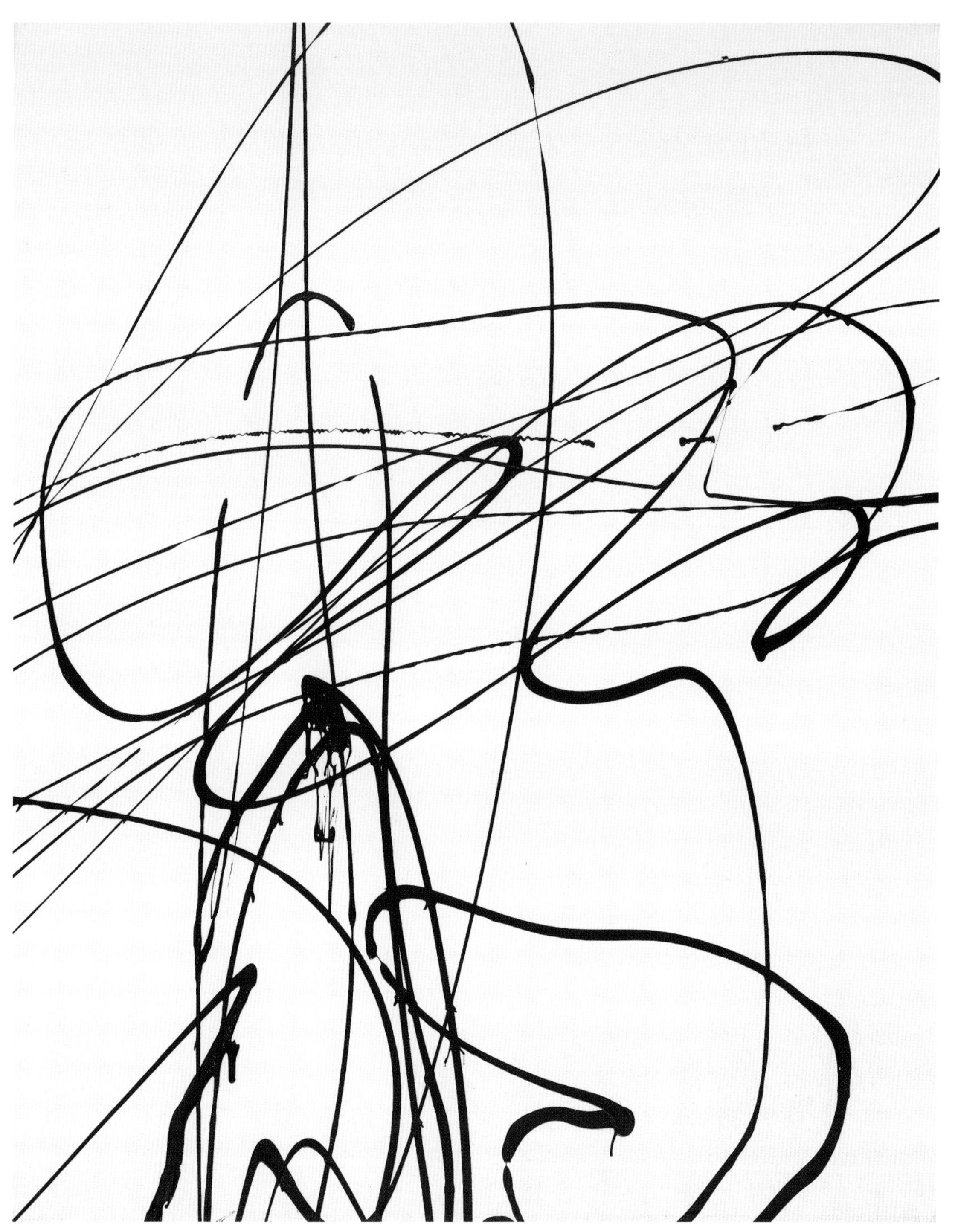

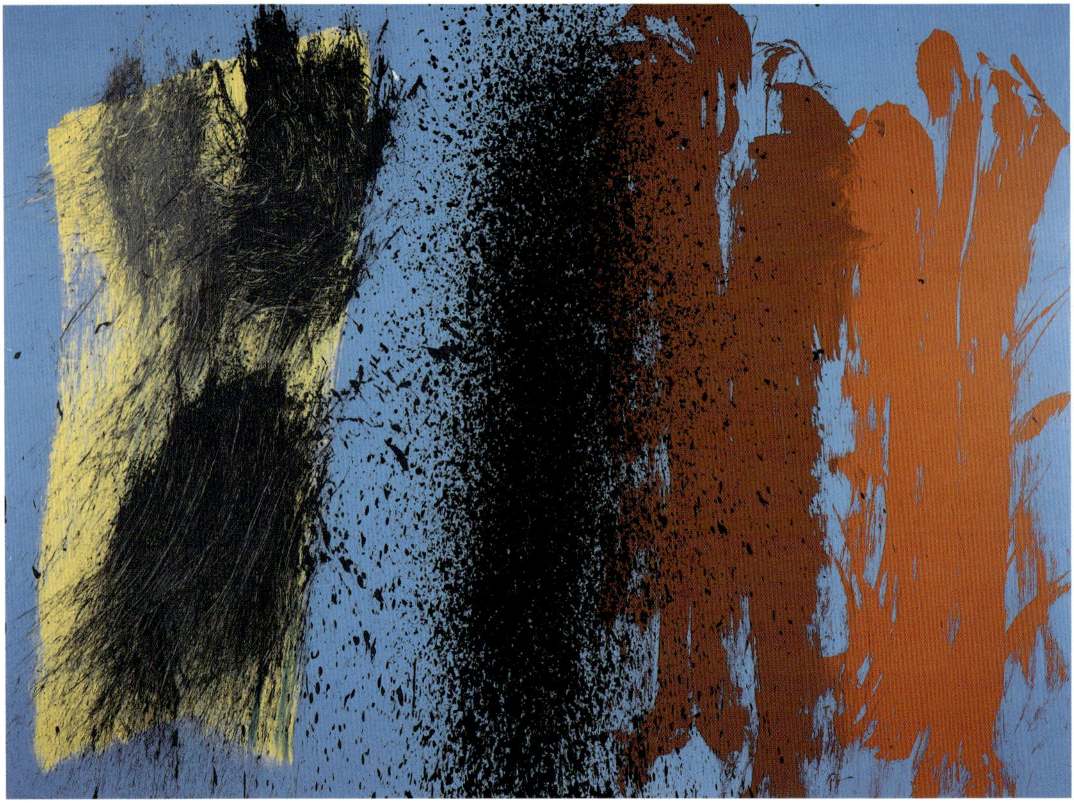

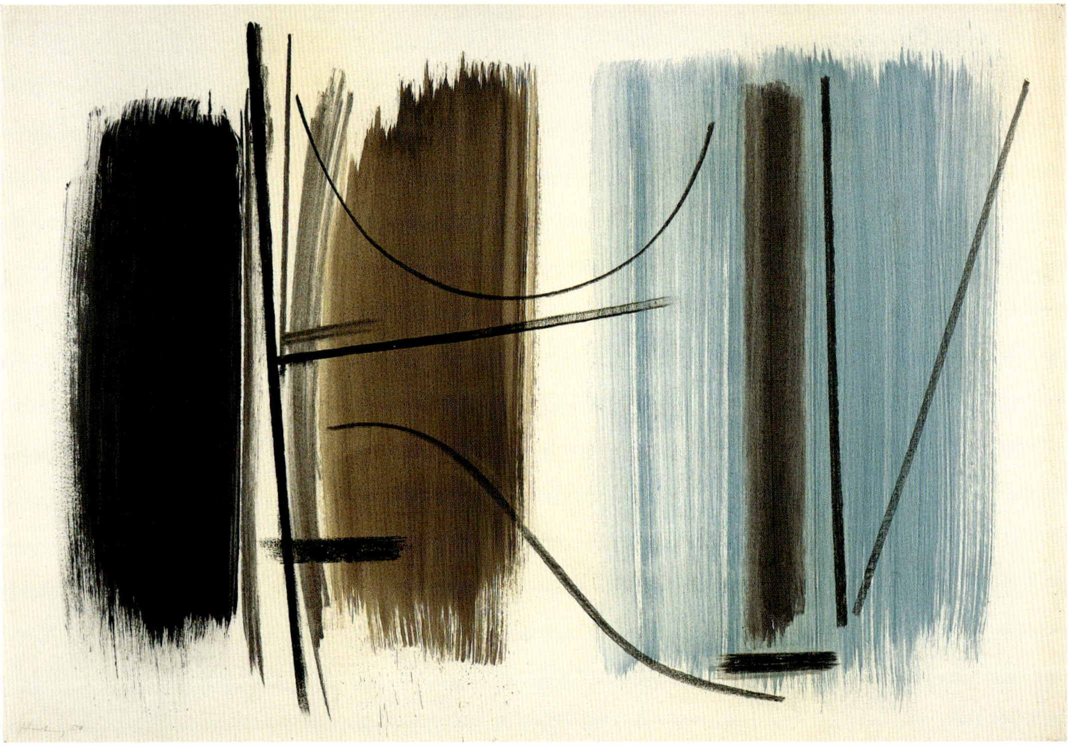

 Christopher Wool

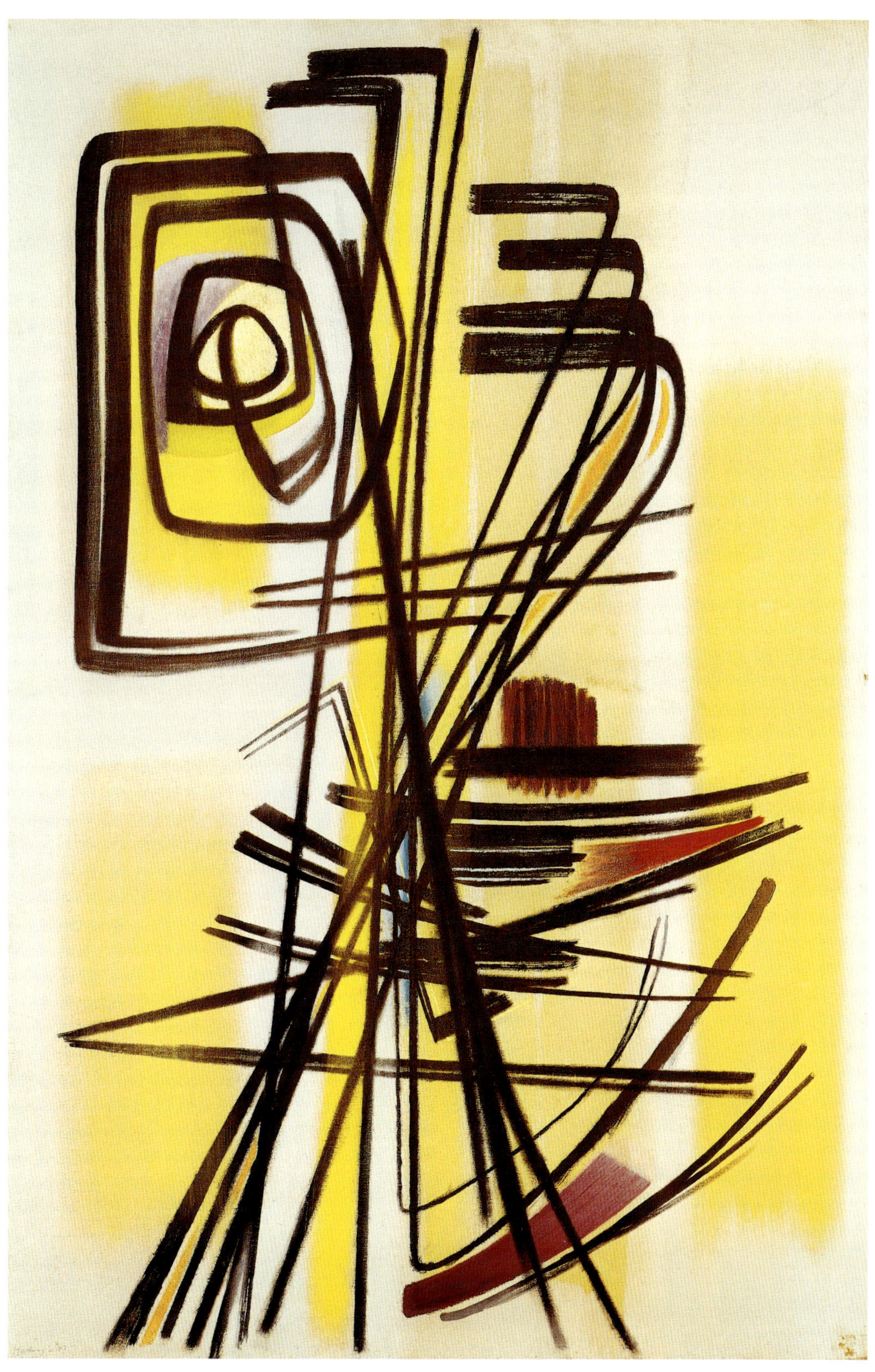

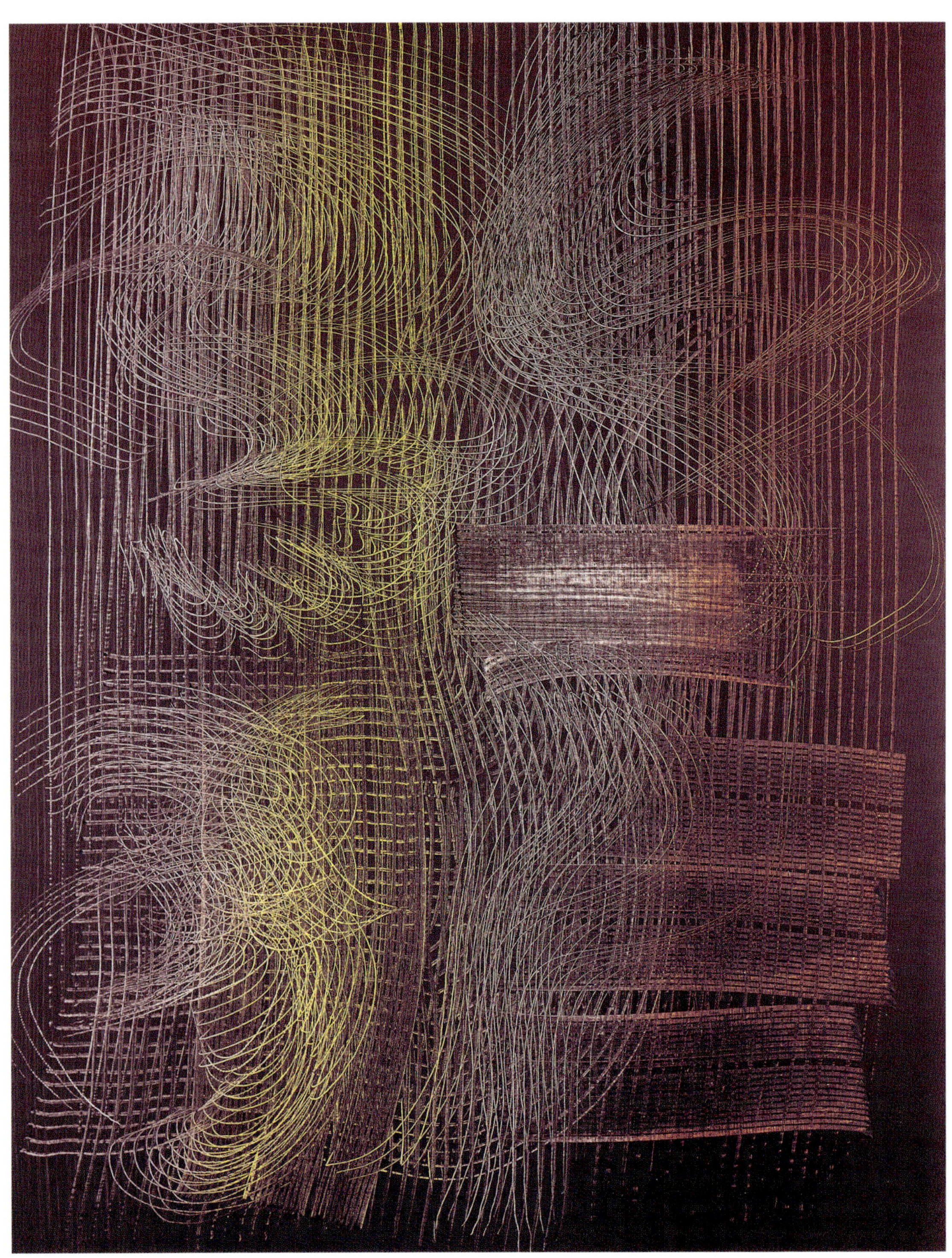

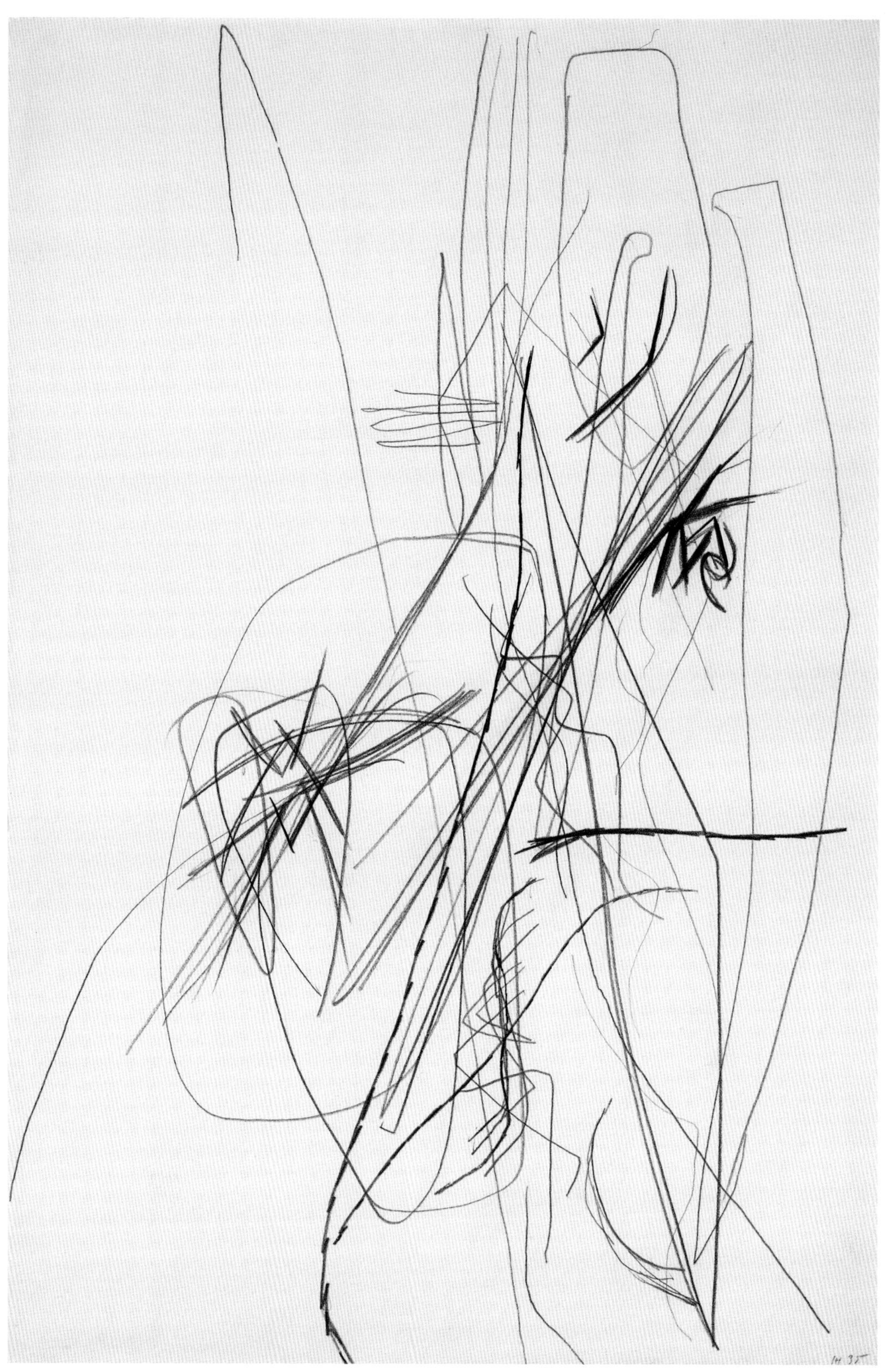

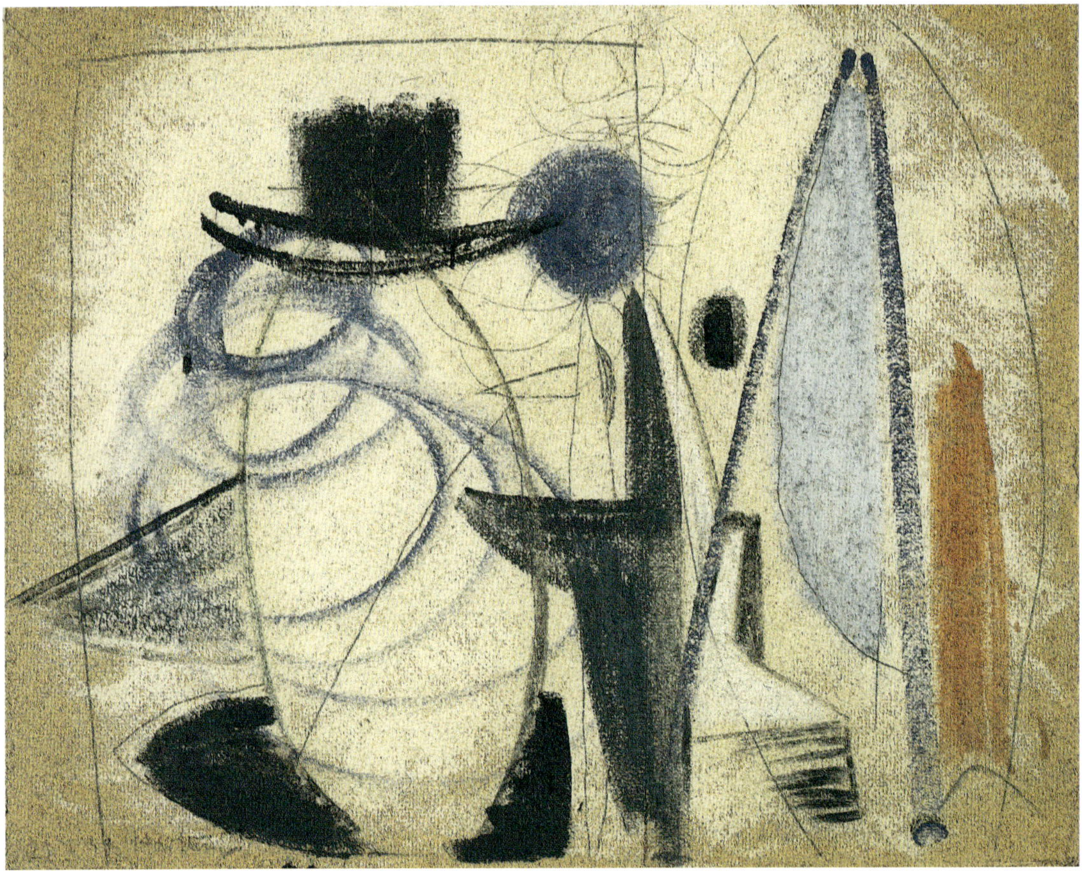

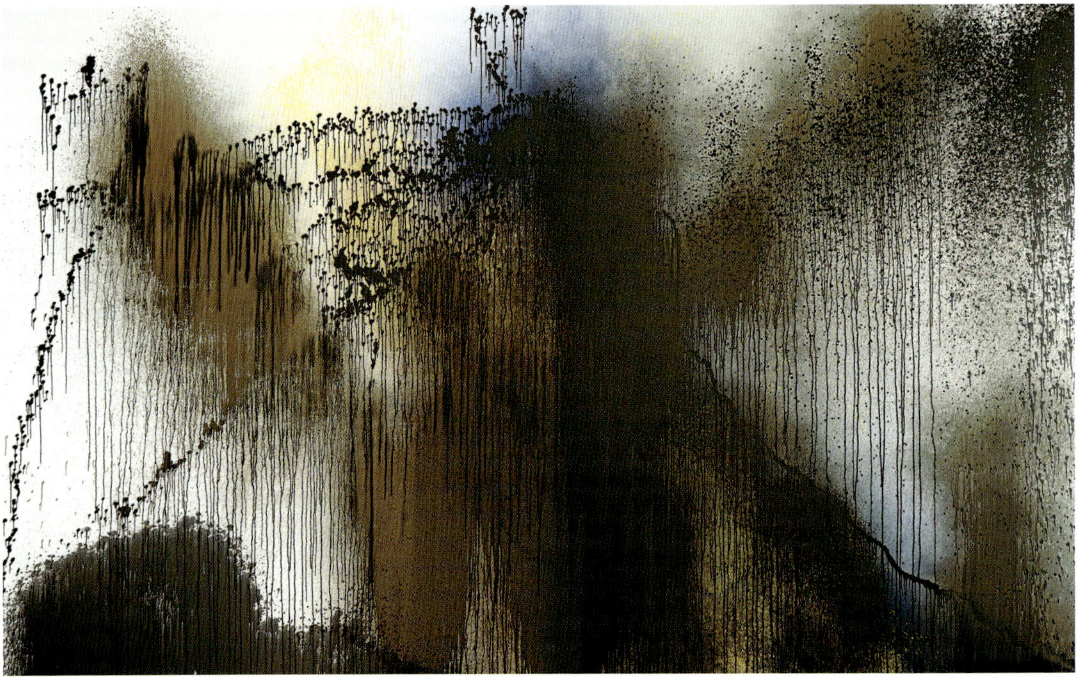

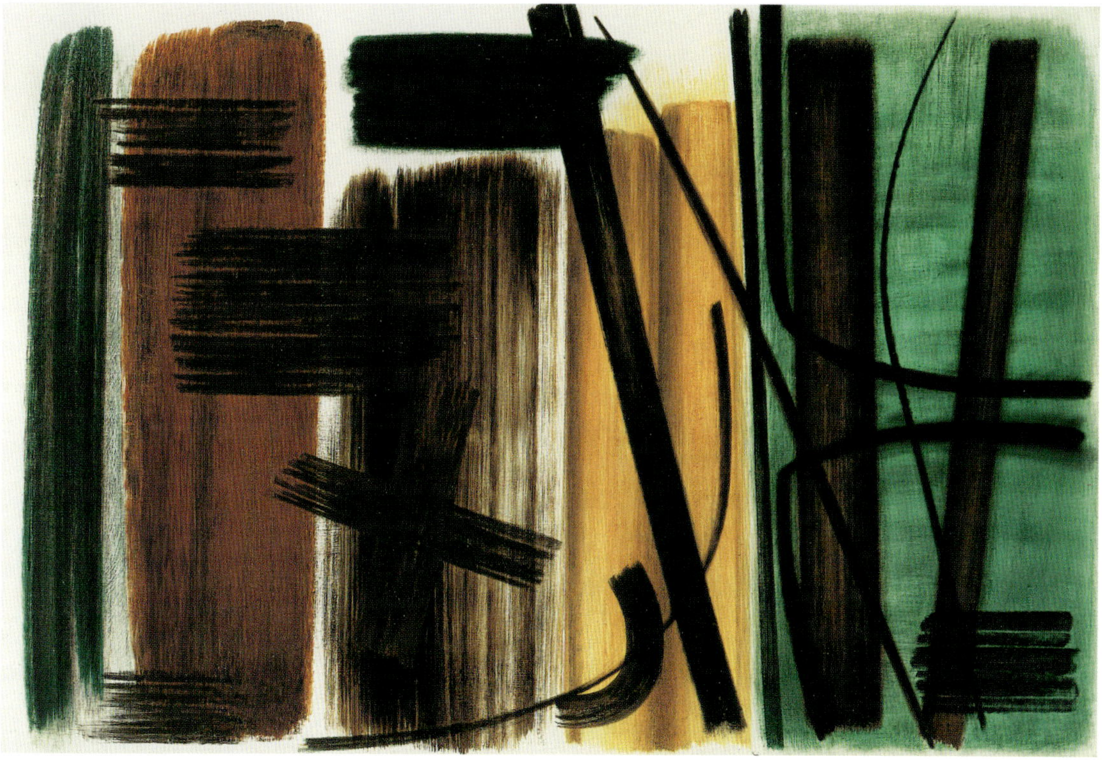

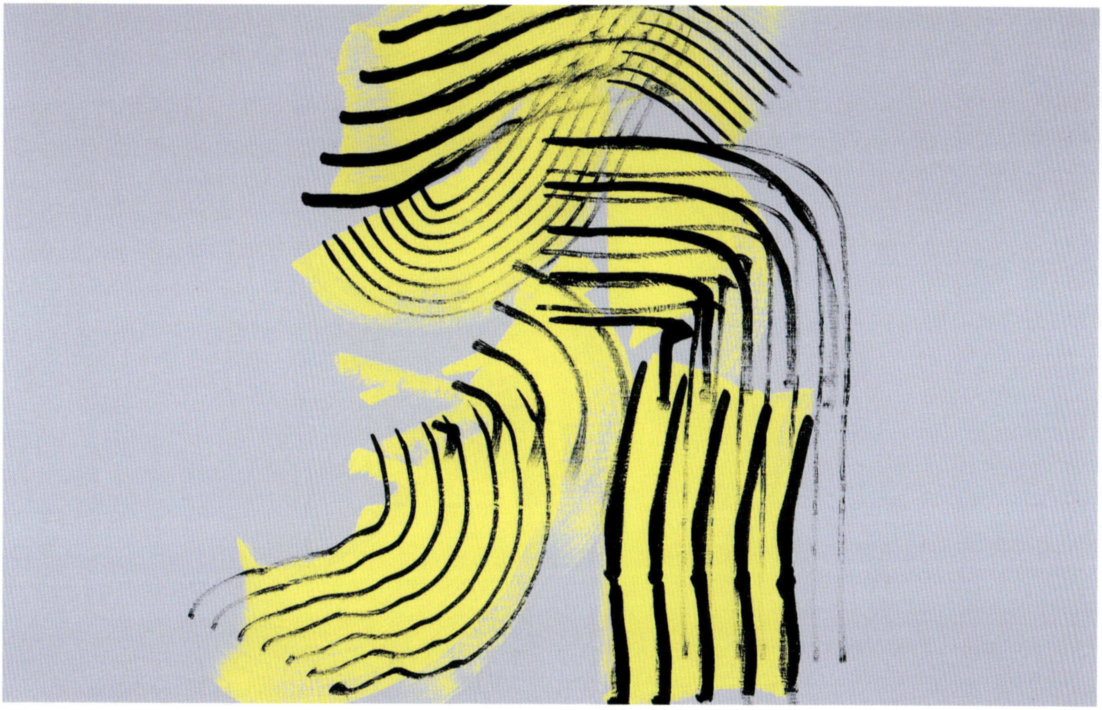

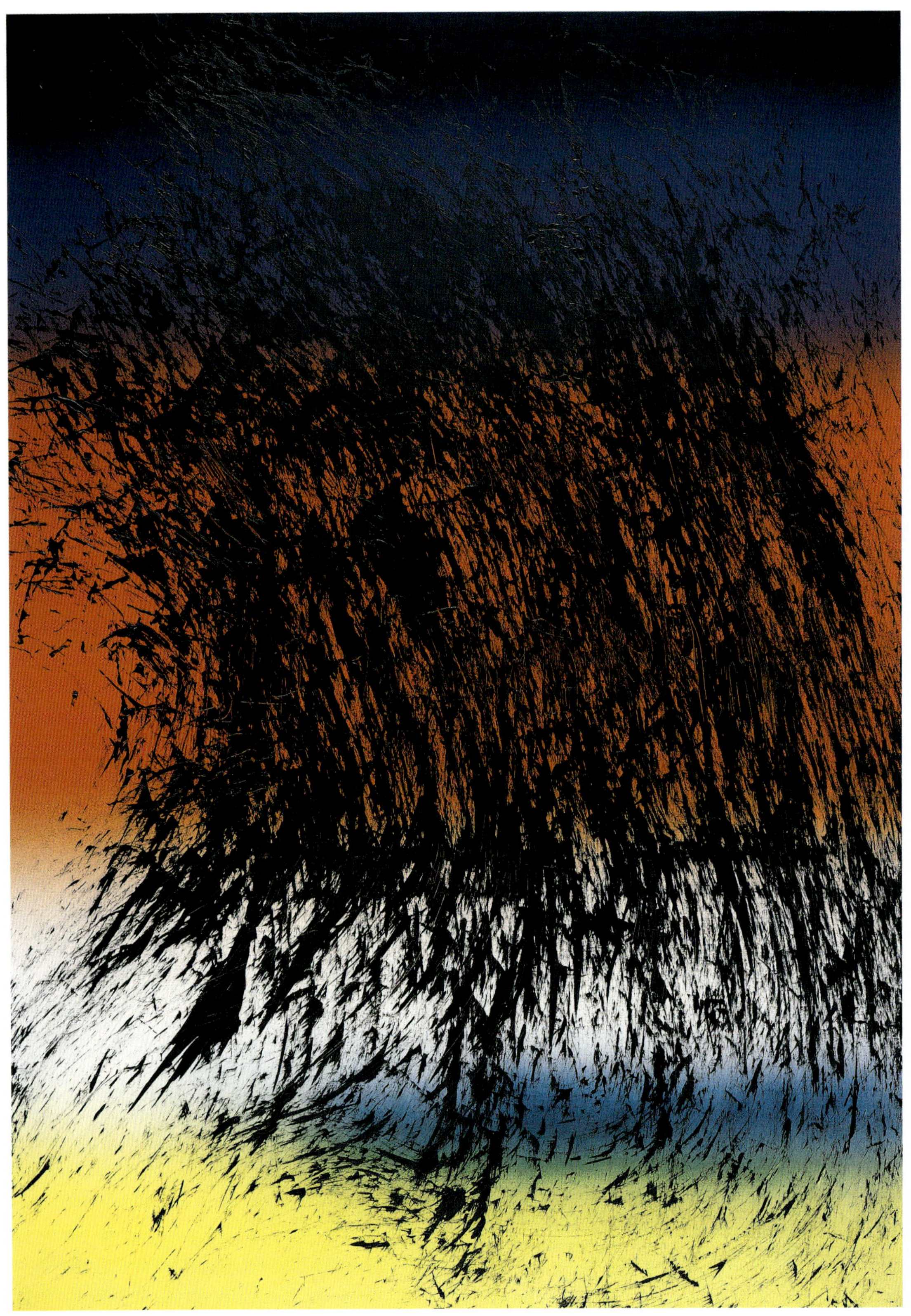

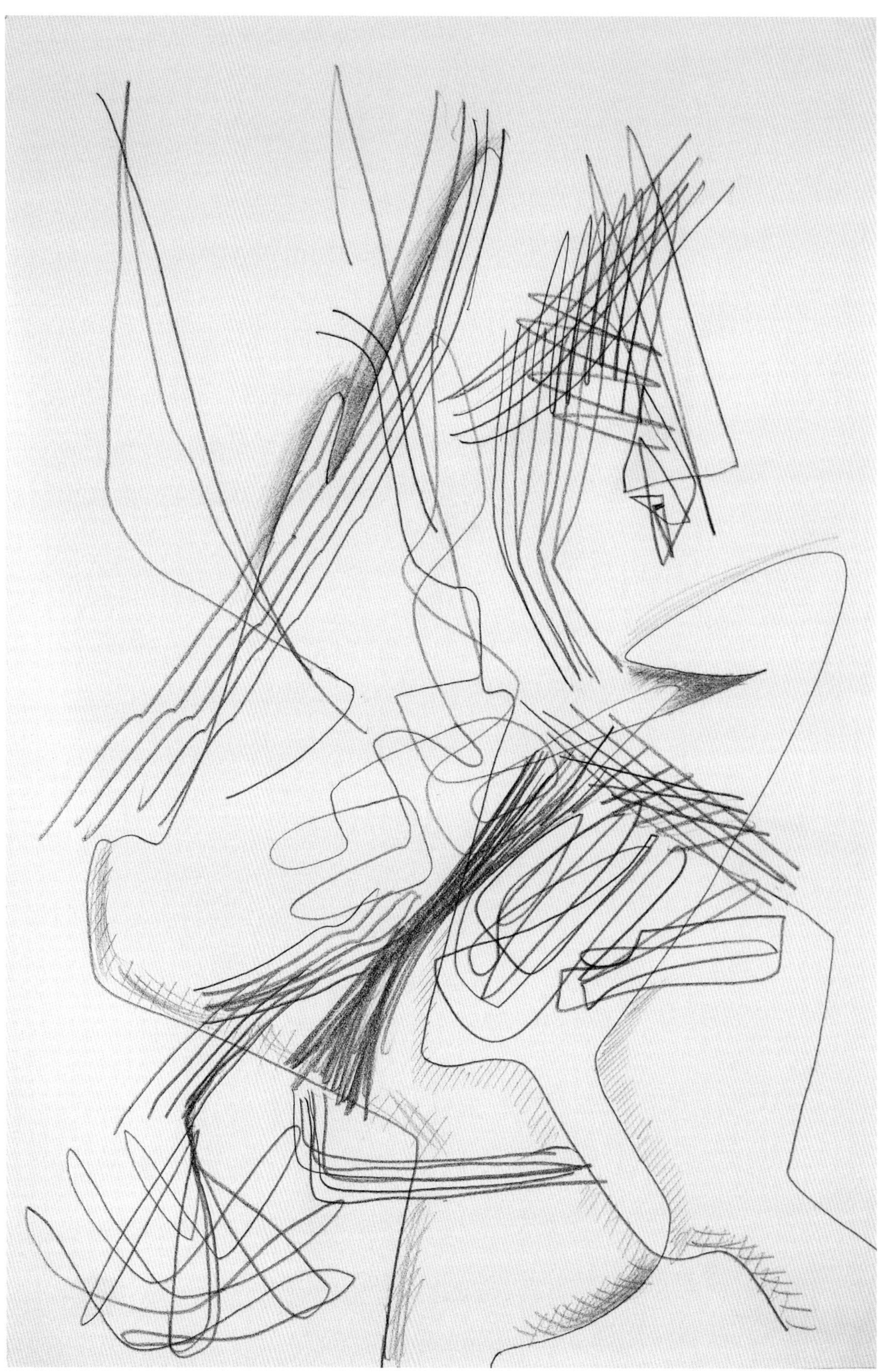

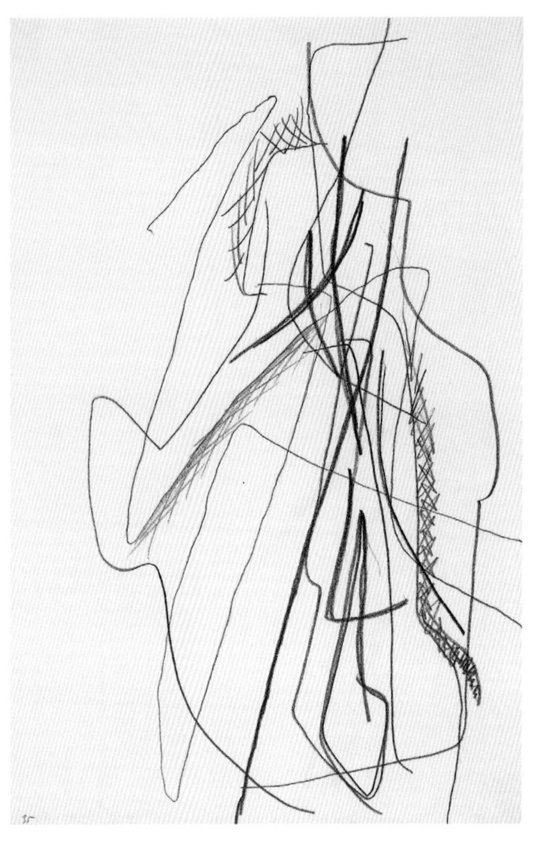
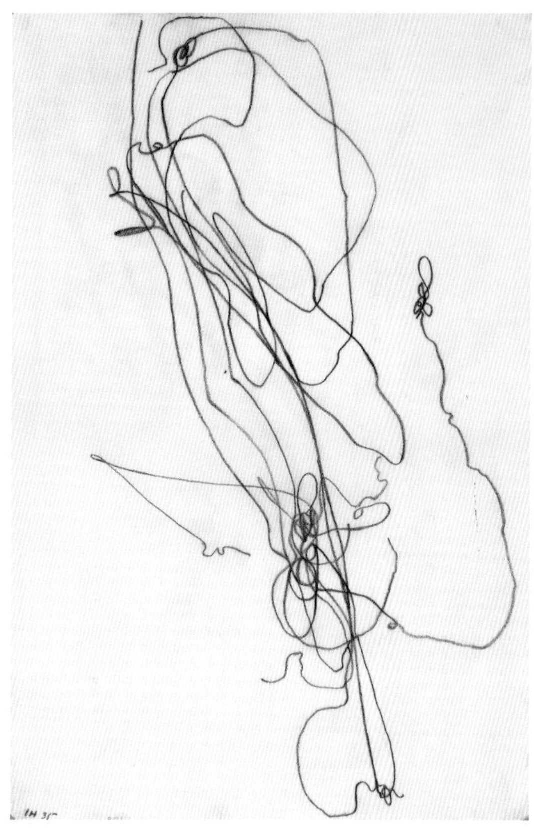
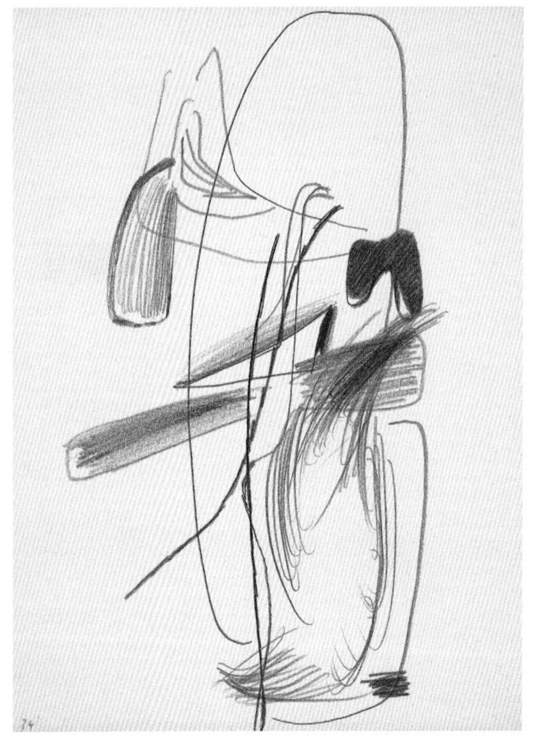
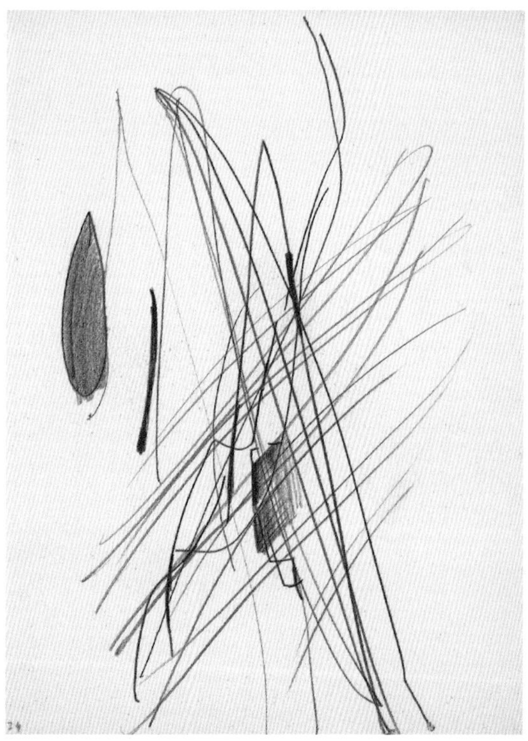

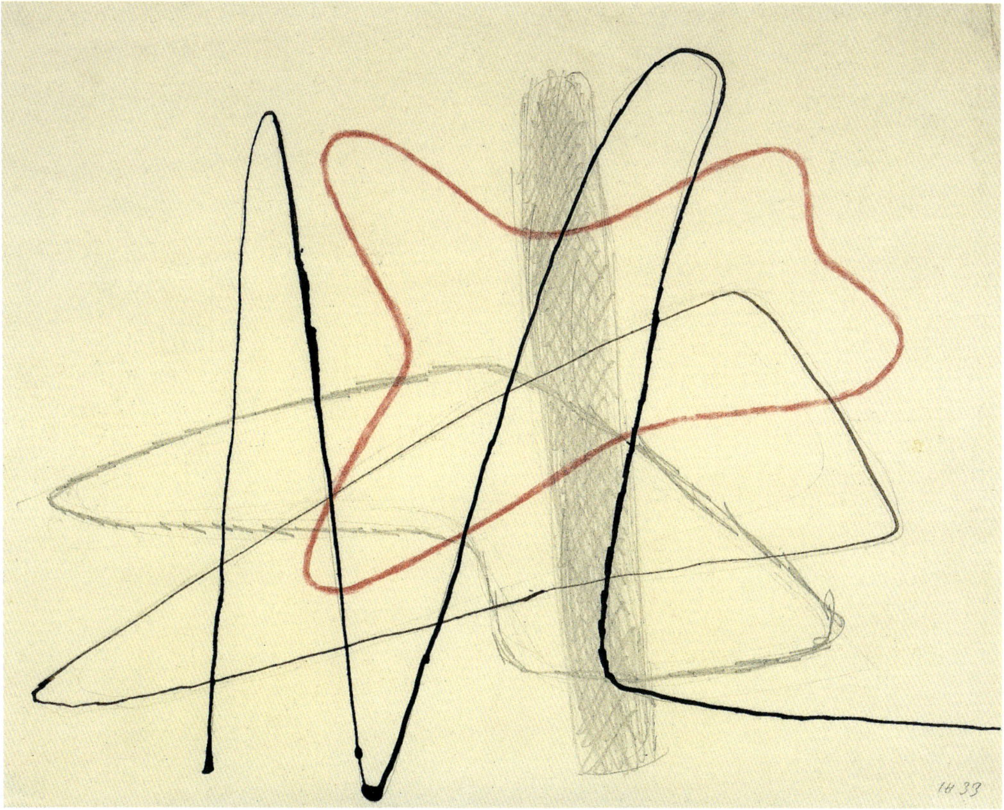

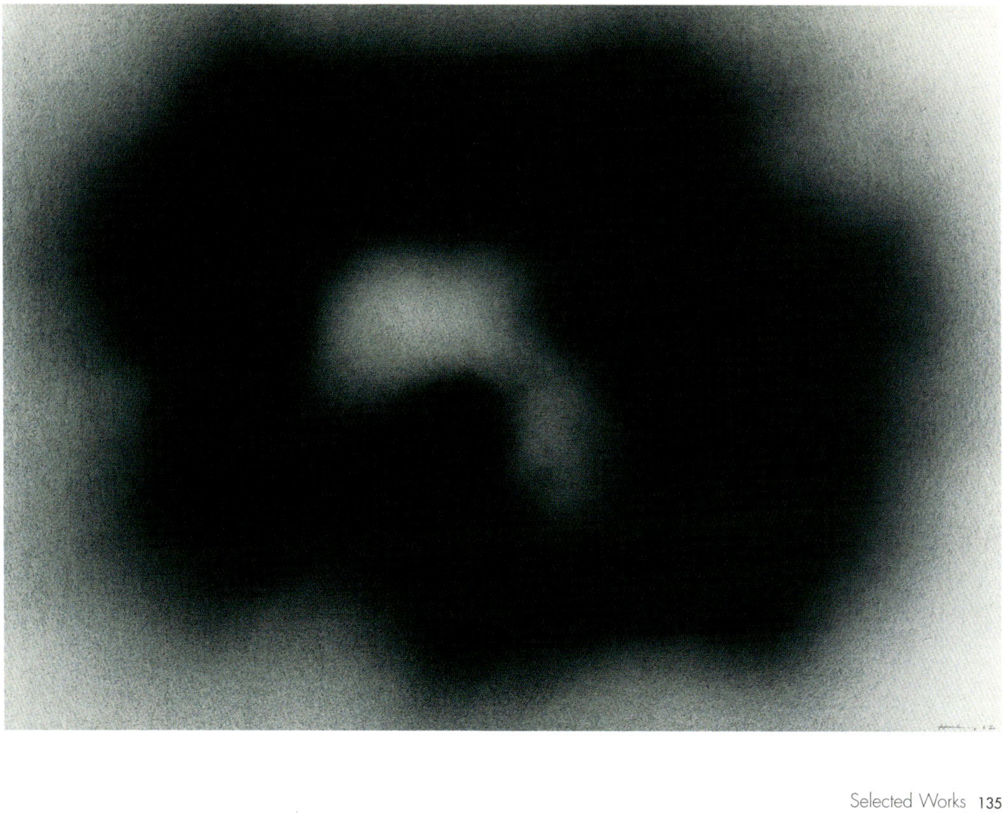

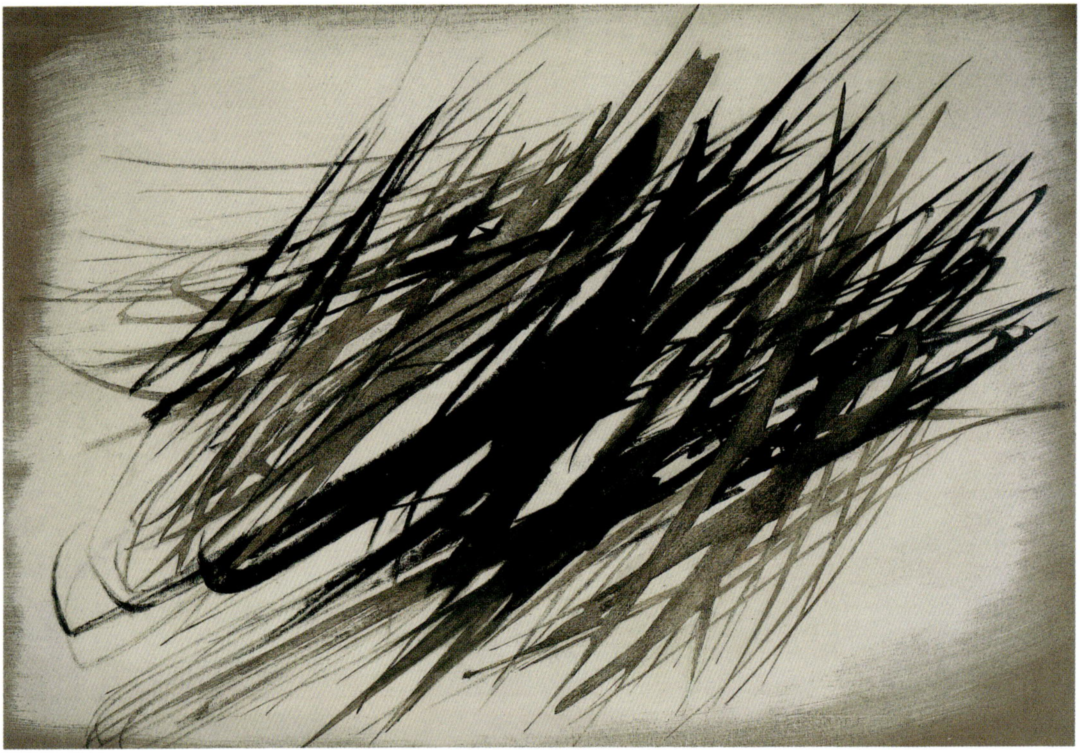

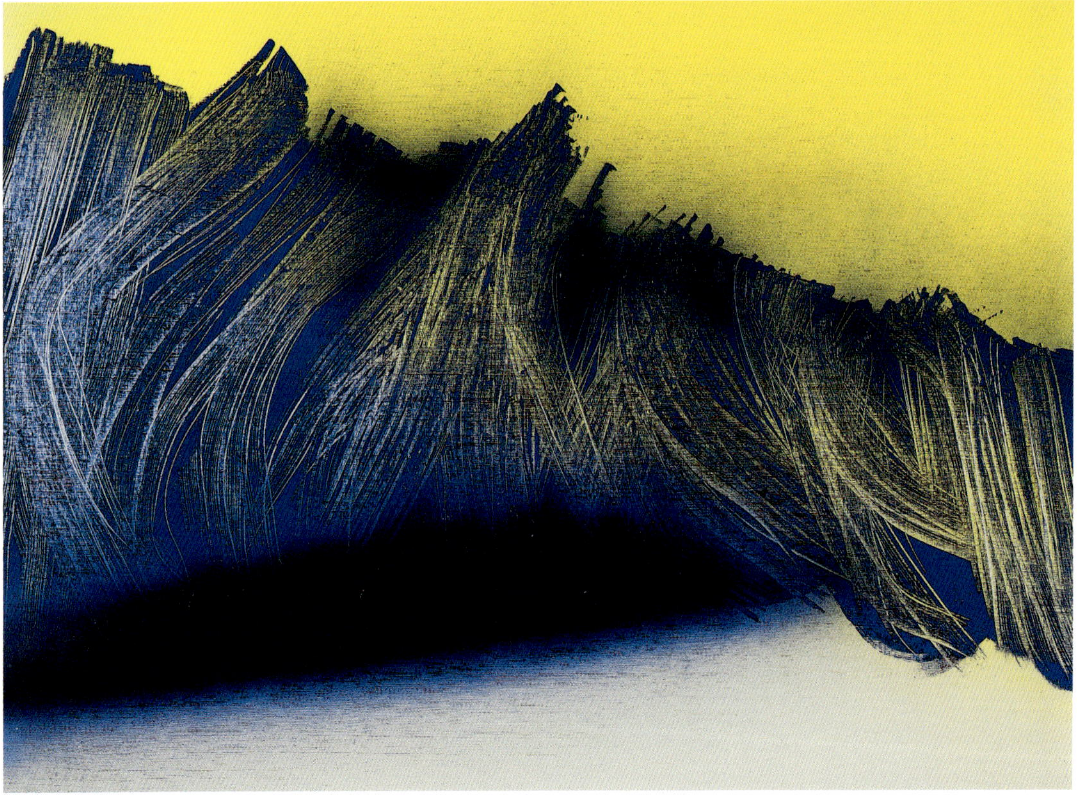

 Christopher Wool

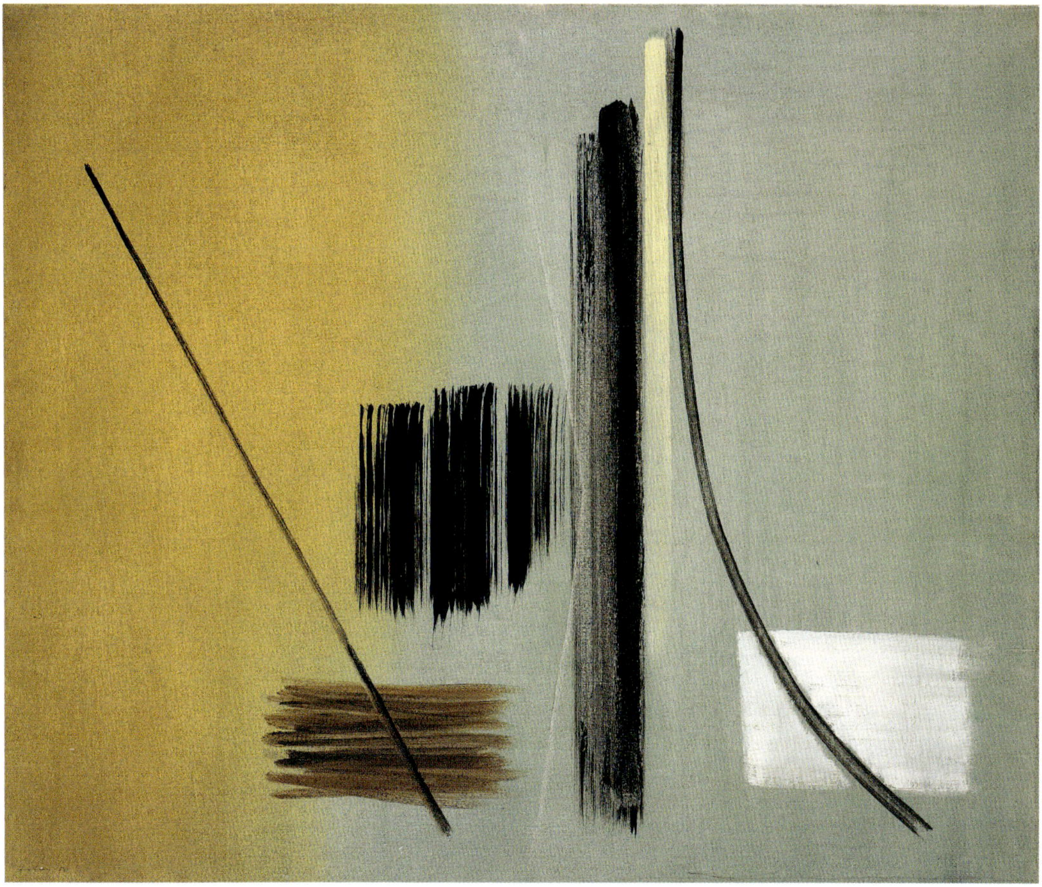

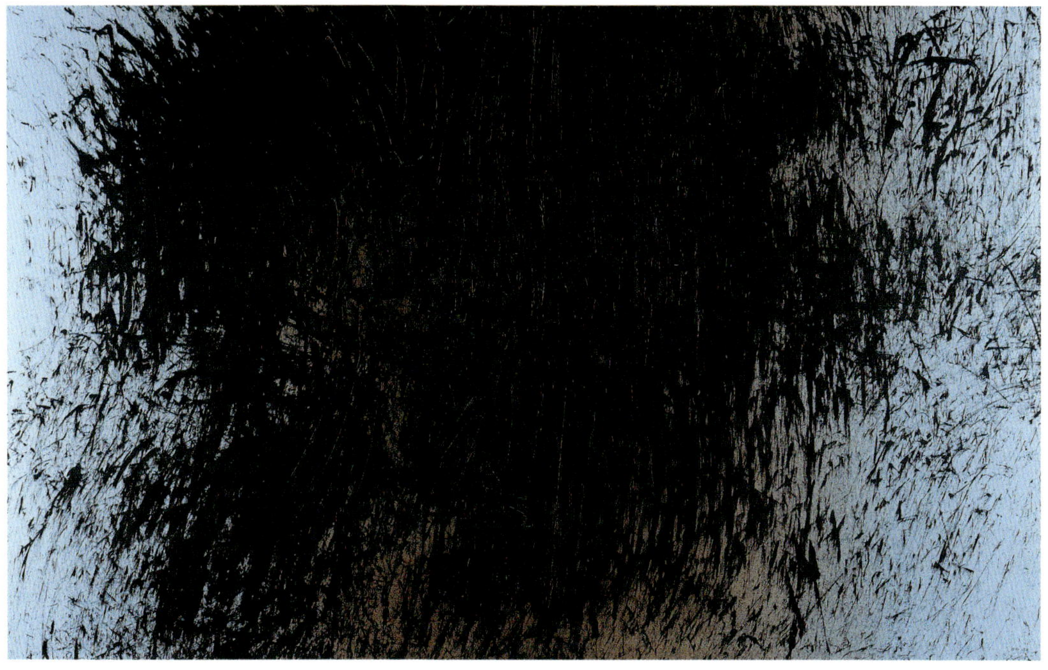

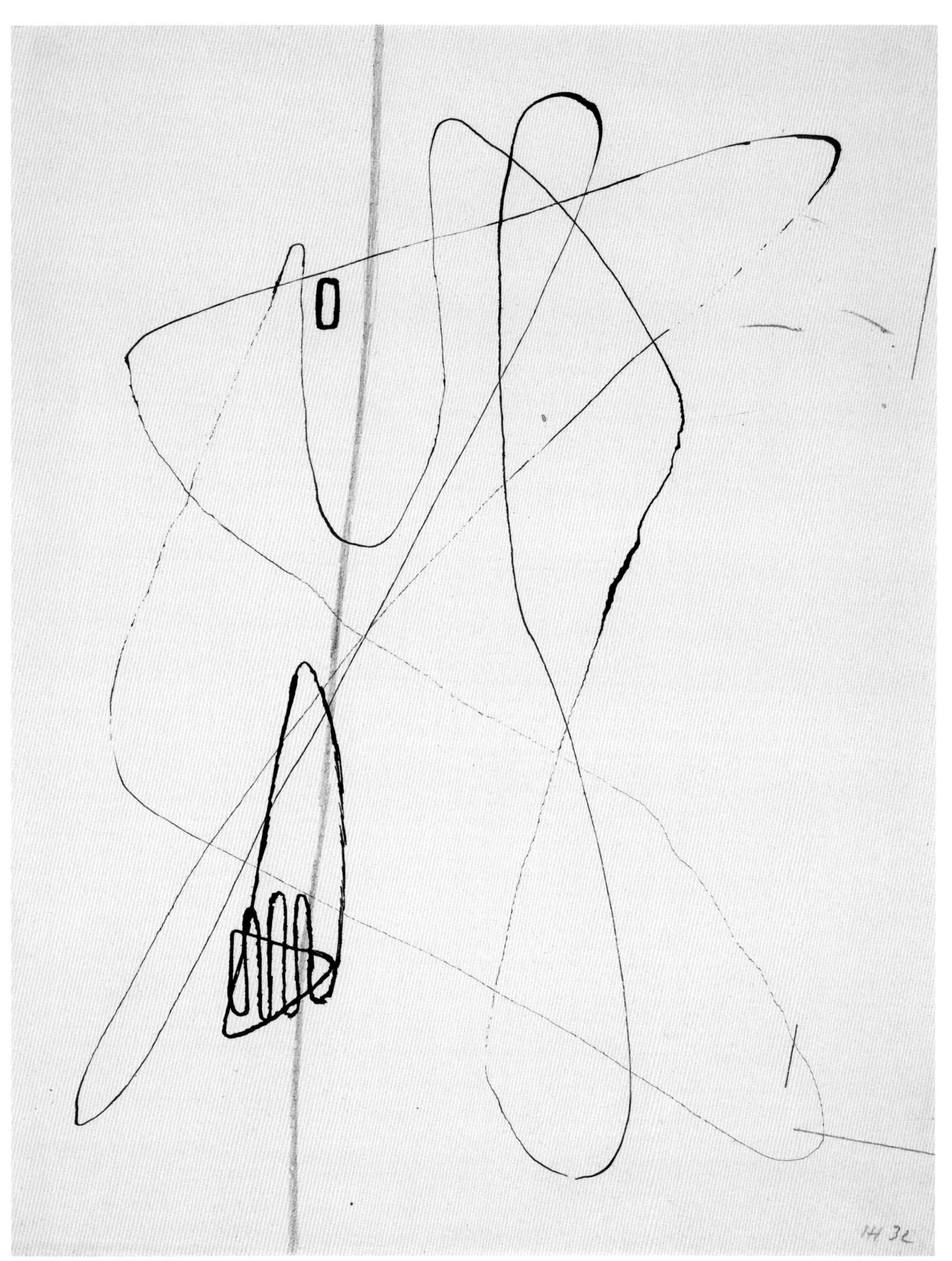

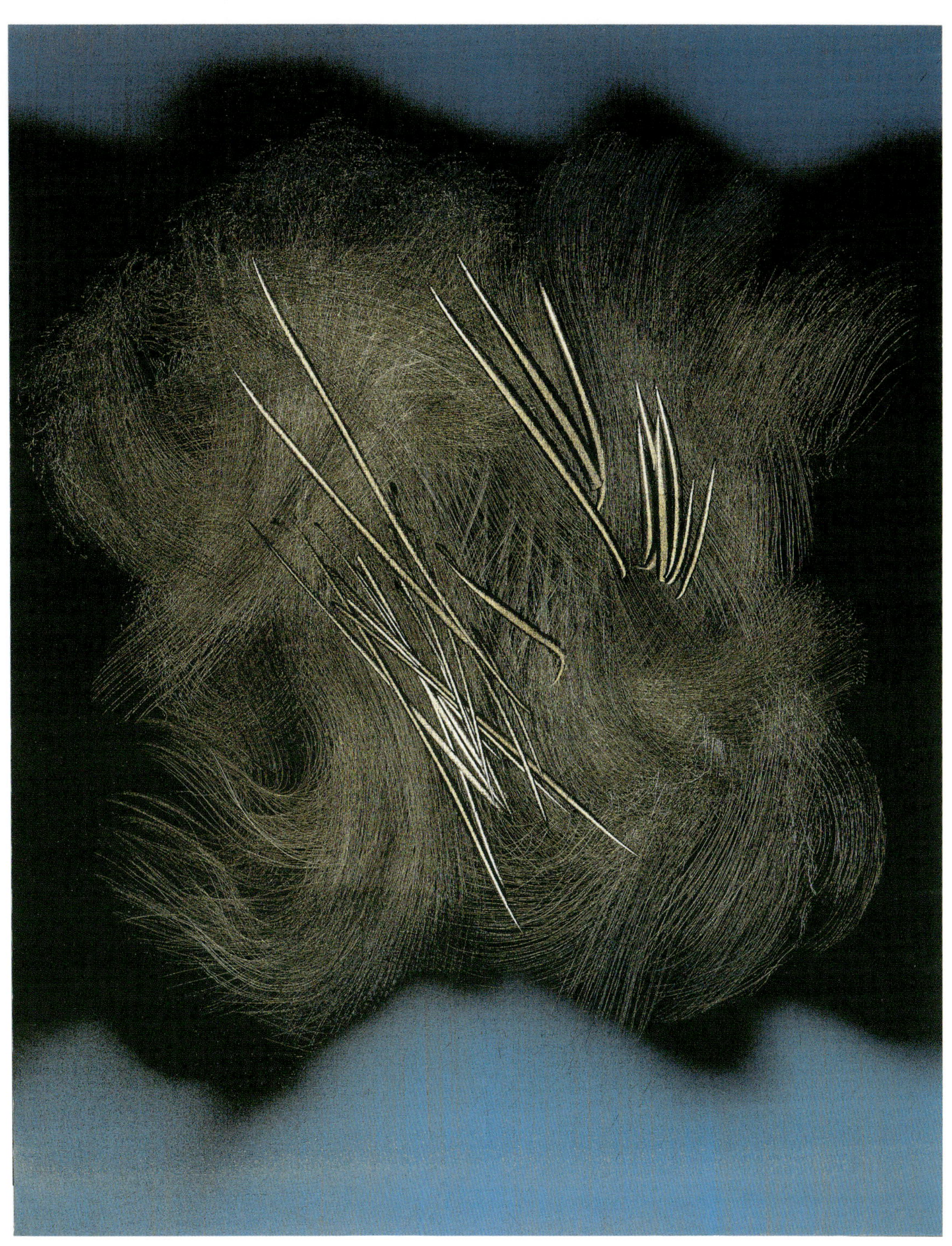

John C. Welchman Hans Hartung

Abcedarium: Reading Between the Lines

Franz-W. Kaiser A Case Study

on the Caducity of Categories

in Art Criticism Annie Claustres

Hans Hartung

Clandestine Artist

1937-1942: the Decisive Years

Christine Mehring Hans Hartung

Mid-Century Modern

Rainer Michael Mason Hartung

and Printmaking Christopher Wool

Selected Works

Anne Pontégnie 1975

Hartung at the

Metropolitan Museum

Chronicle of a Failure Chantal Eschenfelder

Hans Hartung in Germany

Laurence Bertrand Dorléac

Germany and France

Two Parts in One Jennifer Mundy

The Very Late Style of Hans Hartung

a Problem?

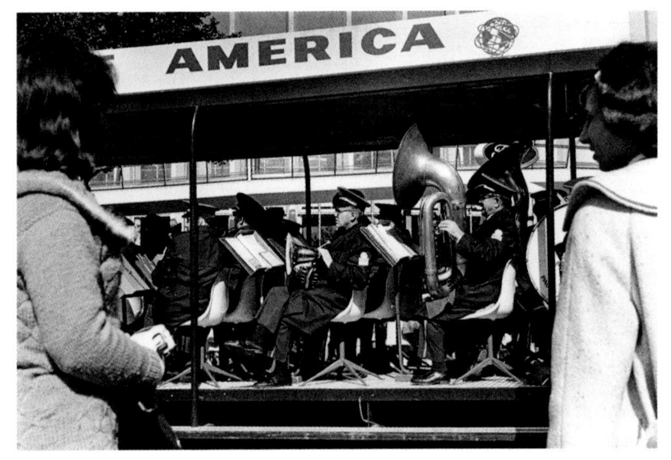

It may seem paradoxical to want to study the first monograph about Hartung, issued as part of his exhibition at the Metropolitan Museum in New York in 1975, since the show will go down in history as one of the most bitter failures of his career. Still, the story of this disappointment, which crowned fifteen years of effort by Hartung and his entourage, is a perfect illustration of how the artist's work was never accepted, or understood, in the United States. Certainly the political and cultural wars that raged between the United States and France since the end of World War II had a hand in the affair, but I have opted instead to approach it through a factual account that connects a whole cast of characters, their strategies to introduce Hartung's work to the American scene, and the systematic resistance of this scene to their efforts.

Hans Hartung's work had only been introduced to the United States from within the context of the second School of Paris, which went from the end of the 1940s to the 1950s. His work was included in group exhibitions like: 'Painted in 1949: European and American Painters' at the Betty Parsons Gallery, where, notably, it was shown alongside paintings by Pollock, and 'Advancing French Art' in 1950 at the Louis Carré Galleries, part of an exhibition that would eventually travel to the Museum of Art in San Francisco, the Art Institute in Chicago, and the Museum of Art in Baltimore. On top of that there were, in 1957 and 1959, exhibitions at the Kleeman Gallery and another in New York. American museums, either because they acquired or received them as a donation, came into possession of one or two 'palm-shaped' paintings emblematic of Hartung's production in the 1950s. Today MoMA, the Guggenheim, the Albright-Knox Gallery, the Fogg Art Museum in Cambridge (Massachusetts), and the Carnegie Museum in Pittsburgh are among the few institutions in the United States with something by Hartung in their collection. To my knowledge, no significant institutional collection in the United States owns anything Hartung produced after the 1950s.

This situation, linked as it was to the growing success of abstract American artists in Europe, had been a source of constant concern to Hartung and Myriam Prévot-Douatte, the director of the Galerie de France and Hartung's representative from the end of the 1950s onwards. It was also at that time, a good fifteen years prior to the exhibition at the Metropolitan Museum, that one of the key players in making the exhibition happen first appeared on the scene: the gallery owner John Lefebre. I have not been able to unearth any traces of the first meeting between Lefebre and Hartung, but it seems they had known each

1. HH, Trip to New York, 1964
2. HH, *T1948–17*, 1948, oil on canvas, 97 x 146 cm

other since the end of the 1940s, when Lefebre, a Berlin Jew who emigrated to New York in the Thirties, was posted to Paris as director of distribution for 20th Century Fox for Europe and the Middle East.[1] Hartung and Lefebre were both born the same year and emigrated during the same period. An enthusiastic collector of modern art, Lefebre eventually returned to New York towards the end of the 1950s, and the ensuing correspondence[2] between the two men is a testament to the fact that they spoke the same language, literally and figuratively. The tone of their exchanges reveals a great deal of familiarity, with each side dotted with allusions to their family lives. Clearly, though, it was John Lefebre who kept the relationship going in his hopes, more or less stated, of becoming Hartung's ambassador to the United States. Lefebre's ebullient enthusiasm for Hartung's work, and even for that of his wife, Anna-Eva Bergman, never once wavered. The beginning of the 1960s saw John Lefebre deciding to open a gallery in New York where he planned to present only European artists: Bissier, Corneille, Poliakoff, Alechinsky, etc. He never gave up trying to convince Hartung, and even Bergman, to allow the gallery to represent him. It was also roughly around this time that Lefebre started alluding to the possibility of convincing a big American institution of organising a Hartung retrospective. He wrote to Hartung on 15 February 1961: "As for the Hartung retrospective, I've been waging a relentless campaign, but a project of such magnitude cannot be mounted overnight—I'll keep working, though". It is clear that this was what eventually convinced Hartung to join his ranks—to the great dismay of Myriam Prévot-Douatte, who was herself working very hard to get an institution to take on such a retrospective via a more established network than the one commanded by the rookie Lefebre.

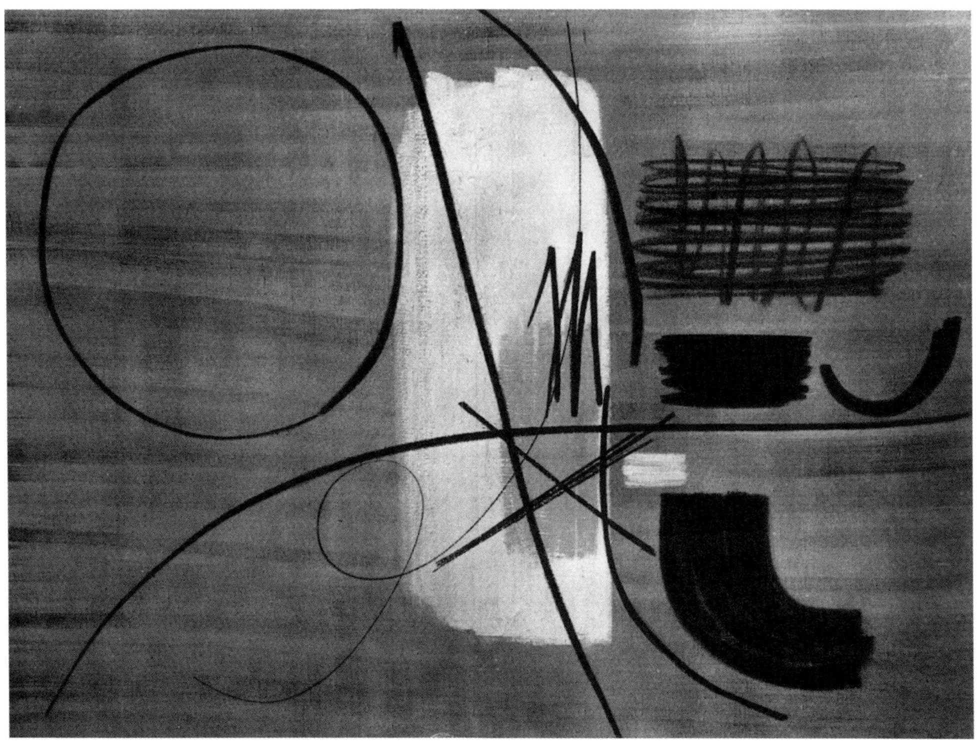

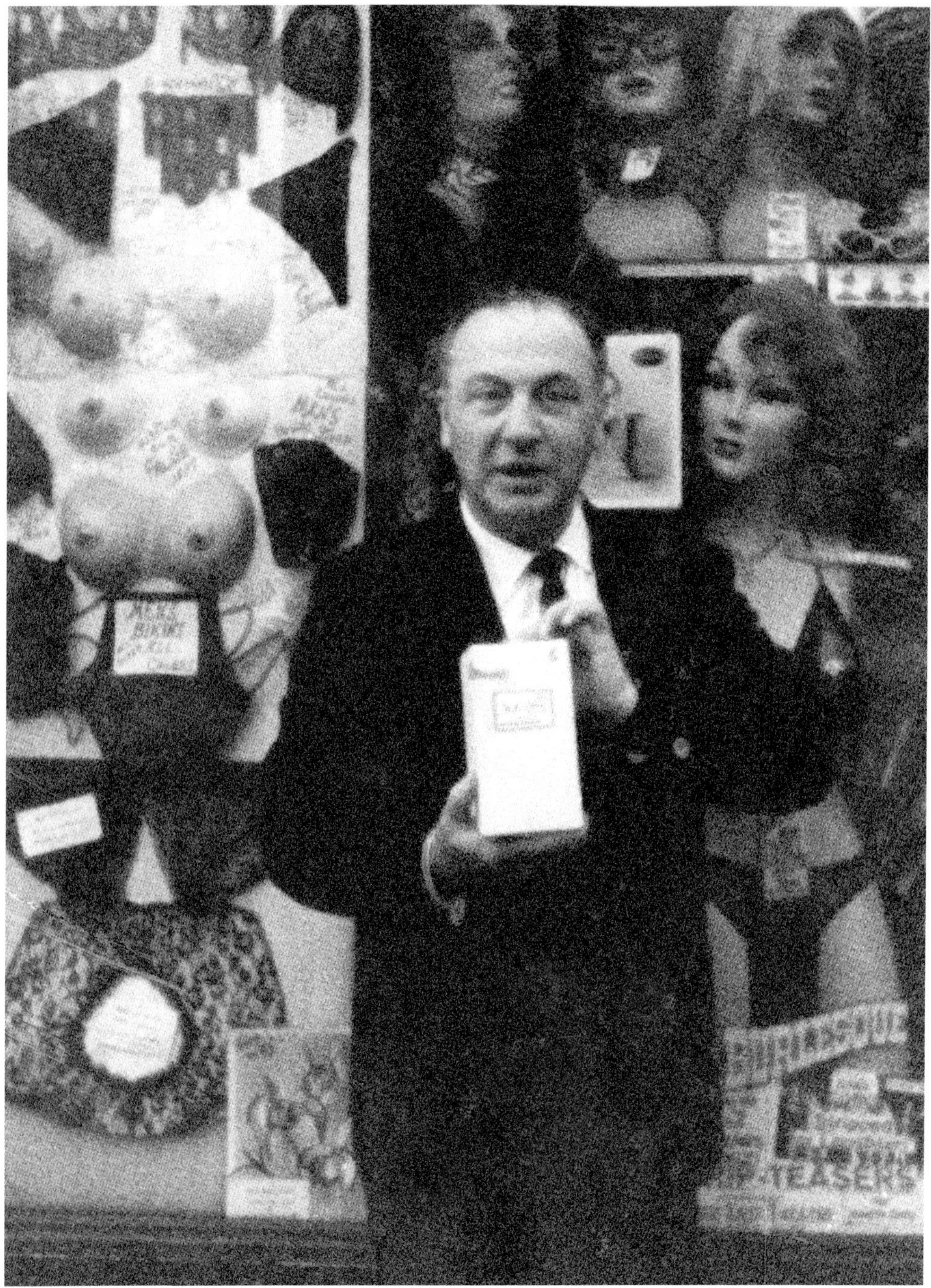

3. HH, Portrait of John Lefebre, New York, 1964

4. HH, Guggenheim Museum, 1969

5. Exhibition at the Emmerich Gallery, 1966

6. Exhibition at the Lefebre Gallery, 1971

In July 1962, Lefebre wrote to Hartung: "I talked to Thomas Messer[3] yesterday... We discussed the possibility of an exhibition at the Guggenheim. I reiterated to him that I had your agreement to discuss the matter with him. His answer was that, for the Guggenheim, we had to wait a little while still". On 24 December 1962, Prévot-Douatte received a letter from Thomas Messer telling her about his discussions with Lefebre and apologising for having to turn down the exhibition, citing the Guggenheim's already "over-committed" schedule as the reason. A little further on he added, quelling all hope: "I am therefore reluctantly reconciled to the possibility that we may lose out on now existing opportunities".

Three years later, Myriam Prévot-Douatte wrote to Hartung from the Beverly Hills Hotel to tell him that Larry Aldrich—a well-known art collector who opened his own museum in Connecticut—had agreed to being in charge of a retrospective of his work and of making it travel around the United States with the aid of the Smithsonian Institution. This particular retrospective finally materialised in 1969, though instead of the promised American tour, Hartung had to "settle" for the Fine Arts Museum in Houston, followed by the Musée du Québec and the Musée d'Art Moderne in Montreal. In a letter

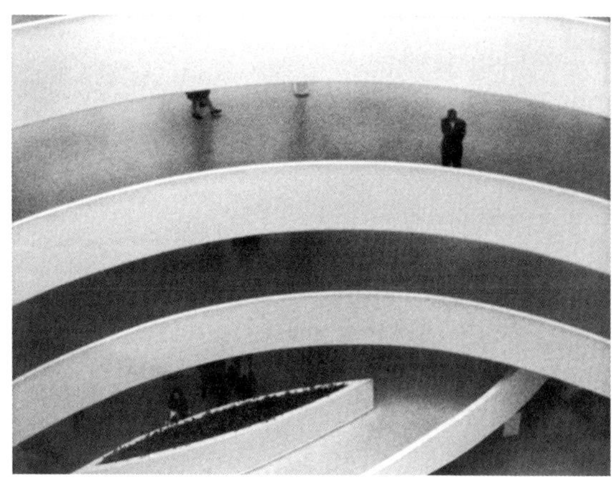

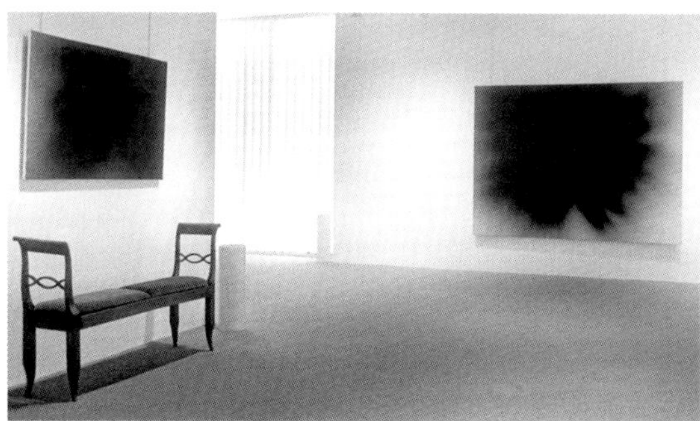

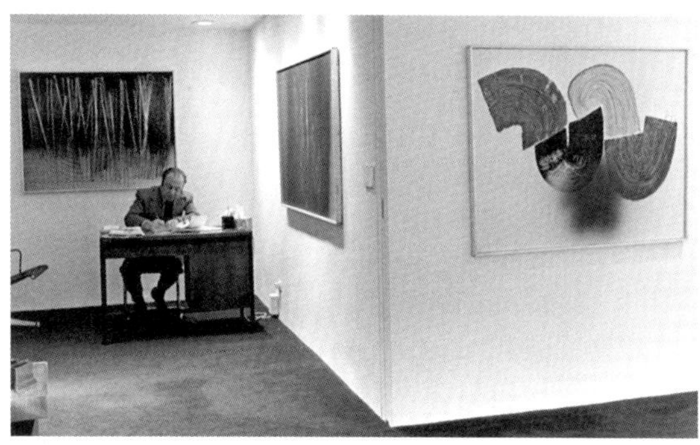

written on 26 March 1965, Prévot-Douatte says: "the only embarrassing thing is that John Lefebre 'has jumped in', no one quite knows why, and wants a carbon copy of the correspondence, etc". The reason for this "embarrassment" became clear a few lines later. Myriam Prévot-Douatte recounts her meeting in the bar of the Hotel Pierre in New York with gallery owner André Emmerich, who represented Helen Frankenthaler, Morris Louis, Kenneth Noland and Jules Olitski. Emmerich was enthusiastic about organising an exhibition of Hartung's recent works for the spring of 1966. What's more, he committed himself to guaranteeing twenty thousand dollars in sales, which, as Prévot-Douatte remarked, "is not bad at all considering the circumstances 'abstract expressionism' is in". She added, a little troubled: "It's not even that they are against the School of Paris here—it's more as if Paris didn't exist at all and nothing from there could interest them".

recession was then hitting its stride, for Hartung to decide to work with John Lefebre. Hartung and Lefebre signed a commercial contract at the very beginning of the 1970s.[6] They decided to organise a first exhibition for the following year, for which Hartung prudently selected only recent works: twelve paintings on paper and six on canvas. John Lefebre succeeded in selling six of the ones on paper and two canvases, and that "in spite of the recession", as he mentioned in many of his letters.[7] Critical reception is again lukewarm. In September 1971, he announced to Hartung: "I've spoken again with the director of the Metropolitan, Henry Geldzahler, and he is very interested in the possibility of acquiring a Hartung".[8] Some of the works reproduced in the catalogue of the Pittsburgh International Exhibition, held at the Carnegie Institute in Pittsburgh, 1967, had stuck in Geldzahler's mind.[9] In a letter dated 25 October 1971, Hartung replied to Geldzahler's selection: "the watercolours of 1922 were all done with aniline colours and hence can tolerate no light at all. Which is why I've already had to refuse selling them many times"—let's not forget that five years earlier Hartung himself had urged Emmerich to introduce precisely one of these works to the United States—"I'm afraid the same is true about the watercolour from 1938... which is, by the way, so small that I have a hard time imagining it in a museum... The painting reproduced on page 124 was bought by the Rome Museum. All that's left is the painting on page 201 *(T1966–H 33)*. I am particularly attached to this painting, but, if you tell me that it will always be on display at the Metropolitan Museum, and not just periodically (I would like to be certain on this point), I would sell it for 90 thousand francs for myself... That would be quite a mark down already". Geldzahler had settled on his final choice by 9

10. HH, *T1965-E33*, 1965, acrylic on canvas, 154 x 250 cm
11. Hans Hartung in his exhibition at the Metropolitan Museum of Art, 1975

November, by which point he had suddenly come to think that the painting selected, which had been the last choice of his original selection, was a "masterpiece".[10] In Paris in March 1972, Geldzahler asked to see the painting in Hartung's studio. Lefebre sent word of Geldzahler's plans to visit the Hartungs in Paris both to Hartung himself and to Myriam Prévot-Douatte, who was no more than a spectator in the latest developments. Back in New York, Geldzahler finally decided for a different *Nuage* painting, *T1965–H33*, which was subsequently sent to Lefebre. Geldzahler dropped by at the gallery to see the piece in April. The Trustees of the Metropolitan Museum met on 12 June and Lefebre predicted a "happy ending" to the deal. On 23 June, Geldzahler wrote to Hartung to let him know that the Trustees had agreed to buy the work.

The time seemed ripe for Lefebre to launch the offensive he'd been preparing for ten years. In February 1973, Geldzahler sent a note to Hartung thanking him for the gift of a small painting that the artist had offered him through Lefebre. Henry Geldzahler then went to see Hartung in Paris in November 1973 to make a preliminary selection of the works for the exhibition at the Metropolitan Museum. The list from 28 November 1973, now in the care of the Fondation Hartung, comprises a selection of crayons and watercolours from the 1920s and a set of more recent, larger works. In the autumn of 1974, Geldzahler again visited the Hartungs, in Antibes this time, to prepare the exhibition which was scheduled to open in October 1975. The list of selected works underwent some alteration,[11] though I have found no clues as to what motivated the changes. The exhibition was then to be composed only of recent works: 20 large paintings, all dating from some time between 1971 and 1975. Lefebre, for his part, organised an exhibition of drawings, old and new, that was also due to open that same October. Lefebre had also been trying to convince the gallery of Associated American Artists, where Hartung had already exhibited some prints in 1965, to organise an exhibition during the same period. Sylvan Cole, the gallery's director, wrote to Myriam Prévot-Douatte

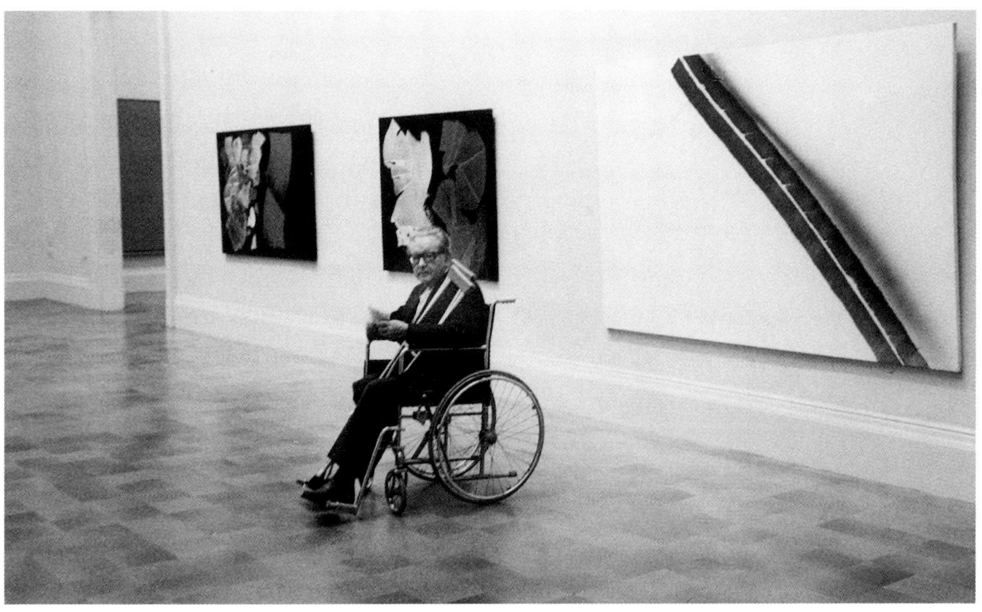

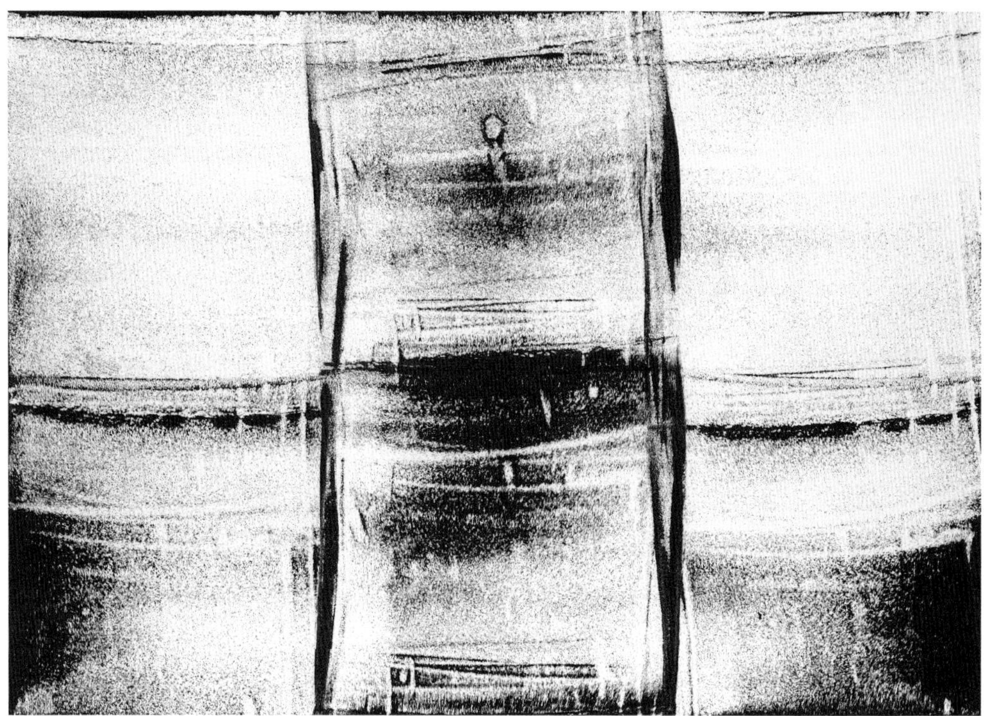

and to Hartung on 21 August 1975: "John Lefebre has called me... to discuss our having an exhibition of Hans' graphics during the show at the Metropolitan Museum and Lefebre Gallery... My schedule is fairly rigid, but by juggling a few exhibitions, I can have an exhibition of Hans' prints opening 3 November and running through 26 November. Lefebre requested that I open a week later, but I cannot do this". The lithographs and etchings exhibited there were also all new, done sometime between 1971 and 1973. In short, all the works on show in New York were recent: the paintings at the Metropolitan Museum, the paintings on paper at Lefebre, and the prints at the AAA.

Hartung celebrated his seventieth birthday in 1974. An enormous retrospective, *Hans Hartung Retrospektive 1921–1974*, was organised for the occasion in Germany, where it travelled to the Wallraf-Richartz Museum in Cologne, the National Gallery in Berlin and the Lenbachhaus in Munich. *Cimaise* dedicated a special issue to Hartung that covered his entire oeuvre;[12] the issue included a text by Geldzahler that essentially restates what he had to say about Hartung in the text published in the catalogue for the exhibition at the Metropolitan Museum, and a text by John Lefebre about Berlin in the 1920s. Hartung's work passed into history, much to the delight of the artist, who had always craved to have his role as a pioneer recognised. Hartung continued, from the beginning of the 1970s up until his death in 1989, to produce a great body of new work, to experiment and renew his style, and he never once doubted the pertinence of his new production. This belief, coupled with commercial reasons,

12. HH, *T1975-E20*, 1975, acrylic on canvas, 114 x 162 cm, Centre Pompidou, Paris
13. HH, *T1975-R35*, 1975, acrylic on canvas, 180 x 180 cm

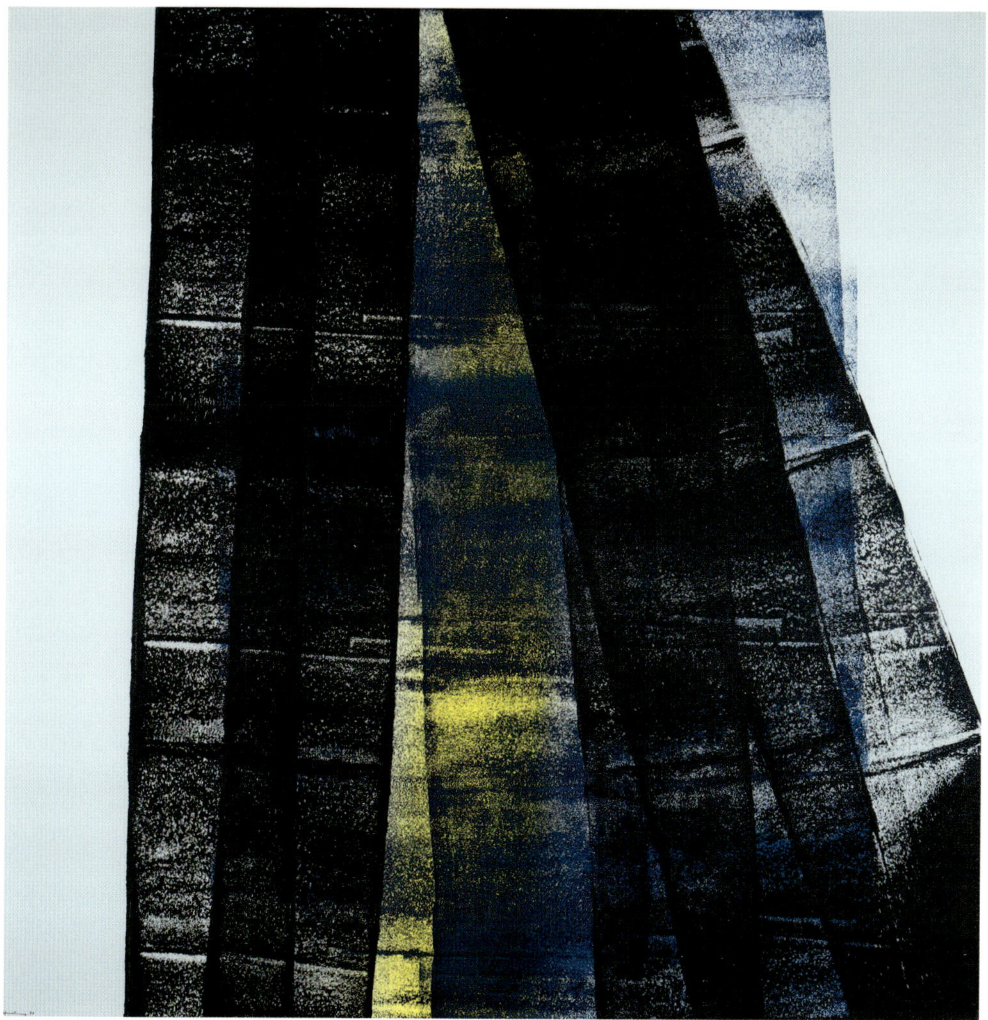

explains why he always stuck to the idea that his new output should be recognised as being on a par with the now historical works. In his *Autoportrait*, Hartung wrote: "Since 1970, I have had the feeling of a renewal. As if I had been granted new energy, a new youth. And, above all, the need to make great paintings".[13] In an interview with *Le Quotidien de Paris* a short while before the exhibition at the Metropolitan Museum, Hartung said: "It was only at the end of their lives that Michelangelo, Goya, Rembrandt and Bonnard produced what is essential in their art".[14]

But did Hartung really think that the two retrospectives dedicated to his work, in Houston in 1969 and in Germany in 1974, were enough to secure his place in history? Or that the exhibit at the Metropolitan Museum of Art was sure proof of the vitality of his recent work, as well as the opportunity to be considered with the giants of American Abstraction? Geldzahler had sent Hartung a list of questions in an attempt to define Hartung's position on American artists. "I saw exhibitions of American painting in the years 1951, 1952, 1953, I think, especially at the Galerie de France, the Galerie Fachetti, and the Galerie Maeght. The exhibition at the Galerie de France included, among others, works by Kline, Pollock,

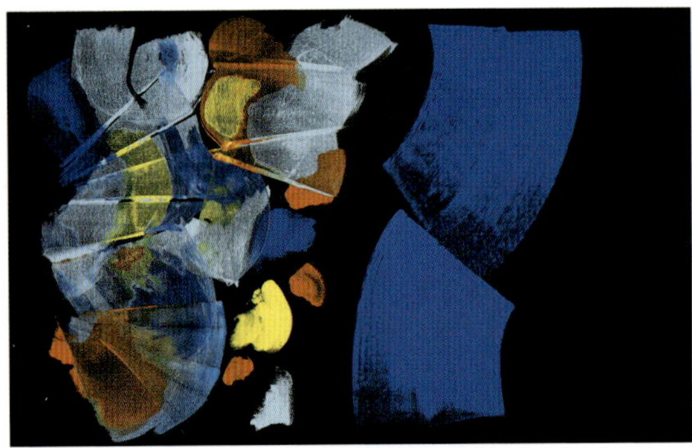

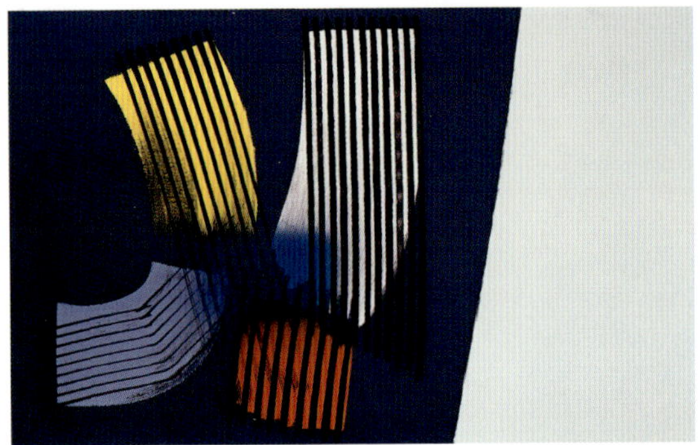

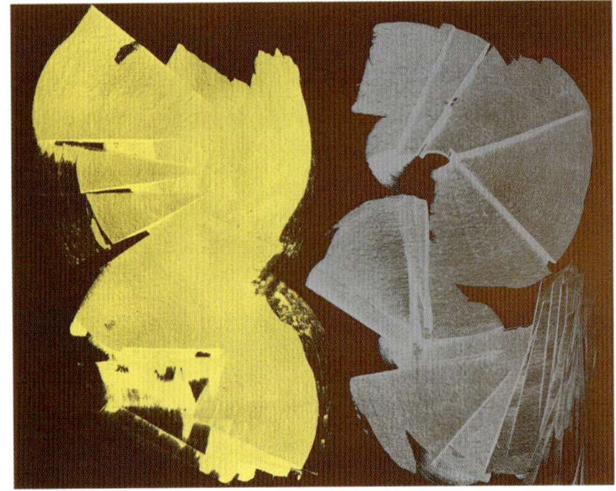

Motherwell… and I thought we had infected them" he replied with pride.[15] When he brought up Kline a little later, he wrote: "The canvases were very large details whose sense and content had become something other than what had given them birth". From after the war up to the beginning of the 1960s, Hartung worked by transferring onto canvas signs he had previously drawn with ink or pastel on small sheets of paper. Whether as a precursor or colleague, Hartung seems to have been claiming a kinship between his work and the work of American abstract artists. He wrote in *Autoportrait*: "I think it's important to insist on the enormous difference between 'geometrical' abstract art and another movement that only found its real voice after the war. By which I mean the art that got tagged with many, and quite inexact, names such as Lyrical art, Non-Figurative art, Abstract Expressionism, Art Informel, Action Painting, Tachism, etc."[16] Still, a little further on in his replies to Geldzahler's questions, he added: "When I saw American paintings in the 1950s, the enormous dimension of the canvases left me stupefied, even a bit jealous at what was certainly a very fertile environment where people could dare works of such dimensions and where one could grow differently than how we did here". Hartung made his wish to align himself with American artists very clear in each of his answers: "They gave me a second great confirmation of everything I defended, and that was very comforting". But, as we shall see, Hartung had much harsher words for American abstract art once the failure at the Metropolitan had been fully consummated.

The doors of the exhibition opened on 10 October 1975 with twenty-seven paintings distributed across three galleries on the ground floor of the museum, the one normally reserved

14. HH, *T1971-R15*, 1971, acrylic on canvas, 111 x 180 cm

15. HH, *T1973-R13*, 1973, acrylic on canvas, 154 x 250 cm, private collection

16. HH, *T1971-R12*, 1971, acrylic on canvas, 114 x 146 cm

17. HH, *T1973-R14*, 1973, acrylic, 154 x 250 cm

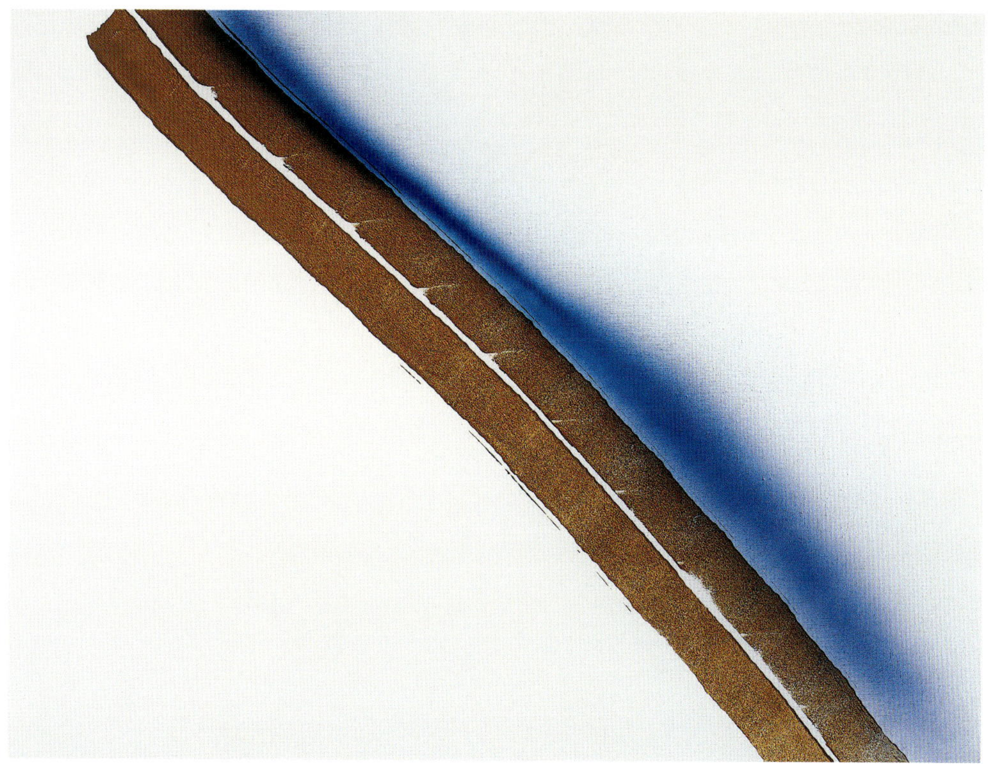

for temporary exhibitions. Hartung, who was always very attentive to this aspect, arranged the paintings airily and elegantly. All the works are medium-sized to large, ranging between 100 x 162 cm and 185 x 300 cm. Characteristics of the work from the beginning of the Seventies were the use of pure colours, with blues and yellows dominating, and of violent contrasting combinations. The traces that cross the paintings resulted from Hartung's experiments with different tools. There is very little expressivity, no gesture save for that produced mechanically, few if any material effects, and motifs running like imprints through the space of the canvases. During those years, Hartung was working exclusively with tools that introduced a distance between the gesture and the medium. He was using a wide variety of instruments: brush handles that he elongated with five or eight very small rollers (multiple rollers), with five or eight brushes (multiple brushes), or with brooms (very large brushes); and he was also working with rollers that had been altered to some degree by blank spots, postage stamps, and by different types of paint propellers (airbrush, airgun, roughcasting machine). Hartung was working with a set of tools that create a temporal and/or material distance between the gesture of the painter and the result on the pictorial surface. He himself pointed out that his work from the 1970s resulted to a large extent from his work in lithography, where the tool prevents all direct relationship between pictorial intention and its realisation. When looked at through the internal prism in Hartung's work, the freshness of these paintings is indeed remarkable and their inventiveness a clear sign of the artist's capacity to renew himself constantly. However, they proved unreadable when examined by a public who knew next to nothing about the artist's history and were enmeshed in the American artistic context of the

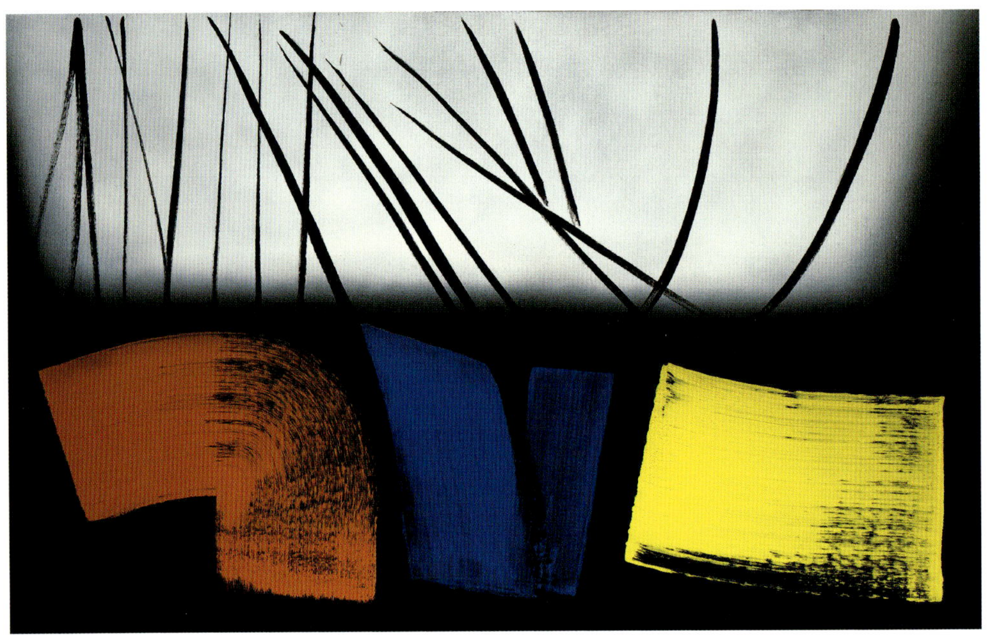

early 1970s dominated by Minimalism and Pop. There is, for instance, a noticeable embarrassment with regard to the more recent works in the text Geldzahler wrote for the catalogue. Although his text was ostensibly about them, he spends 10 out of the 12 pages retracing Hartung's career. When Geldzahler actually addresses the new works, he evokes Brahms and Leonardo da Vinci, talks about vigour and vitality, and discusses the largeness of the format and the institutionalisation of the work, but carefully sidesteps every formal analysis of the works themselves as well as every attempt to situate them in the contemporary art scene. On 18 October Hilton Kramer's slashing review appeared in the *New York Times*: "Why? Why Hartung? This is the question that fills the air, like a barking dog that won't shut up, as one goes around the exhibition of paintings by Hans Hartung that came to the Metropolitan Museum of Art this week. Why, out of the hundreds of living artists whose work might conceivably commend itself for exhibition in this august establishment, single out a painter of such surpassing mediocrity and dullness?"[17] Kramer goes on to criticise the total absence of justification for his choice on Geldzahler's part before retracing, briefly and unkindly, Hartung's career. He concludes by expressing his astonishment at Geldzahler's choice for recent works over mounting a retrospective of this "minor and essentially graphic talent".[18] The article is sprinkled with disparaging words about the School of Paris, France and the French, all of which had already received a few pokes from Kramer in an article from 28 September of the same year: "Once the unrivalled artistic capital of the Western world, the principal source... of ideas worth entertaining and new pictures worth acquiring, Paris as a center of the visual arts has declined in recent decades to something very like a provincial

18. HH, *T1973-E12*, 1973, acrylic on canvas, 154 x 250 cm, private collection
19. Exhibition at the Museum of Fine Arts of Houston, 1969

metropolis. The Louvre and other famous repositories of the past reign undiminished in their glory, but the world of living art no longer commands the old prestige. Its liveliest minds now look to New York for inspiration, and its liveliest institutions likewise look to ours as models of organization and taste. The center of intellectual gravity has shifted decisively".[19] Hartung latched onto this argument to explain the failure of the exhibition. In an interview with the *Le Quotidien de Paris* he says: "Mainly, what I felt there was a very anti-French attitude. The whole country bowed down to this attitude, but France kept its head up. Now that things are not going so well for the Americans, the old grudges spring up anew, and when it comes to painting, the grudge is even older: Americans just can't stomach the fact that Impressionism and Cubism didn't happen there".[20] However, even if the context of strategic rivalry that developed during the aftermath of the war was still continuing in the 1970s, and even if it was partly accountable for the resistance Hartung's work encountered in the United States, it doesn't suffice to explain everything. All the articles about Hartung in the American press, both before and during the exhibition, repeat the same arguments. Thomas Hess, in the *New York Magazine*, talked about a planned and decorative spontaneity, of a meaningless virtuosity, of expediency of execution, of "calculated risks",[21] the title of his article. Deborah Rosenthal talked about an excessive, but unjustified, beauty, of a controlled painterliness.[22]

The press may have speculated on Geldzahler's motives for the exhibition, but what Kay Bearman, who was working with Geldzahler at the time, remembers is simply that he had loved Hartung's exhibition at Lefebre in 1972 and that he had been particularly impressed by his recent work.[23] There is very little about Hartung or the exhibition in Geldzahler's correspondence, journal, or personal papers.[24] Earlier in 1975, Geldzahler had organised a Francis Bacon retrospective at the Met, and he had justified his choice using arguments very similar to those he was later to use to justify the Hartung exhibition: the freshness of the works and the need to allow the American public to become familiar with recent developments in European art. The Philip Guston exhibition Geldzahler organised in 1973, his friendship with David Hockney, his subsequent involvement and commitment to the Italian Transavanguardia and American painting of the 1980s all lead one to believe that he was trying to complicate a slightly too orthodox reading of Modernism by presenting eccentric artists capable of questioning the history of Modernism. There is no doubt that Hartung's work, with its autonomous and asynchronous developments, reveals the complexity and paradoxes of the history of modern art, just as there is no doubt that Geldzahler's words would have found more receptive ears ten years later, when the context was more open to such types of questionings. Nor is there any doubt that a retrospective would have met with a better critical reception. It is not certain that Geldzahler can be held

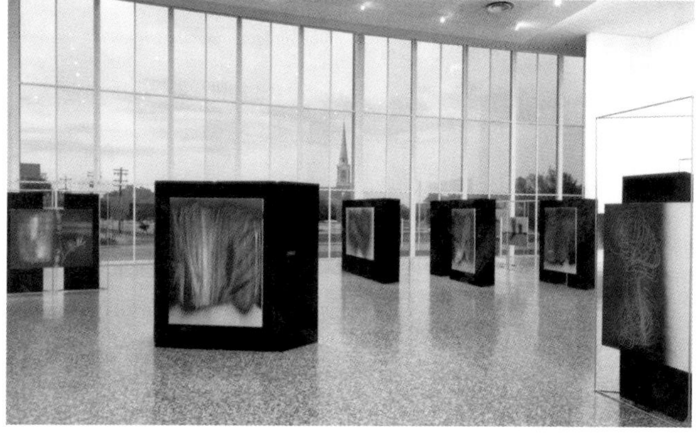

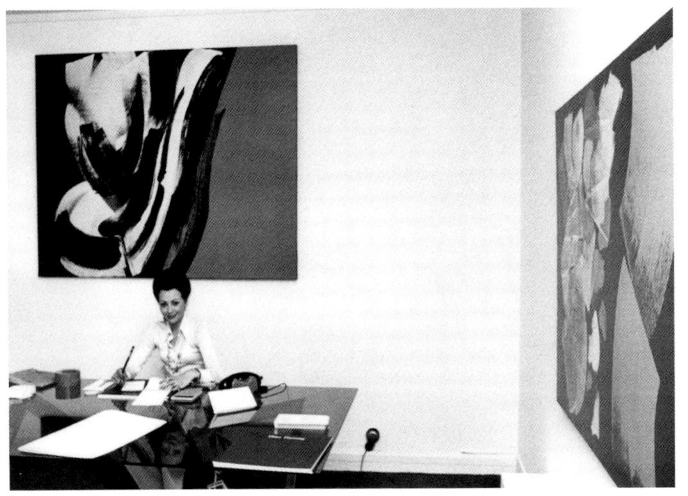
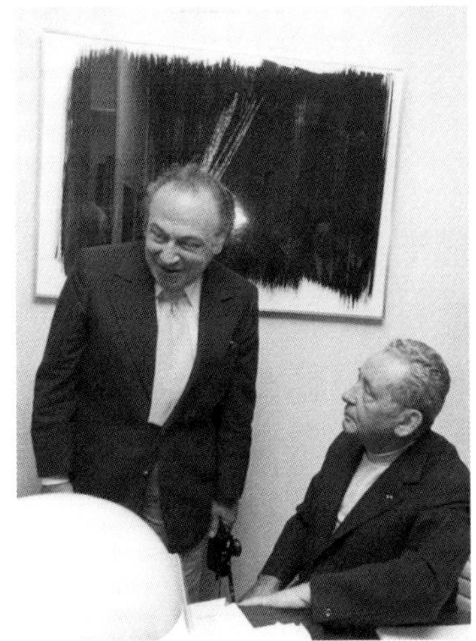

solely responsible for the choice of recent works only. The 1970s were difficult times economically, and Hartung had to find a new market. Indeed, nearly all the works exhibited came from the Galerie de France and were still up for sale. The stakes were enormous for Myriam Prévot-Douatte, who was having a hard time honouring the financial contract she had with Hartung. According to Pierre Alechinsky, who at that time was also represented in Paris by the Galerie de France, the failure of the exhibition at the Metropolitan Museum had profound repercussion for Myriam Prévot-Douatte, who was then on the verge of bankruptcy.[25] She committed suicide the following year.

In a letter to Hartung from 19 November 1975, Geldzahler explained that the "chauvinistic" New York public found it difficult to be receptive to a work they were not familiar with. He insists on the fact that artists—Frank Stella, James Rosenquist, Alex Katz, Richard Hennessey—all liked the works very much. Alex Katz recalled recently: "I liked the painting technique, the strokes rhythms [sic]. I liked the lucidity of the images, clear, with nothing extra".[26] Geldzahler even mentioned in the letter the public success of the show, which received over 85,000 visitors. On 5 January 1976, Geldzahler wrote to Hartung to apologise for having "overestimated the accessibility of Hans Hartung's work to the New York audience", and recognised that he would have done better had he organised a "retrospective heavily emphasizing recent works rather than the recent work by itself". Hartung responded by giving him a painting (*T1974–R24*, 111 x 180 cm).

Lefebre, for his part, accused Hilton Kramer of having had "a very negative impact on sales".[27] Still, he hoped, like Geldzahler, that the "three Hartung exhibitions" in New York would bear good fruit in the future. Their wishes, however, were never heard. Hartung's work was never again shown in the United States and the relationship binding Hartung and Lefebre was forever compromised. From that moment on, their epistolary exchanges boil down to the occasional greeting. As far as I can tell from my research, they never saw each other again.

20. Myriam Prévot–Douatte at the opening of Hartung's exhibition, Galerie de France, 1974
21. Hartung and Lefebre at the opening of Hartung's exhibition, Galerie de France, 1974

1. Information acquired in the course of a phone conversation (28 August 2004) with Pierre Alechinsky, who was represented in New York by John Lefebre.

2. Their correspondence, indeed all the letters cited in this article, is now in the archives of the Fondation Hartung in Antibes.

3. Then director of the Guggenheim.

4. James Mellow, "New York", *Art International* (Lugano, vol. XI, 2, 20 Feb. 1967), p. 64.

5. Moses Hager, "Bewildering Abstracts by Hartung", *The Jersey Journal* (Greenfield, Ohio: Jan. 1967).

6. A handwritten (by Marie Aanderaa) rough copy of this contract survives and is now in the archives of the Fondation Hartung.

7. Letters from 28 Jan. 1970 and 2 Mar. 1972.

8. Letter of 21 Sep. 1971.

9. Letter of 21 Sep. 1971.

10. Lefebre quotes Geldzahler's words in a letter of 9 November 1971.

11. Different lists composed throughout the month of October 1975 have survived and are now in the archives of the Fondation Hartung.

12. *Cimaise*, special issue on Hartung, 21st year, 119, 120, 121 (Paris: Sept., Oct., Nov., Dec. 1974).

13. Hans Hartung, *Autoportrait* (Paris: Bernard Grasset, 1976), p. 238.

14. Gilles Plazy and Annick Pely, "Les entretiens du *Quotidien*: Hans Hartung, l'aventure plastique", *Le Quotidien de Paris* (10 Nov. 1975).

15. Geldzahler's questions and Hartung's answers are now in the archives of the Fondation Hartung.

16. *Autoportrait* p. 154

17. Hilton Kramer, "Art: Hartung Exhibition at Met", *New York Times* (New York: 18 Oct. 1975).

18. Kramer, "Art: Hartung Exhibition at Met."

19. Hilton Kramer, "Ironies of the French Cultural Exchange", *New York Times* (New York, 28 Sep. 1975).

20. Plazy and Pely, "Les entretiens du *Quotidien*".

21. Thomas B. Hess, "Art: Calculated Risks", *New York Magazine* (17 Nov. 1975).

22. Deborah Rosenthal, "Hans Hartung", *Arts Magazine* (Jan. 1976).

23. Kay Bearman is the administrator for Modern Art at the Metropolitan Museum of Art. E-mail from 25 Aug. 2004.

24. The Geldzahler archives are at the Beinecke Library at Yale. Bernard Zirnheld looked through Geldzahler's papers at the author's request (Aug. 2004). Geldzahler was born in Antwerp, Belgium. Given that John Lefebre represented many Belgian artists (Folon, Alechinsky, Dotremont and Pol Bury), for a while I entertained the notion that there may have been a link to explore there. But, even though Kay Bearman has assured me of Geldzahler's attachment to his Belgian roots, neither Folon, nor Alechinsky, nor Geldzahler's own archives have lent any substance to the hypothesis of a "Belgian link".

25. Phone interview with Alechinsky, 28 Aug. 2004.

26. Alex Katz, in a fax from 13 Aug. 2004. Stella and Rosenquist never responded.

27. Letter of 11 Dec. 1975.

John C. Welchman Hans Hartung Abcedarium: Reading Between the Lines

Franz-W. Kaiser A Case Study on the Caducity of Categories in Art Criticism Annie Claustres

Hans Hartung Clandestine Artist

1937-1942: the Decisive Years

Christine Mehring Hans Hartung Mid-Century Modern

Rainer Michael Mason Hartung and Printmaking Christopher Wool

Selected Works

Anne Pontégnie 1975

Hartung at the

Metropolitan Museum

Chronicle of a Failure Chantal Eschenfelder

Hans Hartung in Germany

Laurence Bertrand Dorléac

Germany and France

Two Parts in One Jennifer Mundy

The Very Late Style of Hans Hartung

a Problem?

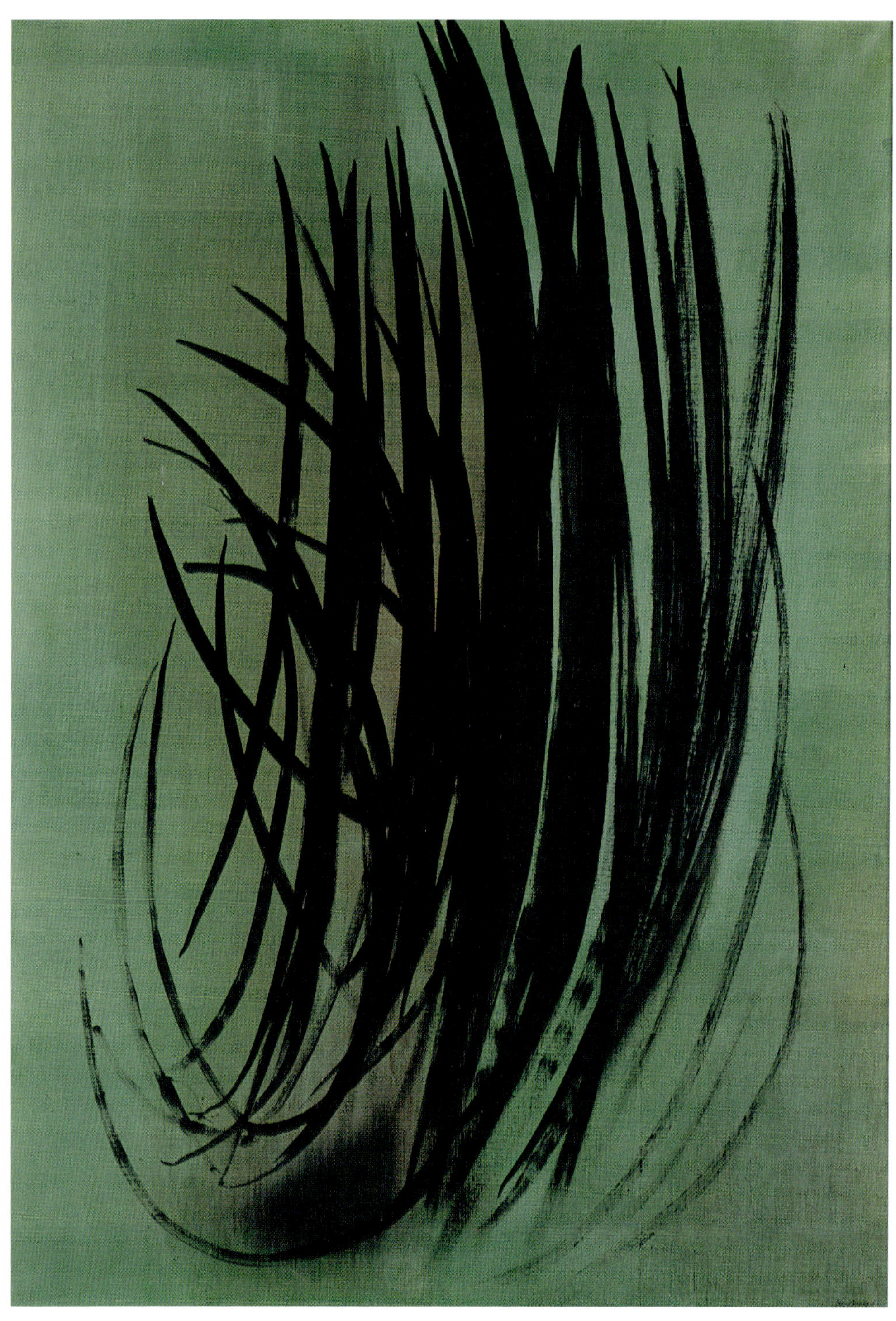

1. HH, *T1955-3*, oil on canvas, 1955, 100 x 81 cm, Museum Ludwig, Cologne
2. First exhibition at the Heinrich Kühl Gallery, Dresden, 1931

"A simple line—violent, surging, bursting; or calm, orderly, stable—translates what we feel. It corresponds with our life..." (fig. 1)[1]

Since the mid-twentieth century, Hans Hartung has been considered one of Europe's most important artists.[2] For art history, this German-born artist represents the École de Paris of the 1950s and counts as one of the most significant figures of French painting in the Modern period. Interestingly, though, his first artistic successes were in Germany, where his work had been shown in an exhibition of 29 paintings, watercolours and drawings at the Heinrich Kühl Gallery in Dresden as early as 1931 (fig. 2). Then, as now, Hartung was mostly seen as a mediator, not just between the tradition of German Expressionism and the informal painting style of the post-war era, but also between the German and French painting traditions, the former influenced by the spirit of Romanticism, the latter shaped by rationalism and the pursuit of clarity. While French interpretations of his work tend to emphasise his German roots, in Germany it is the very union of artistic forms from both nations in his work that is emphasised—not least as a successful example of a non-representational artistic stance within the international avant-garde: "His biography describes a European life and career that is at once individual and exemplary. His painting comes not only from the milieu in which he lived, but, in its pictorial roots and choice of subject matter, also from reflections on traditional European painting. It falls within the world-view of German Romanticism, transposed to the twentieth-century and in the register of the French '*clarté*', purity and rationality that permeate his images. It also bears witness to the artist's longing to represent beauty."[3]

The rich and but also tension-filled relationship between the nations of Germany and France is reflected in Hartung's artistic and personal development. After studying at the art academies of Leipzig, Dresden and Munich, and after his encounter with German Expressionism, he found himself drawn for long stays in Paris and southern France, where he encountered Cubism and the figural precepts of Cézanne. Soon enough, though, the political situation began to dominate his artistic development, which would prove decisive for how he would be understood thereafter. Under pressure from the Gestapo, Hartung was forced to flee National Socialist Germany in 1935, and emigrated to France under the sponsorship of Will Grohmann and Christian Zervos. There he took part in the 1937 exhibition of International Modernism at the Jeu de Paume in Paris, which was organised by Zervos as a reaction against the 'Degenerate Art' show presented by the National Socialists in Munich. When war broke out, he volunteered to fight

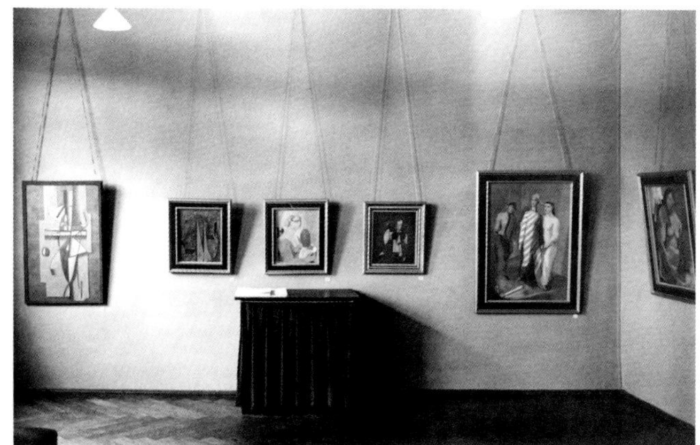

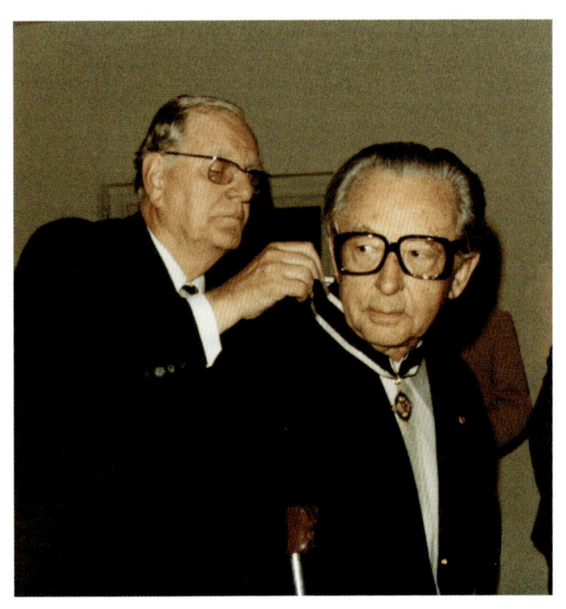

against Nazi Germany, heading immediately to Africa with the Foreign Legion. Upon fleeing German troops later, he was interned in the Méranda del Ebro prison camp in Spain; then, in the battle against the Germans at Belfort in 1944, he was so badly wounded that his right leg had to be amputated. He was honoured as a war hero in France with the Croix de Guerre, the Medaille militaire and French citizenship. These honours were followed in 1961 by his induction into the Legion d'honneur, his appointment as Commandeur in 1968, his 1977 acceptance as a Membre de l'Institute of the Académie des Beaux-Arts and, finally, his elevation to the rank of one of the Grand Officiers de la Légion d'honneur by the French President in 1989. Nor was the Federal Republic of Germany reticent in decorations and honours for the artist: in 1956, Hartung was inducted into the Berlin Akadmie der Künste [Academy of the Arts] and, in 1958, into the Bavarian Akadmie der Künste. In 1964, he earned the Große Bundesverdienstkreuz [Great Cross for Service to the Nation]; in 1977, he was conferred the Orden pour le Mérite für Wissenschaften und Künste [Medal of Merit for the Arts and Sciences] (fig. 3), to name but a few.[4]

When, upon the artist's death, legal difficulties arose concerning the stipulation in his will for the creation of a foundation in France, the former Chancellor of the Federal Republic of Germany, Helmut Schmidt, and the serving Chancellor, Helmut Kohl, both intervened on behalf of the artist's wishes.[5] That, after the war, an artist like Hartung had such great political weight on both sides of the Rhine is simply astounding. A passage from the preface to the catalogue of a 1981 exhibition in Munich dedicated to Hartung suggests a deeper consideration in this matter: "Since the mid-twentieth century, Hans Hartung has been considered one of the most prestigious painters in Europe. As a French citizen of east German origin, in his life and work he embodies as no other the spirit of mutual Franco-German understanding that, since the days of Konrad Adenauer and Charles de Gaulle, has come to characterize the relationship between France and the Federal Republic of Germany."[6]

One might suspect that, even aside from his achievement as an artist, Hans Hartung might have been in the right place at the right time to seal governmental efforts at German-French rapprochement on the cultural level. This rationale for his public accept-

3. Hans Hartung being presented the "Order of Merit", Antibes, October 1978
4. HH, *CP*, 1922, watercolour on paper, 22 x 17.7 cm

ance has already provided the key to several idiosyncrasies, particularly in German interpretations of his work, specifically: 1) the summary dismissal of his artistic development, which entails that both his abstractions of the Twenties and his turn to expression after 1960 are ignored; 2) the fact that in the Fifties, his success in Germany was greater than it was in France; and 3) the lack of interest in his late work in Germany as of the Sixties.

Today the works of this artist, who has won at one time or another nearly every international prize and recognition, may be found in prestigious museums around the world. In Germany alone he is represented in 25 museums, including Berlin, Hamburg, Munich, Cologne, Stuttgart, Mannheim and Hanover; and yet Hans Hartung's significance has become relatively diminished since the Sixties, his meteoric rise in the Fifties written off as a mere historical phenomenon. Despite the fact that Hartung had developed a form of abstraction between 1922 and 1929 that was completely independent from other art movements (fig. 4), in nearly every large exhibition well into the Seventies, his work from before his first solo exhibition at Lydia Conti in Paris in 1947 is not considered his most "authentic". This only furthered the impression that the abstract style of the École de Paris, characterised by the terms *tachisme* or *abstraction lyrique,* as a representative of which Hartung had been presented to German audiences since 1947 at the latest, was invented only after the end of the war and at the same time as American action painting. It is no coincidence that, in the process, the artist's fully autonomous development was ignored and that Hartung was claimed for other movements; rather, there were deep-seated reasons for it that had their roots in the complex political and historical situation of post-war Germany.

Initiatives for resurrecting the arts after the war, along with the cultural activities of the occupying powers, were important factors in Hartung's reception in Germany. Under the auspices of de-Nazification, the German populace, which of course had been cut off from international developments in art's avant-garde for twelve years, was suddenly confronted with the most important aspects of classical Modernism.[7] Nearly all exhibitions of the early post-war period were concerned first and foremost with rehabilitating the

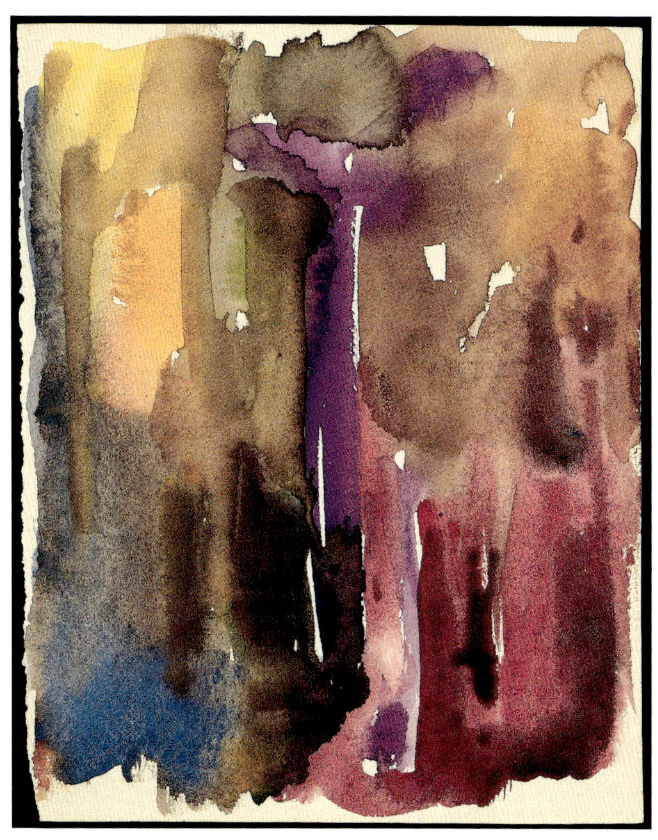

art movements rejected by the Nazis, above all Expressionism, Cubism and Constructivism, but also such recent non-objective directions as the École de Paris and the legacy of the Bauhaus.

The reasons for this overt promotion of non-objective art have not been sufficiently explained to this day.[8] However, chief among them was the beginning of the Cold War after 1946, which led to support for abstract art because one could see it as the exact opposite of "unfree" Socialist Realist painting and propagate it as the symbol of individualistic, Western, democratic values. As early as 1949, in a conference of German art historians, Werner Haftmann had made an impassioned case for the motif of freedom as inherent in Modern art, thus equating artistic freedom with freedom from state control. This was understood to signify Fascist dictates on art as well as state interference in art in the German Democratic Republic after 1948–49.[9] Thus the complete autonomy of artistic creativity as embodied in abstract art took on a political dimension, which was then combined with the element of internationalism; this much is clear, at any rate, from the title of a book printed in 1958: *Abstrakte Kunst, eine Weltsprache* [Abstract Art, a World Language] by George Poensgen and Leopold Zahn.[10] That this union of absolute freedom and internationalism found one if its most significant protagonists in Hartung, an artist working with abstraction and living between two nations, is easy to understand. Furthermore, the language of abstract forms and an apparently content-free form of art effectively allowed artists and consumers of art to escape any real confrontation with the legacy of National Socialism.[11]

The turn to abstraction was also encouraged by its great affinity with the positivist understanding of Modernism rapidly gaining currency in the Fifties, and an unmitigated belief in science and technology, according to which an abstract painting seemed to come the closest to grasping the essence of the modern world. This last reason was offered again and again in the French reception of Hartung.[12]

The many initiatives and events that swiftly built Hartung such a great reputation in Germany after the war give the impression that his fame could only be the result of perfect coordination between a number of benefactors, art critics, galleries and museums, particularly since the activities that made Hartung known to a broad public were had been pursued much more actively in Germany than in France.

One of Hartung's most important benefactors was Will Grohmann, mentioned above, who supported the artist even before the war and, as his good friend, was in close contact with the artist once again after 1946. He introduced Hartung to collectors and museums and wrote catalogue essays and reviews. Grohmann can be largely credited with Hartung's being awarded the Rubens Prize in 1958.

That said, Hartung's impact on the public was chiefly due to the engagement of Ottomar Domnick, a neurologist from Stuttgart.[13] Domnick was a self-appointed advocate of abstract art and had put together what was at that time a peerless collection of non-objective paintings. But mainly his impressive financial support, which made exhi-

5. Hans Hartung at the Galerie Otto Stangl, Munich, 1958

bitions, publications and film projects possible, played a decisive role in Hartung's growing popularity in Germany. For example, Domnick organised the famous 'Wanderausstellung französischer abstrakter Kunst' [Travelling Exhibition of French Abstract Art] in 1948–49, which toured seven cities in Germany. Through activities like these he ensured that he was not only one of the most important initiators of Franco-German cultural exchange, which was officially sanctioned in 1954 with the signing of the Franco-German cultural treaty by Adenauer and Pierre Mendès-France, but also one of abstract art's most outspoken defenders. His greatest contribution to Hartung's reputation in Germany was his publication of the first monograph on the artist, published in Stuttgart in 1949 in a lavish, trilingual edition.[14] For this ambitious project, Domnick secured the contribution of essays, in addition to his own text, from some quite prominent authors: James Johnson Sweeney, Curator at the Museum of Modern Art in New York, wrote the preface, and Madeleine Rousseau, editor of the journal *Le Musée Vivant* and professor at the Institute des hautes études cinématographiques, wrote the main text, in which she sought to place Hartung's work in the context of general developments in abstract art. Her reading of Hartung's use of line, drawing and expressive colour as an "expression of the deepest human emotion" and an "authentic manifestation of contemporary Western culture"[15] strongly influenced his reception in Germany. Rousseau also promoted Hartung in France and in 1947 convinced one of her students, Alain Resnais, to make a film about the artist. This came to accompany the 'Wanderausstellung französischer abstrakter Kunst' in Germany, too, and was crucial in establishing the artist's growing popularity.

Also contributing to Hartung's acclaim in Germany were two galleries: in addition to the gallery Der Spiegel [The Mirror] in Cologne, the Moderne Galerie Otto Stangl [Otto Stangl Modern Gallery], founded in Munich in 1947, made pioneering strides. The engagement of the young gallerists Etta and Otto Stangl for an artist like Hans Hartung is symptomatic of his reception in Germany (fig. 5) and reflected the cultural and political situation at the beginning of the Fifties. As with other post-war attempts to rehabilitate modern art, which had been considered "decadent" under National Socialism, the Stangls' early activities were at first focused on the spiritualistic, abstract innovations of the group known as Blaue Reiter [Blue Rider], above all Kandinsky, Marc and Klee. They hoped to offer an alternative to the idea of Munich as the "birthplace of the fascist movement" with an image of the city as central germination point for abstract art. But for them it was also a matter of a new generation finding its identity between tradition and its dissolution, of bridging

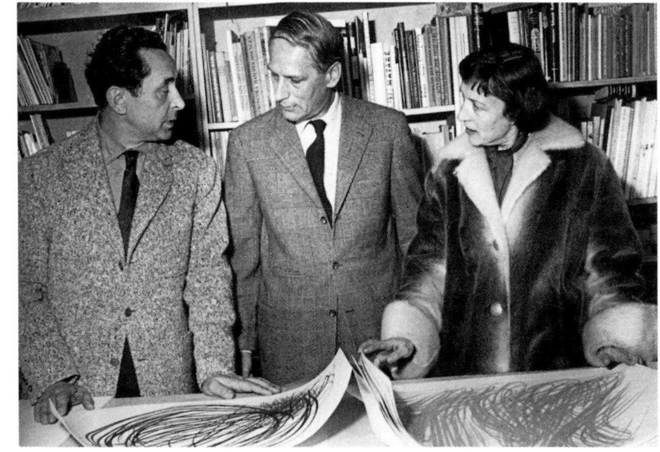

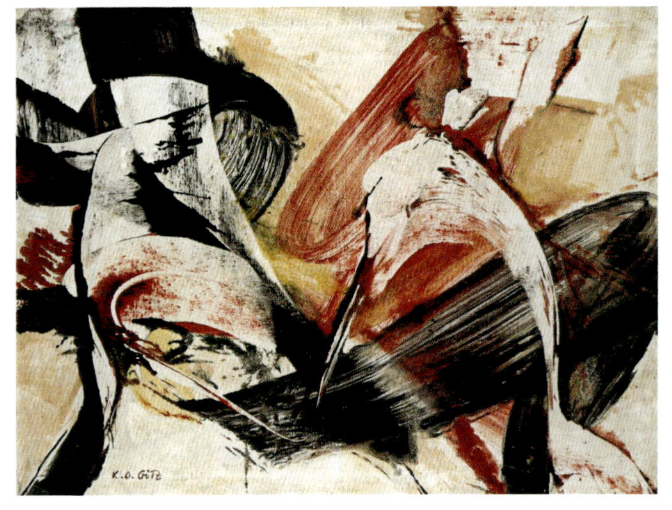

the gap between the early avant-garde movements of the twentieth century and the recent representatives of Modern art after 1945, lending the former an sense of modern continuity. In rehabilitating the abstract art of the Blaue Reiter group, the Stangl gallery also paved the way for international contemporary art. Together with the English Vice-Chancellor and later art critic John Anthony Thwaites, and with a circle of his artist and art-historian friends, the Stangls founded an initiative to popularize abstract art that eventually led to the creation of the *Gruppe der Gegenstandslosen* [Group of Non-Objectivists] in 1949 (later called *ZEN 49*). This group was founded against the backdrop of sharp disagreement between the proponents of abstract and of figurative art that informed the cultural debate at that time.

In parallel with this, the Stangl gallery presented contemporary French art of the recent École de Paris, including Poliakoff, Soulages and Hartung. Hartung's works in particular influenced the German art scene of the time, inspiring painters like Fritz Winter (fig. 6) and Rolf Cavael to pursue a freer gestural and informal painting style, though strictly speaking they cannot be called "gestural" painters. Here we encounter one of the greatest misunderstandings of Hartung in post-war Germany: at this time, Hartung's work method consisted almost solely in the exact translation of much earlier drawings into large-format oils, a process that actually runs counter to the spontaneous, gestural form of expression for which he was incorrectly being celebrated.[16]

In 1948, the same year that Hartung was first represented at the Venice Biennial, the Stangl gallery showed several of his works on paper, followed in 1949 by a show of pastels and watercolours; the latter was Hartung's first solo exhibition in Germany, marking the beginning of his rapid international success in the years that followed.[17] At the peak of his international breakthrough, public collections began acquiring works by Hartung from the Stangl gallery, such as the Karl Ernst Osthaus Museum in Hagen and the city museums of Mannheim and Kaiserslautern.[18] It is interesting, though it needn't diminish the significance of this gallery in the promotion of non-objective art, that its shows tended to be relatively moderate, striving, it seems, for harmony and balance. By the same token, vehement expressions such as those of Karl Otto Götz (fig. 7) or Bernhard Schultze were entirely absent; Jackson Pollock and Willem de Kooning, too, were rejected. The same was true for certain works of the École de Paris: "They [the

6. Karl Otto Götz, *Image from 14.9.1954*, oil on canvas, 95.5 x 131.4 cm, Museum Ludwig, Cologne
7. Fritz Winter, *Nocturnal Rain*, 1952, oil on canvas, 95.5 x 131.4 cm, Museum Ludwig, Cologne

Stangls] avoided any extreme positions and for the most part neither exhibited in their gallery artists who used an uncontrolled painting process (such as, for example, Mathieu) and thus expressed an unfettered search for freedom and independence, an approach that had made some headway even during the Nazis' reign of terror, nor did they make room for the provocative anti-aesthetic and anti-bourgeois art of the Cobra-Gruppe [Cobra

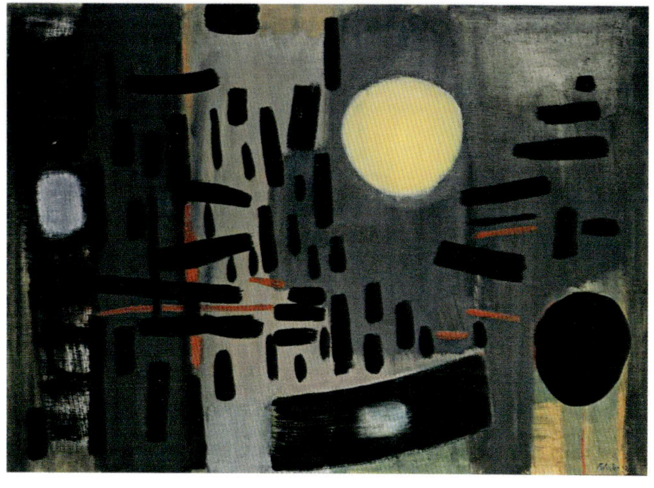

Group]. Hans Hartung's work, shown in the gallery after 1948, is exemplary of this approach. This exiled German, who used vehement and unbridled gestures when under pressure during the Thirties, behaved much more calmly in the Fifties; cosmic harmonies and tones arise, transcending subjective states."[19]

Similar considerations also played a role in Hartung's participation in the first two exhibitions of the Documenta in Kassel in 1955 and 1959, which brought him official recognition. The governing principle of the first Documenta in 1955 can be subsumed under the headings of "coming to terms with the past" and "taking stock of the present".[20] It was bent on illustrating the thesis that it was possible to pick up the threads of the forcefully interrupted progression of the first third of the twentieth century, and to seamlessly reconnect to German Modernism's disrupted experiments with form and content. But it was also meant to reconnect Germany's post-war art with the rest of Europe's, and especially to French Modernism, as it was choreographed in the so-called "main gallery" of the Museum Fridericianum in Kassel by Werner Haftmann, who was responsible for the overall concept. The art of "classical Modernism" was placed in dialogue with post-1945 works; in addition to Picasso and Fritz Winter, four works by Hartung were shown alongside others by Nay, Vasarely, Soulages and Bazaine.[21] Hartung's work was easily integrated into Haftmann's understanding of Modernism as the symbolic language appropriate to self-reflective, twentieth-century human beings. The tension-laden ambiguity of the two determining characteristics of Hartung's art—its freedom, gesture and emotion together with the rather calm manner of its linear structure—could be seen as related to the dramatic circumstances of his life (as Madeleine Rousseau had already attempted to demonstrate) and were granted an existential significance that helped defuse arguments about the meaninglessness of non-objective art. "With the line, as the trace of a forward-moving energy, Hartung found his first means of expression, making affective moments of his feeling for life spontaneously visible and able to be experienced by others [...]. The image is the concrete expression of a moment of human existence"[22] (fig. 8).

In contrast to the first Documenta, the second, in 1959, concentrated almost exclusively on post-war art. With their thesis that "art has become abstract", the curators staked out a clear position in the intensifying battle over contemporary art between the abstract and figurative camps. Werner Haftmann, again responsible for the overall curatorial plan, this time documented his thesis that abstract art had become an internationally unifying world-language, a universal medium of artistic communication, most importantly through a massing of American works of "Abstract Expressionism". "This contested ground was now forcibly entered by an entirely new, dramatic-dynamic, abstract expressive painting. It was conveyed by Hartung, Wols and Pollock, fully independent of one another and in very personal forms. Hartung, coming from German Expressionism, and Kandinsky had found a language of signs based on the expressive capacity of the line and accompanying suggestive colour, made up of dynamic, taut, regular brushwork and spacious, latticed forms and quick snarls of strokes, with which he could sketch, with convincing legibility, moments of human existence in all its drama on the suggestive background of the painting. Every situation that the modern experience of life throws at human beings can be visibly objectified with this language of signs, quivering with excitement and power but reigned in, solemn."[23]

Even in the face of increasing criticism of the one-sidedness of the works chosen for Documenta II, Hartung's popularity continued uninterrupted; indeed, he found himself at the peak of his success in Germany. Two years before, Werner Schmalenbach, Curator of the Kestner-Gesellschaft [Kestner Society] in Hanover and member of the selection committee for painting, sculpture and prints, not to mention the exhibition advisory committee of Documenta II, had organized the first large solo exhibition of Hartung in Germany in collaboration with the Galérie de France. This retrospective presented 85 paintings, drawings and watercolours from the years 1922 to 1956 and was shown in Hanover, Stuttgart, Berlin, Hamburg, Cologne, and Nuremburg. For the catalogue, Schmalenbach graced the artist with a nuanced introduction, seeking to grasp his roots in German Expressionism (Kandinsky and Klee) as well as to trace the influences, through France, of Miró and Gonzales. He explained Hartung's later works as a change from "subjective handwriting to an objective symbolic writing."[24] For Hartung, the exhibition was a success in that a number of museums acquired his works as a result (the Folkwang Museum in Essen, the Kunstmuseum Düsseldorf, the Nationalgalerie in Berlin and the Niedersächsische Landesgalerie in Hanover).

The real culmination of Hartung's reception in 1950s Germany, in which all the issues involved were again made clear, was his being awarded the first Rubens Prize in Siegen in 1958 (fig. 9). The bestowal of this prize on an abstract painter with French citizenship, two years before Hartung won the International Prize at the Venice Biennial, was a courageous decision linked to a cultural and political controversy. A highly qualified jury, which included Will Grohmann, Werner Haftmann, John Anthony Thwaites and Georg Meistermann among many others, decided to award the prize to Hartung "for

| 8. HH, *T1956-21*, 1956, oil on canvas, 180 x 114 cm, Museum Ludwig, Cologne

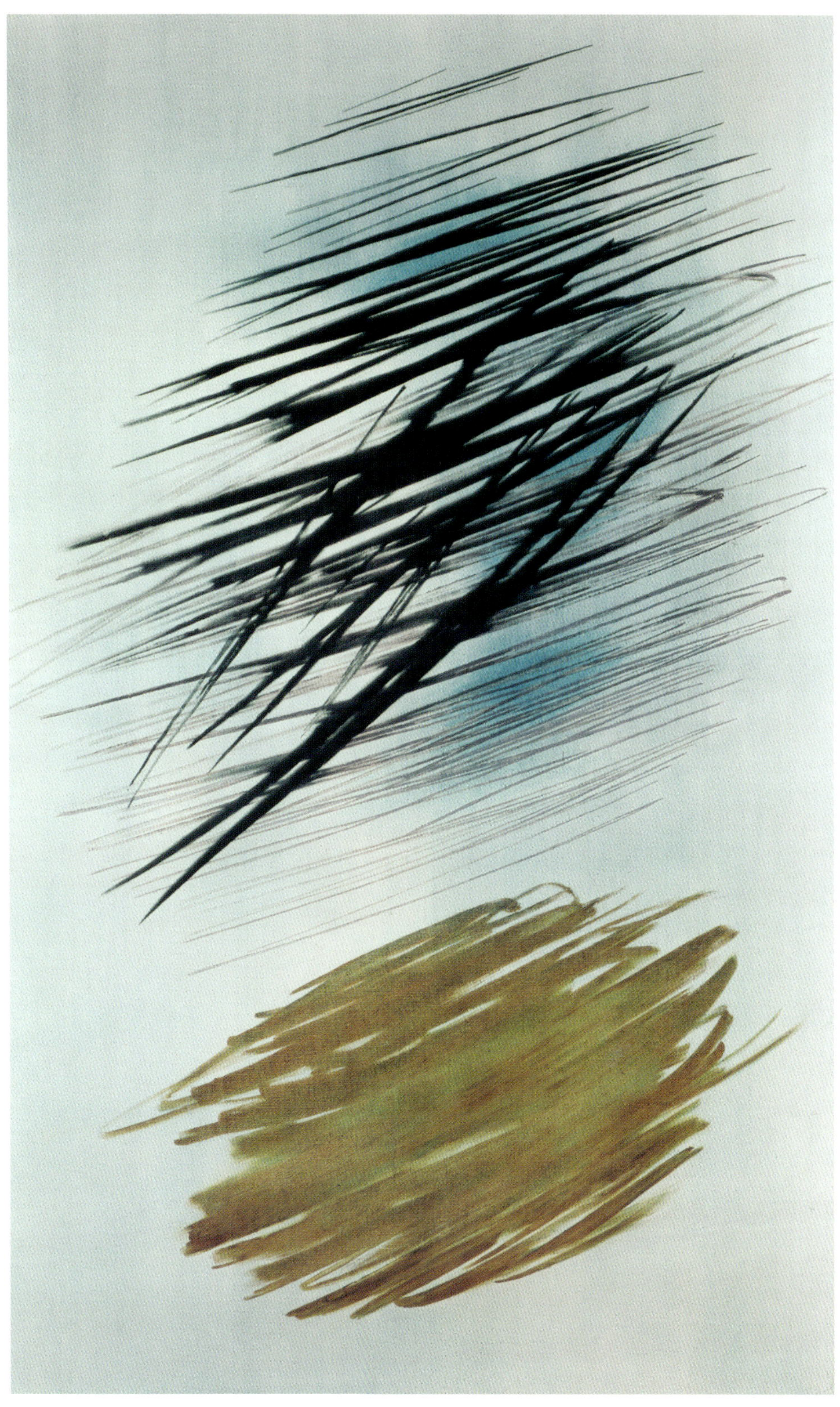

thirty years of artistic achievement on every level" but this decision unleashed a wave of protest from the citizenry, who voiced their displeasure mainly in the form of letters to the editor in local papers.[25]

This incident should serve to put into perspective the description above of Hartung's acclaim in Germany. These facts conveyed the impression that the victory of abstraction in Germany in the 1950s was so widespread that an artist like Hartung could easily steer a course to fame and recognition. However, as Ulrike Wollenhaupt-Schmidt pointed out during the first Documenta in 1955, "the advocates of Modern art were faced with a remarkable phalanx of opponents" and the arguments for avant-garde art were still quite overtly defensive ones.[26] Besides Hans Sedlmayer—who in his piece "The Loss of the Middle" (1948) had concluded that art was being dehumanized and culture sickened, leading him to formulate a critical position on Modern art—Wilhelm Hausenstein, Karl Scheffler, Max Picard and other notable scholars and critics were united in criticising what they, in their conservative view, considered to be the collapse of Western Christian traditions and values discernible in Modern art. These debates were conducted with considerable bitterness and led, in the "Darmstadt Dialogue" of 1950, to the argument between Sedlmayer and Baumeister. The tremendous effort it took to champion abstract art and the arguments that now seem so one-sided should thus be considered in the context of the historical situation, when its opponents were in the majority and operating under cultural and political standards suspiciously close to those of the Third Reich. The cultural conservatism present not only among the populace, but also among many critics, was in the last analysis not clearly enough differentiated from National Socialistic thought, and it unleashed an almost missionary zeal among the defenders of the avant-garde that was only strengthened by the atmosphere of the Cold War.

For this reason, Hartung received more attention in Germany than he did in France, the French apparently not having any use for this kind of cultural–political about-face. Both countries tried to rehabilitate themselves by looking back at their own traditions. In Germany this tradition was the abstraction of a Kandinsky or Klee, while in France there was greater recourse to figurative artists, such as Matisse, Braque, Picasso, Léger and Rouault, with the result that quite different conditions were in place for Hartung's reception in the two countries.[27] This also helps explain why his actual path of development as an artist has been so stubbornly ignored, and why there was such over-emphasis on the supposed affinity of his works in the Fifties to international movements of gestural painting, from Abstract Expressionism to Tachism, as a consequence. As a German exile with a French passport, difficult biographical circumstances and a vigorously persecuted abstract form of painting, he was perfectly situated to become the very symbol of the movement of the renewal of cultural politics in Germany. But it was precisely the intricacy of the relationship between the reception of his works and the historical and political situation of post-war Germany that was responsible for the fact that his significance on the German art scene, after the height of his success and quite independently from his

9. Receiving the Rubens Prize, Siegen, August 1958

individual artistic development, all too quickly became treated as relative. The victory march of abstraction ended abruptly at the beginning of the Sixties when Modernism was said to have begun all over again in a second "zero hour", not without recourse to the past, but neither on the basis of any supposed political non-commitment. "Art—parallel to the radical political tendencies of the Sixties— demanded a direct relationship to the political reality."[28] Turning its back on abstraction, object-based art like Pop and Minimal art found itself in a completely different context in the Sixties. Abstract tendencies, and thus the works of Hans Hartung, were no longer relevant precisely because they embodied a retreat to formal, decorative and content-free modes of expression that were supposed to have been overtaken by reference to societal realities.

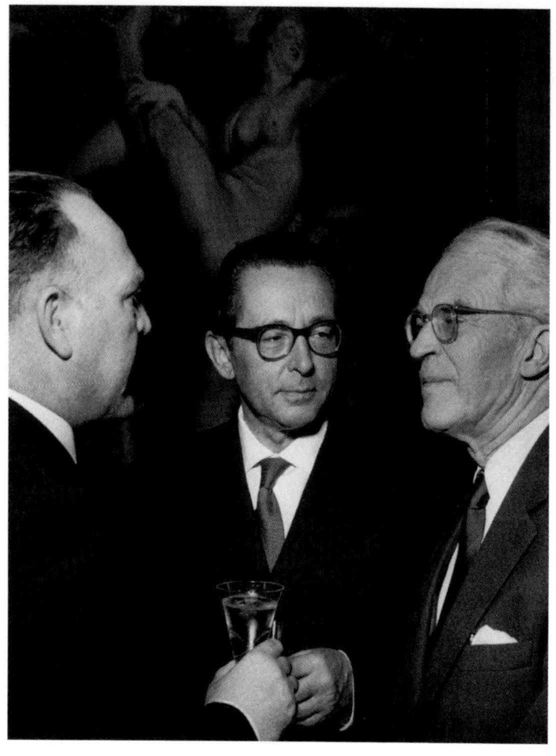

It is worth examining this issue further with a look at a contemporary of Hartung, the painter Alfred Otto Wolfgang Schulze, whose alias was Wols (fig. 10). The connection between these two artists can be seen on several levels. Both were born in Germany and later emigrated to France. Both were seen as artists who belonged to the representatives of a new beginning in art within the École de Paris and so-called Tachism.[29] They were supported by the same advocates, like Werner Haftmann, Will Grohmann and the Der Spiegel gallery in Cologne, and they were exhibited together (for example in 1951 at Nina Dausset in 'Véhemences confrontées' or in 1952 in 'Un art autre' by Michel Tapié); both were active as photographers, albeit in different ways. Nevertheless, their respective receptions in Germany turned out very differently. Although Wols' artistic achievements were well recognized on the German side, he never became a symbolic figure of post-war painting the way Hartung did, and not just because of his personality-induced crises. Rather, Wols seems first to have been successful abroad, at least before a greater acceptance of his work resulted from the retrospective by Ewald Rathke (1965–66) in Frankfurt and the large exhibition conceived by Werner Haftmann in Berlin in 1973. Interestingly, it was precisely during this time that Hartung's star was on the decline in Germany, where he was considered outdated because of his supposed lack of social or political relevance. In contrast, Wols now benefited from the fact that his art had always been credited with an affinity to the philosophical position of Existentialism, which could protect his achievements from being held as meaningless or merely decorative. A look at the works of the two artists makes clear, though, that despite

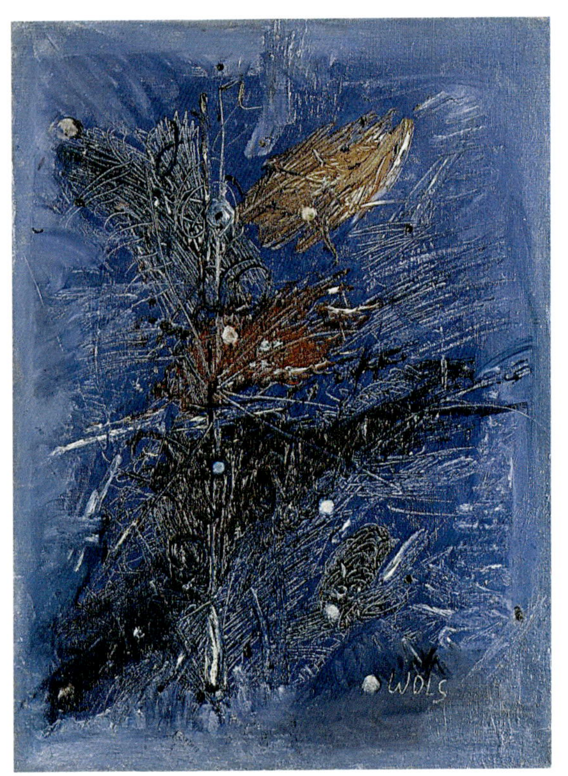

all their artistic divergence, the differences are not so striking as to justify such different receptions. There were other factors, beyond the realm of the visual arts, that were responsible for that.

On the other hand, Hartung was able to continue exhibiting internationally unabated well into the Sixties. In 1966, Grohmann published an edition of Hartung's early watercolours from 1922, attempting in this way to bring attention to the artist's early work. It would take until the Seventies and Eighties, however, for Hartung to become central in the public's interest once more. But when it happened, he was honoured not as the representative of an artistic avant-garde, but as a classic hero of a past artistic mode.

On the occasion of Hans Hartung's seventieth birthday in 1974, the artist received two honours in Cologne: the Stefan Lochner Medallion and an ambitious retrospective at the Wallraf-Richartz-Museum, which travelled to the Nationalgalerie in Berlin (fig. 11) and the municipal gallery at the Lenbachhaus in Munich. The exhibition comprised an imposing selection of 105 works from the years 1922 to 1973 but the accompanying catalogue showed a certain reluctance to comment on the artist's standing. This is remarkable given that precisely in the 1970s, with the rise of new artistic movements such as Pop art, the Nouveaux Réalistes and other trends that were abandoning the classical pictorial genre, a renewed presentation of an abstract direction in art would seem to require some explanation.[30] "Immediately after World War II, Hartung's gestural painting was representative of the reaction of an entire generation to a pre-fabricated, externally determined existence. Uncompromising individualism and the most extreme subjectivism provided the basis for a new determination of self-image. The idea of freedom was interpreted as the uninhibited realisation of personal liberty. And for this mindset, the painting of Hans Hartung is like an outward sign. Magnificent, but today… history."[31]

In this context, the award of the Stefan Lochner Medal to Francis Bacon, Sonia Delaunay, Naum Gabo, Jasper Johns and Antoni Tàpies in addition to Hartung is interesting.[32] This selection shows that the award was not meant to help promote any particular direction in art; rather, the Cologne-based jury had an interest in making a balanced

10. WOLS (Alfred Otto Wolfgang Schulze), *Vowels*, 1950, oil on canvas, 61 x 76 cm, Museum Ludwig, Cologne
11. Opening of the Hans Hartung retrospective at the Neuen Nationalgalerie in Berlin, 24 January 1975

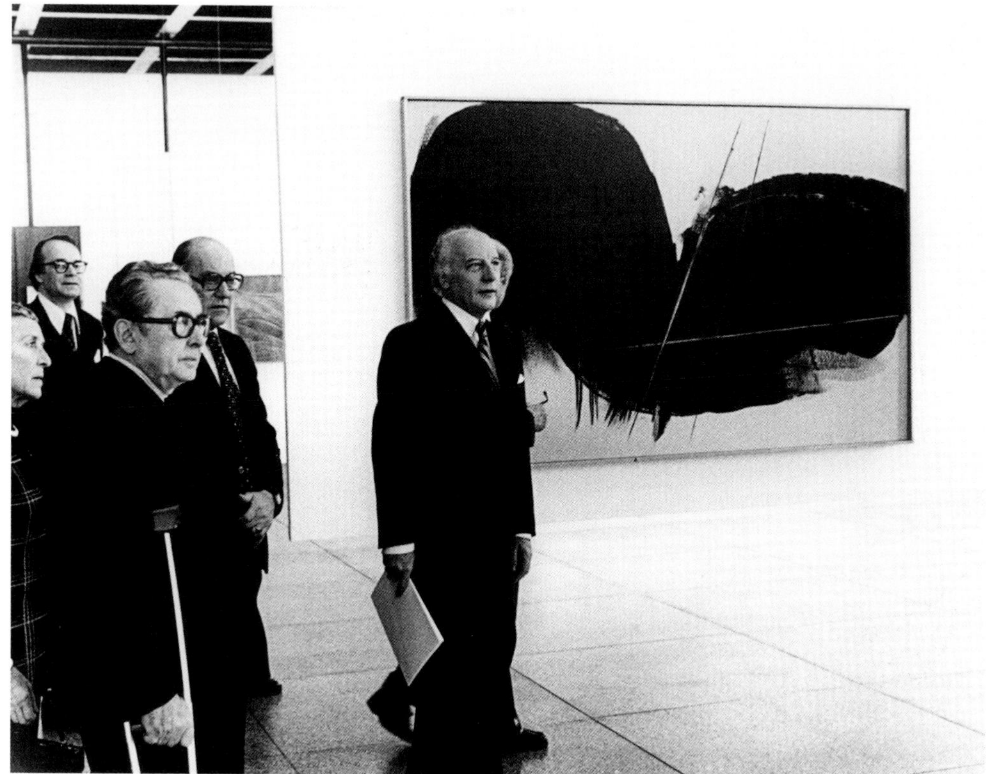

selection of very different stylistic directions within Modern art, from Surrealism to Pop art. Hartung, as the representative of the École de Paris, was chosen to receive the recognition long due this art movement, even though its meaning was rather diminished for being just one among many.

And so it seems only logical that, in 1981, the authors of the catalogue accompanying the Cologne exhibition 'Westkunst' [Art of the West] found precisely this decline in significance worthy of mention in connection with Hartung's Rubens Prize: "That this phase of triumph would be so short and that the unveiling of abstract-informal art at the '59 Documenta would be not only its acme, but also already its decline can only be described as one of the great surprises of the Sixties."[33] The exhibition was intended to take stock of art between 1939 and 1972 in order to contribute to a new understanding of the art of its day. This evaluation of Hartung was already a matter of historical contextualization, a view of his abstract art from a certain temporal distance.

In the same year, the large Hartung exhibition at the Staatsgalerie Moderner Kunst in Munich together with the Nationalgalerie in Berlin gave rise to a new critical viewpoint on the artist. Eschewing the images from the otherwise very well-known period from the end of the Fifties to the beginning of the Seventies, as Jörn Merkert explained fully and with some subtlety in the previously mentioned catalogue, works from Hartung's early phase (after 1922) were meant to be "pointedly juxtaposed" with the most recent works.[34] The goal was to refute the misconception of a temporal accordance between the goals of Hartung's work and those of the art movements Lyrical Abstraction and Tachism, which characterised the spirit of the immediate post-war era. Instead, Hartung was to be presented chiefly as a loner who found himself staking out positions largely outside the prevalent style of any given time, and whose visual innovations took place nearly always independently of, and generally at a different time to the various contemporary movements. Seen in this way, his early abstractions of 1922 were too early—at least as far as concerns the development of informal art—and at the same time too late for the invention of non-objective painting, as it existed already with Kandinsky. Only during the short period after the war did his art appear to accord with the *Zeitgeist*, while with the emergence of Pop art it was felt to be out of step again already. This more differentiated approach has remained relevant to this day. While it doesn't attempt to grasp Hartung's rigorous approach to his artistic career, it does offer a convincing enough explanation for his unusually rapid acceptance, even though his period of success remained limited to the 1950s.

At the beginning of the Eighties, Hartung became a talking point once again through his grants and philanthropic gifts. Through major gifts from the artist, a "Hans Hartung Room" was instituted in 1982 at the Staatsgalerie moderner Kunst in Munich[35] with a gift of ten paintings and in 1984 at the Hessischen Landesmuseum in Darmstadt, in connection with the artist's eightieth birthday. This more recent popularity should be seen in the context of the dominance of Post-Modernism in the interceding years, together with the rise of new painterly tendencies in the Eighties, which had been documented shortly before with the success of the Neuen Wilden [New Fauves / Neo-Expressionists] at Documenta 7. There was a logical concern with Hartung not only as an artist who, owing to his biography, was especially appropriate for such honours, but also as a link to a great painterly tradition in Germany, from "the classical Expressionism of '*die Brücke*' and the avant-garde German Neo-Expressionists..."[36] It is symptomatic of the history of Hartung's reputation that both the rooms once dedicated to his works no longer exist and that his works are now only selectively presented in contemporary art museums.

Of note was an exhibition of graphic works by Hans Hartung in the Kupferstichkabinett [Engravings Gallery] in Dresden (fig. 12) in 1983, which was prompted by a gift from the artist of 61 lithographs and etchings. In the former East Germany, representatives of post-war abstract art were not generally popular, since they stood in opposition to the prevailing doctrine of Socialist Realism and, worse, had been utilised since the mid-Fifties in the propaganda of the Cold War as the very symbol of the Western concept of freedom. It is amazing, though, in how little the keynote address at the opening differed from reviews in the West.[37] This can certainly be attributed in part to the great personal integrity of the Director, Werner Schmidt, who, in the realm of graphics, had striven over the years to stay connected to current developments in art. But it also shows how strongly Hartung's reception in East Germany, too, was influenced by his peculiar biography. For one thing, Hartung had never completely given up contact with his home cities of Leipzig and Dresden[38]—as early as 1964,

12. Hans Hartung exhibition, *Prints 1953–1973*, Leipzig 1984

his works, two graphic pieces, were first shown in Dresden. For another, his past as a fighter against Nazi Germany and his switch to French citizenship appear to have made a neutral approach to his art possible; still, given the otherwise prevalent political terminology, this was quite a surprising development.[39] The positive integrative effect the artist had, as a result, on the situation of art in a divided country cannot be overstated.

In the catalogue for the exhibition 'Deutschlandbilder. Kunst aus einem geteilten Land' [Pictures of Germany.

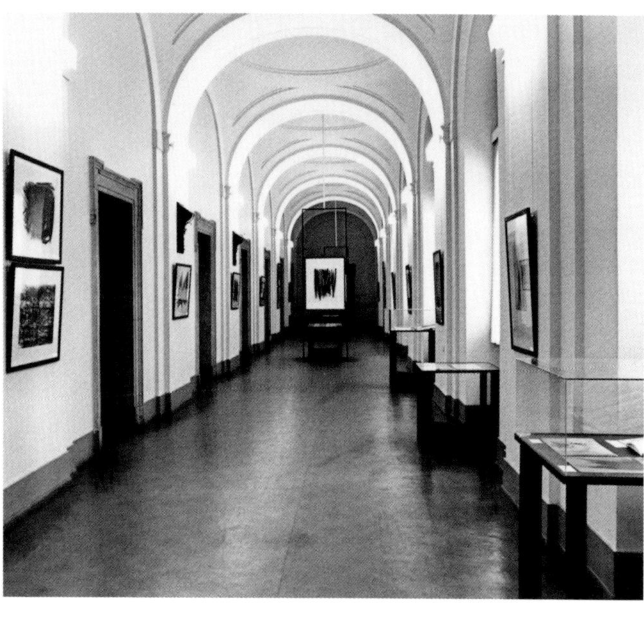

Art from a Divided Country] at the Martin-Gropius Bau in Berlin in 1997–98, Robert Fleck attempted to re-evaluate Hartung across a now great historical distance, with the goal of extending his significance beyond the immediate post-war era and establishing his relevance to contemporary art. Based on examples from his paintings from the Thirties and the discourse surrounding his political and biographical status, he came to the conclusion that Hartung's work was an example of his unmistakable rootedness in German Expressionism and so should be considered as a bridge between Nolde's generation and the post-abstract generation of Gerhard Richter, Sigmar Polke and Georg Baselitz.[40] Even here we see an effort to proffer an antidote to Germany's historical and political disunity through the artistic integrity and continuity of Hans Hartung's work, which, indeed, is meant to overcome it in a kind of healing act. Whether or not this thesis is compelling remains to be seen, particularly as concerns Hartung's relationship with the German art of the Eighties.

The analysis of the reception of Hans Hartung's work in Germany to date shows how strongly it was affected, to a greater degree than with other artists, by an appropriation of his specific biographical development and shaped by cultural and political necessities and demands. It also bears pointing out that Hartung made such a good figure for the young Federal Republic of Germany to identify with as it strove for a new cultural beginning because, while he had fought against National Socialist Germany, unlike many of his colleagues he never became active in communist or socialist groups—something that made social rehabilitation even for victims of the Nazi regime all but impossible during the Cold War. Instead, Hartung's situation as a disabled war veteran who stood well back from party politics, as well as concentrated on his artistic goals, was a good match for the all-encompassing need in post-war Germany to redress previous wrongs against the Modern tradition. The concentration on Hartung's artistic significance for post-war

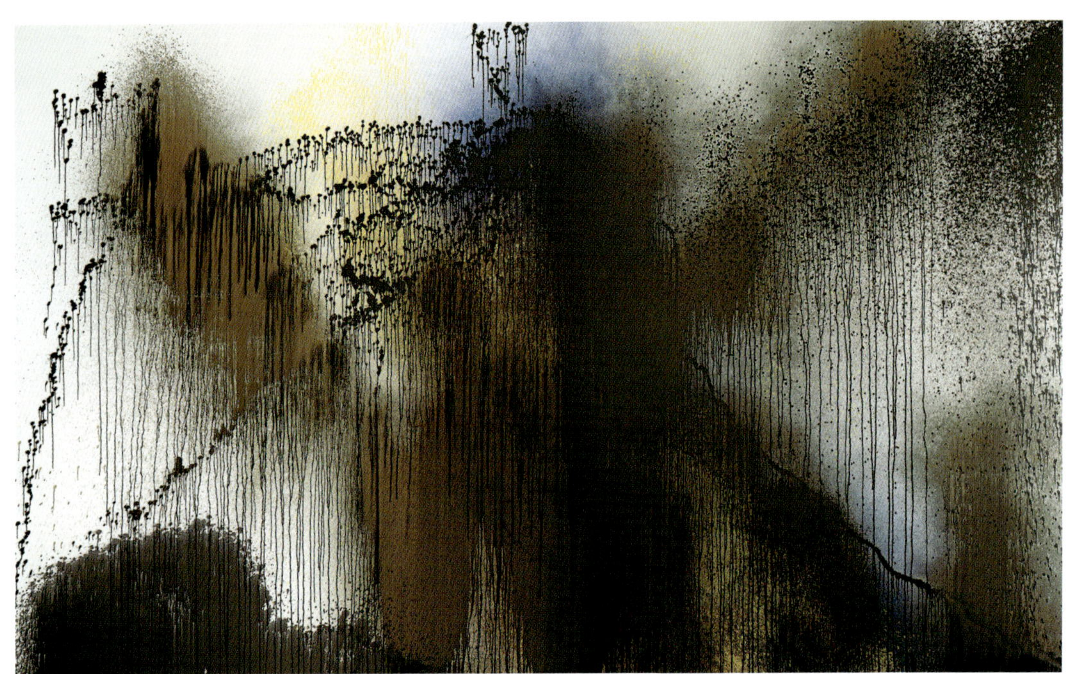

Germany, though, is the reason that his very prolific late work, in which, since the Sixties, he had decided to change his painting method to develop spontaneous action and wild gestures on the canvas (fig. 13), has yet to be widely appreciated in art criticism, at least in Germany.[41] As the rather disappointing interest in the latest Hartung exhibition at the Museum Ludwig in Cologne[42] makes clear, the time for a careful look at his work is not yet ripe. However, this latest chapter of the reception of Hans Hartung's work in Germany is not yet closed.

13. HH, *T1989–R17*, 1989, acrylic on canvas, 300 x 500 cm

1. Hans Hartung in: "Pour ou contre l'art abstrait",
    answer to a questionnaire, *Cahiers des Amis de
    l'Art*, 2/1947. "A chacun sa réalité", answer to a
    questionnaire, *XXe siécle*, Paris, 99/1957. Quoted
    from the exh. cat. *Alternativen. Malerei um
    1945–1950* (Wuppertal: Von der Heydt-Museum,
    1973), p. 27.

2. Eduard Trier, "1945–55. Fragmentarische Erinner-
    ungen" [Fragmentary Recollections] in exh. cat.
    Kunst in der Bundesrepublik Deutschland 1945-85
    [Art in the Federal Republic of Germany 1945-85]
    (Berlin: Nationalgalerie, Staatliche Museen
    Preussischer Kulturbesitz, 1985), p. 12. By the end
    of the Fifties, there were entries on Hartung in var-
    ious art-history books intended to familiarise an
    educated, middle-class public with art of the mod-
    ern period; see, for example, Leopold Zahn, *Eine
    Geschichte der Modernen Kunst–Malerei, Plastik,
    Architektur* [A History of Modern Art–Painting,
    Sculpture, Architecture], (Berlin/Frankfurt: Lizenz
    d.Ullstein-Verlag, 1958), p. 122; Georg Schmidt:
    Malerei in Deutschland 1918-55 [Painting in
    Germany, 1918–55] (Königstein: Taunus, 1960), p.
    61 ff.; and the German edition of the 1956 Parisian
    publication "L'art abstrait" by Marcel Brion, in
    Geschichte der abstrakten Kunst [History of
    Abstract Art] (Cologne: DuMont Schauberg, 1960),
    pp. 197–200.

3. Jörn Merkert, in exh. cat. *Hans Hartung. Malerei,
    Zeichnung, Photographie* [Hans Hartung. Painting,
    Drawing, Photography] (Munich and Berlin:
    Staatsgalerie Moderner Kunst, HWS Verlags-
    gesellschaft, 1981), pp. 11–31.

4. The unusual situation of being decorated with mil-
    itary medals by the formerly warring nations of
    France and Germany was not lost on Hartung, who
    later commented in his autobiography with some
    irony: "And as in France I was decorated with the
    Croix de guerre and the Médaille militaire and I
    was made commander of the Légion d'Honneur, I
    believe I was one of the only civilians–neither
    ambassador nor politician–to have received deco-
    rations from both sides!" Hans Hartung,
    Autoportrait. Récit recueilli par Monique Lefebvre
    (Paris: Bernard Grasset, 1976), p. 209.

5. Robert Fleck in *Art*, Hamburg, 5/1996, p. 37. The
    correspondence between Hartung and Chancellors
    Helmut Schmidt and Helmut Kohl and Vice-
    Chancellor Walter Scheel is kept in the archive of
    the Fondation Hans Hartung et Anna-Eva Bergman
    in Antibes. I thank Mme, Marie Aanderaa for
    sending me the documents.

6. Introduction to the catalogue for the exhibition in
    Munich and Berlin, 1981 (see note 3, above), p. 7.

7. See Martin Schneider, *Expansion/Integration. Die
    Kuntsausstellungen der französischen Besatzung in
    Nachkriegsdeutschland* [Post-War German
    Exhibitions of Art from the Occupation of France]
    (Munich, Berlin: t. Kunstverlag, 2004), esp. p. 14 ff.

8. The following remarks refer mainly to the disserta-
    tion of Ulrike Wollenhaupt-Schmidt: *Documenta
    1955. Eine Auseinandersetzung um die Kunst der
    Avantgarde 1945–1960* [Documenta 1955. An
    Analysis of the Art of the Avant-Garde, 1945-
    1960] (Frankfurt: Lang, 1994), p. 119 ff.

9. *Ibid*, p. 52.

10. "In fact, the development of abstract art was
    meant to be understood as internationalist and
    path-breaking, as was already documented early
    on by way of numerous exhibitions early on in
    the American and French zones." Beate Frosch,
    "Abstrakte und gegenständliche Malerei–die
    Diskussion im Spiegel zeitgenössischer Zeit-
    schriften" [Abstract and Figurative Painting–the
    Discussion as Reflected in Contemporary
    Newspapers], in *ZEN 49. Die Ersten Zehn Jahre–
    Orientierungen* [ZEN 49. The First Ten Years–
    Orientations], (Baden-Baden: Jochen Poetter,
    1986–87), p. 117.

11. Rupprecht Geiger, one of the founding members
    of the group ZEN 49: "At the time, abstract paint-
    ing seemed to us the most fitting means for
    rebuilding German culture. To acknowledge the
    atrocities, to then repeat them through images, all
    the while damning them and saying 'never
    again'–this was not an issue for us." Quoted from
    Clelia Segieth, *Etta und Otto Stangl. Galeristen,
    Sammler, Museumsgründer* [Etta and Otto Stangl.
    Gallerists, Collectors, Museum Founders], edited
    in collaboration with the Zentralarchiv des inter-
    nationalen Kunsthandels [Central Archive of the
    International Art Market] (Cologne: 2000), p. 48.

12. This interpretation is also shared by Pierre Daix in
    the exh. cat. *Les années 50* (Paris: Centre
    Georges-Pompidou, 1988), where he describes
    Hartung as an artist "who treats the space of his
    canvas like a field in the physical sense of the
    world... The graphic signs are configurations of
    forces of energy, knots of tension", in exh. cat. of
    Les années 50, Paris Musée national d'art mod-
    erne, Centre Pompidou, 1988, p. 76. Hartung him-
    self confirmed in a 1959 interview with Georges
    Charbonnier that he, like many others, was influ-
    enced in his art by recent theories in physics. In
    Georges Charbonnier, *Le monologue du peintre,
    Entretiens* (Paris: R. Julliard, 1959), p. 76. This
    interpretation has in turn been relativized in
    recent French criticism: see Anne Malherbe, "Le

réel et le sensible. Quelque mythologies dans le milieu de l'abstraction lyrique" in *Les Cahiers du musée national d'art moderne*, Paris, 84/2003, p. 67.

13. See exh. cat. *Sammlung Stangl. Von Klee bis Poliakoff*. [The Stangl Collection. From Klee to Poliakoff], (Munich: Ostfildern-Ruit, 1993), p. 304.

14. This volume was planned as the first in a series of international publications; however, owing to difficulties in sales, the advertised second volume, which was to have been on Mirò, was never produced.

15. Madeleine Rousseau, "Leben und Werk" [Life and Work] in Ottomar Domnick (ed.), *Hans Hartung*, (Stuttgart: Ottomar Domnick, 1949), p. 44 ff.

16. In this context, see Annie Claustres, "La fabrique de Hans Hartung. Un faux expressionisme pictural" in *Les Cahiers du musée national d'art moderne*, Paris, 80/2002, pp. 56–79. Hartung himself never denied the situation.

17. Segieth, p. 214 ff. His international breakthrough happened through the gallerist Louis Carré, whose show 'Advancing French Art' made Hartung known to the American market. Afterward, Hartung was one of the most sought-after artists of the early École de Paris.

18. *Ibid.*, p. 218, note 106.

19. *Ibid.*, p. 208 ff.

20. See also, Harald Kimpel: *Documenta. Die Überschau. Fünf Jahrzente Weltkunstausstellung in Stichwörtern* [Documenta, an Overview. Five Decades of the World Art Exhibition in Outlines] (Cologne, DuMont, 2002), p. 11 ff.

21. Wollenhaupt-Schmidt, see note 8, p. 84 ff. Haftmann used this opportunity to illustrate, now with real artworks, his thesis that abstraction was the only appropriate form for conveying the reality of the modern age in art.

22. Werner Haftmann, *Malerei im 20. Jahrhundert. Eine Entwicklungsgeschichte* [Painting in the 20th Century, a History of its Development] (Munich: Prestel, 1954), p. 472.

23. Werner Haftmann, "Malerei nach 1945" [Painting After 1945] in exh. cat. *II. documenta '59. Kunst nach 1945. Internationale Ausstellung, 11. Juli–11. Oktober 1959, Bd. I Malerei* [2nd Documenta '59. Art After 1945. International Exhibition, July 11–October 11, 1959. Vol. 1 Painting] (Cologne: DuMont Schauber, 1959), p. 17.

24. Werner Schmalenbach, in the exh. cat. *Hans Hartung* (Hanover: Kestner-Gesellschaft, 1957), p. 8. Schmalenbach's text in specific is still considered a standard in the French criticism.

25. The jury was accused of having chosen the artist not on artistic grounds but rather "in the spirit of compensating the emigrant Hans Hartung". Paul

Sieber, in the *Siegener Zeitung* [The Siegen News] of 25 Jan. 1958. Dr. Friedrich Weber, publication archivist for the *Siegener Zeitung*, kindly gave me access to this material.

26. Wollenhaupt-Schmidt, see note 8, p. 124.

27. Scheider, see note 7, p. 62.

28. Martina Dobbe, "Malerei im Bilderstreit. Eine Revision aus Anlass des Rubenspreis-Jubiläums" [Painting and the Image Debate. A Revision on the Occasion of the Rubens Prize Anniversary], in *10 x Malerei. Rubenspreis der Stadt Siegen in Werken der Sammlung Gambrecht-Schadeberg* [10 x Painting. The Rubens Prize of the City of Siegen, Works in the Gambrecht-Schadeberg Collection] (Siegen: Museum für Gegenwartskunst Siegen, 2002), p. 26.

29. "Alfred Otto Wolfgang Schulze, known as Wols, was a photographer and painter who emigrated from Germany to France in 1930 and among the founding members of a new direction in painting called variously 'art informel', 'lyrical abstraction' and 'Tachism'. Represented during his life and after his death at all the most important exhibitions, he was already a 'classic' Tachist in 1958 at the Venice Biennial." Barbara Wucherer, *Ein Phänomen des Stolperns–Wols' Portraits, 1932-51: in den Medien Fotografie, Malerei und Zeichnung. Studien zur Problematik der Portraitdarstellung im 20. Jahrhundert* [A Phenomenon of Stumbling–Wols' Portraits, 1932-51, in the Media of Photography, Painting, and Drawing. Studies on the Problematics of Portrait Representation in the 20th Century] (Berlin: Gebr. Mann, 1999), p. 9. See also exh. cat. *WOLS* (Düsseldorf, Zurich: Kunsthaus Zurich and Kunstsammlung Nordrhein-Westfalen, 1989).

30. In the *Neuen Rhein Zeitung* [New Rhein News] of 21 Sep. 1974, it was suggested that one could "perceive the sneaking impression of all-too pleasant decoration". Annegret Großkopf wrote, in the Cologne paper *Kölner Stadtanzeiger* on 21 Sep. 1974: "The Wallraf-Richartz-Museum missed an opportunity to analyse Hartung's position critically, the position of a painter who, in his own lifetime, found himself atop the pedestal as a classic of Modernism". She also characterised his late works as "decorative". I thank Mr. M. Fuchs for granting me access to this press material.

31. K. Reinke, in the newspaper *Handelsblatt*, Düsseldorf, 27 Sep. 1974.

32. "I commend above all the artists who have been awarded the Stefan Lochner Medal. Since the jury, correctly, took account of the entire art world, the majority of those honoured preferred their studio to the presentation stage, and have postponed their trips to Cologne for another

time. The awardees of the Stefan Lochner Medal are Sonja Delaunay, Naum Gabo, Hans Hartung, Jasper Johns and Antoni Tàpies...". Excerpt from the speech by Mayor John van Nes Ziegler at the ceremony marking the occasion of 150 years of the Wallraf-Richartz-Museum, on Friday, 29 March 1974, 4:30 p.m. in the Gürzenich district of Cologne: Historical Archive of Cologne, ZS V/101/1443.

33. Exh. cat. *Westkunst. Zeitgenößische Kunst seit 1939*] [Art of the West. Contemporary Art Since 1939], ed. Lazlo Glozer (Cologne: DuMont Buchverlag, 1981), p. 219. The catalogue contains not only texts on the creative context of the various artistic positions, but also historical documents, such as excerpts from, among others, Haftmann, Thwaites, Tapié and others.

34. Jörn Merkert in exh. cat. Munich and Berlin, 1981, see note 3, p. 12.

35. C. Schulz-Hoffmann in a press statement on 25 August 1982. Archive of the Fondation Hartung-Bergman, Antibes. I thank Mme, Marie Aanderaa for this information.

36. C. Stabenow: "Hans Hartung—Geste und Zeichen" [Hans Hartung—Gesture and Symbol] in *Die Kunst und das schöne Heim* [Art and the Beautiful Home], June 1984, pp. 434–41. In a text accompanying the collection, the celebration of his work is described as an "act of compensation to a painter who, with his innovations, led art in new directions". Information text from the Hessischen Landesmuseum in Darmstadt, 2/84, p. 9 ff.

37. See Werner Schmidt, "Ansprache zur Ausstellungseröffnung" [Address at the Exhibition Opening] in *Dresdener Kunstblätter* [Dresden Art Pages], Dresden, 27/1984, pp. 12-16.

38. R. Fleck, "Mann im Dunkeln. Hans Hartung—Bildbeispiele aus den dreißiger Jahren" [A Man in the Dark. Hans Hartung—Image Examples from the Thirties], in exh. cat. *Deutschlandbilder. Kunst aus einem geteilten Land im Martin-Gropius-Bau in Berlin 1997/98* [Pictures of Germany. Art from a Divided Country at the Martin Gropius Building in Berlin in 1997-98] (Cologne: DuMont Buchverlag, 1997), pp. 78, 84.

39. Ingrid Adler characterises Hartung as an "anti-fascist and humanist" in her article in *Union* (27 Oct. 1983), p. 4, but otherwise her review is quite free of ideological overtones.

40. R. Fleck, 1997, p. 84.

41. Recent portrayals of Hartung, which suggest that Hartung's serial manner of working and his systematisation of his production place him closer to conceptual art, have opened new directions in interpretation but do not yet seem particularly compelling. See Franz W. Kaiser, "konzeptuell 'avant la lettre'", in *Hartung x3*, ed. Franz W. Kaiser, Anne Pontégnie, Vincente Todoli (Angers: Expressions contemporaines, 2003), p. 84 ff. Also, see Annie Claustres, note 16, pp. 56–72.

42. See exh. cat. *Hans Hartung "So beschwor ich den Blitz"* [Hans Hartung. "And so I Conjured the Lightning"], ed. Stephan Diederich (Cologne: Verlag der Buchhandlung Walther König, 2004).

John C. Welchman Hans Hartung
Abcedarium: Reading Between the Lines
Franz-W. Kaiser A Case Study
on the Caducity of Categories
in Art Criticism Annie Claustres
Hans Hartung
Clandestine Artist
1937-1942: the Decisive Years
Christine Mehring Hans Hartung
Mid-Century Modern
Rainer Michael Mason Hartung
and Printmaking Christopher Wool

Selected Works

Anne Pontégnie 1975

Hartung at the

Metropolitan Museum

Chronicle of a Failure Chantal Eschenfelder

Hans Hartung in Germany

Laurence Bertrand Dorléac

Germany and France

Two Parts in One Jennifer Mundy

The Very Late Style of Hans Hartung

a Problem?

Orderly Emotions

During an interview in the summer of 1975, Hans Hartung struggled to answer his interviewer's questions concerning his German identity.[1] He saw well enough what attracted him to artists of different nationalities just after the War, whether it was the American Franz Kline or the French Pierre Soulages: the emotional state, the gesture, the famous beams. He accepted, nonetheless, to try to distinguish what in him came from his fatherland and what tied him to his adopted country.

He said his studies in Classics, in Latin especially, which he excelled at, distanced him some from the German language. Unlike German, Latin is "extremely clear, distinct, dry, visible; it instils a more careful, a firmer, discipline in thought that avoids the pitfalls of the Germanic languages. Everything you express in German has many meanings at once, nothing is ever clear and distinct".[2] This same craving for clarity drove him to find the Golden Section. Hans Hartung had also fallen in love with French literature, which he discovered through Alphonse Daudet's *Les Lettres de mon moulin*: "so charming, beautiful, pure, and lyrical, so clear and distinct! The polar opposite of Germanic murkiness".[3] Daudet's *Lettres* were also what first awoke in him the desire to go to Provence. He was equally enamoured of French architecture, which wasn't "enormous", but boasts to its credit a Romanesque style that is in very short supply in Germany as well as a more ancient Gothic. He loved Montparnasse and its characteristic lifestyle, the Paris Casino, the Folies Bergères, and Joséphine Baker, his "great love". The "great shock",[4] however, came during his visit to the Exhibition of International Art in Dresden in 1926; there, he says, he was so "fascinated" with "French painting"[5] that he couldn't tear himself away from it. In Dresden he learned that "expression and emotion could go hand in hand with order and clarity".[6] In Germany, on the other hand, "we had lost the habit of purity, clarity, and beauty. The Expressionists thought that the strongest painting was always the painting that sought to stigmatise the ugliness in humanity. We were working only on the level of the horrible, of the nightmare".[7] When his interviewer insisted on the German side, Hartung said that it was there, in his taste for graphic art ("a favourite of the Germans"), in his attention to perfection, in the "stronger tendency towards the emotional" than one finds in French art, which, especially after 1926, put such stock on the clarity that the analytical Cubists, Picasso, and Braque had brought to it. He didn't think Expressionism had been born in Germany, though he hesitated as to how it had entered the country: "maybe it was through Van Gogh and Munch", and he reminded us that "in Belgium, too, there were people who were already basically Expressionists".[8] Hartung saw many tendencies in Expressionism: there is a "pantheist or humanist side" in Van Gogh, while in Munch, who was strongly influenced by France and Toulouse-Lautrec, there is a side that is "very heavy and nostalgic, very sad, and also in great despair".[9] That was what would have been seen by the German Expressionists, whose art was "more rebellious and a bit adrift in nature".[10]

More or less consciously, Hans Hartung rehearsed in his answers all the clichés the century tagged onto the German and French identities. As one listened to him, one could not but recall the caution advised by the historian Meyer Shapiro, who said in 1953 that "hearing the incessant repetition that German art is by nature tense and irrational, that its grandeur depends on its fidelity to the national character, has contributed to making one accept the idea that these traits were inscribed in the destiny of this people".[11] In this interview about his identity, Hartung kept running into a slew of contradictions: he was certainly well settled in his new homeland, he had been amply decorated in France and Germany, and he was claimed by both countries.[12] In Germany, where he started exhibiting his work in 1931, Hartung was traditionally assigned the role of ferryman between the Romantic German tradition, with its Expressionist side, and the

French tradition of clarity and rationality. In 1981, during an exhibition at the National Gallery of Modern Art in Munich, Jörn Merkert relied on this role to claim for Hartung a "European destiny, of course a particular one, but exemplary nonetheless".[13] It became possible to claim, thenceforward, a European identity for an artist who, a mere twenty years earlier, had occupied a very ambiguous position, at least in France. Back then, his art and his status touched the obsessive fears of the realm of the imagination in French art, which hadn't yet accepted the German part of European culture, particularly its "Expressionist" part, which could so readily be associated with the regrettable excesses that France had always tried to escape.

Where is France going?

The discourse about the specificity of French art, the aim of which is essentially to argue for its supremacy, survived World War II, unscathed by an experience that so cruelly denounced its assumptions as outdated and otherworldly. As for German art, the spectre of Nazism did nothing more than shed light on some already deep-seated preconceptions and on an artistic scene where the artists were the only ones who avoided the pitfalls of preconceived opinion and prejudice given that they actually knew quite well what was going on in the artistic scene across the border. This is borne out in the survey Julien Alvard conducted in the 1950s with ten young French painters. His research revealed that, outside of Picasso, the names that came up most frequently were Klee and Kandinsky, with "a marked preference for Klee, who everyone thought had a greater poetic power. Hartung's name came up every time and his work is highly esteemed".[14] Julien Avelard concluded by noting that the "German School" as a whole seemed to be held in high regard by young painters: German Expressionism—"the only, the authentic one of Klee and Kandinsky and not that of Kokoschka"—remained a "pole of attraction". The circumscription is important as it rejected a form of excess that was still intolerable and from which the whole world would struggle to distance Hartung's work while aligning him to the French tradition.

Just after the Liberation, the works of Paul Klee and Kandinsky were still virtually unknown to the public so that all subterfuges were allowed; suffice it to note that when the Musée d'art Moderne reopened in 1947 under the direction of Jean Cassou, whole sections of international modern art were still not represented on its walls. A year later, when Jean Cassou had to account for Expressionism, he turned to Le Fauconnier and La Patellière, to Gromaire and Goerg, as well as to some masters of the School of Paris, like Pascin, Modigliani and Chagall. It was also at this time, when the Musée still owned nothing[15] by Soutine, that the entirely justified possibility of mounting a temporary exhibition of Paul Klee's work was first mentioned (the show was held in 1948). Bernard Dorival, an art historian and former curator at the Musée d'Art Moderne, said that Klee "is the only foreign painter—along with Ensor—who can be compared to our painters in France ..."[16]

For Dorival, it was a matter of striking the most radical opposition between the good seed and insobriety: he compared, weighed, classified and ultimately pitted the French against the others because "French Expressionism", linked on all sides to international Expressionism, had an essentially original figure.

By 1955, the critic Michel Ragon was able to denounce as ridiculous an overly chauvinistic and rational definition of the School of Paris. Yet, he showed compunction by counting among its members the "former German Hartung", once one has managed to divest it of historically false aspects, such as the sense of measure and the Cartesian approach that clearly had no relevance to Pascal, Sade, Gérard de Nerval, nor to Rimbaud, Berlioz, Antonin Artaud, or the French revolutions.[17]

This critical position at last gained some credibility in the 1970s and 1980s, when the notions underlying art history became less narrow-minded, less chauvinistic, and more conscious at heart of what had really taken place during the century haunted by nationalistic wars, wars that art history really did not escape by crippling, under duress, its appreciation of contemporary art.[18] This is what bothered the critic Michel Tapié. In defending the category of Art Informel, he very carefully sidestepped the spectre posed by Expressionism, noting that "in 1944, the days that immediately followed the war revealed with the most disconcerting violence, at least at first, a handful of authentic individuals whose message the public was not ready for and who, fortunately for them, could not be grouped under a common label: Dubuffet, Fautrier, Wols, Hartung, Tobey, Pollock, Mathieu, Soulages, de Kooning, Ubac, Henri Michaux ...".[19]

In point of fact, the incomprehension of the "Expressionist" strands of European art led to other instances of intellectual blindness after the war concerning artists who either didn't fit, or fit only very badly, the criteria stemming from the phantasm of national identity built around the ideas of reason, measure, controlled courage, *beau métier*, and the assembling—unique in the world—of qualities that might even be contradictory. Hence the famous existence of a French "tension" lined by a superiority complex that flared up over every quarrel of antecedence—Robert Delaunay and Picabia have, more than once, been claimed to have preceded Kandinsky.[20]

Franco-German Reconciliation

While Hartung was very well represented at international gatherings that emphasised Abstract art, in France he enjoyed an efficient defence backed by such high-profile Germans as the art historian Will Grohmann and the great art collector Ottomar Domnick, who played an important role in the development of Franco-German cultural relations after the war. The French press paid a lot of attention[21] to Hartung, who, in this landscape where the border between good and evil in matters of excess was clearly traced, held an interesting position as an index of the spirit of the times.

Denis Chevalier had already announced this after his fashion in the winter of 1946 in the *Petit dictionnaire des artistes contemporains*. Chevalier saw an oscillation in Hartung and argued that his expression was "sometimes Constructivist and free of affective contingencies, and at others lyrical and resolutely emotive".[22] Chevalier discerned in Hartung a "discreetly Romantic temperament"[23] before he was influenced by the "School of Paris", which demanded "more precision"[24] from him, and before he gave free rein to a "nervous and expressive drawing", one that harked back to an "emotional art in love with liberty and poetry, Romantic in its conception and expression".[25] Romanticism for Chevalier served as a pointer to the notions one has of German culture, but there were others who argued that France influenced this milieu of emotion that fitted in so well with a "French-like" lyricism. Just after the war, when Léon Degand recounted the life of "Jean" Hartung (note the Gallicised name), he borrowed Hartung's "plastic poems", which, he claimed were "clearly a part of the incomparable éclat of Paris, capital of the arts".[26] Hartung had to be naturalised, civically and artistically.

Jean-José Marchand's thinking was even more tortuous, in part because at first sight he did not seem to want to de-naturalise Hartung's "Expressionism". In the issue of *Combat* in March 1946, Marchand laid out the elements of Hartung's biography that would tie him to the German Expressionism he might have become acquainted with in the museums of his native town and that might have spurred him towards abstraction: Corinth, Kokoschka, Franz Marc and Nolde. He only silenced his "anger"[27] to link Hartung, via the "scream of a solitary man"[28], to Van Gogh. For Marchand, Hartung hadn't emerged from any school, but was simply destined to posterity in line with a French tradition that Marchand described a few months later as a "unity", a "plastic expression of the world" capable of integrating any and all foreign elements that sprang up.

Marchand essentially restated the ecumenical conception of a new School of Paris that flourished anew after the war (and the time of the exclusions), but in order to bring together rather than to exclude, as Bernard Dorival had wanted to do. Dorival thought that one had to distinguish French art from other arts and that, within France itself, one had to distinguish art from insobriety and from the School of Paris, which he regarded simply as the unfortunate result of an "influx that developed into a crowd during the first years of the century".[29] Some twelve years later, Frank Elgar came up with his own rather obscure mixture as he outlined the outcome of the first significant exhibition of German art in the Volney circle by René Drouin. Elgar noted the echoes of French art in German painters, and he appropriated Wols and Hartung to the "influential" French scene that also included Manessier, Bazaine and Schneider.[30] He also thought that "the new German art is, in truth, not German" but that it was interchangeable with American art. This was all in the effort to mount a bitter critique of the "pale brats" who "pour onto immaculate canvases the waste from their kitchens". As for German art, after stating that it was "more cosmopolitan than German", Elgar corrected himself: "in the lines (when there are any), in the colours (where there are any), one sees the traces of the old Expressionism, of an incurable Romanticism, a sadness that nothing can remedy. Love of life, the taste for matter, sensual excitement all seems to be unknown to the artists now hosting us, as are the classical qualities of measure, serenity, and logic".[31]

Less subject to opinion, Michel Ragon took advantage of his visit to the Blaue Reiter exhibition in Munich in 1948 to draw up a comprehensive picture of art in Germany. After the "chromo painting and bank-note style of the Hitler period" he saw in Germany a "natural disarray", a tendency to abstraction. Moreover, he thought it "significant" that "among abstract artists in Paris a large number are German immigrants".[32] In 1952 the 26th Biennial in Venice devoted a section to Expressionism, and the critics had a fun time coming up with their definition of the term. Robert Vrinat considered Hartung one of the few interesting abstract French artists with real "Expressionist roots"[33], in spite of his (Hartung's) preference at the end of the day for "expressive" expression. Vrinat's larger claim was that art stems from the "situation of the modern man, who is plunged in disquiet and disequilibrium",[34] and corresponds to "certain races, to certain geographic and social milieus, to certain conceptions of culture".[35] Vrinat's verdict, however, could be contradicted by Hartung's trajectory if one accepts that the artist should not be imprisoned within the concept of "race", which, evidently, was not completely bankrupted by the Shoah.

A year later, in 1953, Herta Wescher included Hartung among the artists who found a "lasting place" in the School of Paris by fleeing Nazism. Remarking that "it is often quite difficult to delimit the German and the French sources of the styles" of these artists, Wescher proceeded to make Hartung, who was inspired by the revolutionary movement Kandinsky unleashed in Germany, a representative case. On the French side, she suggested that if, at first, "the expansive force of the line, the primary element of his painting, was given to nervous and turbulent movements, his years in France deepened his awareness of structure, which in turn has served to increase the interior dynamism through forced stabilization".[36]

The same idea, though this time without any reference to France, resurfaced a little later in Michel Tapié, who included Hartung in the category of Art Informel by pitting his patience and his method, "which continues to be unfailingly efficient"[37], against the "the passions deranged to the point of paroxysm in the certainty of an unhinged mysticism"[38] characteristic of Hartung's compatriot Wols.

Abstract Identity

Hans Hartung won the prize at the 30th Biennial of Venice in 1960, and critical reception managed to save him once and for all from hubris by insisting on the fact that in his work "expressive content ... never assumes primacy over the plastic".[39] That same year, Giuseppe Marchiori composed a eulogy to Hartung that isolated him, if not from the world, at least from those strands of it that we may be inclined to associate him with. He loved the watercolours Hartung produced between 1920 and 1922 for the extreme freedom of the patches of colour which, he argues, "can only indirectly be tied to the culture of Expressionism. They are different from Kandinsky's abstractions. For more intimate reasons, they differ from the most typical forms of German Expressionism, with its determination to unveil the crisis of a society, to denounce its frightening lacks, with its inability to shake obsession and fear. In the most difficult contingencies of a period dominated by the "remorse about the war", which functioned as a motif of self-critical analysis pushed to the extremes of annihilation and despair, Hartung assumed Abstract art in a purely intuitive experience, without reference to the attempts of the Cubists or Mondrian, and limited only to an indirect relationship with Kandinsky".[40] In this way, Giuseppe Marchiori outlined the figure of a modern and free hero by evoking the "period of 'Mediterranean' painting that started during his stay in Minorca following his departure from Germany (then, as always, in order to be a free man)", a hero who unfolded "this graphic experience in a light free of Romantic nostalgia, in the pure light of the dreams and myths of an ideal country".[41]

The year before, 1959, during the second Documenta in Germany, Werner Harftmann set his contemporaries on the right track by proposing abstraction to them as a universal mode of language that, among other things, allowed European artists to exist side by side with their American colleagues, the power of whose work was then visible everywhere. Even if he viewed Hartung as coming from German Expressionism and Kandinsky, he contended that his type of abstraction was such that it could exist beyond nationalistic distinctions, in a zone where individuality and liberty claimed for him a higher form of independence.

Only a little while later, the return to new forms of realism meant a new and bitter rejection that would be tinted with nationalistic overtones—Beuys' ascendancy is a perfect illustration of this. But the fact remains that Hartung's career didn't just come to a full stop at that point, and that lately it has been considered in a new light, as the work that provided the link between historical Expressionism and Polke and Richter's generation, whose work Hartung's last paintings are so reminiscent of. Now that Hartung's oeuvre has become European, history will no doubt prefer to accentuate his qualities as a ferryman between two identities that are both present and a phantasm. It will, at any rate, be seen as a production that was by and large split from those bellicose elements that had for so long made art an imaginary battlefield that prolonged the war.

As for the question concerning his origins that haunted Hartung after the Sar, he seems to have preferred to turn it to his advantage by not always hiding his own doubts. In other words, even if it had been a serious question for him, it was undoubtedly less urgent than the paramount events that had made him, first, a stateless person and, second, a person with a double identity who was committed to working and who produced even to excess, as if in reparation. There is no doubt that Hartung, like his admirers, preferred the rebellious aspect of his nature, which had led him to renounce certitude in order to experiment "with very different things". It is hard not to think that he was being ironically playful when he said in the summer of 1975: "Now, if that is a German trait, I don't know, I don't think so ... I've never seen Germans who play up their own characters so much ...".[4]

My thanks to Annie Claustres and Jean-Luc Uro for their precious assistance.

1. See Hans Hartung, *Autoportrait. Récit recueilli par Monique Lefebvre* (Paris: Bernard Grasset, 1976).
2. Interview with Monique Lefebvre, Summer 1975, excerpt of the transcriptions, Coll. Fondation Hartung.
3. *Ibid.*
4. *Autoportrait, op. cit.*, p. 62.
5. *Ibid.*
6. *Ibid.*
7. *Ibid.*
8. Interview with Monique Lefebvre, *op. cit.*
9. *Ibid.*
10. *Ibid.*
11. Meyer Shapiro, *Style, artiste et société*, Fr. trans. Daniel Arasse, (Paris: 1982, p. 73).
12. Hartung jokes about it in his *Autoportrait, op. cit.*, p. 209.
13. Jörn Merkert, in the exh. cat. *Hans Hartung*, Munich, Staatsgalerie Moderner Kunst (Berlin: Akademie der Kunst, 1981), quoted by Chantal Eschenfelder, *in* "Hans Hartung in Deutschland. Hans Hartung so beschwor ich den Blitz" (Cologne: Museum Ludwig, 2004).
14. Julien Alvard, "Enquête auprès des jeunes artistes", *Art d'aujourd'hui,* 6 (Boulogne sur Seine: May 1950).
15. Jean Cassou, "L'ouverture du Musée d'art moderne", *Bulletin des Musées de France*, 6 (Paris: July 1947).
16. Bernard Dorival, "L'exposition Paul Klee", *Musées de France* (Paris: Mar. 1948).
17. See Michel Ragon, "L'Ecole de Paris se porte bien", *Cimaise* (Paris: Dec. 1955).
18. Roland Recht tried it out on the cases of the four art historians: Aloïs Riegl, Wölfflin, Aby Warburg and Erwin Panofsky, in "L'Ecriture de l'histoire de l'art devant les modernes (remarque à partir de Riegl, Wölfflin, Warburg et Panofsky)", *Les Cahiers du Musée National d'Art Moderne*, 48 (Paris: Summer 1994).
19. Michel Tapié, "Messages sans étiquettes", *XXe siècle*, June 1955.
20. See in particular Waldermar George, who attacks an article in *Match* on the birth of Abstractionism in Munich with the Blaue Reiter, *in* "Au Musée National d'Art Moderne Robert Delaunay ou le nouvel Orphée", *Prisme des arts*, 13, 1957, p. 28; and Bernard Dorival, "La Vie des Musées. Nouvelles acquisitions. Musée National d'Art Moderne", *La Revue des Arts*, III (1959), p. 218.
21. On the reception of the work of Hans Hartung, see: Annie Claustres, *Peintures de Hans Hartung (1922–1989). Histoire d'une réception*, PhD thesis, Paris IV-Sorbonne, 2001; and *Hans Hartung. Les aléas d'une réception* (Dijon: Presses du réel, 2005).
22. Denys Chevalier, "Portrait. Petit dictionnaire des artistes contemporains. Hans Hartung", *Art* (Paris: 3 Dec. 1946).
23. *Ibid.*
24. *Ibid.*
25. *Ibid.*
26. Léon Degand, "Jean Hartung", *Juin* (Paris: 3 Dec. 1946)
27. Jean-José Marchand, "Un néo-abstractiviste: Hans Hartung", *Combat* (Paris: 31 Mar. 1946).
28. *Ibid.*
29. Bernard Dorival, *Les Etapes de la peinture française contemporaine*, vol. 3 (Paris: Gallimard, 1946), p. 187.
30. Frank Elgar, "Tel est l'art moderne allemand", *Carrefour des Arts* (Paris: 13 Apr. 1955).
31. *Ibid.*
32. Michel Ragon, "Les tendances actuelles de la peinture allemande", *Arts* (Paris: 17 Sept. 1948).
33. Robert Vrinat, "L'aventure plastique dans l'expressionnisme", *L'Âge nouveau* (Paris: Dec. 1952).
34. *Ibid.*
35. *Ibid.*
36. Herta Wescher, *Art d'aujourd'hui* (Boulogne sur Seine: Aug. 1953).
37. Michel Tapié, "Messages sans étiquette", *op. cit.*
38. *Ibid.*
39. Guy Habasque, "La XXXᵉ Biennale de Venise", *L'Œil* (Sep. 1960).
40. Giuseppe Marchiori, "Hartung : l'œuvre première", *XXᵉ siècle* (June 1960).
41. *Ibid.*
42. Hans Hartung, Interview with Monique Lefebvre, *op. cit.*

John C. Welchman **Hans Hartung Abcedarium:** Reading Between the Lines

Franz-W. Kaiser **A Case Study on the Caducity of Categories in Art Criticism** Annie Claustres

Hans Hartung Clandestine Artist 1937-1942: the Decisive Years

Christine Mehring **Hans Hartung Mid-Century Modern**

Rainer Michael Mason **Hartung and Printmaking** Christopher Wool

Selected Works

Anne Pontégnie

1975

Hartung at the Metropolitan Museum

Chronicle of a Failure   Chantal Eschenfelder

Hans Hartung in Germany

Laurence Bertrand Dorléac

Germany and France

Two Parts in One   Jennifer Mundy

The Very Late Style of Hans Hartung

a Problem?

Issues surrounding the very late style of artists
remain relatively unexplored...

Gary Garrels on de Kooning, 1995[1]

The title sequence of the film commences: "HARTUNG 1989. That year he turned eighty-five. He painted 360 paintings. He died 7 December." These brief sentences—all there is by way of commentary in the film—can perhaps be said to encapsulate the problem of the very late style of Hartung. Towards the end of December 1986 Hartung had suffered a severe stroke and subsequently required nursing to help him dress and bathe. In his last years he was no longer able to stand, and relied on a wheelchair and the help of others to move. He had lost much of his fine motor control and signing documents became something that might only be attempted on "good" days, which became fewer and fewer over the period 1987–89. In his last year his short term memory became patchy, to the point where he might forget the names of his assistants; conversations were limited in scope. More distressing for those around him, Hartung's character seems to have changed. From being a man who was ever in control, precise and decisive, he became quiescent, accepting, and either unwilling to impose his will on the running of his studio or incapable of doing so. This change in disposition made the task of looking after Hartung the invalid much easier. But it poses fundamental questions about the authorship role of Hartung the artist, who as the film's title sequence stated, was able to produce in his very late years what for most other painters would have been a phe-nomenal rate of production, completing eighty-five canvases in 1987 following his recovery from the stroke in March of that year, 202 in 1988, and, as the film noted tri-umphantly, 360 canvases in 1989.

The film, shot by assistants over a period of several months in 1989 and edited into a montage of sequences in 1996 for an exhibition of Hartung's late works,[2] attempted to deal with two of the most obvious questions posed by these very works. First, did Hartung—a man too physically incapacitated to stand and at times too confused to con-verse fluently—actually paint these canvases which were often spectacular in scale and dominated by imagery that spoke of explosive energy? Secondly, was Hartung in full control of the technical means used in the production of his late canvases?

The film would appear to deal with the first question, and, as we shall see, the sec-ond has tended to be answered in the affirmative by a number of writers. But it is per-haps helpful to return to these fundamental questions in order to arrive at a reasoned assessment of the significance of these late works and their place in Hartung's œuvre as a whole. After all, depending on one's response to these questions, the late canvases can

| 1. Hartung with a sprayer in his studio, 2 October 1989, Photo by André Villers

be seen as either a triumphant culmination of essential aspects of Hartung's approach to art or a mere postscript to a career which deserves to be remembered for other works.

Hartung 1989 comprises sequences of the artist at work. Throughout the film Hartung is shown in his wheelchair before a succession of changing canvases. These are brought and taken away by two assistants, who step gingerly over the paint-spattered studio floor. (Hartung's use of "*pulverisateurs*" or sprayers to shoot paint of various degrees of liquidity at a canvas left a slippery mess on the ground.) The film was shot on different occasions in the spring and summer of that year. Some sequences show a video-recorder date, others do not, but they are not presented in the edited film in chronological order.

This is perhaps a clue to the fact that the film, however informative, was not quite a neutral record of the making of the works. In the mind of the film's editor there was clearly a need to use the film to focus on the creativity of the artist rather than on what may have been perceived as the less interesting aspect of the process of producing the paintings. In the beginning of the film, for example, Hartung is shown from the left; the work of getting the various canisters of paint ready for use, which took place on the right and behind the artist, is not shown until halfway through. Also, in the first half of the film, editing has eliminated pauses in the process. With the use of cuts and lap-dis-solve, tools change in the artist's hand; similar tools produce different thicknesses of paint with no apparent change to the sprayer's nozzle; and assistants, when they are shown, are at times reduced to ghostly traces. Significantly, the film is silent and does not record the admittedly minimal conversation that took place between Hartung and the assistants in these sessions.

This lack of conversation, however, is itself revelatory. Hartung tended to work with assistants over a long period of time, and so they came to know intimately the artist's requirements and preferences. When Hartung was wheelchair-bound and infirm, some of the assistants became more involved in the physical tasks of looking after him; in some ways, they felt as close to him as to a family member. Requiring attention day and night, Hartung might have lived the end of his life in a nursing home, were it not for the practical and moral support provided by his wife, the artist Anna-Eva Bergman, before her death in July 1987, by his long-term personal assistant, Marie Aanderaa, and by the team of studio assistants. Key figures in this team in

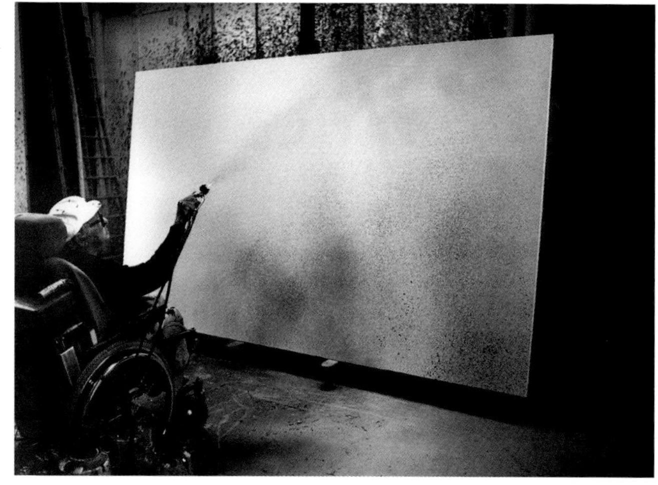

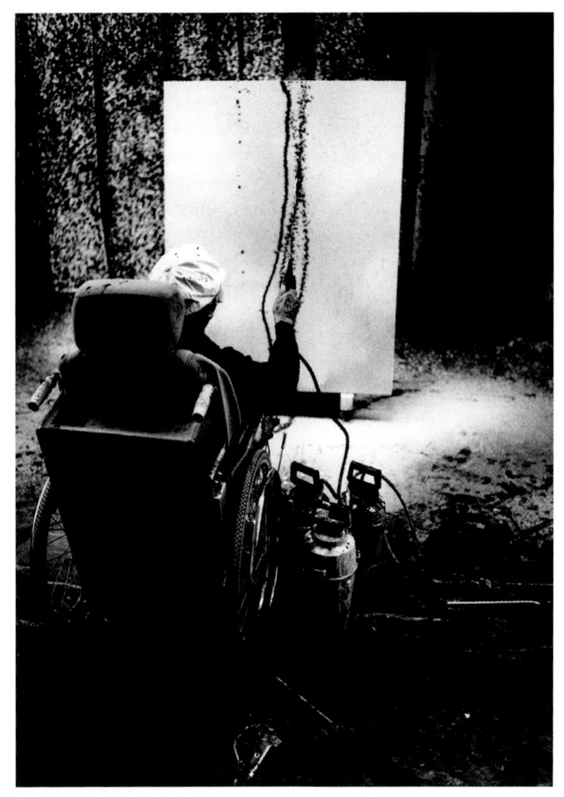

Hartung's later years were Hervé Coste de Champeron, who joined in March 1988, Bernard Derderian, who, after having worked in the studio between 1980 and 1982, returned to work for Hartung in April 1987, Pascal Simonet, who worked in the studio from March 1985, Jean-Luc Uro, who started in October 1988, and Alkis Voliotis, who worked at the studio from 1974 to March 1988. Generally working in pairs, the principal assistants in these years lived and worked at the studio complex on the basis of two weeks on and two weeks off.

Hartung had long employed assistants to help him prepare canvases and paints, as well photograph and catalogue his works. The first joined him in the mid-1950s, at a time when he was becoming famous in France and abroad as a gestural artist.[3] Hartung's reputation, however, was based on a partial misunderstanding, one which he did little to correct. As was only fully established in the 1990s, his famous paintings of the 1950s were in fact carefully transcribed enlargements of drawings.[4] In the early 1950s Hartung would have done this work himself. Once he began to use assistants, however, it seems highly likely that assistants would not only have prepared the canvas and painted the ground but also, in some cases at least, drawn the outline shapes that Hartung would then have carefully filled in, creating the illusion of sweeping, gestural strokes. This way of working continued until the early 1960s when Hartung began to use compressed-air spray-guns to create his images, thereby becoming truly a gestural painter.

Videoed interviews with assistants who worked with Hartung in the 1960s and later reveal that Hartung would ask an assistant early in the morning to prepare a different number of canvases, of certain sizes, and mix a number of specified colours for a painting session that evening (he generally painted at night). During the day the assistant would bring samples of the colours requested, showing how the paints had dried or responded to fixing for Hartung to approve. Volker Schultheis, an assistant from 1964 to 1967, recalled, "after a while I knew what he wanted pretty well"; but he added that

2. Hartung with a sprayer, 1989 (photo by André Villers)
3. Hartung with Bernard Derderian, 1989 (photo by André Villers)

Hartung was difficult to please when it came to mixing up sombre colours, always wanting them "*plus noir*" [blacker].[5]

Assistants who stayed with Hartung for a long period naturally came to understand and anticipate Hartung's wishes. In 1985 Hartung was quoted in an interview as saying that he did not need to instruct his team of assistants much. "The sort of telepathy you establish after working together for a while", Hartung claimed, "makes everything run smoothly when you need it". The interviewer, however, went on to note that Hartung–although more or less in a trance-like state while painting, partly induced by wine and an insulating barrier of Baroque music played extremely loudly–was careful to remain in contact with reality "to make sure his assistants, who prepare this colour or fetch that brush, are on their feet".[6]

Following his illness in late 1986, and subsequent bouts of worsening health, it seems that Hartung was no longer concerned to impose his will in quite the same way as before. The size of canvases on which Hartung worked was determined on a day to day basis by the assistants. They also chose the colours of the grounds of the canvases, which they painted, and prepared the range of colours that were to be used in any one day, without much, if any, consultation with the artist. While Hartung painted, the assistants stood ready with the next sprayer to hand to him, following an agreed understanding of what tool was necessary and when. One type of sprayer would produce a fine mist of paint or, with an adjustment to the nozzle, more defined areas of colour with more or less random patches of opacity, while another made the great arcs and nervously wandering lines that were the hallmarks of Hartung's late works. (The film shows the assistants explaining to the artist what effect a particular nozzle setting would achieve, and Hartung testing the effects by spraying onto the ground beside him.) Different degrees of liquidity were also used to create effects ranging from mist-like droplets to quite messy splashes of paint.

Hartung could have rejected the assistants' choice of canvases and coloured grounds; he could also have declined to use the particular colours they mixed up for each day's work. However, for the most part, he accepted what was done for him. Infirmity seemed to have made him either unwilling to seek to control such matters or simply accepting of the situation. For Derderian, it was as if Hartung was willing to accept and play with the cards dealt him as in a game, the rules of which he him-

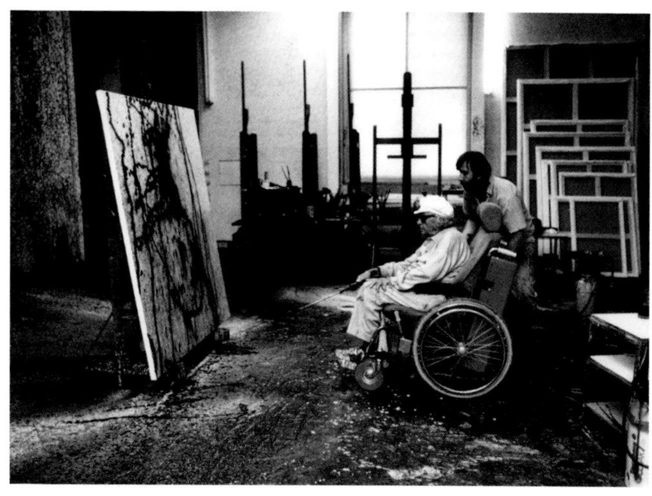

self had established before his stroke. It could be said that, rather than being in control of the studio system, Hartung was now sustained by it. But it was, nonetheless, the system he had put into place.

As demonstrated in the film, Hartung was fully capable of producing the late canvases whose energy and ambition astounded so many contemporary commentators. Hartung painted all the marks on the surface of the canvases and, crucially, decided when a painting was finished and was to be taken away. At one point in the film, the assistant Bernard Derderian appears to lean over to ask Hartung whether a work is finished; Hartung nods and says a few words; Derderian gives a thumbs-up sign and jokingly shakes Hartung's hand in congratulations; and the painting is removed. Amazingly, the process of painting most canvases, even the largest, did not take more than a few minutes. The only limit to the numbers that would be produced in a day was the floor space needed to lay the canvases flat to dry without paint runs spoiling the effect—an effect, of which the film makes clear, Hartung was in control.

However, Hartung's physical incapacity, the growing number of lapses in his attentiveness and short term memory, and, above all, the introduction of the new expansive imagery in the late years lent credence to rumours that the assistants painted some or all of these late works. The video of Hartung at work in 1989 was made expressly to refute these rumours, which nonetheless still surface from time to time today. Technically simple, the late works might seem easy to imitate, but it is worth remarking that, had assistants wanted, for whatever reason, to fake Hartung's work, they surely would have chosen to stay within the compass of his previously established style, using colours, formats and techniques that were recognised as typical. Instead of this, the very late works surprised all those who knew Hartung. The director of the Kunstsammlung Nordrhein-Westfalen, Werner Schmalenbach, for example, was astonished by what he saw as the youthfulness of the works he saw during a visit to Hartung's studio in 1988: "These are not at all the paintings of an old man. They exude the amazing youth Hartung has managed to preserve despite old age, illnesses, and the death of his wife, Anna-Eva."[7]

A New Phase

Writing about the late works of the abstract painter, Willem de Kooning, Robert Storr addressed not only the specific issues arising from the American artist's creeping Alzheimer's over the course of the 1980s but also the more general question of the constraints and opportunities brought to a painter by old age. He wrote:

"Age and sickness debilitate, but they are also catalysts. Those stricken (and eventually no one is spared) might seem less themselves in gross terms, but in subtler ways

---

4. HH, *T1982-E15*, 1982, acrylic on canvas, 185 x 300 cm. Tate Modern, London

they may be simply "other", or different than they were, in order to maintain a more essential continuity of being. Whether a person succeeds in adapting positively to extreme conditions is a consequence of self-knowledge, discipline, support, and unforeseeable good luck in the unfolding of natural misfortune. It is not so much that miracles happen as that the infirmities that inevitably betray us are not always so simple or complete as their onset and symptoms portend. Thus, while the forfeiture of strengths is implicit in the human condition, so too is their constant metamorphosis."[8]

As Storr notes, it is a mistake to generalise about the weaknesses imposed by age and infirmity: the debilities are rarely constant, and while some faculties may be lost, others may continue and even, in stripped down form, flourish. There were clearly "good" days and "bad" days for Hartung. An analysis of his production by month, for example, shows an enormous variation in his ability and desire to paint (see Appendix A). In 1987 he produced twenty-nine canvases in March, the first month he returned to painting after his stroke, but more or less nothing again until the autumn. In 1988 he produced twenty-six canvases in January and twenty-four in February, but this was followed by a period of five months when he again produced almost nothing until August. However, this pattern was entirely similar to that of the early 1980s, when travels and ill health contributed to sometimes extensive periods of inactivity. In 1981, for example, he produced only nine works in January and nothing again until August. In 1984 he worked only in February, March and April. In other words, Hartung's ability and desire to paint may have waxed and waned but it may perhaps be assumed that he only painted when he both wanted to do so and felt that he could.

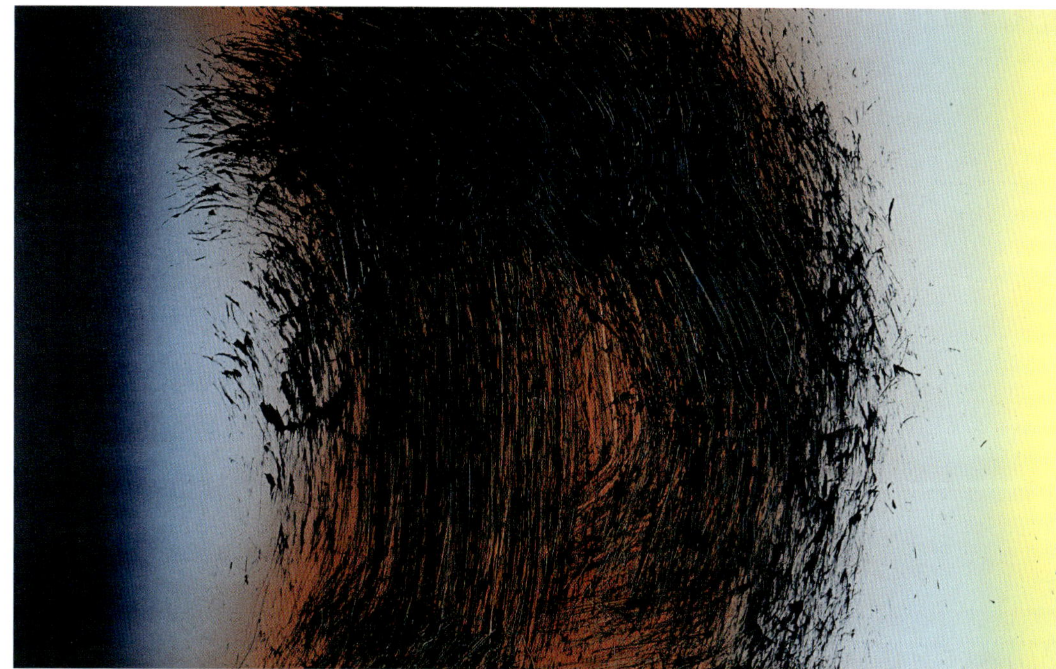

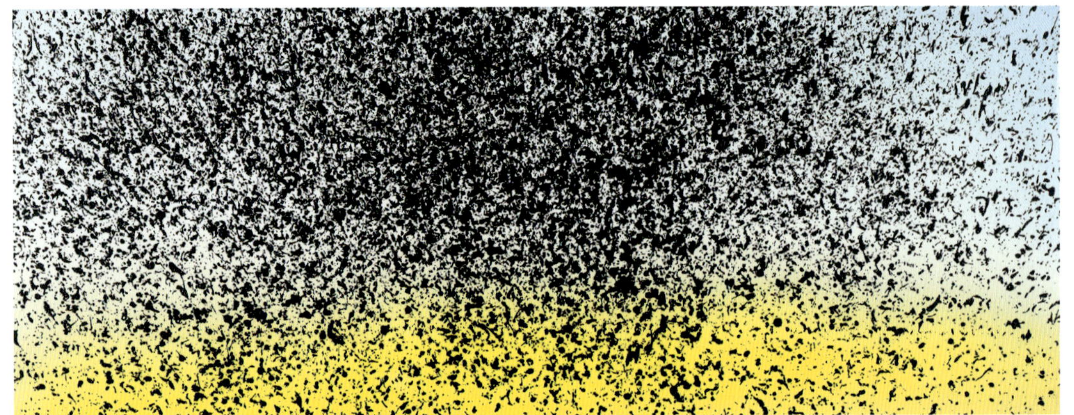

Against this background of an uneven working pattern, how do the late works relate to what had preceded them, and when did significant shifts in style and technique occur? From 1979–80 to late 1986 Hartung used branches, taken from the olive trees that surrounded the studio, with which to paint. Typically, he would thrash the paint-dipped branches against the canvas. Such was the force used by Hartung—a man who had strong upper arms from having walked with the aid of crutches since 1944—that the canvases had to be laid on wooden supports, or isorels, to prevent damage (these were then removed and the finished canvases were placed on conventional stretchers). Alternatively, two assistants would stand with a wooden support behind a canvas while Hartung thrashed the branches onto it.[9] In works such as *T1982-E15* (fig. 5), mechanically sprayed vertical borders of blue and acid yellow frame a central red area over which brushes and branches dipped in black paint have been swept up and across the canvas. Such works spoke of a controlled contrast between order and unleashed energy.

Ever open to change, Hartung had introduced into his already extensive armoury of implements the "*tirolienne*" in July 1985. This is a handheld tool with which house painters spatter pebble dashing onto the walls of houses. In the first works in which the device was used (fig. 6) Hartung created amorphous areas of black spatterings, relatively dense in the centre and airy towards the edges, on grounds painted pale blue or blue with yellow. The effects of this tool were relatively crude, and, because it was quite heavy to carry when filled with paint, it was not a solution to the problem of Hartung's declining physical strength. In a video interview the assistant Alkis Voliotis recalled that in 1986 Anna-Eva had telephoned him to ask if he might be able to find a new tool with which to help Hartung continue to paint.[10] His solution was a sprayer, or "*sulfateuse*", normally used by gardeners to spray herbicide or water in gardens and by viticulturists to spray copper sulphate solutions on vines. It consisted of a metal canister with a flex-

5. HH, *T1985-H30*, 1985, acrylic on canvas, 70 x 190 cm
6. HH, *T1986-R22*, 1986, acrylic on canvas (sprayer), 65 x 81 cm, private collection

ible hose leading to the handle which had a trigger and a long spraying rod. The canister needed to be pumped ten or so times to create enough pressure to force liquid through the nozzle when the trigger was depressed. Hartung had used compressed air to spray paint since the 1960s but this had involved lifting relatively heavy canisters of paint and wearing a protective mask in order not to inhale the spray. It was difficult, too, to achieve anything other than an even—and clearly mechanical—application of paint. With a "*sulfateuse*", however, the canister could be left on the ground and all that had to be held was the light wand of the spraying rod. Above all, with its adjustable nozzle, the sprayer could be used to create both fine and thicker lines of spattered droplets, as well as areas of solid colour. The spray might last only for a minute or so but this drawback could be overcome by having several canisters available. Light and small, it allowed Hartung to project great sweeping lines of paint with a simple flick of a wrist. The artist may have had difficulty controlling a pen in his last years but, as the film shows, he was able to twist his forearm and when necessary lift his right arm to shoulder height—and these small movements were sufficient to paint canvases that were several metres wide and high.

Hartung immediately took to the sprayer. The records show that on the first day he used the "*sulfateuse*"—6 August 1986—he experimented with black acrylic on canvas and ink on board, creating sometimes simple, sometimes more complex, images of wandering lines (fig. 7). Clearly entranced with the new tool, Hartung produced no fewer than 106 canvases and works on paper that month.

When Hartung returned to the studio after his stroke, in March 1987, his options for painting were, of course, limited. As had already been clear in 1986, he no longer had the strength and manual control to paint vigorously, an enormous blow for an artist whose whole career had been predicated on and sustained by a decisive, almost violent, gesturalism. But rather than return to painting in a tentative or timid way, he specifically asked to work on large format paintings. On 10 March, his first day back in the studio, he worked on two canvases each measuring 250 x 154 cm and a diptych measuring in all 180 x 360 cm (figs. 9, 10). With the use of the "*sulfateuse*" and a palette of pale blue, a darker blue, a lemon yellow and black, Hartung was able to create images that were gestural and painterly, combining interlacing lines with

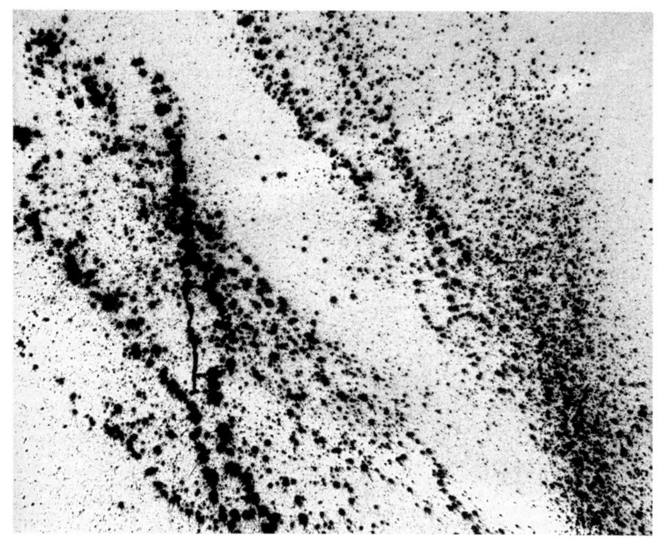

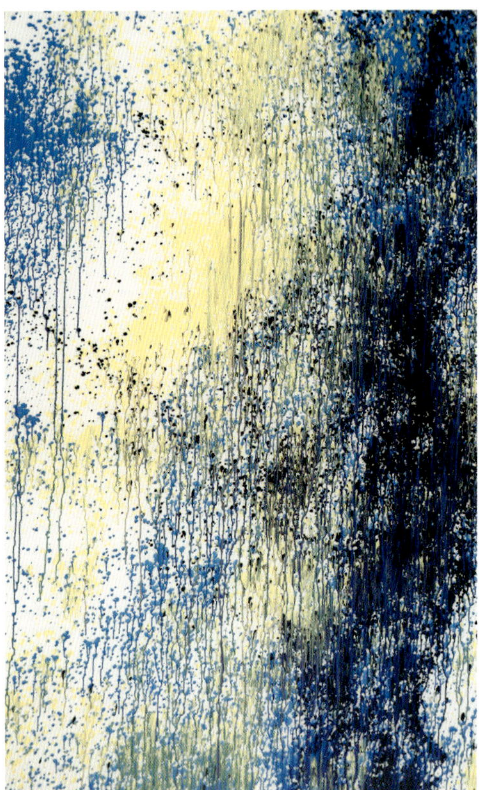

sometimes textured patches of colour of various degrees of density. This choice to work on large format canvases—something that became the norm in this later period—spoke of confidence in himself and in the tools at his disposal. This confidence was to be increased by his use of a second type of spray, known as "*l'airless*", from the beginning of 1989.[11] Used normally by house painters to paint large areas, or car mechanics to paint the body-work of cars, this spray could be used to create relatively even mists of background colour or random patches of greater density. In 1988 Hartung briefly used the five-brush tool, similar in form to a rake, that he had used in the 1970s, but the resulting few paintings offered no way ahead and the experiment was not extended (fig. 12). Fine mists, thicker "clouds", paint runs and freely doodled lines were to be the formal language of Hartung's last years. None of this would have been possible without the simple, if unorthodox, tech-nology discovered by the studio assistants. This was, in Storr's phrase, the piece of "unforeseeable good luck in the unfolding of natural misfortune" that made it possible for Hartung to continue to work as an artist.

7. HH, *T1987-H1*, 1987, acrylic on canvas, 250 x 154 cm
8. HH, *T1987-H2*, 1987, acrylic on canvas, 250 x 154 cm
9. HH, *T1987-H3*, 1987, acrylic on canvas, 180 x 180 cm
10. HH, *T1987-H4*, 1987, acrylic on canvas, 180 x 180 cm

From this point on—albeit somewhat spasmodically—Hartung went on to paint some of the freest, most ambitious, largest and most colourful works of his entire career. Enormous scale held no terrors, and he painted several grand canvases of 5 metres width. Some of his paintings presented radically off-centred images of freely doodled lines that went off the edges of the canvas. Combined with areas of colour and texture, some of the wilder images showed a knowing disregard for traditional composition, and even tested the stylistic conventions that had characterised much of Hartung's work to date. Some canvases, for example, relied not on line but on colour applied in layers of wet paint that were allowed to run together, creating a highly textured patterning. With their splashes and seemingly random lines, other images could be read as both manifestations of energised paint and images of inchoate matter within the natural world. Spontaneous and experimental by nature, not all the late works can be judged successes, but the best of them spoke of a grand ambition and a complex interplay of moods and emotions.

Were these freer compositions expressions of a "late style" or an "Alterstil"? Should the distinct changes in Hartung's style in these last years be compared to the fresh ambition and shift away from naturalism shown in the late *Water-lily* paintings by Monet? Or the radical simplification of forms and joyousness of Matisse's late paper cutouts? Or the schematic quality and focus on mortality found in Picasso's late works? Whatever answers are given to these questions, it is easy to believe that advancing age and physical decline gave Hartung an incentive to focus on exploring those aspects of his artistic identity that he could still access. Where he had once been forceful, explosive, decisive and in control, he was now more open to expressing through gesture chance, disorder and emotions that embraced awe, delight and foreboding.

Both these aspects had always been present in his work, even if the former had generally dominated. The free cursive gestures, the courting of chance and even the use of

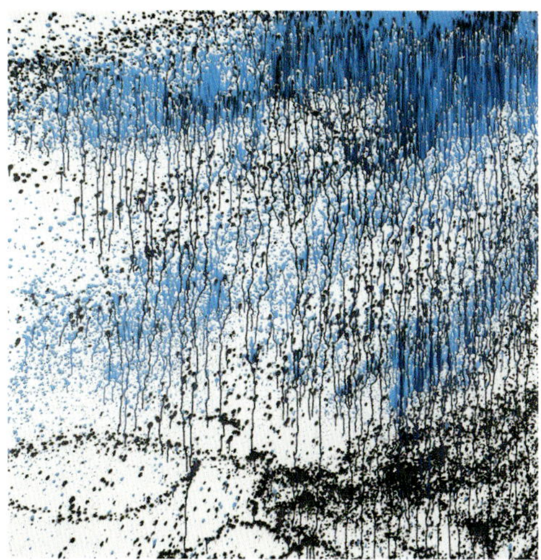
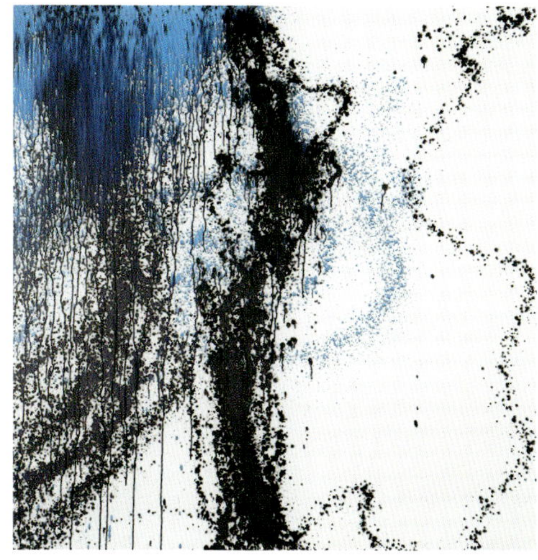

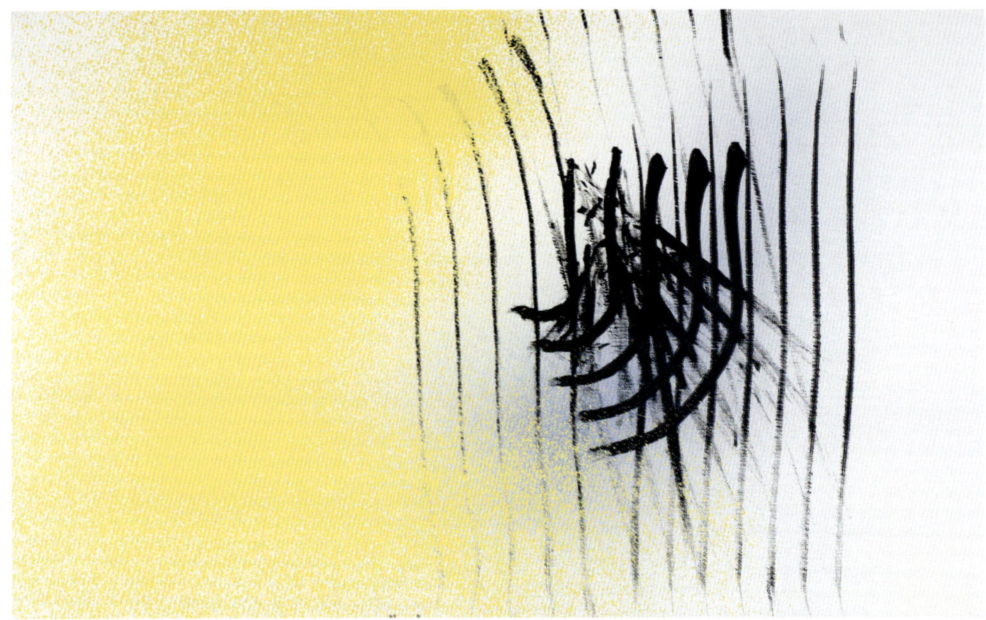

sweeter colours in the late years had antecedents in earlier works. Although on a quite different scale, various drawings that Hartung made in the 1920s and 1930s seem to anticipate the graphism of the later works (see figs. 13, 14). The atypical colours found in the late works, however, marked a distinct shift. Hartung had often said that he preferred sombre colours and actively disliked sweet colours, particularly pinks and reds,[12] though in the 1970s he did for a period begin to use warmer colours.[13] This is an area where the assistants seem to have played a particular role, choosing colours that were not typical of Hartung's tastes but which nonetheless had been used by the artist at some point in the past (fig. 15). A comment made by Hartung in an interview of August 1988 to the newspaper *Libération* may indicate that he did not feel strongly about the choice of colours in his paintings of this period: "I abuse them. Usually, they're the ones who decide".[14] This should perhaps be read as code for the simple fact that the colours, and the sequence of their use in particular paintings, were generally decided by the assistants. For good or ill, the assistants broadened Hartung's typical palette, but did so in the knowledge that he himself had experimented from time to time with a range of colours. Hartung's acceptance—and perhaps even welcoming of the intervention of others—in this area can be seen as an expression of his weakened faculties. It may also be seen, however, as another aspect of the complex interplay of control and chance involved in the late works.

11. HH, *T1988-H9*, 1988, acrylic on canvas, 89 x 146 cm
12. HH, untitled, 1927 (?), ink on paper, 12 x 7.2 cm
13. HH, untitled, 1935 (?), crayon on paper, 49 x 65 cm

Reception

The new developments in Hartung's art were not viewed uniformly positively by those around him. One assistant, who, it should be noted, was trained as a restorer and had had enormous respect for Hartung's mastery of technical matters, found it difficult to accept these very late works, which seemed to him to be lacking in authorial control and to be a product of infirmity. For a period in 1987 the atmosphere in the studio was poor, and this affected Hartung's ability and willingness to paint. The arrival of Bernard Derderian in April 1987 and the recruitment of other, younger assistants changed the situation. As Derderian noted in an interview given in 1996, the newer assistants tended to be much more aware of the conceptual underpinning of the development of modern art, and had no difficulty in accepting the technical simplicity of Hartung's late paintings as being as valid as more complex ways of working. He added that throughout Hartung's career there had been teams of assistants whose particular skills and interests corresponded to the needs and direction of Hartung's painting at the time. "Those who admired the gesture of the 1950s or the virtuosity of the 1960s started to leave when they thought Hartung's paintings had become too random", he said. "Those of us who were just arriving belonged to a new generation that was not really that interested in technique. And, anyway, stretching canvases and using vinyl paint had become very easy".[15]

Hartung's recent works were included in a number of exhibitions in the years 1987–89[16] and engendered a uniformly positive response from press critics. Writers typically marvelled at Hartung's inventiveness at an age when other artists had long since ceased to paint at all, and were struck by both the scale and what they saw as the sheer beauty of some of the late works. One reviewer of an exhibition of Hartung's recent works, for example, commented in *Art Press* in January 1988:

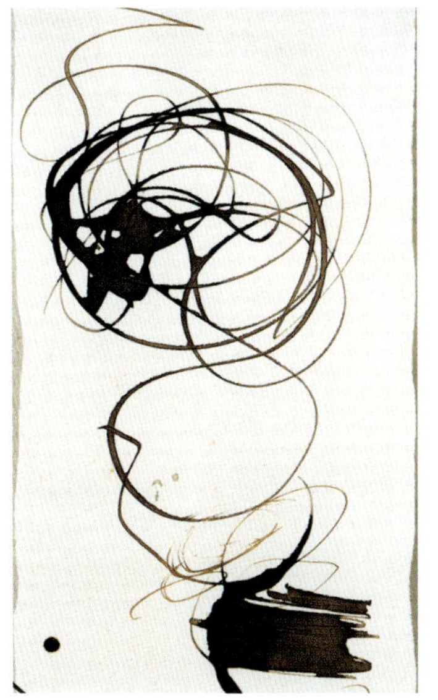

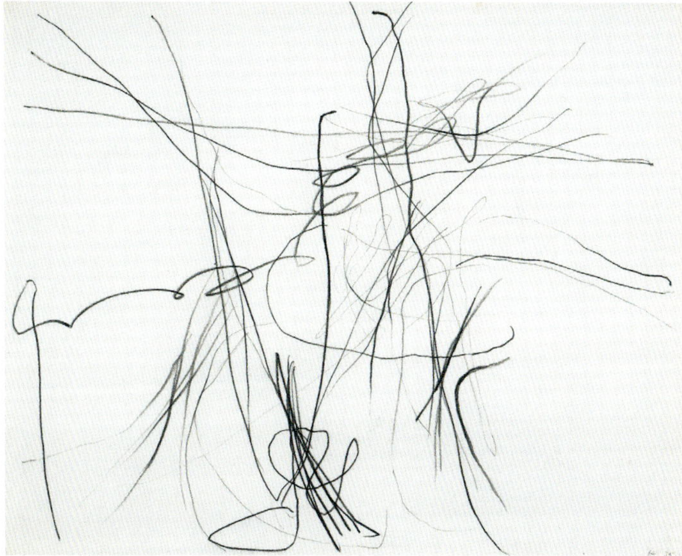

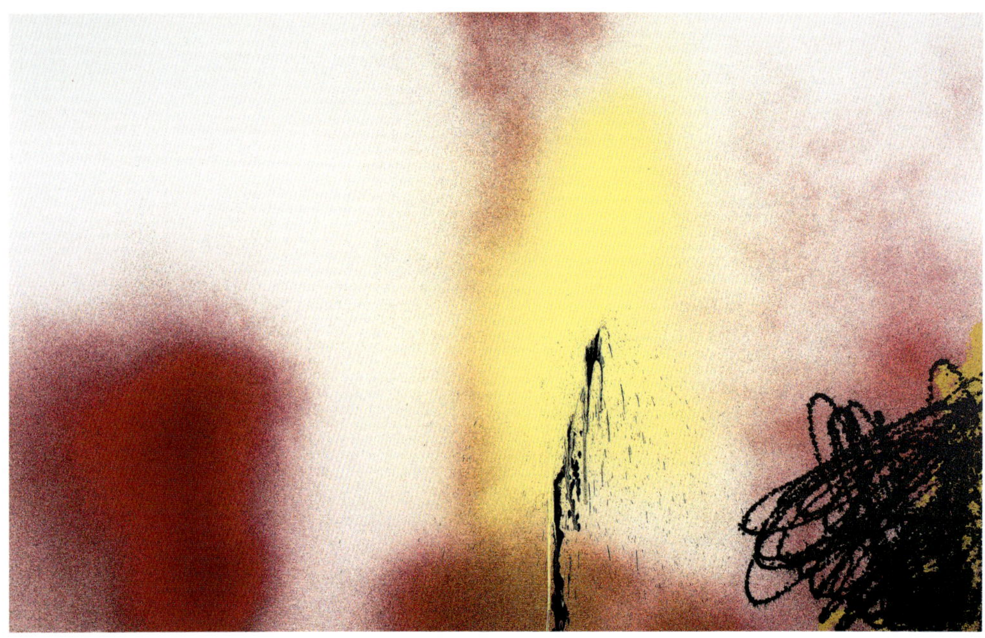

"From 1986 on, Hartung slowly started replacing the big brushes he had been using—and which left such large and colourful evidence of their passage on the canvas—with paint sprayers. He had alighted upon the means of projecting, by means of different systems, the liquid colours of his palette onto a vertical frame... The energy of the spontaneous act he had achieved by the concentration of the gesture is still there, in the way the paint atomises the moment it hits the canvas. With the resulting graphic and coloured lines (black being much more present in his recent paintings) Hartung opens up a new world of immense beauty for abstraction, where the dozen or so paintings on display at the Daniel Gervis Gallery are so many planets."[17]

In the preface to the catalogue of a showing of Hartung's recent work held in autumn 1988 in Paris, the artist's age was contrasted with the youthfulness of the work, and a parallel with late Picasso was drawn: "In a creative outpouring reminiscent of Picasso's last efforts, Hartung, who's already past eighty, is still making the most unexpected and the 'youngest' paintings you could imagine, and in astonishing numbers".[18] In the same catalogue the writer Daniel Abadie noted that the simple "*sulfateuse*" allowed Hartung such freedom to create that each canvas had its own individuality and tonality. He went on to suggest that the expansive imagery created by the droplets of paint was, in effect, a metaphor for Hartung's vision of nature:

"In many of the paintings from this series, Hartung juxtaposes canvases with an elongated format... By thus recreating a unity with disparate elements, he shows that the

14. HH, *T1989–R45*, 1989, acrylic on canvas, 154 x 250 cm
15. HH, *T1989–L37,* 1989, acrylic on canvas, 250 x 154 cm

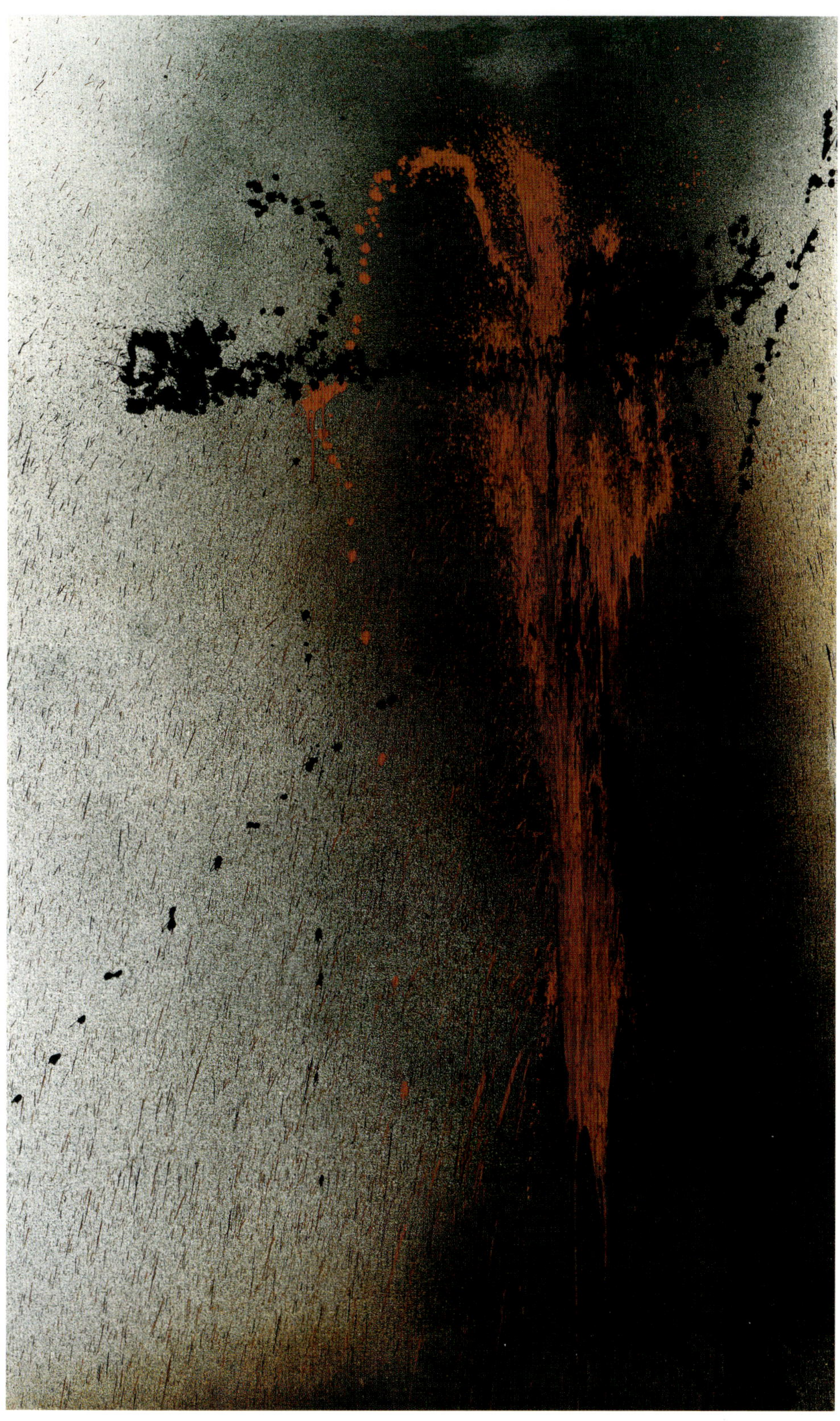

painting is just a fragment from a much vaster body, much as the lines that cut across them are, to the attentive viewer, no more than myriad points in succession. It is the same discontinuity that governs the universe: an atomic structure that his paintings, in their fragmentation, try to echo."[19]

Hartung himself appears to have believed that his new works expressed profound aspects of his vision of painting's relationship with material reality and energy. In the interview given to *Libération* and published in August 1988, he said: "The age, the view of the world, now aggressive, now sweet, positive or negative depending on the moment, and this wish to live, to be part of life, are the things I try to express in my paintings". He also spoke of his continued fascination with energy and speed. "They allow me to evoke atmospheric and cosmic tensions, the energies and forces that govern the universe. These are the vital, natural, and physical forces that I have always expressed in the gesture. That's only normal: if you're furious, you smack someone in the face. Well, the same goes for painting: the vigorous sign you make is always the expression of something. It must be as accurate as possible... I like the gesture to be definitive; I don't want to have to come back to it, unless of course it didn't come out quite right. From this improvisation on the canvas, this spontaneity, comes the rhythm and the intensity".[20] In this interview Hartung seemed very much aware of his personal situation. He had been unable to paint recently because of a back problem, commenting ruefully: "I'm not painting at all right now. I worked very hard at the beginning of the year, on large paintings especially, and maybe it was because of the effort they demanded that I've had to take a break from working following a compression of the spinal column". The records of the Fondation Hans Hartung et Anna-Eva Bergman indicate that Hartung had produced practically nothing in the previous four months, but that from August, recovered from his back problem, he returned to a more regular rate of production, completing 206 canvases and ten works on paper that year.

The steady and prolific rate of production of the last year of Hartung's life is one of the most telling points in the story of the late works. If 1987 saw a slow recovery from the stroke and a trying resolution of difficulties within the studio, and if 1988 saw a steadier production but one nonetheless dogged by the pain of his collapsed vertebrae, 1989 saw Hartung averaging nearly thirty-three paintings a month for the eleven months he worked, or, alternatively expressed, between five and six canvases a day for the sixty-two days he worked in the studio that year.[21] Each work was unique in its colours and composition, and each had its own distinctive mood and emotional quality. The variety and quantity of his production can be seen as an expression of Hartung's profound sense of the eternal flux that lay at the core of the material world and our apprehension of it, something which had underlain his work from the earliest days of his recording lightning

| 16. HH, *T1989-L37*, 1989, acrylic on canvas, 195 x 130 cm

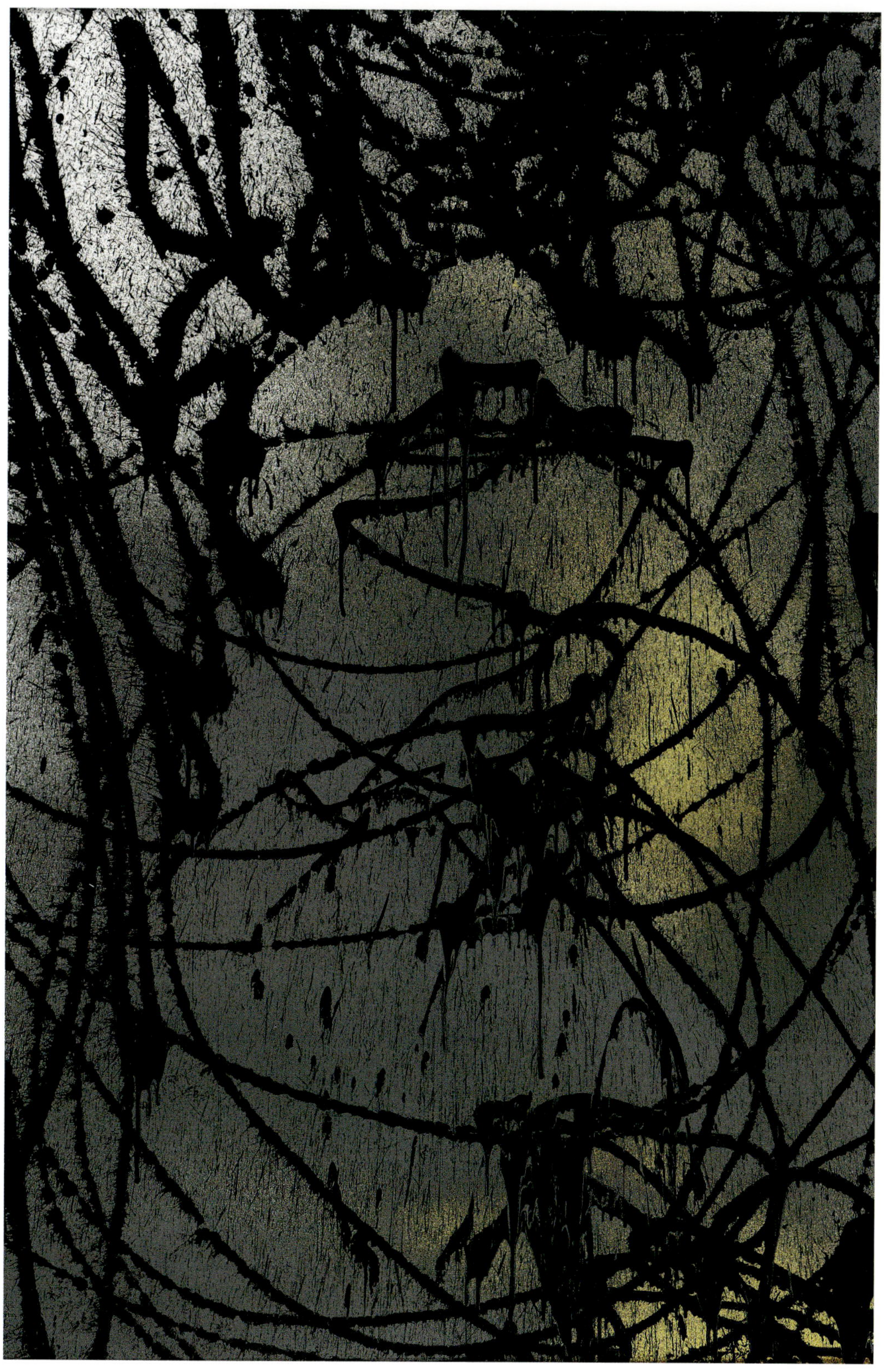

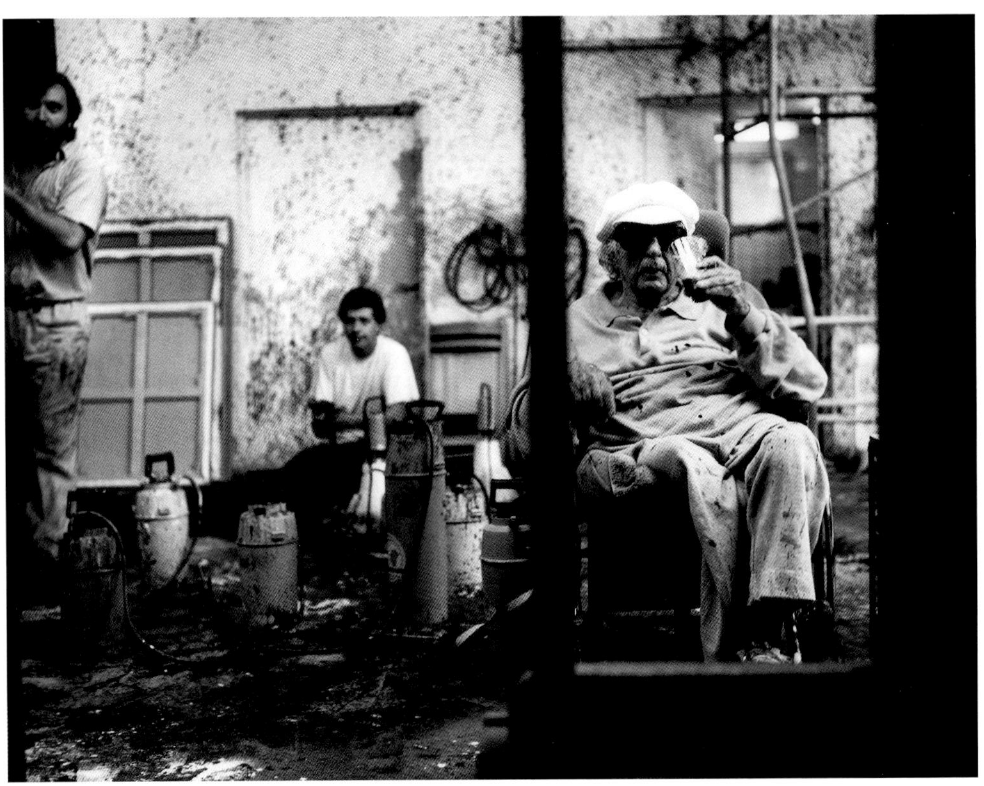

flashes while still a boy. No longer bothered to suppress accidental figurative allusions within his works, Hartung allowed some images to suggest crucifixions, a motif of his early figurative work and thus, perhaps, made a knowing allusion to his early preoccupations.

In 1988 Hartung commented, "Our position to life changes because life itself is constantly changing. So that there is always something else to express, you're always trying to go one step further. You enjoy painting as you enjoy life. You can't stop". Those who knew him and worked alongside him believe that in these last years Hartung focused on what he could do, and did not bother himself with the negative aspects of his condition. Marie Aanderaa, his long-term personal assistant, said of him, "Hartung in his latest years, being freer than ever, only lived for his painting. Not having much time left over, he knew or chose (or does one really know or choose?) what was essential to him and left aside everything else".[22] The late paintings would not have existed were it not for the somewhat fortuitous discovery of the sprayers, Hartung's openness to working with new tools and his need to do so. But clearly there is something more at play in these works than these material circumstances, fundamental though they

17. Bernard Derderian, Jean–Luc Uro and Hans Hartung in Hartung's studio, 11 September 1989.
Photo by André Villers

were. Paradoxically, it would seem that the proximity of death allowed Hartung a freedom to go beyond what was familiar, while the reduction in his physical strength and his mental faculties permitted a renewed enjoyment of the sensuous aspects of painting. Astonishingly, old age and a stroke had not denied Hartung the ability to remain in contact with the forces within himself that had always driven his work forward. Instead, Hartung was able to continue to find pleasure in painting, and maintain the link between expression and energy that lay at the core of his work.

Appendix – Hartung's production in the 1980s

	1981	1982	1983	1984	1985	1986	1987	1988	1989
January	9	27	59	0	0	0	0	26	51
February	0	87	27	9	0	99	0	24	21
March	0	101	30	31	0	7	29	0	9
April	0	0	55	16	0	38	0	0	19
May	0	1	8	0	0	3	5	4	36
June	0	13	6	0	11	0	0	0	25
July	0	2	0	0	54	37	0	0	35
August	49	36	6	0	31	106	10	34	63
September	0	0	3	0	0	26	6	17	41
October	14	0	0	0	0	18	23	39	29
November	162	1	0	0	0	74	12	31	31
December	7	0	0	0	24	29	0	41	0
	241	268	194	56	120	437	85	216	360
Total number of canvases	175	229	141	16	61	210	76	206	360
Total number of works on paper	66	39	53	40	59	227	9	10	0

Acknowledgements

I should like to express my profound thanks to the team at the Fondation Hans Hartung et Anna-Eva, and in particular to Marie Aanderaa, Bernard Derderian and Jean-Luc Uro, who with great kindness and patience provided much of the information contained in this essay.

1. Gary Garrels, "Three Toads in the Garden: Line, Color, and Form", in *Williem de Kooning: The Late Paintings, The 1980s*, exh. cat. (San Francisco: Museum of Modern Art, 1995), p. 12.

2. *Hartung, peintre moderne, oeuvres ultimes*, Fréjus, Centre d'Art Contemporain (Milan: Skira, 1996).

3. The first assistant was Dieter Ruff, who, when he joined Hartung in 1956, was only eighteen years old. As Marie Aanderaa has pointed out, Hartung must have transferred the motifs to canvas himself before this (letter to author, dated 11 Dec. 2004).

4. See J. Mundy, *Hans Hartung: Works on Paper 1922–56*, exh. cat. (London: Tate Gallery, 1996). Also Franz-W. Kaiser, "Conceptuel avant la lettre," in Franz-W. Kaiser, Anne Pontegnie, Vicente Todoli, *Hartung x 3* (Angers: Expressions Contemporaines, 2003), especially p. 64 ff.

5. Untitled video held at the Fondation Hans Hartung et Anna-Eva.

6. Jacques Michel, "Hartung, L'Abstracteur lyrique", *Le Monde Aujourd'hui* (Paris: 3 June 1985), n.p.

7. Werner Schmalenbach, "Pour Hans Hartung", in *Hans Hartung (1904–1989): Les Oeuvres ultimes*, exh. cat., Galerie Marwan Hoss (Paris: n.p., 1990).

8. Robert Storr, "At Last Light", in *Williem de Kooning: The Late Paintings, The 1980s*, exh. cat., San Francisco Museum of Modern Art, 1995, p. 51.

9. Bernard Derderian: "A point que certaines séances avec les genêts ressemblaient à des séances de kendo. 'En retour'", in *Hartung: Peintre moderne*, exh.cat., Frèjus, *op. cit.*, p. 133.

10. As remembered by Alkis Voliotis in an untitled video of interviews with studio assistants, Fondation Hans Hartung et Anna-Eva, 2004.

11. This tool was found by Bernard Derderian.

12. In his autobiography Hartung mentioned that he did not like pink and hardly ever used it (Hans Hartung, *Autoportrait: Récit receuilli par Monique Lefebvre* [Paris: Bernard Grasset, 1976], p. 186). He also said he did not like red, "this brutal, impertinent, provoking colour" (p. 239). Both colours, however, had featured in early works, and were to do so again in the 1970s.

13. *Ibid.*

14. Henri-Francois Debailleux, "L'Art selon Hartung", *Libération* (Paris: 18 Aug. 1988), p. 20.

15. Derderian, "En retour", note 9, pp. 131–32.

16. Hartung showed recent works in a number of exhibitions in the years 1987–89: *Hans Hartung. Œuvres récentes* (Paris: Galerie Daniel Gervis, Nov.–Dec. 1987); *Hans Hartung* (Ferrara: Palazzo dei Diamanti, May.–Sep. 1988); *Hans Hartung. Travaux récentes 1986–1987–1988* (Carcassonne: Musée des Beaux-Arts, June–Sep. 1988); *Hans Hartung: Neue Bilder*, (Saint Gall: Erker-Galerie, July–Sep. 1988); *Hans Hartung: Peintures 1974–88* (Luxembourg: Galerie de Luxembourg, Sep.–Oct. 1988); *Hans Hartung (Peintures 1986–1988)* (Paris: Chapelle de la Sorbonne, Sep.–Oct 1988); *Hans Hartung: L'Epoque d'Antibes 1973–1988*, Nov.–Dec. 1988; *Hartung: Peintures 1988* (Nice, Galerie Sapone, Feb.–Apr. 1989); *Hans Hartung: Zum 85. Geburtstag. Acryl auf Leinwand*, Sep. 1989; *Hartung: Œuvres du début des années 80 à l'occasion du 85e aniversaire de l'artiste* (Paris: Galerie Patrice Trigano, and stand at FIAC, Paris, Oct. 1989).

17. Jean-Louis Andral, "Hans Hartung. Galerie Daniel Gervis, 12 novembre–19 décembre 1987", *Art Press* 121 (January 1988), p. 78.

18. Jean Tiberi, "Fêtes d'Automne," in *Hans Hartung*, exh. cat. (Paris: Chapelle de la Sorbonne, 1988), n.p.

19. Daniel Abadie, "Hartung, ce qui fait style...", *ibid.*

20. Debailleux, 1988, note 14, p. 21.

21. Figures supplied by the Fondation Hans Hartung et Anna-Eva show that Hartung worked the following number of days per month in 1989:

January	9
February	3
March	2
April	3
May	8
June	7
July	6
August	10
September	6
October	4
November	4

22. Marie Aanderaa, letter dated 11 Dec. 2004.

Selected Works

Anne Pontégnie 1975

Hartung at the

Metropolitan Appendices Museum

Chronicle of a Failure Chantal Eschenfelder

Hans Hartung in Germany

Laurence Bertrand Dorléac

Germany and France

Two Parts in One Jennifer Mundy

The Very Late Style of Hans Hartung

a Problem?

Chronology

1904	Born in Leipzig on 21 September.
1912-1914	Family moves to Basle.
1915-1924	Lives in Dresden. Specialises in Classics at high school. Is attracted by nature and religion, but eventually painting emerges as his main interest.
1921-1924	Very impressed by Rembrandt, and then by Nolde.
1921-1922	First informal watercolours and pieces in Indian ink.
1926-1929	Travels to Italy, Holland, Belgium and, most importantly, to France, where he gets to study French Impressionism and Cubism up close.
1929-1932	Marries Anna-Eva Bergmann. Lives in Dresden, France, and Norway.
1931	First exhibition at the Heinrich Kühl Gallery in Dresden.
1932-1934	Builds a house in Minorca where he lives and works for two years.
1935	Following a brief stay in Berlin, he flees Germany and the Nazi regime for good and settles in Paris.
1937	Participates in the exhibition "From Cézanne to Non-Figurative Art" organised by Christian Zervos at the Jeu de Paume.
1938	Participates in the "Exhibition of Twentieth Century Art" at the New Burlington Galleries in London.
1939	He and Anna-Eva Bergmann divorce. He marries Roberta González and later enlists in the Foreign Legion.
1943	Forced to flee to Spain where he falls prisoner. Released seven months after his capture, he joins up with the Foreign Legion in North Africa.
1944	Seriously wounded on the Alsatian front. His right leg is amputated.
1945	Returns to Paris and starts working again after six years of interruptions.
1946	Is awarded the Military Medal and granted French citizenship.
1947	First solo exhibition in France, at the Galerie Lydia Conti in Paris.
1953	Moves to 7 Rue de Cels, in the 14th *arrondissement*, with Anna-Eva Bergmann, who had returned from Norway in 1952.
1956	Receives the Guggenheim Prize for the Europe–Africa continental selection.
1959	Has a new studio, which he designed himself, built on the Rue Gauguet in the 14th arrondissement.
1960	Is awarded the Grand Prix for painting at the Venice Biennale with the unanimous vote of the jury.
1967	Is elevated to the rank of Commandeur de l'Ordre des Arts et des Lettres.
1968	Begins planning the studio and his villa in Antibes
1969	A retrospective of his work at the Musée National d'Art Moderne in Paris.
1973	Construction of the villa and studio in Antibes.
1974-1975	A travelling retrospective exhibition organized at the Wallraf-Museum in Cologne, the National Galerie in Berlin and the Städtische Galerie im Lenbachhaus in Munich.
1975	Solo exhibition at the Metropolitan Museum of Art in New York.
1977	Elected member of the Académie des Beaux-Arts.
1980	Solo exhibition at the Musée d'Art Moderne de la Ville de Paris.
1981	Opening of a room permanently dedicated to Hartung's work at the Staatsgalerie Moderner Kunst in Munich.
1984	Receives the Great Cross of the Order of Merit of the German Federal Republic. His work is shown at the Venice Biennale (Palazzo Sagredo).
1987	Anna-Eva Bergman dies on 24 July.
1989	Is elevated to the rank of Grand Officier de la Légion d'Honneur by the French President.
1989	Hartung dies in Antibes on 7 December.
1994	Inauguration of a foundation of public interest under the name Fondation Hans Hartung et Anna-Eva Bergman.

Monographs

1949   Rousseau, Madeleine and Domnick, Ottomar
        Hans Hartung, preface by James Johnson Sweeney
        Stuttgart: Domnick Verlag
1960   Gindertael, R.V.
        Hans Hartung
        Paris: Pierre Tisné Editeur
        English edition – New York: Universal Books, 1961
        German edition – Berlin: Rembrandt Verlag, 1962
1961   Aubier, Dominique
        Hartung
        Paris: Éditions Georges Fall
1962   Tardieu, Jean
        Hans Hartung
        Paris: Fernand Hazan
1965   Schmücking, Rolf
        Hans Hartung. Werkverzeichnis der Graphik 1921–1965
        Brunswick: Verlag Galerie Schmücking
        New edition – *Hans Hartung: Das graphische Werk, 1921–1965*
        Basel: Verlag Galerie Schmücking, 1990
1966   Grohmann, Will
        Hans Hartung. Aquarelle 1922
        Saint-Gall: Erker-Verlag
1967   Appolonio, Umbro
        Hans Hartung
        Milan: Fratelli Fabbri, 1966
        French edition – Paris: ODEGE
1968   Siblik, Jiri
        Hans Hartung
        Prague: Odeon
1976   Hartung, Hans
        Autoportrait. Récit recueilli par Monique Lefebvre
        Paris: Bernard Grasset
        German edition – Berlin: Akademie der Künste, 1981 (Schriftenreihe der Akademie der Künste. B.14)
        Italian edition – Turin: GAM, 2000
1977   Descargues, Pierre
        Hartung
        Barcelona: Ediciones Poligrafa S.A
        French edition – Barcelona: Ediciones Poligrafa S.A., and Paris: Cercle d'Art, 1977
        English edition – Barcelona: Ediciones Poligrafa S.A., and New York: Rizzoli International
        Publications Inc., 1977
        German edition – Barcelona: Ediciones Weber-Poligrafa, 1983
1990   Daix, Pierre
        Hartung
        Paris: Bordas, Daniel Gervis, Éditions de Grenelle
2003   Kaiser, Franz-W., Pontégnie, Anne et Todoli, Vicente
        Hartung x 3
        Angers, Expressions contemporaines et Antibes, Fondation Hartung-Bergman, 2003
2005   Claustres, Annie
        Hans Hartung. Les aléas d'une réception
        Dijon: Les presses du réel, 2005

Joint exhibitions (selection)

1932   Berlin
        Galerie Flechtheim
        Junger Künstler
1935   Paris
        Les Surindépendants
1936   Paris
        Les Surindépendants
        Paris
        Galerie Pierre
        Œuvres récentes de Arp Ferren Giacometti
        Hartung Hélion Kandinsky Nelson Paalen
        Taeuber-Arp
1937   Paris
        Les Surindépendants
        Paris
        Musée du Jeu de paume
        De Cézanne à l'art non figuratif
1938   Paris
        Les Surindépendants
        London
        New Burlington Galleries
        Exhibition of Twentieth Century German
        Art
1939   Paris
        Salon des Réalités nouvelles
        London
        Guggenheim Jeune
        Abstract and Concrete Art
1945   Paris
        Les Surindépendants
1946   Paris
        Les Surindépendants
        Paris
        Salon des Réalités nouvelles
        Paris
        Salon de Mai
        Paris
        Salle du Centre de recherche
        Domela Hartung Schneider
        Paris
        Galerie Denise René
        Peinture abstraite
1947   Paris
        Salon des Réalités nouvelles
        Paris
        Salon de Mai
        Paris
        Galerie Denise René
        Peintures abstraites
1948   Paris
        Salon des Réalités nouvelles

        Paris
        Salon de Mai
        Venice
        Venice Biennale
        Paris
        Galerie Denise René
        Tendances de l'art abstrait
1949   Paris
        Salon des Réalités nouvelles
        Paris
        Salon de Mai
        Stuttgart
        Munich
        Düsseldorf
        Hanover
        Hamburg
        Frankfurt
        Freiburg
        Wanderausstellung französicher abstrakter
        Malerei
        Paris
        Galerie Lydia Conti
        Peintures abstraites : Hartung, Schneider,
        Soulages
        New York
        Betty Parsons Gallery
        Painted in 1949. European and American
        Painters
1950   Paris
        Salon des Réalités nouvelles
        Paris
        Salon de Mai
        New York
        Galerie Louis Carré
        Advancing French Art
1951   Paris
        Salon des Réalités nouvelles
        Paris
        Salon de Mai
        Turin
        Peintres d'aujourd'hui France Italie
        San Francisco
        Museum of Art, San Francisco
        Advancing French Art
        Chicago
        Art Institute of Chicago
        Advancing French Art
1952   Paris
        Salon de Mai
        Venice
        Venice Biennale

Baltimore
Museum of Art
Advancing French Art
Stuttgart
Württembergische Staatsgalerie
Sammlung Domnick
London, Birmingham
New Burlington Gallery,
Birmingham Art Gallery
School of Paris
Berlin
Akademie am Steinplatz
Berliner Neue Gruppe-École de Paris
Zurich
Kunsthaus
Malerei in Paris heute

1953 **Paris**
Salon de Mai
Turin
Peintres d'aujourd'hui France Italie
Brussels
Palais des beaux-arts
Collection Domnick
Stuttgart
Staatsgalerie Stuttgart
Collection Domnick
New York
Guggenheim Museum
Young European Painters

1954 **Paris**
Salon de Mai
Venice
Venice Biennale
Bern
Kunsthalle
Tendances actuelles de l'école de Paris
Sao Paolo
Museu de Arte Moderna
Artistas de Vanguarda da Ecola de Paris

1955 **Paris**
Salon de Mai
Ljubljana
Moderna Galerija
International Exhibition of Engraving
Kassel
Museum Fridericianum
Documenta 1
Pittsburgh
Carnegie Institute
The Pittsburgh International Exhibition
Sao Paolo
Museu de Arte Moderna
Biennale de Sao Paolo 3

Tokyo
Metropolitan Art Gallery
Tokyo Biennial

1956 **Paris**
Salon des Réalités nouvelles
Paris
Salon de Mai
Paris
National Museum of Modern Art
Prix Guggenheim 1956

1957 **Paris**
Salon de Mai
Ljubljana
Moderna Galerija
International Exhibition of Engraving

1958 **Paris**
Salon de Mai
Basel
Galerie Beyeler
Peintures informelles
Pittsburgh
Carnegie Institute
The Pittsburgh International Exhibition
Brussels
French Pavilion
Exposition universelle
Paris
National Museum of Modern Art
De l'impressionnisme à nos jours
Paris
Galerie Rive droite
Origines de l'art informel

1959 **Paris**
Salon de Mai
Turin
Peintres d'aujourd'hui France Italie
Ljubljana
Moderna Galerija
International Exhibition of Engraving
Kassel
Museum Fridericianum
Documenta 2
Pittsburgh
Carnegie Institute
The Pittsburgh International Exhibition
Tokyo
Metropolitan Art Gallery
Tokyo Biennial
Paris
Musée Cernuschi
Orient Occident

1960 **Paris**
Salon de Mai

Venice
Venice Biennale
Tel-Aviv
Jerusalem
Haifa
Tel Aviv Museum of Art
National Museum
Modern Art Museum
La peinture française d'aujourd'hui
1961 Paris
Salon de Mai
Turin
Peintres d'aujourd'hui France Italie
Pittsburgh
Carnegie Institute
The Pittsburgh International Exhibition
Moscow
Art français
Eindhoven
Stedelijk Van Abbe Museum
Paris : Carrefour de la peinture 1945-1961
1962 Paris
Les Surindépendants
Venice
Venice Biennale
Pittsburgh
Carnegie Institute
The Pittsburgh International Exhibition
Warsaw
Exhibition of French Art
London
Tate Gallery
School of Paris
1963 Vienna
Museum des 20. Jahrhunderts
Kunst von 1900 bis heute
Amsterdam
Stedelijk Museum
Schrift und Bild
1964 Venice
Venice Biennale
Kassel
Museum Fridericianum
Documenta 3
London
Tate Gallery
54 / 64 Painting and Sculpture of a decade
1965 Ljubljana
Moderna Galerija
International Exhibition of Engraving
Boston
Institute of Contemporary Art
Painting without a brush

Cologne
Wallraff-Richartz Museum
Traum – Zeichen – Raum
1967 Saint-Paul-de-Vence
Fondation Maeght
Dix ans d'art vivant 1955-1965
1968 Paris
New York
Boston
Chicago
Tokyo
National Museum of Modern Art
The Metropolitan Museum
Museum of Fine Arts
Art Institute
National Museum of Modern Art
Painting in France 1900-1967
1977 Paris
Centre Georges Pompidou
Paris-New York
1981 Paris
Centre Georges Pompidou
Paris-Paris
1988 Paris
Centre Georges Pompidou
Les Années 50
1995 Geneva
Musée Rath
Les figures de la liberté
Paris
Musée d'art moderne
Passions privées
1997 Paris
Musée d'Art moderne de la ville de Paris
Années 30 en Europe
1998 Vienna
Secession
Das Jahrhundert der künstlerischen Freiheit
Vis-à-vis Deutschland-Frankreich
1999 New York
Guggenheim Museum
Rendezvous, Masterpieces from the Centre
Georges Pompidou
2001 Strasbourg
Musée d'art moderne et contemporain
Kandinsky, retour en Russie 1914-1921
2002 London
Bilbao
Royal Academy of Arts
Guggenheim Museum
Paris, Capital of the Arts 1900 - 1968

Solo exhibitions (selection)

1931 **Dresden**
Galerie Heinrich Kühl
1932 **Oslo**
Blomqvist Kunsthandel
1939 **Paris**
Galerie Henriette
1946 **Zurich**
Hans Ulrich Gasser
1947 **Paris**
Galerie Lydia Conti
1948 **Paris**
Galerie Lydia Conti
1949 **London**
Hanover Gallery
Munich
Moderne Galerie Otto Stangl
1951 **Basel**
Galerie d'art moderne
Cologne
Galerie der Spiegel
1952 **Basel**
Kunsthalle
1953 **London**
Lefevre Gallery
Bern
Galerie Marbach
1954 **Brussels**
Palais des beaux-arts
Paris
La Hune
1956 **Paris**
Galerie de France
Paris
Galerie Craven
1957 **New York**
Kleemann Galleries
Hanover
Kestner-Gesellschaft
Stuttgart
Württembergische Staatsgalerie
Berlin
Haus am Waldsee
Hamburg
Kunsthalle
Nuremberg
Germanisches National Museum
1958 **Munich**
Moderne Galerie Otto Stangl
Rome
Il Segno

Milan
Galleria Blu
Siegen
Rathaus
Paris
Galerie de France
1959 **New York**
Kleemann Galleries
Antibes
Musée Picasso
1960 **Venice**
XXX International Biennial of Art
London
Gimpel Fils
1961 **Madrid**
Ateneo
Rome
Libreria Einaudi
Paris
Galerie de France
Beirut
Centre d'art contemporain
1962 **Arras**
Cercle Noroit
Paris
Galerie de France
1963 **Saint-Gall**
Galerie Im Erker
Zurich
Kunsthaus
Vienna
Museum des 20. Jahrhunderts
Düsseldorf
Kunstverein
Brussels
Palais des beaux-arts
Amsterdam
Stedelijk Museum
1964 **Paris**
Galerie de France
1965 **Brunswick**
Städtisches Museum
Pittsburgh
University of Pittsburgh
New York
Associated American Artists
1966 **Saint-Gall**
Galerie im Erker
Paris
Galerie de France

Turin
Galleria Civica d'Arte Moderna
New York
André Emmerich Gallery
Madrid
Sala Nebli
1967 Belgrade
Muzej Savremene, Umetnost
Skopje
Museum of Contemporary Art
1968 Birmingham
City Museum and Art Gallery
Prague
Galerie Hollar
1969 Paris
Musée national d'Art moderne
Paris
Galerie de France
Marseilles
École des beaux-arts et d'architecture
Quebec
Musée de Quebec
Houston
Museum of Fine Arts
Montreal
Musée d'art contemporain
1970 Brunswick
Kunstverein Braunschweig
Venice (Mestre)
Galleria Meneghini
1971 New York
Lefebre Gallery
Saint-Paul-de-Vence
Fondation Maeght
Paris
Galerie de France
1972 Siegen
Städtische Galerie Haus Seel
Mannheim
Mannheimer Kunstverein
1973 Zurich
Galerie Maeght
Milan
Centro Arte Internazionale
Paris
Palais de l'Élysée
1974 Paris
Galerie de France
Cologne
Galerie der Spiegel
1975 Cologne
Wallraf-Richartz Museum
Brest
Palais des arts et de la culture

Berlin
Nationalgalerie
Munich
Städtische Galerie im Lenbachhaus
Munich
Galerie Stangl
New York
The Metropolitan Museum of Art
New York
Lefebre Gallery
New York
Associated American Artists
1976 Paris
Grand Palais
Arras
Cercle Noroit
1978 Nice
Galerie Sapone
Saint-Gall
Erker-Galerie
Paris
Galerie de France
1979 Antibes
Musée Picasso
Nice
Galerie Sapone
1980 Chalon-sur-Saône
Musée Nicéphore Niepce
Paris
Musée d'art moderne
Musée de la Poste
1981 London
Fischer Fine Art Limited
Klagenfurt
Kulturamt der Stadt
Hövikodden
Fondation Sonja-Henie-Niels, Onstad
Düsseldorf
Städtische Kunsthalle
Munich
Staatsgalerie Moderner Kunst,
im Haus der Kunst
1982 Paris
Musée national d'art moderne, Centre
Georges Pompidou
Vienna
Hochschule für Angewandte Kunst
1983 Antibes
Musée Picasso
Dresden
Kupferstich-Kabinett der
Staatlichen Kunstsammlungen
1984 Venice
Palazzo de Sagredo, Venice Biennale

Leipzig
Museum der Bildenden Künste
Siegen
Städtische Galerie Haus Seel
1985 Antibes
Musée Picasso
Paris
Hôtel de Ville de Paris
Cavaillon
Chapelle du Grand Couvent
Paris
Galerie Daniel Gervis
1986 Nice
Espace niçois d'art contemporain
Paris
Galerie Daniel Gervis
1987 London
Institut français
Antibes
Musée Picasso
Paris
Galerie Daniel Gervis
1988 Tokyo
Galerie Art Point
Ferrara
Palazzo dei Diamanti
Carcassonne
Musée des beaux-arts
Mougins
Musée de la photographie
Pérouges
Maison des Princes
Paris
Chapelle de la Sorbonne
1989 Colmar
Musée d'Unterlinden

Posthumous exhibitions

1991 Paris
Centre Georges Pompidou
Valence
Ivam Centre Julio Gonzalez
1992 Paris
Galerie de France
1993 Royan
Centre d'arts plastiques
1995 Antibes
Musée Picasso
1996 Fréjus
Le Capitou Centre d'art contemporain
London
Tate Gallery
1997 Taiwan
Taiwan Museum of Art
Dijon
Le Consortium
1998 Nagoya
Aichi Prefectural Museum of Art
Monaco
Printemps des arts de Monte-Carlo
1999 Balearic Islands
Travelling exhibition
2000 Turin
Galleria Civica d'Arte Moderna
e Contemporanea
2003 Montbéliard
Musée du château des ducs de Wurtemberg
2004 Cahors
Musée de Cahors Henri-Martin
Mondovi
Former church of Santo Stefano
Cologne
Museum Ludwig
The Hague
Gemeentemuseum den Haag
2005 Beijing
Palais des beaux-arts
Nankin
National Museum

Laurence Bertrand Dorléac

Laurence Bertrand Dorléac is an Art Historian, a Professor and a member of the Institute Universitaire de France. She met Hans Hartung while working on her dissertation on World War II, which she has since edited into two books, one of which is *L'Art de la défaite. 1940–1944* (Paris: Seuil, 1993). She has written extensively on art and the art world in the twentieth century. Her most recent publication is *L'ordre sauvage. Violence, dépense et sacré dans l'art des années 1950–1960* (Paris: Gallimard, 2004).

Annie Claustres

Annie Claustres is a Lecturer in Art History at the Université Lyon 2 and an art critic. A revised version of her doctoral dissertation has just been published: *Hans Hartung. Les aléas d'une reception* (Dijon: Les presses du réel, 2005). Her monograph on Hartung has served as a springboard into an area of research concerned with deconstructing and rereading non-geometric Abstraction in Europe; see her article: "L'abstraction lyrique ou le mythe de la spontanéité" in *Pratiques. Réflexions sur l'art*, 16, (Spring 2005), pp. 6-25.

Chantal Eschenfelder

Chantal Eschenfelder was born in Darmstadt, Germany, in 1965. She studied art history and German and American literature in Munich and Paris. In 1996 she earned her doctorate with a dissertation on the ballroom at Fontainebleau. She joined the Cologne Museum Services Association (*Museumsdienst Köln*) in 2000, where she is responsible for communications at the Museum Ludwig and the Museum of Applied Art in Cologne. As a Lecturer at the Institute for Art History at the University of Düsseldorf she taught several seminars on French art, including one on the École de Paris in the 1950s. She was also a contributor to the catalogue accompanying the Hans Hartung exhibition at Museum Ludwig in 2004.

Franz-W. Kaiser

Franz-W. Kaiser is a Historian, Art Historian and Philosopher. He has been director of exhibitions at the *Gemeentemuseum* in The Hague (Holland) since 1989. In his role as director, as well as independently of it, he has curated numerous exhibitions of modern and contemporary art, among them the travelling exhibition "Conceptual avant la lettre", part of the project *Hartung x 3* organised by the Fondation Hans Hartung et Anna-Eva Bergman.

Rainer Michael Mason

Rainer Michael Mason was born in Hamburg (Germany) in 1943. An Art Historian and critic, he joined the Print Room of the Musée d'art et d'histoire in Geneva, which he went on to direct from 1979 to 2005, during which time he showed equal dedication to eighteenth-century Venetian prints, the Russian avant-garde and Georg Baselitz. He has written more than a dozen catalogues raisonnés (among them of Jean Fautrier, Henri Michaux and Markus Raetz). He has been working on a descriptive inventory of the print works of Hans Hartung since 1998. He is currently working on general catalogues of the paintings and drawings of Henri Michaux and Bram van Velde.

Christine Mehring

Christine Mehring is Assistant Professor of Art History at Yale University. Following studies in *Angewandte Kulturwissenschaften* at the Universität Lüneburg, Germany, she received an M.A. in Art Criticism and Art History from SUNY Stony Brook, an M.A. in Fine Arts and a Ph.D. in History of Art from Harvard University. She is the co-author with Pamela M. Lee of *Drawing is Another Kind of Language* and the author of *Wols Photographs*, the catalogue of an exhibition she curated at the Busch-Reisinger Museum in Cambridge (Mass.) in 1999. Her essays on postwar European art, abstract art, and photography have appeared in journals such as *Artforum, Art Journal, Grey Room, History of Photography, Modernism/Modernity* and *Texte zur Kunst*. She is currently completing a book-length study of the German abstract painter Blinky Palermo and is at work on an examination of relations between abstract art and design in the twentieth century.

Jennifer Mundy

Jennifer Mundy is Head of International Art and Head of Research at Tate, London. She first worked with the Fondation Hans Hartung et Anna-Eva Bergman in preparation for the exhibition catalogue *Hans Hartung: Works on Paper 1922–1956*, produced by the Tate Gallery in association with the Fondation in 1996. She curated "Surrealism: Desire Unbound" for Tate Modern in 2001.

Anne Pontégnie

Anne Pontégnie is an Art Historian. As an independent curator, she has organised shows on Mike Kelley, Christopher Wool and Douglas Houber, and she also worked on such production initiatives as Les Nouveaux Commanditaires and Microproductions. She is a regular contributor to *Artforum* and to catalogues. For the project *Hartung x 3* she curated the exhibition "Hans Hartung, 1973". In 2005 she was appointed director of exhibitions at Wiels, a contemporary art centre in Brussels.

John C. Welchman

John C. Welchman is Professor of Art History in the Visual Arts department at the University of California, San Diego. His books include *Modernism Relocated: Towards a Cultural Studies of Visual Modernity* (Allen & Unwin, 1995), *Invisible Colours: A Visual History of Titles* (Yale UP, 1997) and *Art After Appropriation: Essays on Art in the 1990s* (Routledge, 2001); he is co-author of the *Dada and Surrealist Word Image* (MIT Press, 1987) and of *Mike Kelley* in the Phaidon Contemporary Artists series (1999); and editor of *Rethinking Borders* (Minnesota UP, 1996). He has written for *Artforum, Screen, The New York Times, International Herald Tribune* and other newspapers and journals, and has contributed catalogue essays for exhibitions. His current projects include editing the collected writings of Mike Kelley (the first vol., *Foul Perfection: Essays and Criticism*, was published by MIT Press in 2003). Welchman authored a catalogue essay for the exhibition *The Uncanny* (Tate Liverpool/Vienna Museum of Contemporary Art (Spring-Autumn 2004), is finalising two books on the relation between art, film and the representation of faces (*The Celluloid Face* and *Faces and Powers*), and is contracted to write a major survey, *Global Art Now* for Phaidon (London).

Christopher Wool

Christopher Wool was born in 1955 and lives and works in New York City. Like Hartung he is primarily a painter who also works in photography.